W9-BTE-682

ET FAVXBOVRGS DE PARIS AVEC LA DESCRIPTION DE SON ANTIQVITE
ET SINGVLIARITES

LA RIVIERE DE SEINE

Imp. Ch. Chardon aîné.

1615

hieu Merian

THE EMERGING CITY

For Mollie

The emerging city

PARIS IN THE AGE OF LOUIS XIV

LEON BERNARD

Durham, North Carolina

DUKE UNIVERSITY PRESS

1970

© 1970, Duke University Press

L.C.C. card no. 71-86478

I.S.B.N. 0-8223-0214-4

PRINTED IN THE UNITED STATES OF
AMERICA BY THE SEEMAN PRINTERY

PREFACE

One of the sorest problems facing the human race today is world-wide urbanization. Whereas a short century and a half ago only about 3 percent of the world's inhabitants dwelled in cities of more than 5,000 population, today almost a third live in such communities. When the nineteenth century began, only 45 cities of over 100,000 could be counted on the surface of our planet; today there are 875. Forty-nine cities now number over a million.[1] As modern technology frees ever larger numbers from the obligation of providing foodstuffs for urban dwellers, the flight from countryside to city accelerates. Political leaders, town planners, social thinkers of all varieties despair at the sight of millions of people insisting upon crowding into physical environments seemingly incapable of affording minimum human happiness. Books on the subject of the city's role and future in modern society come endlessly off the presses, and the study of urbanization has become one of the newest academic preoccupations. Universities of the world now compete in evidencing their social awareness and topical orientation by organizing departments of urban studies. Endless interdisciplinary symposia meet to ponder the "future of the city," invariably marked by the experts' understandable inability to find practical solutions for problems of such vast scope and complexity. (One participant in such an academic assemblage was driven after several days of patient listening to remind the participants of Lewis Mumford's warning of the futility of speculation on the future of the city until the future of the bomb had been settled.[2])

The present work, needless to say, offers no solutions for the problems of urbanization. Our very modest aim is to enhance the understanding of Western urban history by focusing on one of its principal exemplars—Paris—at a hitherto neglected stage in its development.

Commonly, modern Paris is said to have begun with the great "urban renewal" of Napoleon III and Haussmann in the 1850's and 1860's. This book attempts to put the history of the city in larger perspective. Long before Haussmann, forces were shaping the city in a manner which can only be termed "modern." Far from marking the transition from medieval to modern Paris, Napoleon III and Haussmann are in reality links in a chain which stretches back to the seventeenth century and forward to present-day urbanists. The problems confronting the urbanists of the age of Louis XIV were minuscule compared with those of today's urban planners. But they were the same kinds of problems— of circulation, physical security, health, pollution of the environment, education, urban aesthetics, and so on. In the seventeenth century, for the first time at least since ancient times, urban administrators became aware of such problems in something more than a haphazard way and began to seek rational solutions. That idea is, of course, not new. The great French urban historian Pierre Lavedan recognized tendencies in the seventeenth century "so new that one would date from this era the start of modern urbanism." He pointed out that from the seventeenth century until the end of the Old Regime there was hardly a leading architect in western Europe who did not proudly consider himself an *urbaniste*. In the Paris of Louis XIV these new tendencies were in clear view.

This book lies somewhere in the misty region between urban and social history. As a contribution to urban history, it touches on the topographical and physical changes which permit us to see in seventeenth-century maps of Paris the outlines of the city of Haussmann and of today. It takes note of the beginning of the *grands boulevards*, a consequence of the razing of most of the medieval walls and many of the old gates; of the erection of new kinds of *places* (the modern Places des Vosges, des Victoires, Vendôme, and others), all reflecting a new urban philosophy; of the appearance of opulent new residential neighborhoods; of the start of systematic and rational programs for straighter, wider, and better-paved streets, as well as for a larger supply of city water, and other such matters.

But, more than with buildings, streets, *places*, and other topographical matters, this book deals with how seventeenth-century Parisians dealt with the challenges resulting from what, for that period, must have been an explosive growth. Change in history is, of course, normal. In any generation of Paris's 2,500 or so years for which adequate records exist the historian could surely discern a clash between conservative forces and the forces of change. But the relative intensity of such conflict varies greatly from one generation to another. We believe the forces of change were particularly strong in the reign of Louis XIV, after many generations of relative dormancy. One can see the new dynamism at work in urban transportation and communication, in the transformed theatrical scene, in new attitudes towards the poor, in the condition of labor, in the formation of a totally new kind of urban administrative machinery, in the creation of new street-lighting and fire-fighting systems, in the revolt against a time-hallowed system of education, and much else—even in new habits of eating bread.

It would be well to state what we exclude as well as what we include. Institutions of national rather than local importance, such as the Parlement and other administrative and judicial organs centered at the Palais de Justice, will receive only passing mention, as will the cultural academies founded in the 1660's and 1670's. Our assumption is that they belong to the history of France rather than that of Paris. On something of the same principle, we exclude the University except as it impinges on secondary education. The Arts faculty, therefore, comes within our scope, but not the Faculties of Theology and Law.

A word about sources. We make no claims to original archival research; this book is one of synthesis. Its author acknowledges his indebtedness to those scholars, nearly all French, who by immersing themselves in the archives to a degree virtually impossible for an American, produce monographs which make this sort of book possible and which in turn are mainly justified by works of synthesis. A wide variety of printed contemporary sources has, of course, also been employed. Probably the most indispensable of these is the four folio volumes of laws and regulations relating to the police of Paris compiled by Nicolas Delamare. Not the least of the accomplishments of this remarkable *commissaire* of the Cité quarter was his unconscious ability to let his

concern for the well-being of ordinary Parisians show through his musty and long-forgotten compilation.

Our thanks are extended particularly to the Librarians of the Universities of Chicago, Michigan, Duke, and Minnesota for making available scarce books in this area, as well as to the administrators of the Bibliothèque Historique de la Ville de Paris, where the final touches were put on the manuscript. The sumptuous new quarters of the latter in the seventeenth-century Hôtel Lamoignon afford an incomparable atmosphere for any Old Regime historian. I also gratefully acknowledge the editorial assistance and encouragement of my wife, as well as the patience and good cheer of Mrs. Lee Pacholke in preparing the manuscript. They both successfully coped with a handwriting which would have driven to violence any of those seventeenth-century writing masters whom we shall have occasion to discuss.

The illustrations in this volume have all been furnished by the Cabinet des Estampes of the Bibliothèque Nationale. To its curators we express our sincere thanks.

Finally, we are happy to acknowledge our debt to the University of Notre Dame and its Program of Western European Studies directed by Dr. Stephen Kertesz for making possible a year in France in 1968-1969.

LEON BERNARD

Le Mesnil-St.Denis
January 1969

CONTENTS

THE EMERGING CITY

CHAPTER ONE

The changing face of Paris

EARLY in his personal reign, Louis XIV conceived a scheme for the embellishment of Paris which one of his most fulsome, but in this instance puzzled, admirers could only describe as "singular."[1] The self-confident young monarch defied Nature by stocking the pestiferous waters of the Seine within the city limits with large numbers of exotic white swans imported at considerable expense. Not only would Paris be made more beautiful thereby, the King reasoned, but the courtiers journeying along the river banks en route to Versailles, then under construction, would be treated to a most pleasing spectacle. Laws protecting the birds and their nests were hopefully promulgated. Surprisingly enough, some of the creatures must have survived, because the police were still issuing ordinances on their behalf a generation later,[2] and for a long time thereafter a small island just below the Invalides, now joined to the mainland, was known as the Ile-aux-Cygnes.

Ludicrous as may appear the Sun King's swans, they serve nevertheless as apt symbols of a new era in the development of Paris. We may smile at the impracticality of breeding swans in the filth of the Parisian Seine, but somehow in Louis XIV's reign such a thing was no longer entirely inappropriate. If flocks of white swans convey the image of grace, stateliness, opulence, and the like—as surely Louis must have intended—then he was perhaps not too far amiss. Paris, in part at least, had come to stand for many of these qualities along with the squalor and filth of the medieval city.

Testimony to the new physical glories of the city is easy to come by, although one must, of course, be cautious in appraising such statements. Visitors to Paris throughout the ages have been prone to gush over the

3

marvels of the city; most tourists tend to be enthusiastic about famous sights they visit and describe for their friends back home. But travelers whose writings would recommend them as objective witnesses, and even blasé natives, were very vocal about the change that had come over the city in their lifetimes. In the 1670's, for example, the famous commentator on the Parisian theater, Chappuzeau, whose objectivity we have no reason to question, wrote, "Everything here is going from good to better, and regardless of where one turns, Paris was never so fine nor so stately as it is today."3 The matter-of-fact and distinctly Anglophile physician Martin Lister, revisiting Paris in 1698 after an absence of several decades, observed that it was a "new City within this 40 years . . . most of the great Hostels are built, or re-edified; in like manner the Convents, the Keyes upon the River, the Pavements, all these have had great additions or are quite new."4 Half a century later, Voltaire would echo these words when he wrote: "there is little that was not either re-established or created in [Louis XIV's] time."5 Any visitor to modern Paris would agree with Voltaire if he took the trouble to ascertain the dates of the fine old town houses on either bank and noted how very few edifices antedate the seventeenth century.6

What probably struck observers most vividly was the new opulence of the city. Dr Lister commented on the "Whirlpool" of luxury which he encountered in Paris. "Here," he wrote, with only mild disapproval, "as soon as a Man gets any thing by Fortune or Inheritance, he lays it out . . . ,"7 suggesting what was obvious to readers of his book—that Dr Lister did not consort very much with the frugal middle class of Paris. A Sicilian expatriate and a long-time resident of Paris, Marana, writing at about the same time, concluded that "luxury here is so excessive that anyone who wished to enrich 300 deserted cities need simply destroy Paris."8 (Marana was pleased to note, however, that money had not destroyed good manners, for he acknowledged the exquisite courtesy with which even streetwalkers accosted him.) A contemporary historian of Paris, Sauval, observed that "luxury and vanity are so highly valued" that lodgings in the Place Royale, which at the start of the century were the last word in comfort and elegance, now no longer sufficed for many.9 The city "abounds with opulence and luxury," Sauval commented, "and contains more than 400 people worth three millions [livres]," which, insofar as such things can be reckoned, was equal to at least as many modern dollars.

Seventeenth-century Parisians must have had the sensation of living in a boom town, of feeling a dynamism about them which perhaps only the twelfth-century city could have matched. Given the paucity and unreliability of economic and demographic records, the dramatic expansion of the city in the seventeenth century would be next to impossible to establish statistically. Fortunately, one can easily judge the growth of the city by the expansion—or lack thereof—of the city walls. Readily available maps of Paris offer abundant evidence that from the High Middle Ages to the start of the seventeenth century the city was relatively stagnant. In the first volume of Nicolas Delamare's *Traité de la police* (if one is fortunate enough to possess a copy whose invaluable engravings have not been pilfered) one finds a series of eight folded maps of the city from Roman times to the early eighteenth century. The author, an indefatigable booster of Paris, put them there to illustrate the great and continuous growth of the city, which some of his contemporaries made out to house close to a million souls. (Better evidence would suggest a population in the later seventeenth century of about half that number.)[10]

Contrary to the author's purpose, a scrutiny of Delamare's maps leaves one quite unimpressed with the growth of Paris in the four centuries preceding the Grand Siècle. At the start of the seventeenth century the late-twelfth-century wall of Philip Augustus still stood intact on the Left Bank. On the Right Bank the same wall had been extended outward only some three to six hundred yards by Charles V in the fourteenth century. It is true that on both sides of the river there had been some new construction outside the walls. But this was quite thin, especially on the Right Bank, where it was generally limited to double rows of houses alongside the main roads radiating out from the city. Contemporary engravings bear this out—for example, the well-known and exceptionally detailed panorama of Paris in 1620 by the cartographer Mathieu Mérian.

Delamare considerably exaggerated the pre-seventeenth-century growth of the city beyond the old walls, as one would expect of an inveterate civic booster. If one looks at the Faubourg Saint-Germain as depicted in his Sixth Plan (1589), one gets the impression that this faubourg extended half a mile or so beyond the old wall. But other more detailed and more authoritative maps drawn thirty years later show that much of Delamare's built-up area had in reality been mere pasturage and continued to be such well into Richelieu's time.[11]

It is equally disillusioning that at the end of the sixteenth century— after the Left Bank wall had stood for four centuries and the Right Bank wall for two centuries and a half—there were still large fields under cultivation within the walls. These were especially extensive on the Right Bank. One could walk alongside long stretches of Charles V's wall inside the city without ever having one's way blocked by a house or building. Even on the more populous Left Bank, the pressure of urban growth had been so slight as to permit the continued existence of a number of large monastic gardens, each the size of several modern city blocks. One is led to speculate whether we could not also apply to Paris itself one demographer's conclusion that the overall French population would have shown an actual decrease in those centuries had it not been for the influx of foreigners.[12]

In any case, around the start of the seventeenth century, Paris bestirred itself from its long doldrums. The city began to display a dynamism not seen since the High Middle Ages. One of the most obvious and interesting manifestations of this upsurge was the appearance of a new type of land speculator and developer. The relatively static economy of earlier centuries had left little room for land speculation, but beginning early in the century, the *lotissement dirigé,* or planned subdivision, became a common phenomenon. Fortunes were made and lost in the risky business of buying up large tracts of land in the outskirts, subdividing them, building streets, furnishing water, and (later in the century) erecting street lighting—all on speculation. This was a far cry from the simple *lotissements* of the preceding century, when a great *hôtel* or palace might be leveled and lots sold with but one purpose in mind—realizing a quick profit from minimum capital expenditure. Now we are no longer dealing with helterskelter and unplanned urban expansion, as a glance at a seventeenth-century map of Paris will show. The new developments on both the eastern and western extremities of the city are quickly spotted for their relatively wide streets crossing at right angles, or at least at uniform angles. One of the earliest of these *lotissements dirigés* centered on the Ile Saint-Louis. Used only by occasional merchants for storage yards at the start of the century, this island was transformed into an excellent residential neighborhood in 1614 and thereafter through the talents of an association of land promoters headed by Christophe Marie. The association contracted to build a bridge (the Pont Marie) and a grid of streets, in return for which it received valuable land rights. Within a generation a belt of fine aristocratic houses had been erected on the island's periphery and less pretentious construction in the interior.[13]

The outstanding land developer of seventeenth-century Paris—the Henry Flagler of the time—was Louis Le Barbier, who arrived as an unknown young man in 1610 from Orléans, promptly started making surprising amounts of money in land speculation, tax farming, and public works, and by the early 1620's was ready to head a consortium of five financiers in developing a large rectangle of cultivated fields opposite the Tuileries Palace.[14] The property had once belonged to the notorious Queen Margot, repudiated wife of Henry IV, who willed it to Louis XIII in return for his promise to assume her debts amounting to 1,300,000 livres.[15] The Council of State, hard-pressed by a syndicate of the deceased Margot's creditors (they had organized in self-protection twenty years earlier), decided to sell the land to Barbier and his associates for subdivision. Doubtless the recent success of a similar operation at the Place Royale, the site of an old horse market, along with the development of the Ile Saint-Louis, helped to inspire this transaction. In the next ten years the associates opened up eight new streets (still in existence) through their once open fields, erected a quay, a marketplace, and bridge across to the Tuileries Palace, and contrived a large pump to provide river water for their customers. On his own account, the far-sighted Barbier bought some adjacent land and contracted with one of the King's fashionable architects for the erection of a number of fine *hôtels*. By saving wealthy Parisians the ennui of making all their own arrangements, he made even more money off the sale of the houses than he did off the land.[16] Thus began the famous Faubourg Saint-Germain-des-Prés as a center of *le beau monde*.

From this first important development of the Faubourg Saint-Germain Barbier went on to even larger enterprises. Around 1630 the Council of State finally arrived at the long-delayed decision to move the northwest wall out so as to encompass the Tuileries Gardens, relocating the Porte Saint-Honoré in the process about five-eighths of a mile to the west.[17] Once again Barbier was called in, although the ensuing contracts were signed by two of his subordinates, Pidou and Froger. The master remained cautiously hidden from view, a common procedure among Old Regime financiers.

Perhaps because he was not overinvolved in the Thirty Years' War at this time, Richelieu was emboldened to go far beyond the original project of relocating the northwest wall. He undertook some additional work as ambitious for the times as it was expensive. The Cardinal arranged, apparently as an afterthought, for the construction of a navigational canal 72 feet wide across the north of the city, as well as for the enclosure of the Right Bank's main sewer, which then wound its pestilent course around the northern perimeter of the city.[18] Despite the Cardinal's backing, nothing came of either the canal project or the sewer enclosure. Vested interests, in addition to the belated realization of costs and engineering difficulties, blocked the former, although it continued to be talked about well into the nineteenth century. More than a century later, the northern sewer was finally enclosed. But both projects are of interest as examples of what Parisian urbanizers were then projecting.

In 1633 Barbier, through an associate, signed a second contract, this one modestly limited to the original project of relocating the northwest wall.[19] Never lacking in imagination, Barbier devised a plan which he promised would cost the government not one sou. The contractor agreed to build the new wall (with two gates) and to level the old in return for the land occupied by the old ramparts. All property owners between the two walls were ordered to make an immediate payment to Barbier to defray the cost of streets and public places he promised to construct.

Cardinal Richelieu's obvious self-interest in these public works might have caused him a good deal of embarrassment in a more democratic age. His princely Palais-Cardinal was just being completed as Barbier began tearing down the old wall and filling in the odoriferous moats which cut diagonally across the Cardinal's new domain. The Cardinal profited from the new project not only by the purification of the air around his new residence but, more materially, by a royal grant of a section of the newly reclaimed land behind his palace.[20] To the land given him Richelieu added numerous small parcels purchased from private individuals, finally emerging with a magnificent rectangle of land almost 200 yards deep and 100 yards wide. This became the garden of the Palais-Cardinal.

At this point, the Cardinal, immensely wealthy though he was, took a step which suggests that speculation in urban real estate had become a mania affecting even the mighty. He undertook to parcel off three sides of his garden tract into forty-five small residential lots. Three of these he retained, and the other forty-two he rented for a flat sum to Barbier, with the understanding that the latter would build a house on each lot to sell or rent on Barbier's own account. Richelieu, despite what this transaction might suggest, valued the privacy of his garden, so he stipulated that there should be no windows or openings in the back walls of the forty-two houses. But in insisting on this stipulation he eliminated the location's principal attraction—the view on the great man's garden. Sales were disappointingly slow. When Barbier died in 1641 in a blaze of overspeculation and lawsuits which were still being adjudicated forty years later, only about half the lots had been sold.[21]

Much more significant than Richelieu's private real-estate speculations was the fact that by the time Barbier died the development of a new and important part of the modern city—the Quartier Richelieu— was well under way. This "first great development of the Paris of the Right Bank since the fourteenth century" added almost 50 percent to the walled area on the north side of the city.[22] Corneille's *Le Menteur* in 1642 celebrated the birth of the new city arisen out of the ditches of Charles V. Further impetus to the growth of the neighborhood was given in 1667 by the leveling of the Butte Saint-Roch and the Butte des Moulins. These unsightly mounds had had their start in the construction of the fourteenth-century moats and had gradually grown in size as garbage and trash heaps. Still later in the century, two great exemplars of the new urbanism—the Place des Victoires and the Place Louis-le-Grand—came into being in the same neighborhood, as we shall note shortly. By the end of Louis XIV's reign the entire area north and west of the Palais-Cardinal (renamed the Palais-Royal) between the old and new enclosures and beyond was completely developed.

The start of Louis XIV's personal reign in 1661 and the consequent emergence of Jean-Baptiste Colbert as principal minister greatly intensified urban tendencies apparent in the early part of the seventeenth century. While these two men are difficult to distinguish in the formulation of governmental policies, so close was their association, it is easy to judge which of the two had the more genuine and unselfish love for Paris and the determination to make it not only a beautiful city but a more comfortable community in which to live. Colbert was the Parisian at heart. He shunned Versailles and centered his personal life around his palatial *hôtel* built in the new quarter directly in back of the Palais-Royal. One of the heaviest crosses he had to bear during his ministry was his inability to turn the King's attention back to Paris from the allurements of Versailles. In 1665, when there was apparently still hope of changing the King's course, he wrote a passionate letter to his monarch imploring him to halt the extravagances of Versailles (500,000 *écus* spent in the preceding two years and no one knew where it had all gone) and return it to the Louvre. "Oh, how tragic," Colbert wrote to his monarch, "that the greatest and most virtuous King . . . should be judged by Versailles! . . . There is reason to fear this calamity."[23]

The "calamity" materialized, of course. While Saint-Simon's indictment of Louis XIV on the grounds that he "abandoned Paris" and did nothing for the city other than construct the Pont Royal is unfair, no one can dispute Louis's relative want of interest in the city. Whether he could never put out of his mind his painful experiences with Parisian revolutionaries during the Fronde, or whether he simply desired an entirely fresh setting for his grandeur, his relations with the city seemed to rest simply on his sense of *noblesse oblige*. Paris was his capital and the strongest of all Louis XIV's traits—pride—demanded that Paris should be an impressive city. But his true feelings are revealed in the record of his visits and in his books of account. From 1670 to the end of the century, Paris received at best an annual visit or two. Between 1700 and 1715, Paris was honored by the royal presence on only four occasions.[24]

Even more telling are the books of accounts, which at least in Colbert's day were maintained with perhaps more care and precision than some of the structures themselves. Between 1644 and 1715 Louis spent 9,643,301 livres, 9 sous and 5 deniers on the Louvre and Tuileries combined, compared with an expenditure in the same period on Versailles of 65,651,275 l., 18 s., and 3 d. By far the greater part of the former was represented by Perrault's great Louvre colonnade completed between 1664 and 1676 as a grudging concession to Colbert.[25] In 1671, for the first time, expenses on Versailles exceeded those on the Louvre, and from then on this remained the case.[26] Until 1680 the Louvre occupied the traditional place of honor at the head of the royal ledger, but after that year it was relegated to last.

Judging from the funds expended on their upkeep, the royal edifices in Paris must have become depressing sights. For example, the immense Palais-Royal, willed to the King on the death of Richelieu, received during the years 1664-1680 annual appropriations for upkeep ranging from a modest 20,000 livres down to a miserly 2,000.[27] In the years Louis was lavishing the equivalent of an entire year's national tax revenues on Versailles, he was not unaware of Paris's needs. In 1672 he issued letters patent in which were described with some conviction the physical shortcomings of the Châtelet and the Halles, two city structures whose upkeep was the royal responsibility. He piously promised to raze both buildings and replace them with new ones.[28] But whereas Versailles was completed almost down to the last flower pot, the disgraceful old Châtelet continued in use to the time of Napoleon and the Halles to the Fifth Republic.

While Colbert showed much interest in the more prosaic problems of urban living, the King's concern was with the adornment of the city. Louis XIV's views on urban design, like those of the later indefatigable Haussmann, were in the classical tradition. He thought only in terms of the straight line, perfect alignment, symmetry, the long vista and open spaces. Mme de Maintenon, who had a perfect phobia about fresh air and drafts, complained bitterly of her husband's insistence that interior doors be constructed opposite one another, in reckless disregard of the resultant drafts. "With him," she wrote, "there is only grandeur, magnificence and symmetry . . . we must expire in symmetry."[29]

It goes without saying that there was no room in such thinking for medieval congestion and strangling city walls and gates, especially when the walls were so old and crumbly that had an enemy appeared before the city, mounds of earth would have had to have been piled in front of them to absorb the impact of artillery. The fourteenth-century wall of Charles V in the northeast sector of the capital had so lost its intended function that windmills had been erected in almost continuous line along its surface.[30] The near-five-centuries-old wall of Philip Augustus on the south side of the city had even less military significance.

Although he was on the verge of war with the Dutch, Louis XIV was so supremely confident of his army's ability to keep enemy troops far from his capital that in the summer of 1670 he ordered the city magistrates to raze the old fortifications, fill the double moats still visible in many places, and replace the lot with a tree-lined boulevard extending completely around the circumference of the city.[31] Work was to begin on the north side, always the principal concern of the authorities. Four rows of elms were to form a central *cours* approximately 100 feet wide flanked by two lateral alleys each about 20 feet wide. The new rampart (through force of habit, perhaps, the word continued to be used although the military connotation was nil) was to be banked with a low stone wall. Provision was made for a paved roadway atop the rampart, but apparently it was not intended as an arterial route, for the plans called for a parallel street inside the new promenade to serve this purpose.[32] The King's stated aim was to "provide promenades for the bourgeois and inhabitants"[33]—certainly a new and welcome note for Parisians long deprived of breathing space.

Along with the walls went the archaic old gates. A dozen or more of the minor ones were unceremoniously razed, and black marble plaques were supposedly left behind to mark the date of destruction.[34] The more famous ones were replaced with *arcs de triomphe*, generally located slightly outside the new roadway so as not to detract from the feeling of openness so sought after by the architects. The new Porte Saint-Denis was erected in 1672 commemorating the army's victories on the Rhine, while the Porte Saint-Martin and the Porte Saint-Antoine were completed two years later. All three were the work of the noted architect and pioneer urban planner Blondell, whose urban philosophy was excellent but whose artistic taste, at least as far as attested in these entranceways, was execrable. They were excessively ornate, overburdened with statuary, inscriptions, and medallions in honor of Ludovico Magno, and capped by senseless pyramids and other geometric shapes remindful of a child at play with his blocks. Viewing contemporary engravings of such barbarisms, one can only concur with Martin Lister's lament of the little "relish of the ancient simplicity" in much of the new construction.[35] (He compared the Luxembourg to a London cheesemonger's shop.)

Posterity can be grateful that the most ambitious and ornate of all these monuments was never completed. On a wide avenue leading out of the Porte Saint-Antoine, close to the spot where in 1660 he first received his bride Marie Thérèse for her entry into Paris, Louis XIV began a triumphal arch that was meant to surpass anything ancient Rome could offer. The architect was the great Claude Perrault, designer of the Observatory, the colonnade of the Louvre, and other works of undeniable merit. One can only wonder whether he had tongue in cheek when he presented this plan for Louis's approval. It was to consist of three arched portals set among gigantic Corinthian columns, between which were placed oversized medallions reminding viewers of all Louis's triumphs, alleged and real. At the pinnacle of the structure the plans called for a gargantuan equestrian statue of the monarch. Fortunately, work on the new gateway to Paris was suspended in 1681 for financial reasons, but not until half a million livres had been spent.[36] When Brice described the site in the 1698 edition of his guidebook, the stone still rose depressingly a few feet off the ground. The author, in the manner of writers of travel guides, managed to express cautious enthusiasm for a nearby plaster model.[37] Within a year after Louis's death, the Regent had removed (with all the relish he took in undoing Louis's work) all traces of his uncle's grand entranceway into Paris.

The destruction of the old wall and its replacement with the fine new promenade around the circumference of the city continued, on the Right Bank at least, slowly and painfully from 1670 to the end of the century. By 1684 the halfway point had been reached. To help the municipality, which was footing the bill and having a good deal of trouble doing so, the King authorized the sale for the profit of the Hôtel de Ville of all property on which the old wall and moats had stood.[38] By the close of the century, the promenade, or Cours, as it was called, had been completed on the Right Bank, and it was then possible to travel by carriage or on foot from the Porte Saint-Antoine around to the new Porte Saint-Honoré.[39] Thus were born the *grands boulevards* of modern Paris.

As for the Left Bank, it was relatively neglected and long continued to be so except for the favored Faubourg Saint-Germain. Even Voltaire many years later would complain about the primitive conditions on the south side of the city.[40] The master plan for the modernization and embellishment of Paris presented to the King in 1676 by his architects Bullet and Blondell showed an avenue of trees similar to the one on the Right Bank running from the Porte Saint-Bernard around to a point just east of the Invalides, but no significant progress was made on this work at any time during the reign. An *ordonnance* of 1704 again ordered the construction of the Left Bank promenade,[41] but by this time the city did not have enough money in its coffers even to maintain the municipal water supply. As a result, nothing was done. The only progress made was in the removal of the old city gate on the Left Bank. In the mid-1680's the Portes Saint-Victor, Saint-Jacques, Saint-Michel, and Saint-Marcel disappeared. At the upstream end of the Left Bank, the famous Porte Saint-Bernard, considered the symbolic entranceway to the port of Paris, was replaced in 1670 by one of Blondell's *arcs de triomphe*, this one with a bas-relief depicting Louis XIV at the tiller of a ship in full sail.

Of more lasting significance for both the Left Bank and Paris was the erection beginning in 1671 of the Invalides, Louis XIV's old soldiers' home just beyond the projected Cours. The setting for this huge edifice, an enormous parvis with broad avenues radiating out in many directions, was very much in the new style. Never before had Parisians witnessed such lavish use of space, not even for the Tuileries. This was the setting Louis XIV was in the process of creating for Versailles and which he might have provided for the entire city of Paris had the funds and the inclination been greater. When the Invalides was being erected, Louis XIV ordered his chief landscape architect, Le Nôtre, to continue the perspective of the Tuileries even further to the west with the now familiar quadruple line of trees. For good measure an *étoile* was placed in line with the Invalides across the river. To this maze was later given the name Champs-Elysées. It quickly became a favorite promenade for the bourgeois of Paris "to refresh themselves after the travails of the week." Just a few hundred yards to the south, on the Cours-la-Reine built by Marie de Médicis, perhaps the pioneer formal promenade in Europe, the *grand monde* of Paris consorted nightly, weather permitting. Not until the last quarter of the eighteenth century did the aristocracy begin to show any interest in the Champs-Elysées and to appreciate its possibilitites.[42]

The replacement of the old walls and gates by the magnificent new Cours was, of course, a great step forward in the embellishment of Paris, but such changes on the periphery did little to brighten life within the city. Dr Lister made some interesting observations on living conditions in Paris compared with London. He thought the French capital much more crowded for the "Common People" than the English and attributed this largely to the fact that in Paris "the Palaces and Convents have eat up the Peoples Dwellings, and crowded them excessively together . . . whereas in London . . . the People have destroyed the Palaces . . . and forced the Nobility to live in Squares or Streets in a sort of Community. . . ." The immense areas taken up on a seventeenth-century map of Paris by the gardens and fields of the religious orders, to say nothing of the *hôtels* of the great, confirm Lister's observations. Medieval Paris, like virtually all medieval cities, had given little thought to space for the sake of space. Churches and public buildings had been erected with little or no free area—land was too hard to come by for such waste—so it was next to impossible to step back and enjoy an un-obstructed view of a building. What public squares there were in medi-eval Paris were designed to fill some sort of public function, never aesthetic and generally unpleasant for man's spirit or senses—say the execution of criminals or the sale of meat, fish, vegetables, and a thou-sand wares. Such free areas were, one contemporary observed, "without order and haphazard."[43]

The seventeenth century ushered in a new concept, that of the *place royale*, called by one urban historian the "most perfect expression of classical urbanism."[44] Pierre Lavedan maintains, perhaps controversial-ly, that such *places* were a French invention resulting from the fusion of two Italian elements, the planned public square and the equestrian statue. If indeed they had an inventor, some credit must be given to Henry IV, whose Place Royale (the modern Place des Vosges) in the Marais quarter served as the prototype. In the closing years of his reign, this very inventive monarch had plans drawn for a *place* three sides of which would be given over to aristocratic residences, the fourth to a silk-sheet factory, and the space within to the general welfare of the entire neighborhood. The letters patent creating the project expressed the need for a "promenade for the inhabitants of our city, who are much crowded in their houses because of the multitude of people who flow in from all sides."[45]

The residential part of the project flourished from the start (the identification of the King with the new promotion was a powerful in-centive), but fortunately, plans for the factory languished. Henry IV, apparently as anxious to show a profit as any small bourgeois, therefore authorized his five bourgeois associates to abandon the factory and close in that side with the same sort of façade as had already been erected on the other three sides.[46] What the contracting parties purchased was a specific number of arcades in a beautifully symmetrical façade, behind which they erected their fine *hôtels* according to plans approved by the monarch or his agents. Throughout the century, the tenants of the Place Royale were of undisputed pedigree and always included a handful of bishops, who obviously would have led a more useful, if less glamorous, life back in the dioceses which were footing their bills.[47]

Although the Place Royale was in the first half of the century incontestably the most aristocratic address in the city, life even there could present problems. Surrounded by poorer and very poor neighborhoods, the dark arcades of the Place became a favorite target for the underworld. For reasons that are hard to fathom, the northwest corner of the square remained open to the public, perhaps in deference to the wishes of the democratic Henry IV that the area serve the needs of more than the immediate tenants. This opening was an invitation to the underworld to enter these enticing precincts. The usual ineffective warnings were constantly being issued to the lawless to stay away from the premises, like the ordinance of 1656 forbidding "all women and girls of ill repute, lackeys, idlers, vagabonds and other such" from gathering under the galleries. A couple of years later, the residents erected a wooden barrier around the perimeter of the square, leaving only enough room for a roadway. It must have then become more secure because Mlle de Montpensier, writing of the new enclosure, commented that the fashionable world promenaded there to the strains of violins "without torches."[48] The transition, unfortunate in a sense, to an English-type town square was completed in 1682 when the residents erected a ten-foot iron fence enclosing the often vandalized equestrian statue of Louis XIII along with a large area of the surrounding sward.

Also begun in the closing years (1608-1610) of Henry IV's reign was the unique Place Dauphine at the downstream end of the Ile de la Cité. An awkward point of waste land, for the most part created in the recent construction of the Pont Neuf (the first bridge in Paris uncluttered by houses), became the site of another imaginative residential development. Three rows of graceful brick houses in the form of an isosceles triangle were erected, each with identical façades on outer and inner sides, employing the same type of arched arcade so effectively used at the Place Royale. The famous bronze equestrian statue of Henry IV was located outside the triangle across the roadway of the Pont Neuf. It was the first equestrian statue in Paris (any public monument was a novelty at that time), so Marie de Médicis was forced to solicit the aid of her Italian relatives on behalf of her husband's monument. After a good deal of shopping around, a model was finally found, the statue of Ferdinand I at Leghorn.[49] In contrast to the Place Royale, which still stands today virtually unaltered, all that is left in original form of the Place Dauphine is a couple of houses, preserved for the rather dubious reason of their association with the hostess *extraordinaire* of the Revolution, Mme Roland.

Towards the end of the century, two more *places royales* were undertaken, the Place des Victoires and the Place Louis-le-Grand (the modern Place Vendôme), both the work of the King's premier architect, Jules Hardouin-Mansart. Both also played a significant role in the growth of Paris, but the construction of the Place Louis-le-Grand has been said to have given a "decisive *élan*" to the capital's development.[50]

The origin of the Place des Victoires was rather bizarre. The elderly Maréchal de Feuillade, long-time beneficiary of Louis XIV's friendship and generosity, resolved in 1683 to show his appreciation ("veneration" would not be too strong a word) by erecting a monumental Desjardins statue of Louis in front of his *hôtel*. But the statue was too large, the street too narrow, the perspective, in a day which had come to attach great importance to fine perspectives, impossible. The resolute Maréchal decided to raze a large part of his *hôtel*, as well as some neighboring houses purchased at his own expense, to acquire the necessary space. Before long even the wealthy Feuillade began to feel hard-pressed for money, so the sympathetic monarch accorded him a *gratification extraordinaire* of 120,000 livres.[51] When even this was inadequate, the municipality was dragged most reluctantly into the project. The Hôtel de Ville "received orders" to reach down into its coffers to buy more of the surrounding houses.[52]

Mansart had meanwhile produced an elaborate plan for two semicircular rows of houses much more pretentious than those in either the Place Royale or the Place Dauphine, testimony to Sauval's assertion that what had at the start of the century been good enough for wealthy Parisians no longer sufficed.[53] The style was strictly classical. The pilasters were erected in Ionic, "the favorite order of the modern Architects," Brice observed.[54] Feuillade receded more and more into the background as the plan developed. We find Louis assuming the role—which lesser humans would have found quite awkward—of directing work on his own monument, ordering "the manner in which the statue . . . should be placed."[55] It was finally dedicated in late 1685. The ceremony was marked by so much pagan fulsomeness as to cause some scandalized contemporaries to speculate whether France had forsaken Christianity. The magistrates of the Hôtel de Ville, who had provided roughly half the cost,[56] were told by the King that they could participate in the ceremonies on condition they say nothing about the financial assistance they had rendered to Feuillade.[57] Despite all the efforts and expense, Brice, viewing the site a decade later, found the effect quite disappointing.[58]

The construction of the Place des Victoires led directly to an even more significant project, the Place Louis-le-Grand, eventually to become renowned as the Place Vendôme. The promoters did not repeat Feuillade's mistake of choosing a location in a thoroughly built-up area, where costs were high and long vistas impossible, at least without the resources of a Haussmann. They went farther west, almost to the wall of 1633, now replaced by the great northern promenade. The large area between the former walls of Louis XIII and Charles V had been built up with startling swiftness. Where half a century earlier there had existed only monasteries and fields, there now stood seven churches, six large *hôtels*, one palace, two fountains and more than 1200 houses.[59] But to the west there were still two large enclaves: the vast Hôtel Vendôme and the adjacent Capuchin convent. These now attracted the attention of the urbanizers.

In July 1685 the financial reverses of the Vendômes forced the family to sell its palatial *hôtel* to the King for 600,000 livres and a *pot-de-vin* of 66,000. The King had probably already been persuaded by his superintendent of buildings Louvois and his first architect Mansart to sponsor a project whose boldness would do credit to any twentieth-century urban planner. The two men had convinced their monarch that it was not fitting for a mere courtier like the Maréchal de Feuillade to take the lead in the embellishment of the city[60] and had sketched for the King's personal action "the greatest and most magnificent public place in Europe."[61] Its dimensions would be about 500 by 550 feet. One side would be open on the Rue Saint-Honoré while the other three would be allocated to quarters for the Royal Library, the Académie Française, the Academy of Sciences, various other cultural academies founded by Louis XIV, the Mint, and an ambassadorial residence.[62] While it is difficult to see where the space was all coming from, the rest of the frontage —the larger part of the total—would be sold for private luxury housing. When the King murmured about the expense, he was glibly assured that the sale of lots to private individuals would amply take care of the expense of the public sector.

Somewhat reluctantly, the King went ahead with the project. Expropriating the convent of the Capuchin sisters, he gallantly rebuilt their house a stone's throw distant in so perfect a replica that Sauval assures us the sisters could not tell they had been moved.[63] In accordance with his promise to Louvois and Mansart (both of whom, but especially the latter, can be suspected of considerable financial involvement),[64] Louis undertook at his own expense the construction of the façade, or *murs de face*, of the project.[65] As at the Place Royale and Place des Victoires, purchasers obtained a portion of a false front along with their land. In 1691 Louvois died, and according to Saint-Simon, the King's first action, once free of his minister's persuasive presence, was to order the work halted.[66] For the rest of the century, while Louis XIV was waging still another of his interminable wars, the project was caught up in a web of legal complications which the King seemed to be little interested in untangling. A contemporary engraving shows the first façade of the Place Louis-le-Grand standing like a Hollywood movie set, awaiting the buildings and *hôtels* that never materialized behind it.[67] The great Girardon equestrian statue of Louis XIV, which Saugrain insisted was large enough to hold twenty people around a table in its stomach, was before the end of the century bravely set in the middle of this depressing tableau. Finally, after almost fifteen years and the expenditure of 2,350,000 livres for land, the relocation of the Capuchin sisters, the construction of the ill-fated first façade, and other incidentals, the King abandoned the role of land developer.

The Hôtel de Ville was again asked to pull the royal chestnuts out of the fire, but it quickly and willingly gave way to a syndicate of six professional financiers headed by Jean Masneuf. By this time the novel plans for an administrative and cultural center—centuries ahead of its time for Paris or any other city—had been quietly shelved. Mansart redesigned the site along the familiar octagonal lines of the modern Place Vendôme. The sale of lots at the Place, as well as its environs, proceeded briskly after 1700, giving birth, Nicolas Delamare wrote, to "an entirely new city."[68]

The tenants who in the last twenty-five years of Louis XIV's reign hastened to occupy the prestigious addresses in and around the Place des Victoires and the Place Louis-le-Grand tell a great deal about the growing rottenness of the Old Regime. The fact that construction of *hôtels* at the Place Louis-le-Grand *accelerated* between 1708 and 1710 is in itself a terrible indictment of the government and ruling classes of the times. These three years constituted probably the nadir of the French economy in the last two centuries before the Revolution; it would be difficult to find in modern French history human suffering more appalling than during the Great Winter of 1708-1709. Yet construction of luxury houses in Paris boomed in these very years.

The fortunate few who managed to grow so prosperous in the midst of such widespread distress were the men of finance, known as *maltôtiers, traitants, partisans, gens d'affaires, fermiers*, and other less polite terms. The French monarchy had long employed the services of such men in the collection of the indirect taxes, which had for centuries been farmed out to the highest bidder like any other government contract. In the seventeenth century, however, as government expenditures and deficits rose sharply, these financiers achieved a prominence they had never before known. Many of them became one-man banks, receiving deposits, paying interest, lending money to the always hard-pressed state. They made themselves remarkably useful, especially at the end of the century, by promoting an incredible number and variety of public offices which they would proceed to peddle for the Treasury, always at a fine profit to themselves. They became involved in the sale of privileges and of patents of nobility, in lotteries, loans of all kinds, schemes for recoinage, anticipations of revenue, the alienation of the royal domain, and much more. All these were part and parcel of the *affaires extraordinaires* which, thanks to the ingenuity of the men of finance and the criminal shortsightedness of the state, became routine sources of revenue rather than extraordinary ones. One of the most successful of these financiers, Poisson de Bourvalais, conceived, for example, the creation of new public market functionaries known as the *jurés vendeurs langueyeurs de porcs*, or examiners of pig tongues.[69] The government received a generous capital sum from the purchasers, Poisson earned a liberal commission, and the public suffered for generations thereafter from higher pork prices in order to pay the fees of the new inspectors, who quite possibly hired for a pittance some vagrant to carry out the "inspections." Such officials were multiplied thousands of times over. The Parisian scene was filled with these petty functionaries who, owning their offices, assumed an independence and intransigence which infuriated the public and perhaps explain the attitudes of even twentieth-century French functionaries. On an even loftier scale were men like Samuel Bernard, the greatest financier of the times. His fortune of 60,000,000 livres made him possibly the richest man in the realm after the King, whose banker he became.

The aristocrats resented the *hommes d'affaires* all the more because of their alleged humble origins, although these were liable to be exaggerated. Legend made all the *nouveaux riches* financiers the sons of peasants or of the dregs of the urban population. Commenting on a lavish ball and supper given for the ladies of the Opera by a prominent financier, an aristocratic correspondent of the Controller-General wrote: "I assure you that this conduct revolts everyone and that it is very difficult for us to see a man we all knew once as a shop clerk making such a splash with our money." In truth, most of the financiers descended from good bourgeois professional and commercial stock. They got their start as bright, reasonably well-educated, but obviously less-than-scrupulous young men who in a different society would probably have made large fortunes in commerce or industry. In the economic milieu of seventeenth-century Paris, where large-scale private enterprise was almost an impossibility, they turned to other more questionable outlets for their talents. The cynical irresponsibility of the men who directed the state assured them of ample opportunities.

These were the men who concentrated at the end of the seventeenth century in the newly developed neighborhood to the northwest of the city. An analysis of the addresses of sixty-three prominent financiers listed in Blégny's directory of Paris for 1692 shows that eighteen resided at that time in the new Montmartre quarter, in and around the Place des Victoires.[70] Probably as many more lived in the neighborhood immediately adjacent, and this, we must remember, was almost a decade before the rush by this class to the Place Louis-le-Grand. When this *place* opened early in the new century, its first occupant was Antoine Crozat, one of the greatest and most notorious financiers. By the end of the first decade of the eighteenth century, the Place Louis-le-Grand was the residential Wall Street of its day, boasting such names as Poisson de Bourvalais (whose *hôtel* cost 230,000 livres); the Comte d'Evreux, son-in-law of Crozat (the marriage of blood and money had already begun); Delpech, the farmer-general; Aubert, *receveur des finances* of Caen; Lelay, another farmer-general; Heuzé de Vauloger, treasurer of Alençon; and innumerable others.[71] Virtually the only residents of the Place Louis-le-Grand who were not financiers or relatives of financiers were four architects, including Pierre Bullet and Jules Hardouin-Mansart, who had made fortunes in the new profession of designing *hôtels* and *châteaux* for the wealthy. The populace had very pithily characterized the social divisions of seventeenth-century Paris in a well-known aphorism which alluded, with reference to the three statues of monarchs in different parts of Paris, to "Henry IV with the populace on the Pont Neuf, Louis XIII with the people of quality at the Place Royale, and Louis XIV with the *maltôtiers* in the Place des Victoires."

The popular saying was already a trifle dated in its reference to the "people of quality." While the Place Royale remained a thoroughly fashionable address, it had become by the end of the century something of an oasis of the *beau monde*. Henry IV and Louis XIII were the last monarchs to show any fondness for the east side of Paris. In the second half of the seventeenth century, the very obvious trend was to the west, both on the Right and Left Banks. The construction of the Palais-Royal, the Place des Victoires, and the Place Louis-le-Grand, all well to the west, had much to do with this trend, as did the location of Versailles to the southwest. It became much more convenient to live on the west side of Paris, thus eliminating the need for crossing the city to get back home after a ride to Versailles.

In the most favorable position to take advantage of the location of Versailles was the Faubourg Saint-Germain-des-Prés, which in 1642 had been promoted to the rank of *quartier* (the seventeenth). As we have seen, this neighborhood received its first real impetus in the 1630's. From then on, its growth was continuous. Soon it became for Parisians the Grand Faubourg, termed by Sauval "one of the miracles of the world."[72] In Louis XIV's time it was both the fastest-growing and most aristocratic neighborhood in Paris. If one tracks down the location of 189 notable *hôtels* listed in Saugrain's guidebook of 1716, no fewer than 54 will be found to be in Saint-Germain-des-Prés, compared with 31 in the Marais quarter to the northeast, 27 in the new Montmartre quarter, and 14 in the area around the Louvre and the Palais-Royal. One must remember, too, that the great majority of the *hôtels* located in the Faubourg Saint-Germain were no older than the closing years of Louis XIII's reign. Not only were most *hôtels* being built in Saint-Germain, but the "best people" were occupying them. The *nouveaux riches* clearly did not gravitate in that direction, as we can see from the simple fact that of the sixty-three financiers listed in the *Livre commode* for 1692, only two had addresses there.

The Grand Faubourg was convenient to everything that mattered for the rich; its streets were uncluttered, its air, in the firm opinion of the residents, superior to any in the city. The best hotels for transients were located in Saint-Germain, and a visitor of distinction rarely stooped to residing elsewhere. It was traditional for wealthy young foreigners to take lodgings in the Faubourg for a year or more, availing themselves of the services of the innumerable French tutors, of the seven riding academies, of the various fashionable *maîtres d'exercice*, and the like. Towards the end of the century, Germain Brice, author of the most popular Parisian guidebook of the century, asserted that in one representative winter season there could be found in the Faubourg Saint-Germain "twelve princes of Germany, and more than three hundred counts and barons, without counting a far greater number of simple noblemen."[73]

The sharp upsurge in land development and building activity in the reign of Louis XIV was not limited to the city proper. The environs shared much of this activity. While no census was taken of country estates around Paris in the seventeenth century, common sense supports Marcel Poete's conclusion that the century saw a great increase in such houses. It can be safely assumed that every one of the fine *hôtels* erected in the seventeenth century had its rural complement. For a well-to-do Parisian not to retire to the country with the advent of the summer season in order to recuperate spiritually and financially from the preceding winter's whirl and to prepare for the next, would have been unthinkable. Such was the traditional pattern of living which the new wealth, anxious to be accepted into the old, can be safely assumed to have copied. Many *châteaux* and less pretentious houses would, of course, be at some distance from the city, but the introduction of the carriage in the seventeenth century along with marked improvements in the roads leading out of Paris (Dr Lister was much struck by their high quality)[74] doubtless encouraged the construction of country places readily accessible to the city. The German "gentlemen's companion," Nemeitz, writing at the end of Louis XIV's reign, noted that "many Parisians rent apartments at Saint-Cloud for the entire year or only for the summer in order to taste the delights of this charming spot."[75] In 1656 the young De Lacke brothers, visitors from Holland, were greatly impressed even at this early date by the "quantity of fine houses which seem as if sown in the countryside." This fusion of man's labor with nature impressed many onlookers and provoked Marcel Poete's felicitous phrase, "la campagne arrangée du XVIIe siècle." The contemporary historian Sauval was bemused by the prodigious labors involved in establishing the long avenues of trees, creating the gardens and parks, and "bringing in water in spite of nature." Even as unlyrical a person as the commissioner of police, Nicolas Delamare, waxed rhapsodic over the "enchanted places" in the environs of the city.[76]

As he was completing in 1698 a six-month sojourn in Paris, Martin Lister wrote that "the greatest part of the City has been lately rebuilt." Obviously the greatest part of Paris had not been rebuilt. Nevertheless, significant physical changes were apparent. The destruction of the old wall in the 1670's had symbolized the determination to break out of the medieval cocoon. The great physical expansion of the city after centuries of minimum growth gave evidence of a new dynamism which could be counted on to rebel against the timeworn practices of the past. The many new spacious promenades and streets, the new public squares, the magnificent new setting of the Invalides, were all indicative of a new urban aesthetic.

The change which had come over Paris, however, was more basic than a physical change. One does not have to await the famous Baron Haussmann in the nineteenth century to encounter a systematic, rational campaign of modernization in the affairs of Paris. It may be found in the Grand Siècle, although, of course, in far less spectacular and personal form. One of the most respected historians of European cities, Pierre Lavedan, dates the start of modern urbanism to the seventeenth century. By "urbanism" he means the overall view of the city and its problems, something much more than the old notion that the embellishment of a community could be achieved by a few fine buildings and houses. The new urbanism demanded that city magistrates plan the total needs of the community in terms of water and sanitation requirements, circulation, recreation, provisioning, open spaces, and the rest.

Serving as unofficial director of Parisian public works in the early years of Louis XIV's personal reign was a royal architect and pioneer urbanist named François Blondell. Blondell's background, one might be tempted to say, was strangely unprofessional, except that in those days the notion of an architectural profession was quite amorphous— any master mason might well assume the name. He probably first attracted Colbert's attention while helping in the engineering of the new naval port of Rochefort, then served briefly as a mariner in the King's service, and at some time developed enough of a reputation as a mathematician to be entrusted in 1672 with the mathematical education of both the Dauphin and Colbert's own son, Seignelay.[77] In the same year he for the first time emerged into architectural prominence by designing the new Portes Saint-Antoine and Saint-Bernard and was shortly thereafter made "Directeur" of the new Royal Academy of Architecture. Being close to the royal presence, he must have served as a convenient intermediary between the King and Council on the one hand, and the Hôtel de Ville (responsible for Parisian public works) on the other.

For the Academy he wrote his *Cours d'architecture* (1675), one of the first theoretical considerations of modern urbanism. His dedicatory letter to the King spoke approvingly of how his pupil, the Dauphin, had interested himself not only in the military aspects of architecture but in those that relate to "the public comfort and improvement of the cities, to pleasure as well as grandeur." While by far the largest part of the *Cours d'architecture* dealt with technical architectural matters, Blondell devoted several chapters to the "Public Works of Paris" then being executed: street improvements, new quays, pumps, water lines, fountains ("most of them new"), the recently opened Cours north of the Bastille ("Is there anything on earth grander and more pleasant?").[78] Blondell also referred to the new city plan, incorporating his own ideas but drawn by Pierre Bullet, "skilled draughtsman." This Bullet-Blondell plan, possibly the first of its kind for Paris, showed all recent as well as projected improvements. Blondell alleged in his book that the King had ordered all future public works to conform to the new master plan.

As a result of this new urban thinking, Paris had probably become by the end of the century a far better place to live in than at the start. A few people at least had begun to think about the city, its problems and its needs. The rational approach to the business of government, so much a part of Colbert's thinking and of the early decades of Louis XIV's personal reign, inevitably influenced the administration of the capital, since Paris was essentially a department of the national government. The old ways of administering the city, of policing it, of maintaining its streets, of caring for its sick and poor—these and much more were reexamined. Newly established learned groups such as the Royal Academy of Architecture devoted entire sessions to solving such problems as the maximum height of Parisian houses, the optimum street width, the precise water requirements of the population.[79] The Academy was doubtless too classically minded and obsessed with the ideas of the ancients (in its death throes in 1793 it was still discussing Vitruvius),[80] but the mere fact that men were again concerning themselves with such questions is significant.

CHAPTER TWO

Paris acquires a chief magistrate

ONE of the striking aspects of the seventeenth-century expansion of Paris was the uneasiness it provoked among officials responsible for the city's welfare. Not unlike hard-pressed mayors of certain modern urban agglomerations, seventeenth-century French monarchs and Parisian magistrates expressed the fear that at some point in their growth cities might become so unwieldy and complicated as to be ungovernable. That they suspected this point may have been reached when the population of Paris was still short of half a million is not surprising when one considers the city's primitive administrative machinery—inherited essentially from the time of the Crusades.

Historically, Parisian magistrates had discouraged urban expansion beyond the walls, principally on military grounds. In actual fact, the question had remained rather academic, since the population had never grown so fast as to warrant much building outside the walls. Delamare assures us that during the Hundred Years' War such construction was so negligible that whenever necessary it was simply set afire, the owners first being allowed to remove whatever they wished. The first formal interdiction against building outside the walls, and the first law to set limits for Paris, dated only to Henry II in 1548. Even in this instance the fear of excessive growth was only incidental. The main motive was the protection of the city's guildsmen. It seems that "free" trades and shops were springing up in the faubourgs and enticing recruits from both the walled city and outlying communities. (The law of 1548 also mentioned moral considerations: the vice and corruption of the faubourgs were allegedly affecting the youth of Paris.)[1]

But the qualms shown in the seventeenth century by Louis XIII, and even more by Louis XIV, as they watched their capital spill across its walls, were no longer related to military, economic, or moral concerns. As we have noted, Louis XIV was so little concerned about the defenses of Paris that he replaced half of the city's walls with promenades and would gladly have completed the task had he had the resources. What lay behind seventeenth-century attempts to put reins on the city's growth were administrative considerations. In three laws issued in 1627, 1633, and 1638, Louis XIII took note of the "extraordinary disorder" resulting from the recent expansion of the city. The growth of the faubourgs, he alleged, had corrupted the air, made it difficult to dispose of filth, created havoc in the food supply, and given occasion to uncontrolled larceny, robbery, and murder.[2] Fields which from time immemorial had been devoted to supplying the markets of the city had been converted into residential lots with "intolerable" consequences to the cost of living. To arrest this budding catastrophe, Louis XIII ordered thirty-one markers—some of marble with gold lettering, others of stone, still others of wood—placed around the perimeter of the city, warning that anyone constructing beyond these markers was liable to have his house razed and be fined 3,000 livres.[3] The new markers left little room for future building. On the Right Bank they mainly coincided with the existing wall; on the Left they extended as much as half a mile beyond, but unaccountably sliced off a segment of the promising new residential development in the Faubourg Saint-Germain-des-Prés. Louis XIII and his advisers seemed determined not merely to slow things down but rather to halt expansion completely.

Predictably, little attention was paid to Louis XIII's thirty-one markers. The city continued to grow. In 1672, in search of funds ostensibly to repair certain buildings in his capital but more likely for his senseless war on Holland, Louis XIV threatened to invoke his father's laws unless the violator came forward with payment equivalent to 10 percent of his property's value.[4] Louis strongly defended the need for such limits. "It would be useless," he wrote, "to have lavished so much care on the embellishment, comfort and security of our city of Paris" if no attention were paid to what was "of greatest consequence," namely, keeping the city within manageable bounds. In the King's opinion, the proper policing of a large city was impossible; he feared for Paris the fate "of the larger cities which found in themselves the principle of their own ruin."[5] (One wonders how much Louis XIV's fears of a growing Paris rested also on his unpleasant boyhood experiences with the *frondeurs* and on his financial needs.)

Historical circumstances had dictated that the citizens of Paris be burdened with not one but two principal organs of administration, the Hôtel de Ville and the Châtelet. The Hôtel de Ville—the Parisian municipality properly speaking—was currently housed in the graceful Renaissance structure on the Right Bank which until destroyed by the Communards in 1871 served as the focal point of so much Parisian and national history. In front of this edifice lay the largest open space in the inner city, the famous Place de Grève, where at the start of Louis XIV's personal reign it was estimated that two or three people were executed daily.[6] Judging from the journal of the "two young Hollanders" written about the same time, the estimate seems quite credible. *En passant,* they mention witnessing the execution of two "cavaliers" for robbery; the following day, the hanging of six more robbers; and soon afterwards, a beheading so botched by an inept executioner that troops had to be summoned from the nearby Bastille to protect him from the allegedly angry spectators.[7]

At the Hôtel de Ville presided the municipal officers, the Prévôt des Marchands and the four Echevins—one is rarely mentioned without the other. Their principal function was overseeing the ports and the traffic on the Seine, Marne, Yonne, and Oise rivers by which most of the city's needs were filled. Like all administrators in those days, they served as judges as well; legal cases arising among the rivermen and merchants in the several ports of the city went to them for adjudication.

Subordinate to the Prévôt des Marchands and the Echevins, and serving as connecting links between them and the public, was an ancient and badly outmoded bureaucracy of neighborhood officials. When the five-year-old Louis XIV began his reign in 1643, Paris was divided administratively into 16 *quartiers* each headed by a *quartenier*, and subdivided into 64 *cinquantaines* and 256 *dizaines,* each in the charge of a neighborhood official. This complex organization had originally been created for the purpose of raising a militia, elements of which were still to be observed on seventeenth-century ceremonial occasions, although their ranks were by now badly depleted. The professional army of Louis XIV had little use for the ceremonial-minded urban militia. The *coup de grâce* for the *quarteniers-cinquanteniers-dizainiers* resulted from their marked antiroyalist activities during the Fronde. In subsequent years, Louis XIV stripped them of what remained of their former functions.[8] Even the old honor accorded the *quarteniers* of acting as custodians of the city keys fell a cropper when most of the gates were replaced by *arcs de triomphe*.[9]

Deprived of their old military and police functions, the *quarteniers* and their subordinates in the later seventeenth century did little more than keep a watchful eye on their neighborhoods. Theoretically, at least, they reported crimes, fires, contagion, and so on to the officials of the Châtelet and rendered minor assistance in the collection of certain municipal taxes. Since they (like the Prévôt des Marchands, the Echevins, and nearly all the officials at the Hôtel de Ville) received no salary, one may question the seriousness of their labors. Such offices were only rewarding for the distinction and financial exemptions they brought their holders, which were by no means inconsiderable, to judge from a newspaper advertisement of May 1, 1689: "For sale—A city office of *cinquantenier* carrying exemption from *tutelle, curatelle,* lodging of troops, and several others. About 500 livres."[10]

Like the bureaucracy of local officials, the Hôtel de Ville itself had shown too much sympathy with the rebels in the Fronde and had to pay the consequences. After mid-century it ceased to play a significant role in the political life of Paris and France. Once chosen from among the merchant aristocracy of the city, the Prévôts des Marchands were now invariably crown officials. The historian of the Parisian municipality, Le Roux de Lincy, ended his history of the Hôtel de Ville at this point, remarking that henceforth its role was purely administrative and festive.[11] Louis XIV thoroughly distrusted the institution, but it was much too venerable (as well as financially convenient) to suppress. The election of the Prévôt des Marchands continued to take place every two years, as it had for centuries, but it became a comedy, meaningless as it was colorful and complicated. Louis XIV, by some not so devious means, would announce well beforehand whom he intended to be the next Prévôt des Marchands. In D'Ormesson's journal, for example, one finds an entry for 1668 recounting how M. Le Pelletier had just been stopped in a corridor by the King, and informed that "he was selected to be the [next] Prévôt des Marchands."[12]

A visitor to Louis XIV's Paris, arriving from the north or from one of the Channel ports, ordinarily entered the city by the Porte Saint-Denis. Traveling southward on the street of the same name, one of the few arterial routes in the city, passing such landmarks as the Convent of the Filles-Dieu, the Cour des Miracles, the crusader Church of the Holy Sepulcher, and the Church and Cemetery of the Holy Innocents, he would finally have had to come to a halt before the ugly twelfth-century fortress of the Châtelet. The seventeenth-century tourist would probably have taken a street around the structure in order to get to the Pont au Change. In earlier times, this having once been the famous Porte de Paris (the name was still retained), he would have been forced to pass beneath the Châtelet through a narrow opening to reach the only bridge from the Right Bank to the Island of the Cité.

With the construction at the end of the twelfth century of the wall of Philip Augustus, half a mile or so to the north, the Châtelet lost its military significance and began to serve simply as the seat of justice for the Prévôt de Paris, the King's representative in the city. Enlarged by succeeding monarchs, the Châtelet served this purpose for five centuries, until the Revolution destroyed both the building and the justice it symbolized. Like all edifices in the Old Regime connected with the administration of justice, the Châtelet enjoyed a very sinister reputation, even worse than the storied Bastille. Relatively few Parisians of common stock were ever able to claim the dubious distinction that a relative or friend languished in the dungeons of the Bastille; many more could make the claim for the dank chambers of the Châtelet, inherently far more fearsome than the dry and relatively comfortable prison a mile to the east. When the King wrote in 1672 of replacing this old prison with a new one, he mentioned that the illnesses generally contracted during a sojourn in the Châtelet were more dreaded than the loss of liberty itself.[13]

The roadway which passed under the Châtelet (in effect the continuation of the Rue Saint-Denis) set apart the municipal prison on the eastern side of the structure from the various magisterial chambers to the west. Below these chambers lay the city morgue, where the numerous bodies found daily in the river and on the streets were brought to be exposed for possible identification before burial—probably at the nearby Holy Innocents Cemetery. Since the end of the fifteenth century, the Prévôt de Paris, who should be carefully distinguished from the Prévôt des Marchands at the Hôtel de Ville, had permitted a growing number of middle-class lieutenants to try cases in his name. Meanwhile, his office became the sort of empty but highly prized and prestigious sinecure so typical of the Old Regime. Legal decisions at the Châtelet were rendered in his name, although all the magisterial offices were venal and their occupants responsible to no one, least of all the Prévôt. The feudal assemblage of the Parisian nobility for military service was his responsibility. He in theory led the valorous knights in battle, except that even on paper such obligations came to an end after Louis XIV made a couple of disastrous efforts at exacting feudal service from the untrained, undisciplined, and unwilling nobility. Nevertheless, the Prévôt collected a liberal emolument from the Treasury which he earned after a fashion by appearances at occasional processions and other ceremonial functions. The magistrates, the Prévôt's theoretical subordinates, who actually ran the Châtelet in Louis XIV's day were the *lieutenant civil*, the *lieutenant criminel*, and two *lieutenants particuliers*, each of whom presided over different civil and criminal sections of the courts.

The administrative history of Paris would have been enormously simplified had not Louis IX in 1246 encouraged the powerful merchant community to organize the municipal authority which ultimately became known as the Hôtel de Ville. As a consequence, the main theme of the city's administrative history for centuries was the clash between the Châtelet and its upstream neighbor. The monarchs tried valiantly to establish peace between them by asserting that the Hôtel de Ville had cognizance over all matters pertaining to water commerce and the Châtelet to commerce on land. But this was like trying to settle medieval church-state controversies by invoking the Biblical order to give to Caesar what belonged to Caesar and to the Lord what was His due. The most notable peace-making effort by the King was the long and detailed Ordinance of 1415, but it enjoyed only indifferent success. Louis XIV's laws of 1672 and 1700 were little more than weary efforts to update that of 1415. On both occasions, the Sun King noted, in classic bits of understatement, the existence of "some difficulties" between Hôtel de Ville and Châtelet.

The law of 1700, for example, tried to end the hoary quarrel pertaining to jurisdiction over the sale of oysters. The Hôtel de Ville had long claimed the right to oversee their commerce since oysters were obviously connected with water. But painful experience had shown that oysters also constituted a health hazard, which enabled the Châtelet to claim they fell within its jurisdiction. (Needless to say, what was really at stake was which officials would collect the fees for the inspection and sale of the bivalves.) Another vital issue perennially debated between Châtelet and Hôtel de Ville was the right in times of dangerous floods to order the bridge residents to leave their domiciles (all bridges except the Pont Neuf supported houses). On the question of the oysters, the Châtelet won hands down, but the issue of the bridges was apparently more difficult. The law of 1700 provided that if an order to evacuate a bridge became necessary, the representatives of the Châtelet and the Hôtel de Ville would give the order concurrently. If, on the other hand, they could not agree on whether such an order was necessary, they were required to consult the Parlement for a final decision.[14] The fate of the unfortunate bridge dwellers pending a judicial ruling appeared of secondary concern. Wearily, Louis XIV in his ordinance of 1700 requested that the two parties "avoid as much as possible all kinds of conflicts of jurisdiction and settle, amicably if they can . . . those that developed."[15]

Two conflicting and warring centers of administration—Hôtel de Ville and Châtelet—hardly made for good municipal management. But complicating matters even further was the existence of a maze of conflicting and overlapping seignorial jurisdictions inherited from medieval times. Each of these authorities was bent on guarding and possibly extending his own bailiwick; all seemed unaware of the conception of public service. In large areas of Paris the officials of both the Châtelet and the Hôtel de Ville were forced to give way to these "feudal" magistrates, whose authority could extend to judicial, police, and administrative matters alike, since the Old Regime rarely distinguished among them. Not unusually, legal cases hinged on which side of a street an offense had been committed, and the original issue might well be forgotten over the "larger" question of which authority had legal cognizance.

A typical story of conflicting police and legal jurisdiction was told by two young Dutch visitors in 1656. Arriving in Paris, the two strangers stopped in the Saint-Germain quarter at an auberge managed by a quarrelsome compatriot named Regina de Hoeve. Her unadmiring but apparently experienced guests quickly dubbed their landlady Regina de Hoer. One thing led to another and before long they were out on the street, their horses held hostage for allegedly unpaid bills and the animals' owners in obvious need of legal assistance.

The problem was to whom to turn. The auberge being in the Saint-Germain-des-Prés quarter, the case from one point of view fell in the jurisdiction of the abbot of Saint-Germain-des-Prés. Historically his claim was hard to dispute, going back as it did to the sixth-century foundation of the monastery. For a thousand years the abbey had enjoyed virtual solitude, but by Louis XIV's time it was surrounded on all sides by the burgeoning and fashionable quarter whose name was derived from the abbey. The abbot's ancient claim as *seigneur* of the entire neighborhood was by then the subject of continuing dispute with the royal magistrates. (The matter was by no means trivial, since the seignory included the most famous and richest fair in the city, held each spring in buildings just south of the abbey. The value of the seignory can be judged by the willingness of laymen to pay in the vicinity of 50,000 livres for the office of bailiff, or judge, of Saint-Germain-des-Prés.)[16]

It was to this bailiff of Saint-Germain that the young visitors now appealed for return of their horses. Their case was either denied, or what is more likely, put aside. Disappointed, they crossed the river to the Châtelet. There they met with much more success. They were sent to the house of the police commissioner residing in Saint-Germain and "after waiting for him a long time" accompanied him to the de Hoeve auberge. After such argument, the woman finally surrendered their horses.[17] However, we may be sure that the judge of Saint-Germain was as disgruntled by this "invasion" of his bailiwick as the magistrates at the Châtelet were happy to disregard his claims.

This small incident affords a glimmer of the complications caused by the presence of numerous anachronistic seignorial judges in Paris. Sauval wrote that in the middle of the seventeenth century more than half of Paris "belonged" to the *seigneurs*, mostly of the ecclesiastical variety, since the Church, especially abbots and abbesses, had been far more successful in holding on to ancient prerogatives than the lay lords. All these lords still clung to the right of *haute-justice*, that is the right to sentence prisoners to capital punishment (although not without automatic appeal to a royal court). Many streets were divided among different *seigneurs*, and occasionally the line of demarcation even ran through a house. The abbot of Saint-Germain-des-Prés, in addition to being lord of the entire faubourg, was *seigneur* of thirty other streets in Paris; the Archbishop was master of 164; the Chapter of Notre-Dame of 38, the abbot of Sainte-Geneviève, 54; the abbot of Saint-Magloire, 70; the abbot of Saint-Victor, 25; the Chapter of Saint-Honoré, five.[18] Some of these lords—not all—claimed the right of *voirie* over these streets and thus determined which would be opened or closed and who should be fined for cluttering the right-of-way with garbage or for erecting a sign or a balcony projecting illegally into the street. Others of them, notably the abbot of Saint-Germain, even regulated the guilds, or "corporations," lying within their bailiwicks.[19]

Another kind of seignorial autonomy survived into the seventeenth century to plague efforts of reformers to achieve administrative and judicial unity. The autonomies of ecclesiastics like the abbots of Saint-Germain-des-Prés and the Grand Prior of the Knights of Malta stemmed from ancient territorial grants by the kings in what were then the outskirts of Paris. But besides doling out land to a privileged few, medieval kings had given to important officials of their household lucrative rights to oversee certain trades and individuals vital to the provisioning of the court. This even included the power to determine who would be allowed to practice such trades. The Royal Cupbearer (the Grand Echanson), for example, had been given jurisdiction over the wine merchants, the Grand Chamberlain over a great variety of trades concerned with clothing and furnishings, the Grand Master of the Household over everything dealing with the king's table, and so on. As the Châtelet grew in strength, its judges naturally complained that such concessions infringed on their rights to police industry and trade, so the jurisdiction of the household officers gradually became limited to tradesmen who could prove that they were actually engaged in provisioning the court. When Louis XIV came to the throne, over thirty of these privileged merchants were ensconced in the galleries of the Louvre alone,[20] and many more were scattered throughout Paris. They all made themselves highly unpopular with Parisian guildsmen and the Châtelet by claiming complete independence from both. The existence of a special court, the Prévôté de l'Hôtel, to handle their litigation was tangible evidence of their autonomy.

In a category of his own among these old court functionaries, still undisturbed in all the medieval fullness of his prerogatives when Louis XIV became king, was the Grand Panetier. For over four centuries, this official had supervised Parisian bakers. Largely because their guild statutes had remained in the hands of this courtier, whose only interest in bread-making was the tribute he could squeeze out of it, the bakers' guild regulations had remained remarkably unchanged since first being promulgated 450 years earlier.[21] The Grand Panetier collected from each member of the guild—master, journeyman and apprentice—a tribute of one sou every year on the Sunday after Epiphany. New masters paid him an *hommage* of one *louis d'or* upon reception plus five sous for each of their first three years as master.[22] In addition, the Grand Panetier collected lucrative fees in his private court for adjudicating differences among the guild members. The bakers naturally had little love for this anachronistic relationship and tried repeatedly but unsuccessfully to get out from under the Grand Panetier's yoke, placing their cause, as one would expect, in the willing hands of the magistrates of the Châtelet. Not infrequently, dual elections for guild officers, one under the supervision of the Châtelet, the other under the Grand Panetier, were held, resulting in interminable lawsuits financially ruinous to the bakers of Paris.

ܐ܀ ܐ܀

Such were some of the anachronisms that troubled seventeenth-century Parisians interested in rationalizing the city's administration. Fortunately, they were given their innings early in the personal reign of Louis XIV. The 1660's and 1670's were for Paris, as for France as a whole, years of reform bordering on the unique in the 300-year span of the Old Regime. For a few brief years the government seemed fully as interested in shaping a better society for its citizens as in the age-old preoccupations of foreign policy. For a moment it seemed bent on making many of the basic changes and reforms which in the end only Revolution would effect. These were the years when Jean-Baptiste Colbert dominated the ministry, as much as anyone was allowed to dominate it in the reign of the Sun King.

Of bourgeois origins, icily efficient, cordially disliked by nearly everyone around him, Colbert was intent upon drawing a curtain on the dark Gothic past and on reevaluating outmoded institutions in the light of reason and good sense. Not the least bit interested in philosophy and philosophers, he was nevertheless a Cartesian in thought and action. "We are not in the reign of little things," he wrote, and he was determined to make good these words for the capital city. Paris was both his place of residence (he loathed Versailles) and his ministerial responsibility. The King, never at heart a Parisian, permitted himself for the moment to be drawn along by his minister's zeal. Royal pride and prestige were at stake. Besides, Paris was a royal city constitutionally. Unlike nearly all other French cities, it had never obtained the charter of liberties which carried with it a measure of independence from the Crown. The city's destinies lay ultimately in the hands of the King's councilors rather than local officials.

The first important step Louis XIV and Colbert took to modernize Parisian administration was the establishment in 1666 of a special high-level committee, the Conseil de Police, to explore all facets of the city's operations and make recommendations for improvements. The need for change was apparently urgent. Delamare wrote that Paris had become "a Sewer." The new committee worked from October 1666 to February of the following year. From it stemmed the most important administrative reforms of the Old Regime pertaining to Paris. Headed by Chancellor Séguier, it included Colbert, Marshal Villeroy, D'Aligre, and eight councilors of state. Colbert is said to have dominated the proceedings.[23] The full committee met weekly at the Chancellor's residence, but in the intervening days each councilor of state was assigned to two of the sixteen quarters of the city to interview the senior police commissioners and representative bourgeois therein.[24] In addition to mastering the problems of his assigned neighborhood, each councilor was handed a specific assignment. For example, Pussort was assigned the problem of street lighting, another councilor street cleaning, a third public security. The King did not attend any of the sessions himself but remained in close touch. At one point, the Chancellor announced to the members that the King had sent word that he intended to walk the streets personally to ensure that the new directives on street cleaning were being observed.[25]

All these findings and recommendations went on to the King in Council, from which specific decrees and ordinances ensued. Tentative measures were taken against the troublesome *hauts seigneurs* whose medieval autonomy so complicated the task of administering the city. The cleaning and repairing of the streets were reorganized. The night watch was augmented and reformed in the hope of making the streets more secure than the "darkest woods" to which Boileau had recently compared them. A system of street lighting, probably the finest in the world at the time, came into being. All these measures will be discussed in due course, but even more basic was the creation in March 1667 of a chief police magistrate for the entire city under the name of the Lieutenant of Police. Behind this new creation lay a couple of decades of particularly scandalous street disorders. But what impelled immediate action was the recent murders of two high-ranking magistrates, one brutally murdered with his spouse in his own home.[26] Obviously, decisive measures for the reform of the Parisian police were in order.

The edict creating the post of Lieutenant of Police brought into being a wholly new kind of administrative authority. Hitherto, administration and justice had been one; they were now separated. To think of the new officer as simply a chief of police in the modern sense of the term is to misinterpret his significance. What Parisians were obtaining for the first time was the equivalent of a modern mayor or urban executive. It is at this point, Roland Mousnier writes, that evolution begins from "judicial administration to that which we call executive administration, that is to say, administration rendered by governmental organs which derive all executive powers from the government itself."[27] In the words of Louis XIV: "As the functions of Justice and Police are often incompatible, and of too great a scope to be exercised by an Officer alone in Paris, we have resolved to separate them. . . ." Delamare commented sagely that litigation belonged to the bench, while matters concerning public order and security were the province of government.[28] Although the first and many subsequent occupants of the office were trained in the law, their legal function was always secondary to their administrative. Relations between the new Lieutenant of Police and his fellow magistrates at the Châtelet—the latter all exclusively judges— were notoriously cool at best, the basic reason being that the Lieutenant of Police thought of his mission as preventing litigation while the judges lived to promote litigation.[29]

Parisians living under Louis XIV were unusually fortunate in having as their successive Lieutenants of Police two men of exceptional ability. Their zeal, devotion to duty, humanity, and public spirit made them stand out in a society which produced officials of much higher quality than is popularly supposed. Under their direction appeared in broad outline almost all the public services of modern Paris.[30]

The first of these Lieutenants of Police was Gabriel Nicolas de La Reynie, born in Limoges in 1625. His family had for generations produced judges or royal officers of one kind or another. That the newest member of the family continued true to a tradition of public service would be evidenced in many ways but perhaps most strikingly by the terms of his will eighty-four years after his birth. Among his last wishes was one that he be buried in his parish cemetery rather than inside the church as would be appropriate for a man of his distinction. He gave as his reason that he wished to "avoid contributing by the putrefaction of my body to the corruption and infection of the air."[31] This may suggest simple eccentricity unless taken in the context of his lifelong battle to rid Paris of a thousand outrages to the nose.

Becoming the president of the *présidial* (a court just below the level of parlement in the judicial scale) of Bordeaux at the age of twenty-one, La Reynie attracted the attention of government officials close to Mazarin. By 1657 he had moved to the capital and a few years later purchased for 300,000 livres a post in the most prestigious tribunal in France, the Parlement of Paris. When the Conseil de Police undertook the reform of Parisian administration in 1666-1667, he was Colbert's choice as first Lieutenant of Police. He served thirty distinguished years in that office, no mean feat considering the inevitable enemies in high places its occupant was forced to make if he took his duties seriously. Under him the lieutenancy of police was raised in every way except name to ministerial status. He enjoyed the complete confidence of the King and could count on personal access to him whenever circumstances warranted. At the age of seventy-two he finally resigned, having recently alienated two important ministers at Versailles. One he angered by his characteristic leniency towards Protestants; the other by his admirable opposition to financing war by increased indirect levies on foodstuffs, and thus, he wrote, placing an intolerable burden on those who could least afford to pay. At the time of his death twelve years later, Saint-Simon, who rarely said nice things about any man who had been close to Louis XIV, devoted a page to a moving tribute of La Reynie. The famous memoirist wrote that La Reynie was "a man of great virtue and ability who, in an office which he had so to speak created, was bound to attract public hatred [but] nevertheless acquired universal esteem."[32]

La Reynie was replaced by another provincial who had managed to attract the eye of a member of the King's inner circle. He was Marc-

René Voyer de Paulmy d'Argenson, and as the name would suggest, his lineage left little to be desired. Voltaire later wrote that his background was much too good for the office of Lieutenant of Police, yet acknowledged that he earned greater reputation in the post than he did later as minister. "In every sphere," Voltaire commented, "matters became so perfect" that D'Argenson acquired luster comparable to any great man of the age.[33]

Most historians would qualify Voltaire's fulsome praise. Matters were clearly not "perfect" in Paris in the closing years of Louis XIV's reign, but given the character of the times, D'Argenson's performance was excellent. He became indirectly a victim of the King's growing interest in the moral police of Paris, which perhaps was motivated as much by an old man's curiosity about the latest perversions as by Christian duty.[34] He had to spend a great deal of time answering requests (transmitted through Chancellor Pontchartrain and other ministers) for such items as a "full and detailed *mémoire* on the corrupters of young people, . . . in which you will indicate as many cases as you are able to discover. . . ."[35] The admirable spy system he had inherited from La Reynie was perfected. As a consequence, D'Argenson became indisputably the best-informed man in the realm on the activities of Parisians of every class.[36]

But what was most striking in D'Argenson was the quality for which Saint-Simon lauded him—his humanity. In a period when popular misery attained new depths, such a man was sorely needed. One of his most consistent enemies was the Procureur at the Parlement, Robert, who kept accusing him of "softness" in handling bread rioters. Robert's philosophy was to keep the masses in line by "making examples."[37] D'Argenson was known to have descended frequently from his carriage to mix with the poor and talk with them of their problems[38] (in his day, usually the high price of bread). In the near-revolutionary winter of 1709-1710, his house surrounded by a hungry mob bent on incendiarism, he coolly emerged and strode into its midst to restore calm.[39] On still another occasion, when he was brought the customary "gratification" by some contractors, he had them take the money to the Treasury to pay arrears in soldiers' pensions.[40] One can only speculate how different might have been the fate of the Bourbon monarchs had they gained the services of more men of the caliber of La Reynie and D'Argenson.

The jurisdiction of the new Lieutenant of Police was a sweeping one. The edict creating the office devoted twenty-two lines to spelling out his duties. Among them were the supervision of street cleaning; fire fighting; flood prevention; the provisioning of the city; price control; supervision of butchers' stalls; inspection of marketplaces, fairs, hotels, inns, furnished rooms, gaming houses, tobacco shops, and places of ill repute; investigation of illicit assemblies and other disorders; overseeing the guilds; inspection of weights and measures and of regulations pertaining to the book trade; enforcement of the ordinances against carrying weapons; and much more. To expedite his work, and despite what the King had said about separating justice from administration, the Lieutenant of Police was allowed to try minor wrongdoers apprehended *en flagrant délit*.[41] In Louis XIV's day, the court of the Lieutenant of Police was the only one in the Châtelet where minor criminal cases were disposed of without delay or red tape. Another novel feature of the Lieutenant of Police's prerogatives was that in certain broad fields, particularly the provisioning of Paris, his jurisdiction extended over the entire realm. An edict of April 1667, for example, gave him the right to legislate personally over all goods necessary for the provisioning of the capital, a privilege certain to arouse the ire of the Parlement, which had long enjoyed similar jurisdiction.

Obviously, the Lieutenant of Police was meant to head a bureaucracy. This he inherited in the persons of the forty-eight *commissaires enquêteurs-examinateurs* of the Châtelet, commonly referred to as simply *les commissaires*. Long before 1667, they had served as all-purpose agents of the Châtelet in the various quarters of Paris. But by choice and economic compulsion, they had increasingly forsaken their role of watchdogs of public security and had become somewhat discredited fee-grabbers, mainly concerned with such matters as imposing seals on the property of the deceased, taking legal inventories, serving summonses, and imposing a wide variety of fines on which they collected a lucrative percentage.

Immediately upon taking office as the first Lieutenant of Police, La Reynie began the task of forming this unlikely troupe into a dedicated corps of public servants. He persuaded the King to raise salaries, broaden retirement benefits (at the end of twenty years' service) and restore some of the honors formerly attached to these offices—all in the hope of making the *commissaires* more public-spirited officials.[42] But despite their restored honors and new emoluments, the *commissaires* took in very bad grace La Reynie's decision to reduce their old fees. Regardless of his desire to convert the *commissaires* into salaried officials, these fees continued to form probably the larger part of their income. The general regulations of 1688 complained as of old of their regrettable habit of setting up death watches so as to be first on the scene for affixing seals. The statutes warned that any *commissaire* entering the house of the deceased without being solicited by a relative, or who took up residence in an adjoining house in anticipation of the demise, would be fined.[43] It was a losing battle. In 1699 the old fee system was restored in the manner long demanded by the *commissaires*.[44] Like almost everyone in Old Regime Paris they had long been organized in their own tight little *corporations* well suited to protecting their "rights." Entrenched interests had triumphed over La Reynie's reforming zeal and his determination to make the *commissaires* into "the best disciplined and best ordered" corps in the land.[45]

Whatever the shortcomings of the forty-eight *commissaires*, they remained the backbone of public order in Paris. Several kinds of armed, uniformed patrolmen theoretically circulated around the streets of Paris, as we shall see, but in time of trouble the *commissaire's* house (practically all seventeenth-century officials did their work from their residences) loomed as large as Gibraltar. Ordinarily, a criminal case began with someone knocking on the door of the nearest *commissaire* and lodging a complaint against a fellow citizen. The *commissaire's* address was well known to residents of his *quartier*, and he was supposed to be available day and night to hear grievances and settle disputes. By virtue of his office he served as a minor magistrate and was the only judge with whom most inhabitants ever came in contact. In more serious matters he received authority from his superiors at the

Châtelet to summon the disputing parties, receive depositions, and prepare the *procès-verbal* for submission to the magistrates of the Châtelet, where the case would eventually be disposed of. Each *commissaire* was assigned several *sergents* or *huissiers* to assist him in carrying out his civil duties—the only duties most *commissaires* really cared about, since they carried the most lucrative fees.

The Conseil de Police of 1666-1667 recognized that Paris needed some old institutions dismantled as well as new ones erected. In the former category, seignorialism was a logical starting point. But the King showed himself extremely reluctant to approach this very sensitive problem. Early in the deliberations of the Conseil de Police, and apparently acting on its recommendations, he issued an edict forbidding the seigneurs of Paris to interfere in any way with the King's police, which is to say, with the Châtelet, the *commissaires* and their underlings.[46] Colbert was deeply disappointed. This sort of timid prohibition, with no specific sanctions, was a very old and hackneyed story. It had been tried innumerable times in the past and had always been disregarded. The newest version would surely meet the same fate.

However, this setback for the cause of modernization was only temporary. Eight years later the King proclaimed the law which had seemed so imminent in 1666 and which next to the creation of the Lieutenant of Police constituted probably the most important police measure of the reign for Paris. This statute of February 1674 boldly abolished the judicial and administrative prerogatives of all nineteen remaining *hauts seigneurs* as well as lesser autonomies such as those of the court of the Prévôté de l'Hôtel and the merchants serving the Crown. Some of these rights dated back a millennium, so this was a hard blow both to tradition and to some very influential ecclesiastical *seigneurs*. The blow was softened a bit by some rather vague promises of indemnification, as well as by the reminder that the lords would no longer be expected to contribute to the care of foundlings, for whom they had formerly been responsible.[47]

The ensuing reaction to the so-called destruction of feudalism in Paris is enlightening and documents the thesis that only a revolution could correct the abuses inherent in the system. No sooner was the edict published then pressure for exemptions began to be placed on the King by those affected, especially ecclesiastics. He was deluged with appeals to his conscience and reminders of the sanctity of private property. The Grand Monarque began to wither. (Had he shown the same lack of resolution to foreign foes, Europe would never have had cause for alarm.)

The ecclesiastics wisely showed a willingness to compromise. Over the loss of their seignorial street rights, even rights of justice along the streets of their fiefs, they raised no great objection. Their churches, abbeys, convents, and the areas immediately around them were another matter. These they described as untouchable sacred precincts. Their sincerity, unfortunately, was open to question, since churchmen had long encouraged lay people to dwell and labor within their protected domains. In return the church collected large rentals. The difficulty was how to separate the lay precincts from the sacred. The medieval jumble of streets made the task a difficult one, and obviously, churchmen were in no hurry to resolve the confusion.

Rarely inclined to press issues over the resistance of the Church, Louis XIV promptly began to water down the historically inevitable law of 1674. The Abbey of Saint-Germain-des-Prés and the spacious *enclos* of the Temple were the first to receive exemptions, soon followed by Saint-Jean-de-Latran in the University quarter and the domains of the Archbishop and Chapter on the Island of the Cité. Later concessions of the same sort were made to still others, although by no means all, of the nineteen *seigneurs* specified in the original law.[48] Until the Revolution, these ecclesiastical sanctuaries, in large part misused by lay tenants for the profit of the Church, remained a thorn in the side of the authorities.

ご゚   ご゚

One facet of the city's administration which the Conseil de Police made no effort to modernize was its finances. With the creation of the office of Lieutenant of Police in 1667, the burden of administration fell more heavily than ever on the Châtelet. Yet the traditional role of the Hôtel de Ville as the city's treasurer remained undisturbed. It was the custodian of the carefully husbanded municipal patrimony, as well as the recipient of the "rebates" allowed the city on the entry taxes which the government tax farmers collected on wines and other consumer goods. The officials of the Hôtel de Ville performed creditably as financiers. The account books of Paris were said to be in better shape than those of almost any other French city,[49] and the city's credit was so good that the government, unfortunately, had taken to filling its financial needs through loans made in the name of the Hôtel de Ville.

The taxes to which Parisians were subject were quite different from those of the rest of France. The two best-known and most notorious taxes of the Old Regime, the *taille* and the *gabelle*, one a property tax and the other a salt tax, were either unknown or of negligible importance in the capital. Since Charles VII's ordinance of 1449, Paris had enjoyed the enviable status of *ville franche* with respect to the *taille*. Its citizens received exemptions not only for their city property but for country residences as well, provided they did not reside there more than five months each year.[50] As for the famous *gabelle*, Paris had its *magasin à sel*, located near the Pont Neuf and open to the public on Mondays, Wednesdays, and Fridays,[51] but no fixed quotas were set on individuals as was done everywhere else in France. Salt buyers were obliged to obtain their needs at this government outlet at highly inflated prices, but if one found a way to avoid buying any salt at all, he was free to do without.

Even though Paris was free of *taille* and *gabelle* it was by no means a taxpayers' paradise. The inhabitants earned their exemptions thanks to the entry taxes that merchants paid at the city limits, all eventually passed on to the consumer in the guise of higher prices at the marketplaces. Such entry taxes (*aides*) were one of the principal sources of national revenue, and Parisians paid roughly two-thirds the national total. As would be expected, wine and beer, particularly, were affected. Between 1658 and 1708, the *aides* on wine entering Paris had approximately doubled.[52] Consequently, in many of the little villages beyond the barriers of the tax collectors, but still within easy walking distance of Paris, one could find numerous outposts catering to economy-minded imbibers. The term *guinguettes* to describe such establishments—some innocently gay, others downright sordid and affronts to moralists—came into use in the later seventeenth century. Here the oversized measure, the beloved *grande pinte* of the lower classes, prevailed, and as one guidebook advised its readers, "love often goes with the wine."[53] Since such towns could bring in more revenue through entry taxes than by the *taille*, the government was constantly inclined to annex them to the city. Such was the unwelcome fate of Chaillot, made into a faubourg of Paris in 1659 under the name of La Conférence in order "only to increase His Majesty's revenues," one contemporary charged.[54] Winebibbers were apparently being compelled to take more and more exercise to earn their tax-free beverage.

The entry taxes were collected at the outlying barriers or at the quays by government tax farmers. In Louis XIV's day, approximately half of the receipts was handed back to the Hôtel de Ville in the form of *octrois*, which formed the city's principal source of income. This arrangement was confirmed by an ordinance of July 1681,[55] but the city magistrates could never rest completely assured that the *octrois* would be forthcoming. Twice in Louis XIV's reign, in 1647 and 1710, the government pocketed the entire receipts from the entry taxes. That it had at the same time authorized the city to collect an equal amount on its own account, thus in effect doubling the tax burden, had not prevented near chaos in municipal finances.

The remainder of the Hôtel de Ville's revenues came from the city's patrimony: rents from bridge houses, shops, butcher stalls, and the like which the city had come to own over the centuries; water concessions to private users; revenue from municipally owned mills on the river; fees from boat owners in the ports; and other miscellany. All this property was looked upon as jealously husbanded capital, never to be alienated, except, reluctantly, in crises such as those resulting from the occasional withholding of the *octrois*.

In ordinary times revenue from the *octrois* and the *biens patrimoniaux* were sufficient to meet the city's modest needs. In the later seventeenth century, however, the Hôtel de Ville faced a good deal of financial embarrassment because of the unprecedented demands made upon it by the King for costly urban embellishments. We noted earlier how both the Place des Victoires and Place Vendôme projects had been dumped in its lap after the King had exhausted both funds and patience. This was rather typical of the high-handedness Louis XIV often displayed in his relations with the Hôtel de Ville. While Paris was the King's City, Louis expected its citizens to defray the cost of its beautification.

There was no clear agreement about who should pay for public works in Paris—King, Hôtel de Ville, or Châtelet. Even Delamare, whose readiness to shift burdens onto the Hôtel de Ville was very apparent, admittedly was uncertain of the legal precedents. He, of course, leaned to the belief that the Hôtel de Ville, as custodian of the domain and *octrois* of Paris, should stand the burden of public works but conceded that this position was based, not on any statute, but on the "loi générale."[56] The municipality made no such concession, being strongly inclined to rely on "la libéralité du Roi."[57] Sometimes it was not disappointed. For example, when the bridge in front of the Tuileries burned down in 1684, the King erected in record time a graceful stone replacement, the Pont Royal. The entire cost of 675,000 livres came out of the royal coffers.[58]

But this sort of royal generosity was very unusual and in the case of the Pont Royal probably due to the King's impatience to get on with the new bridge. The extensive work done on the *quais* during the reign, the construction of the new promenades, the *arcs de triomphe*, the enlargement of the water supply, and much else, were financed almost entirely by the municipality. If the latter's protests were sufficiently clamorous, and if the work was delayed long enough for lack of funds, the Conseil might be prevailed upon to grant an additional *octroi* or some other concession to the city. For example, the costly lines of trees atop the old ramparts on the Right Bank were paid for, after repeated stoppages and protestations, by conceding to the city most of the vacant lands along the old fortifications.[59] These the city sold at a handsome profit, but even so the new promenade took almost thirty years to complete. The Quai Malaquet was financed in a somewhat similar manner, the King granting to the city the ancient moat and rampart (little remained of either) of Philip Augustus adjoining the Porte de Nesle. On at least one occasion the very conservative gentlemen at the Hôtel de Ville were even persuaded to resort to the modern technique of going into debt to finance a capital improvement. The Quai d'Orsay was financed in the midst of the War of the Spanish Succession by a *rente* of 500,000 livres at 5½ percent which the Conseil authorized the Hôtel de Ville to make.[60]

Although civic improvements were paid for, as logic dictated, by Parisians rather than by the government, the unwritten rule prevailed that taxpayers should be unaware they were footing the bill. Direct proportionate levies, while not wholly unknown, were regarded as an abomination by property owners. If direct taxation was occasionally unavoidable, it was felt that it should be kept on a "voluntary" basis. (One thinks ahead to the aristocrats of 1789 who, threatened with revolution, agreed to pay the *taille* if it were called the *taille noble*.) Even for as worthy a cause as the Hôpital-Général, direct levies were regarded by those best able to pay as *taxes forcées*. It remained axiomatic that the greater the ability to pay—Delamare singled out "the Princes, the *seigneurs*, even the Magistrates"—the less the chances of receiving payments on tax assessments. When Mazarin was casting about in 1656 for ways to finance the costly Hôpital-Général for the poor, he asked for voluntary contributions from all the communities, corps, and corporations of Paris, lay and religious, warning that, this failing, he would tax them whatever amount was necessary.[61] He was true to his word. Since he did not receive the contributions he desired, he introduced a direct tax in the edict establishing the Hôpital-Général, only to have it struck out by the Parlement in the process of registration.[62] Although a great deal of public money found its way into the new poorhouse in the ensuing years, it was always in the form of duties on wines, part of the proceeds from court fines, theater admissions taxes, and other hidden taxes.

In the dreadful winter of 1709, when Paris was on the verge of a mass uprising and the city magistrates felt obliged to provide for special poor-relief funds, they did so only by means of voluntary city-wide contributions. Prominent laymen in each parish were given the task of calling on all parishioners for donations, with the understanding that those who refused would be marked down for forced payments.[63] As the Controller-General was informed, "one of the surest ways to encourage most of the *grands seigneurs* . . . to make substantial contributions is [to make them] fear that H.M. will be informed of their refusal or of the smallness of their offers."[64] Before long, however, it was discovered that the list of nonpayers had been hidden away by the parlementarians, who were probably as affluent an economic group as could be found in the city.

Despite the upper-class aversion to direct taxation, two such levies had been introduced in the first part of the sixteenth century and had somehow survived into Louis XIV's period. One was the poor tax (*taxe des pauvres*), which, although inconsequential in amount, is of some institutional significance as marking the start of obligatory charity in Paris.[65] It constituted a principal support for the Grand Bureau des Pauvres, whose mission it was to arrange for the domiciliary care of elderly deserving poor, in contrast to the vagabonds and other "drifters" under the jurisdiction of the Hôpital-Général and police. In every parish were to be found bourgeois "commissioners of the poor," selected by other bourgeois and required by law to accept their appointments. Their unpaid and unwelcome task was to collect the poor tax and dispense alms to the beneficiaries of the Grand Bureau. (If the *commissaire des pauvres* could afford to do so, he paid some impoverished flunky a few sous to make his collections for him.) The levy was theoretically in proportion to one's "state and condition" in life and no one was supposed to be exempt except domestics and those who could present a certificate of poverty from their *curés*.

The assessments were so small that one wonders why so many people went to the trouble of evading them. For example, artisans paid 13 sous, doctors 26, bourgeois notables 52, councilors in Parlement 5 livres, 4 sous, bishops 10 livres, the great *seigneurs* 20 to 50 livres. Total collections on the poor tax at the start of the eighteenth century were in the vicinity of 35,000 livres,[66] which by any reckoning works out to less than 10 sous per family. At that, many people had always professed to be outraged by having charity based on something other than alms. To circumvent this complaint the law sanctioned voluntary donations which, if deemed adequate for one's "state and condition," freed the contributor from any further obligation. The total budget of the Grand Bureau was about double the amount of the poor tax receipts; thus it appears that many people contributed in this manner. Nevertheless, the *taxe des pauvres* as a means of supporting a public institution can only be considered a monument of unnecessary and wasteful effort.

A more important levy than the *taxe des pauvres*, and the only significant direct tax paid by Parisians in Louis XIV's reign, was known as the *taxe des boues et lanternes*. It financed both street cleaning and the operation of some 5000 new street lanterns. The day had long passed when each citizen of Paris was expected to keep clean his part of the street and maintain a lighted candle in his front window to light the street. To pay for the new services, the "mud and lantern" tax was inaugurated in 1667, but unfortunately for the cause of efficiency, the old principle of decentralization of taxation was retained. The "mud and lantern" tax was assessed and collected by neighborhood bourgeois while the Châtelet remained very much in the background. In each *quartier* of Paris a Direction de Quartier, made up of from two to four top-drawer citizens, drew up tax rolls for the *boues et lanternes*, arranged for collections, and contracted for and paid a neighborhood cleaning entrepreneur. Looming in the background were the officials of the Châtelet, ever helpful (for a fee) in arranging for the seizure of the household effects of recalcitrant citizens or in prosecuting cleaning contractors guilty of permitting filth to slop over the sides of their wagons.

Undoubtedly the most heroic person involved in the *boues et lanternes* levy was the *receveur particulier*, the unpaid citizen who tried to translate the names on the tax rolls into tax receipts. He, also, once selected by the Direction, had no legal alternative but to accept. The oligarchy which controlled the Directions chose their *receveurs particuliers* from a somewhat less distinguished class than their own, as Delamare put it, from "good Bourgeois, Merchants or Artisans, having due regard for their solvency."[67] The assessments they were required to collect twice yearly in January and July were calculated at 1 percent of the rental value of the property. How such men fared when they knocked on the doors of great lords and churchmen is not hard to imagine.

Nevertheless, the system inaugurated in 1667 was by all accounts superior to anything tried in the past. It continued in use until the start of the new century. At that time the "mud and lantern tax" became subject to the sort of financial lunacy so typical of Louis's last fifteen years and so revealing of the techniques by which the financiers acquired their impressive new *hôtels* in the northwest of the city. In a bewildering succession of moves beginning in 1701 and masterminded by the bankers, the King replaced the existing system of neighborhood Directions with a bureaucracy of venal officeholders, established a new "mud and lantern tax" of 300,000 livres, invited the citizens to buy back the imposition for a sum equal to eighteen times their annual payments on the old tax, then quickly spent the large capital sum proffered him to finance his current war. The financiers made a fine profit from the sale of new offices and from funding the new "mud and lantern tax" for property owners enticed into the scheme by the assurance that after eighteen years they would be completely free and clear of expense. Having spent the money on war, however, the King was unable to assume his responsibility to clean the streets. The net effect was that Louis XIV when he died left the streets of Paris in almost as bad shape as he had inherited them seventy-two years earlier.[68]

However, from the administrative viewpoint, it is significant that after all the jugglery had subsided and the Regency had restored order, Paris did not revert to the antique neighborhood organization for cleaning and illuminating its streets. A new professional bureaucracy centered at the Châtelet remained in control. At least one long-time traditionalist welcomed the change. Nicolas Delamare, who earlier in his career as *commissaire* of the Cité quarter had been convinced that the best way to get a job done was to let the people immediately concerned do it themselves, now wrote: "Today street cleaning is done more simply but . . . not less well. If fewer people are employed, it is because the funds for this work are no longer charged to Parisians. Also, there is no question now of . . . raising the money, of Bureaus of

Direction, of Assemblies of the Bourgeois and other similar precautions."[69]

Whether the neighborhood bourgeois who had formerly controlled affairs felt any regret over the new turn of events we do not know, but in any case a new page had been turned in the history of municipal services in Paris.

CHAPTER THREE

A city takes to wheels

NO aspect of the greatly quickened pace of life in seventeenth-century Paris will strike a more responsive chord among moderns than the appearance of traffic congestion.

Traffic is, of course, a very relative thing. From the earliest beginnings of any urban society, citizens can be suspected of taking a perverse pride in the volume of traffic in the streets. Paris was no exception. Even when confined to little more than a small island in the Seine, medieval Parisians could be counted on to complain about the perils of walking the streets. But in the seventeenth century, for the first time, we can take such talk both seriously and sympathetically, for this was the century in which the carriage appeared and transportation was consequently revolutionized. By the end of the century Parisians had learned to steel themselves to the noise and danger of thousands of swiftly moving carriages threading their dangerous way through narrow streets designed only for mules, wagons, and pedestrians. Under Louis XIV is heard, perhaps for the first time, the suggestion that state intervention was needed to reduce the number of conveyances on the streets and reestablish good order. (The King's reply to this suggestion was more reminiscent of a modern democratic politician than of the Roi Soleil. He said he would "leave this freedom [presumably to be maimed] to his subjects."[1])

At the beginning of the seventeenth century, the august presidents of the Parlement of Paris, whose sense of dignity was surpassed not even by the *grands seigneurs*, still made their way to the Palais de Justice on the backs of mules,[2] long the favorite conveyance through the mud of Paris. The historian Sauval, writing in the 1660's and obviously struck by the wonders wrought by modern progress, remarked that he knew an elderly lady who remembered when the first carriage (*carrosse*, to be distinguished from the much older workaday *chariots, charettes, carrioles*, and other vehicles) appeared in the streets of Paris. The proud owner of the vehicle, Sauval's acquaintance told him, was not the haughty duchess one would imagine, but rather the wife of a rich apothecary residing in the Rue Saint-Antoine.[3] Whether or not the old lady was correct in all the details, it is doubtless true that until the start of the new century this latest Italian importation was very rare in Paris. One authority maintains that in 1594 there were only eight carriages to be seen in and around Paris—great cumbersome vehicles owned only by the very rich.[4] The vast majority of even upper-class Parisians continued to get about on foot or on the backs of animals. If they paid a formal call and arrived with muddy feet, they changed footgear in an antechamber before stepping on their hostess's carpets.

Under Louis XIII, the number of carriages in Paris increased sharply. An official report drawn up by the Châtelet in the 1630's set the number at over 4,000.[5] The "two young Hollanders" visiting the Carnival celebrations in the Saint-Antoine quarter in 1656 reported seeing 3,000 carriages in that area alone.[6] According to Voltaire, magnificent new spring-suspension carriages equipped with glass windows began to make their appearance in the streets of Paris shortly after mid-century.[7] He was probably referring to the new French window glass manufactured at the Manufacture des Glaces in the Quartier Saint-Antoine, a factory which by the end of the century employed 400 people and was probably the largest industrial establishment in the city.[8] Voltaire's suspension devices are harder to fathom. The guild regulations of the Parisian harnessmakers for about the time Voltaire was describing tell us simply that the best suspension consisted of "four fine Hungarian hides, the longest which can be obtained."[9] But whatever the nature of the new suspension, its superiority over English vehicles, at least, is well attested by Martin Lister. He wrote that he was less tired after six hours of riding even in public carriages in Paris than after one hour in the finest English conveyance.[10]

The luxuriousness of the carriages of Louis XIV's time can be judged by their regular inclusion, beginning with a law of 1656, in sumptuary laws. Even if Louis XIV was unwilling to curtail the number of carriages on the streets of Paris, he was willing to regulate their owners' wasteful competition (shocking to the mercantilist mind) for elegance and novelty. Alongside the old prohibitions against dressing livery servants in silks (rather than wool), against the use of gold and silver in clothing and furniture, against the fashionable new Canadian beaver hats and all other animal-hair hats costing more than 40 livres, appeared prohibitions against the gilding of carriages and the use of fine fringes, lacework, and embroidery.[11] In the first few decades of Louis XIV's reign, sumptuary laws directed at carriages reached a peak. By the end of the reign, one hears relatively little about carriages and much more about clothing and furniture. Either the novelty of finely gilded carriages wore off or the authorities despaired of curbing them and stopped trying.

By the end of the seventeenth century Brice estimated there were 20,000 carriages in Paris.[12] A new status symbol had been born. The numerous books on etiquette now urged the use of the *carrosse* as the only acceptable transportation for a man of parts. The accepted criterion for deciding on the social desirability of a young man became, Does he have a carriage? Nemeitz, who had a professionally developed sense of what was proper, advised his readers that "gentlemen cannot go about Paris on foot." Compounding the problems of young dandies whose social ambitions were disproportionate to their pocketbooks, he added that "when one wants to operate a carriage, at least two lackeys are called for."[13]

The seventeenth-century carriage phenomenon resulted in changes in habits and patterns of living suggestive of the social impact of the automobile in our own day. One of the most striking social developments was the *promenade à carrosse*. Life took on new dimensions, at least for the well-to-do, as carriage outings became the rage: promenades to the Bois de Boulogne, to Vincennes, to the Luxembourg, to the Saint-Germain and Saint-Laurent fairs, to the innumerable little villages outside the city—Meudon, Mont-Valérien, Saint-Denis, Charenton, Conflans, and the rest.

Even the time-honored techniques of trysting changed. References at the Comédie to a "marriage of the Bois de Boulogne," or such lines as "You talk like a girl who has already made a dozen campaigns in the Bois de Boulogne," were certain to provoke appreciative laughter.[14] Carriages at least made sin more accessible. The drivers of the new rented *fiacres* were noted for their discretion, whether the destination was the Bois or some more remote and lavish establishment like the Moulin de Javel opposite Auteuil, notorious at the end of the century as a "factory of pleasures and the shame of bourgeois families," or the still more scandalous rural complex of Durier at Saint-Cloud, described by John Evelyn as boasting eighty luxuriously furnished rooms in three or four houses, all for the pleasure of "grands personnages."[15]

But, fortunately for the cause of morality, most of the devotees of carriages had more innocent pleasures in mind. In 1656 the visiting De Lacke brothers charmingly described in their journal how they went to Chaillot by carriage with two fashionable ladies, and arriving there, obtained the services of a *pâtissier* for a picnic lunch on the grass.[16] The word *cadeau*, now taken to mean any sort of gift or present, then meant a repast which young gallants gave their ladies, particularly in the country.[17] The Englishman Dr Lister was delighted and surprised by the French passion for "coaching," which he described as the "great and daily Business of People of Quality," and "that which makes the dwelling in this City very diverting."[18] Taken on a carriage ride through the royal gardens at Saint-Cloud, he noted: "These vast riding Gardens are unknown to us in England, and *se promener à cheval, ou en carrosse* is not English. We cannot afford to lose so much Country, as those Gardens take up." Another favorite excursion on hot summer days was a visit to the Porte Saint-Bernard to view the bathers on the banks of the river. The De Lacke brothers testified to the presence of more than 400 carriages lining the south bank one summer day.

Far and away the most popular promenade of the fashionable world was the Cours-la-Reine, which ran far almost a mile alongside the Seine just west of the Tuileries gardens. Thanks to a wall on the north

side and gate houses at both ends, all but the *beau monde* were theoretically kept out. Within were three alleys of fine elms, the center one of
which was reputed capable of accommodating up to six carriages
abreast. An evening visit, generally in summer, was a favorite occupation of the wealthy, and as many as a thousand carriages, Nemeitz insisted, could be seen moving leisurely along the Cours,[19] their occupants exchanging pleasantries and quiet appraisals. For those who required them, messengers were on hand to carry *billets doux* from one
vehicle to another.[20] Saint-Simon's *Mémoires* describe delightful midnight promenades on the Cours "aux flambeaux," accompanied by vio-
lin music and dancing on the capacious turning-circle. Occasionally,
the King attended in person, and one could then expect a great traffic
jam. The De Lacke brothers tell of one such occasion enlivened by a
pitched battle among lackeys striving to get their masters back into the
open.

The seventeenth-century revolution in transportation made an impact on many more than the fortunate few who could afford carriages
and gain access to midnight promenades on the Cours-la-Reine. For the
first time transportation within the city became an industry. Thousands
of simple citizens were affected in one way or another by the new willingness and ability to pay a few sous to be transported about Paris. For
many poor wretches, progress was not an unmitigated cause for rejoic-
ing. Thousands of lower-class Parisians suddenly found themselves
making their livelihood in ways generally associated with less fortunate
Oriental societies—pushing, pulling, or carrying all manner of strange
new conveyances.

The great assortment of rented vehicles which appeared for the
first time on the streets of Paris in the Grand Siècle fell into three main
categories: the portable *chaises*, the *chaises* on wheels, and the famous
fiacres. Within these three general types could be found a bewildering
assortment of styles and models, many of whose names survived into
the era of the horseless carriage. The right to operate these vehicles
was earned and precariously protected by hard-won royal privilege. An
inventor had no choice but to keep his creation off the streets until such
time as he, or more likely, an associate with access to official circles,

could obtain letters patent giving him the right of exploitation. Such permission was obtained for a price, of course. In 1650, for example, a Sieur Charles Villermé deposited 15,000 livres in the royal treasury for the exclusive right to furnish Parisians with certain types of rented carriages and chairs.[21] It is noteworthy that when Louis XIV early in the eighteenth century was looking about for ways to reinvigorate commerce, a deputy from Paris advanced the suggestion that public transportation should be opened to anyone wishing to enter the field and that all the innumerable monopoly rights so costly to the public should be abolished. (Nothing came of the proposal.)

Of the many kinds of public conveyances which transformed the streets of Paris in the seventeenth century, the oldest was the litter chair, carried by two men dubbed "baptized mules." They appeared in the city at the end of the sixteenth century, although the first "privilege" for their use was given only in 1617 to Pierre Petit, captain of the King's Guards. They quickly gained public acceptance and by the 1630's the Châtelet calculated there were 1700 *porteurs de chaise* in Paris. Early in the reign of Louis XIV (1644), the Marquis de Montbrun stole from London the idea of a covered chair, and he and his natural son retained their monopoly well into Louis XIV's reign.[22] The owners leased out the chairs to porters for 5 livres per week with the understanding that the lessee would be responsible for all breakages. Considering the great numbers of such conveyances on the streets of Paris in the later seventeenth century, the source of at least one new kind of private fortune is evident.

Once the litter chair had been well accepted, the next step, obviously, was to attach wheels to it. But this apparently simple development was an inordinately long time coming. For one thing Parisian streets around mid-century were in a particularly poor state of repair, making any kind of wheeled vehicle impractical. Probably more important, the owners of the monopoly for chairs, the Marquis de Montbrun and his partners, strongly opposed the wheeled vehicles.[23] Although the King to ease their fears of competition gave them the right to exploit the wheeled chairs any time they wished, they made no effort to do so. According to Delamare, they were deterred by their inability to procure a mysterious "secret [invention] which greatly improves the rolling power" of the vehicles.[24] The "secret" must have been safeguarded like the crown jewels because not until 1669 did the small two-wheeled contrivances appear. By this time the Montbrun group was no longer on the scene. The new transportation magnates were a group headed by a Sieur Dupin, identified in the letters patent as chief inventor of the new vehicle. The *brouette* was simply the old portable chair suspended between a pair of wheels with the fore-and-aft porters replaced by a single human mule, or *brouetteur*, in the front. A good deal of popular derision and even violence greeted the novel vehicle, and the police were hard put to it to preserve the property of Dupin and his partners. (One may suspect that the operators of the portable chairs did their best to stir up trouble for their new competitor.)

But the *brouette* survived, met public acceptance, and remained on the Parisian scene into the next century. It went under a variety of names: *brouette, roulette, chaise roulante, chaise volante,* and *vinaigrette.* Some variations were horse-drawn, but at the end of the century it was still the original man-drawn model which so scandalized Dr Lister. In describing the variety of coaches in the city he said "there is one more . . . which I was willing to omit, as thinking it at first sight Scandalous, and a very Jest; it being a wretched Business in so Magnificent a City; and that is, the Vinegrette, a Coach on Two Wheels, dragg'd by a Man, and push'd behind by a Woman or Boy or both."[25]

The *brouette* doubtless had its uses—Sauval commented rather scornfully that it was popular with ladies seeking shelter from the rain—but for longer journeys within the city, where more speed and comfort were desirable, still another type of conveyance came into use in the middle of the century, the *fiacre,* or as Englishmen corrupted the word, hack. Until the start of Louis XIV's reign, the *carrosse* had been associated exclusively with the rich and great, but a few years before the outbreak of the Fronde an enterprising stablemaster by the name of Nicholas Sauvage, residing in the Rue Saint-Martin at the sign of Saint-Fiacre, began to rent carriages and horses to anyone who presented himself.[26] So great was his success that all rental carriages as well as their drivers were henceforth styled *fiacres.* However, this confusion of carriages and coachmen never sat well with the latter, especially as their vehicles became equated in the popular mind with something run-down and disreputable. They insisted on the more dignified *cocher* rather than *fiacre*.[27]

Before long the rental carriages were taken out of the stables and made available at designated spots around the city. This was the work of a M. de Givry, who in 1657 received letters patent authorizing him to establish two-horse carriages on the streets of Paris from seven in the morning until seven in the evening (eleven later in the reign). The business arrangement was the customary one: Givry paid the Crown for his privilege, acquired the horses and carriages, and rented them out to the drivers. The state profited in still another way, for some ingenious soul in the government soon thought of making each driver pay a tax (a very high one of 21 sous daily) for the right to use the designated street parking areas.[28]

All seventeenth-century visitors to Paris who have left any record of their impressions agree on at least one point—the disreputable character of the *fiacres* and their drivers. For Lister they were "the most nasty and miserable Voiture that can be. . . ."[29] The Sicilian Marana reflected that Seneca must have written his *Tranquillity of Life* as a reaction to the cab drivers of his own day. Witnessing the brutality of the drivers, hearing their hoarse and frightening voices, he thought "all the Furies were out to make Paris into hell."[30] Like Marana, Nemeitz was struck by the custom of feeding the *fiacre* horses at every stop, so that they nearly always had tufts of hay hanging from their jaws as they walked along dispiritedly. Always conscious of the right and the wrong in social behavior, Nemeitz cautioned that one must never drive up to a fashionable house in such a conveyance. The gatekeeper would so resent having his *porte-cochère* littered with animal feed that he might turn his back and give priority to other more fashionable guests.[31] The brutality of the coachmen to their animals was proverbial: all Parisians knew the aphorism, "Paris is the paradise of women, the purgatory of men, and the hell of horses."[32]

Worse still, it seemed to some, than the brutality of the drivers to their horses was their brutality to their fares. One must always, Nemeitz warned his readers, avoid getting embroiled with them for "there is nothing to be gained from fighting with mud." Besides, he added, the populace was always inclined to take the side of the driver, a dangerous partiality which could lead to all manner of embarrassment. The best course if one *must* ride a *fiacre*, Nemeitz cautioned, was to raise the wooden window, preserve incognito, and pray that you would not be overturned (a frequent occurrence) and forced to crawl out under the curious stares of a crowd of onlookers. But far wiser, for the visitor, at least, was not to rely on the *fiacre* at all, but rather to rent a *carosse de remise* at one of the numerous stables in the Saint-Germain quarter for 300 or 400 livres a month. These, Lister said, "are very well Guilt, neat Harness, and good Horses. . . ."[33]

The most startling of all the many seventeenth-century innovations in Parisian transportation was the system of *carrosses à cinq sous*, the first omnibus system in Paris and probably anywhere else. They antedated the modern Parisian buses by precisely 166 years. According to a well-founded tradition, Blaise Pascal was the inventor and moving spirit of the new enterprise.[34] But obviously, any plan as daring as this required unusually strong protection at court. This was duly obtained in the persons of the Duc de Roannez, Governor of Poitou, the Marquis de Sourches, Grand Prévôt de l'Hôtel, and the Marquis de Crenan, the King's Cupbearer. (Apparently the laws forbidding nobility to engage in commerce did not apply to Parisian transport because the majority of the new privileges were handed out to noblemen.) In January 1662 these three gentlemen received permission from the King to operate public carriages on the streets of Paris according to fixed schedules and routes and a uniform fare of 5 sous.[35]

The first line opened in March 1662. Its terminals were the Saint-Antoine Gate and the Luxembourg Palace. Seven *coches*, very much on the order of the vehicles then being used in intercity transportation, were employed, each seating eight passengers. The scheduled time between the vehicles was to be fifteen minutes, and one had the right to hail them at any point along their route. Pascal's sister, Mme Perrier, described the opening day's ceremonies and operations in a letter so enthusiastic as to suggest that she too was financially interested in the undertaking. Officials and guards from both the Châtelet and the Hôtel de Ville were present for what appears to have been a very gay occasion. The vehicles were colorfully painted, carried the coat-of-arms of the city, and were driven by men clad in the brilliant livery of the Hôtel de Ville.

An ominous note was struck, however, by the police commissioners of the Châtelet in the dedicatory speeches. They asked the bourgeois of Paris to support the new venture, warning the *petit peuple* that if they caused the least trouble, punishment would be severe.[36] It seems that these pioneer common carriers were anything but common. The blue-blooded promoters, in a decision which perhaps affords more insight than many a weighty tome into why France was heading towards a revolution, had decreed that "neither soldiers, nor pages, nor lackeys, nor artisans" would be permitted on the *carrosses à cinq sous*.

The authorities must have expected trouble on the opening day for they placed policemen all along the route. How much trouble actually materialized depends upon which account of the event one accepts. Sauval maintained that the populace followed the *carrosses* with "great hooting and stone-throwing" and that the police commissioners made a number of arrests.[37] Mme Perrier in her eyewitness letter (Sauval, too, was living in Paris, at the time, but did not claim to have been on the spot) to Arnauld de Pomponne maintained that everything went without the "least disorder." She asserted that crowds of spectators, including many artisans, had lined the route to view the progress of the new *carrosses*, and that one saw only laughing faces, "not mocking laughter, but laughter of approbation and joy. . . ."[38] The unanswered question remains whether Sauval, ordinarily a careful historian, got his facts confused or whether Mme Perrier was trying to interest the minister in a venture in which her brother was already involved.

Whatever the reaction of the populace, the second omnibus line opened with almost as much fanfare a few weeks later. This one ran on a half-hour schedule from Saint-Roch Church in the Rue Saint-Honoré clear across Paris to the Saint-Antoine Gate.[39] Subsequently, three more routes were established and success seemed assured. Even the King and the Duc d'Enghien are said to have tried the new service.

It was also very popular with the magistrates at the Châtelet and the Palais de Justice—so popular, Sauval wrote, that the owners advanced the price 1 sou in 1664.[40] But without anyone ever having been able to ascribe a logical cause, the *carrosses à cinq (six) sous* went out of existence sometime well before the end of the century, not to be revived until 1828, when the price, incidentally, was still the original 5 sous.

Longer lived were the nautical equivalents of the *carrosses à cinq sous*, the *bachots*, or small boats which helped meet the seventeenth-century demand for promenades into what Delamare described as "the enchanted places which give a new éclat to the city of Paris."[41] To enable the public to enjoy the "marvels" of the countryside over which contemporary writers waxed so rhapsodic—to permit it to see the fine country houses of the rich, to breathe the "pure country air," to promenade in the innumerable gardens of the princes and great seigneurs "always open for the satisfaction of the public"—the hack drivers were permitted to take passengers up to about twelve miles outside of Paris. This kind of transportation was well beyond the reach of many, so the *bachots* came into use to take passengers for a few sous to Chaillot, Passy, Sèvres, Saint-Cloud and many other points upstream and down. These boats had a legal capacity of sixteen, and like everything else connected with the water, were under the licensing authority and supervision of the Hôtel de Ville. The city magistrates went through the motions of trying to moderate the "swearing and blaspheming" and insults of the *bachoteurs* and to persuade them that they should depart (generally from alongside the Tuileries) at the appointed hour and not only when their boats filled with passengers.

The mass of traffic which came into being in the course of the seventeenth century, alongside the carts, wagons and four-legged conveyances of older times, inevitably created new pressures for street improvements. The latter could no longer be motivated by simple aesthetic and hygienic considerations. (Philip Augustus in the thirteenth century had, according to a well-established story, first felt the need for paving streets when he put his head out of his palace window and smelled the stench of the muddy streets.) In the seventeenth century, especially in the second half, street improvements became essential to the city's functioning and its citizens' well-being. The narrow, crooked, unimproved streets of the medieval past were obviously unfit for the pellmell traffic of the 20,000 carriages reputed to be on the city streets at the century's end. Brice in 1698 complained bitterly of the press of traffic in front of the Petit Châtelet as one entered the Rue Saint-Jacques, "where one is almost always in danger of being crushed if one does not have the patience to wait some time." Striking a note which any modern street commissioner would appreciate, Brice expressed mystification that the authorities managed to widen and improve numerous other thoroughfares while nothing was done about this one.

From the time of Louis XIV, important changes began to take place in street work. The many-fold increase in the paving budget was one sign of changing times (see Chapter VIII). Also noteworthy was the new concern for such matters as the optimum width of streets, an obvious consequence of the many street-construction projects executed in these years. Three classifications were established: the *grandes rues*, which were to be between 42 and 60 feet in width; the *rues de communication et distribution*, from 18 to 30 feet; and the *petites rues* from 6 to 18.[42] By general agreement, 5 *toises* (about 30 feet) was established as the ideal width of the ordinary city street, and this became the size of most of the streets in the new quarters. In the older sections of the city the problem of street modernization was, of course, vastly more complex than in the new neighborhoods to the west. In many parts of Paris little attention had been paid in the past to the proper alignment of houses along the streets, and some residences by being allowed to jut out into the thoroughfares had become formidable bottlenecks. A creditable beginning was now made in street modernization. The standard collection of royal ordinances dealing with projects for widening and straightening Parisian streets begins for all practical purposes with the reign of Louis XIV.[43] From the time that the Rue Ferronerie, running alongside the south side of the Holy Innocents Cemetery, was widened and straightened in 1669 to the end of the century, at least fourteen ordinances (most of them dealing with a number of arteries) emanated from Versailles on this subject. Authorization for the construction of streets in new neighborhoods was the subject of still other ordinances.

The Hôtel de Ville had the responsibility for carrying out these projects. The well-established rule was that the cost of new pavement fell on the adjoining property owners, but a much thornier question was who would indemnify them for land appropriated for street-widening projects. Delamare wrote piously that "all private interests had to give way to the public good,"[44] but this, of course, did not negate the right of indemnification. The latter was always carefully provided for in each ordinance ordering a street improvement. Depending upon circumstances, property owners were indemnified from the King's domain, the royal treasury, the Hôtel de Ville, or by assessments on nearby property owners who stood to gain from the improvements.[45]

ॐ   ॐ

The great advances in transport within Paris in the seventeenth century were easily surpassed by the facilities linking the capital with the provinces and the rest of Europe. A real effort of the imagination is needed to visualize the impact on a community of the sudden burgeoning of stagecoach lines where no public transportation had previously existed and of the appearance on street corners of little boxes in which one could drop letters and for a few sous each have them delivered almost miraculously to correspondents throughout Europe. Such was the happy experience of Parisians in the seventeenth century.

In 1600 there were only three stagecoach lines in all France, and all had been established in the preceding dozen years or so. They ran from Paris to Orléans, Rouen, and Amiens. Paralleling the increase of privately owned *carrosses* on the streets of Paris, the *carrosses de route* or *carrosses de voiture* on the open road multiplied at a rate which must have gratified all those who ever had reason to travel. Long before anyone thought of selling public transportation within the city, Parisians were able to journey by stagecoach to almost every part of France. Although each new line required royal authorization, private entrepreneurs launched and retained control of the industry. During the formative years and well into the reign of Louis XIII the tycoon of French stagecoaching was a lady by the name of Anne du Bueil, Dame de Fontaines, who enjoyed a monopoly of all rolling stock and must have made a tidy fortune leasing it to various operators. According to Delamare, she "neglected nothing to augment public carriages in the Kingdom, they multiplied on the major routes as well as on the lateral."[46] Although her descendants did not retain her monopoly and stagecoaching became a very decentralized industry, the Dame de Fontaines deserves to be remembered for her early promotional efforts.

By mid-century coaching was a flourishing institution in France, far in advance of the rest of the continent and even farther in advance of England. Much of the credit must go to the concern of the French government for the construction and upkeep of roads. In England, for example, very little could be done in intercity transportation until eighteenth-century highway improvements had begun. In France, even at the end of the Thirty Years' War when finances were at low ebb and the country generally demoralized, an English visitor, John Evelyn, noted that "the way from Paris . . . , as indeed most of the roads in France, is paved with a small square freestone, so that the country does not much molest the traveller with dirt and ill way, as in England."

A *Liste des messagers, coches et postes de France* for 1646 shows the startling increase in stagecoach lines since their small beginnings at the start of the century.[47] The schedule listed over two hundred towns in every part of the country which one could reach from Paris, along with the boarding-point in the city for each and the time of departure. The romantic vagueness of the schedule was its most striking characteristic; the traveler was rarely told more than that his stagecoach left "once or twice a week," or what was very common, that it "arrives and leaves when it can." For an operator to commit himself to an hour of departure was unthinkable.

While most stagecoach operators were doubtless happy just to deliver their fares at their destination on the promised day or as soon thereafter as possible, on some of the more traveled routes efforts began to be made in the second half of the century to provide blue-ribbon service. Most famous was the *diligence de Lyon*. It started operation probably in the 1670's, reducing a journey which had recently taken eleven days to only seven.[48]

John Locke wrote a very enthusiastic account of his journey from

Paris to Lyons on the *diligence* in December 1675. He appeared to relish the experience despite riding after dark, spending the night in "miserable Lodging" ("but that must be borne with in France"), and being awakened at four in the morning to face another bone-shattering day on the road. At Chalon on the Saône River, Locke described how the passengers were transferred to one of the new river boats, and how they drifted, seemingly idyllically, down the river to Lyons while he played cards, conversed with his fellow passengers, and saw his strong Protestant prejudices confirmed when one of the clerical passengers "and a woman lay in the same chamber . . . the first night, and so 2 or 3 nights after."[49]

The adventures of stagecoaching even became in 1680 the subject of a popular play at the theater. The valet in this piece, after hearing his master lament the travails of an *honnête homme* journeying by stagecoach from Paris to Orléans, allowed that he found the experience rather pleasurable, despite the young country girls who "emit deafening screams" in fear the carriage will overturn and the inevitable kind old ladies who must always stop the coach to "render tribute to nature."[50]

However, stagecoaches, with all their apparent glamour and adventure, did not appeal to some travelers, who continued down to the end of the Old Regime to prefer the expensive but faster and more private relay service. Such travelers availed themselves of the post stations originated by Louis XI in 1464 and thereafter for the royal mail carriers, and expanded in the seventeenth century into a nationwide facility to serve the needs of private transportation. The masters of the posts began at that time to augment their income by offering escorted trips on horseback between various towns.[51] In 1630, for example, travelers could post from Paris to Lyons for 250 livres, which was perhaps half as much again as fare on the stagecoach. Light baggage was allowed on the horses' hindquarters. To travel in this manner was to *courir la Poste à cheval*, and there was no faster or more physically demanding form of transportation.

The "two young Hollanders," traveling from Calais to Paris in 1656, had "run the post," complaining all the time of the discomfort and wretched accommodations. John Evelyn in the course of his extensive travels in France in the same decade made use mainly of the relay horses and guides, who, in addition to getting their fares to their destination, returned the mounts to their masters. When he first arrived in France in the 1670's, John Locke mentioned hiring a *messager* to take him from Calais to Paris, paying him "for horse and diet . . . 12 crowns, and 3 sous per lb. for baggage, except shoes and 6 lbs. which were allowed." Nemeitz began his guidebook on Paris with the matter-of-fact remark: "One arrives in Paris ordinarily either by *chariot ordinaire* [a colloquialism for stagecoach] or by the *chevaux de poste.*"

For people unable to spend long days on horseback, yet willing to pay to avoid the enforced democracy of stagecoach travel, the seventeenth century invented still another mode of travel. It became possible to "run the post" in any of a variety of rented vehicles, including light two-wheeled carriages for one or two persons and heavier four-wheeled conveyances like the *berline,* the *berline coupée,* the *phaéton* and various other models. One paid at each stop according to the type of vehicle employed and the number of passengers carried, due distinction being made between passengers of quality and simple servants. Weight was an important consideration. Some of the heavier types of carriages had killed so many horses on certain *courses* that an edict of 1708 forbade their use without special permission.[52]

In 1664 the Marquis de Crenan and the Marquis de Sourches, the same gentlemen who were causing a sensation in Paris with their *carrosses à cinq sous*, extended their operations onto the open road. They obtained a privilege to exploit a new two-wheeled vehicle "capable of making extraordinary *diligence* with only one horse." (The inventor was a Sieur de la Grugère; nevertheless, his brainchildren became popularized as the *chaises de Crenan*.) They were put on sale for 300 livres but were also made available on some of the *courses* for 50 sous per relay, the price including rental of both buggy and horse. Of this amount the Maîtres de Poste were allowed to retain 34 sous while the balance was divided among the promoters and the Général des Postes.

Rapid obsolescence being part of the new order of things, the *chaises de Crenan* were soon superseded by a lighter and more convenient carriage fancifully termed the *soufflet* (whisper), which in turn was replaced by a widely used one-seater known more prosaically as *chaise de poste*.

For the delivery of out-of-town letters and packages, the Parisian public, until the early seventeenth century, had to rely almost exclusively on the messengers of the University of Paris. Perhaps as far back as the late twelfth century, school officials had shrewdly judged the need for communication facilities between parents and students and began licensing messengers for this purpose. The service became one of the University's principal sources of revenues. In the first half of the seventeenth century, however, the University gained a competitor which was eventually to drive it out of business. This was the national grid of relay stations.

The Général des Postes who must be given the credit for this achievement was Sieur Pierre d'Alméras. He took office in 1621 and a year later created the first *couriers ordinaires*, authorized to take private mail on fixed schedules from Paris to Lyons, Bordeaux, Toulouse, Dijon, and other cities, making use of the established relay service. In 1627 D'Alméras established the first *bureaux* in the largest towns of France. Here he posted detailed schedules of rates and times of departure. By the end of the decade regular mail service was available between Paris and London for any citizen who could afford 10 sous for postage.[53]

Until well into the reign of Louis XIV, the public was allowed to choose between royal couriers, University messengers, and a number of private entrepreneurs attracted to the postal business. Many Frenchmen out of habit or mistrust of the royal couriers continued to rely on the University messengers. Inevitably, the Grand Monarque attempted to end all this medieval diversity by combining all mail service under one authority. The monopoly was sold in 1672 to a certain Lazare Patin, who paid 1,700,000 livres annually to the Treasury for the exclusive right to carry intercity mail. Just as inevitably Patin became entangled in a jungle of lawsuits as former concessionaires (private and University) strove to remain in business.

Despite the legal entanglements, mail service improved (at least in the sense of broadening) steadily. This can perhaps best be seen by comparing the official mail schedules of 1644 and 1704. The first—in two parts, one for domestic the other for foreign mail—covered barely more than a page in Delamare's *Traité de la police* while the latter took up eleven pages.[54] Unlike most prices the cost of postage changed comparatively little over this sixty-year period. In 1644 a *lettre simple* (folded over and sealed without an envelope) sent between Paris and Lyons cost 4 sous; in 1704 the same cost 6 sous. Postage on letters between Paris and England was unchanged at 10 sous, while between Madrid and Paris it had increased only from 10 to 12 sous.

Perhaps, however, the official rates were a little deceptive. In the Conseil de Commerce belatedly established by Louis XIV in 1700 to hear the grievances and suggestions of merchants, complaints were heard of the arbitrariness of postal officials, of their "dastardly audacity" in raising rates on their own authority and their threats to stop all mail deliveries to patrons who dared object to paying a few extra sous on a letter.[55] (Complaints about the independence of French postal employees apparently began early.)

Nevertheless, the shortcomings of the *fonctionnaires* were of small importance when compared with the enormous convenience of the service which had become available to Parisians in one lifetime. At the Bureau Général de la Poste in the Rue des Déchargeurs, close by the Halles, one could mail letters "at any hour." For the further convenience of the public, eight other letterboxes were located about Paris where one could mail a letter during daylight hours to any European city west of and including Germany and Austria.[56]

৵৹   ৵৹

The absurdity of being able to communicate more easily with the provinces and even foreign states than with fellow residents of one's own city was not lost on Parisians. At least one attempt was made in Louis XIV's reign to correct this anomaly. In Isambert's collection of pre-revolutionary laws one finds the preamble of an unobtrusive little edict dated 1653, refreshingly different from the generality of Old Regime laws.[57] This edict aimed simply at solving the dilemma of the merchant or artisan needing to communicate with another citizen but who "could not leave his shop" and "had nothing he held so dear as the time spent on the work which fed him." In an effort to help him solve his problem, the King authorized the establishment of the *petite poste* in Paris. In every quarter of the city were placed boxes for the deposit of letters bearing postage known as *billets de port payé*, available for 1 sou at designated convents, schools, and prisons. The boxes were supposed to be emptied three times each day, the contents taken to the Palais de Justice on the Cité, sorted, and delivered immediately to the addresses. The Edict boasted it would become possible for individuals to exchange information "two or three times a day," theoretically putting twentieth-century postal practices to shame. The inventor of this visionary scheme was a mysterious gentleman by the name of the Comte de Villayer, a man of minor political prominence who served as a Councilor of State for fifty-five years, was received in the Académie Française in 1659 regardless of a total absence of literary attainments, and was known principally for his inventions.[58]

Despite its obvious merits, Villayer's project failed even more dismally than the equally visionary *carrosses à cinq sous*. The chief villains were reputed to be the professional city messengers, Savoyards for the most part, who, seeing their jobs threatened, took to stuffing rodents and filth in the letterboxes.[59] The *petite poste* aborted. Not until more than a hundred years later did Parisians obtain a permanent local postal service.

The edict of 1653 establishing the ill-fated *petite poste* alluded to the widespread practice of transmitting messages within Paris by one's servants, who would then spend "whole days" in finding an address. It is possible, of course, that the servants were malingering, but anyone who has considered the problem of finding an address in old Paris must sympathize with them. Perhaps the complexities of the system for identifying Parisian streets and houses, as much as the "rodents and filth," explain the failure of the *petite poste*. Progress had been nil in this area since the twelfth century. Streets remained unmarked for the most part, but there was so much duplication in street names that markers would have been of little help. A glance at a list of seventeenth-century Parisian street names reveals a complete unconcern with the difficulties inevitably arising from repetitious nomenclature. There were nine versions of the Rue Notre-Dame, five of Saint-Augustin (Rue Saint-Augustin, Rue des Augustins, Rue des Vieux Augustins, Rue Neuve des Vieux Augustins, Rue des Petits Augustins), three of Sainte-Anne (all identical). Rue des Prêtres was the name of five streets, Rue d'Enfer of three, Rue Pavée of four, Rue de Deux Portes of five, Rue Neuve de Deux Portes of one, Rue de Trois Portes of three, plus a Rue des Portes and a Rue des Douze Portes.[60] It was customary to give one's parish as part of one's address, but even parish priests were often uncertain of parish boundaries.[61] One's *quartier* was rarely used, since it was essentially a police and administrative jurisdiction.

When one had located a street, one's difficulties had possibly just begun. The house seeker then had to start walking slowly down the street looking at the myriads of house and shop signs, comforted only by the knowledge that duplications on the same street were rare. Most Parisians lived in the upper floors of buildings identifiable only by the signs of commercial establishments on the ground floor. Purely residential structures often had their own *enseignes*. These were naturally of a more dignified type, generally carved in stone or molded in clay above or to one side of the principal door and usually painted or gilded.[62] The truly elegant houses, Lister tells us, had name plates over their gates in letters of gold set in black marble. Saint-Simon relates the stir the new-rich caused when they began to use the words *hôtel de* over their doors, for men of birth had long considered the use of this term one of their prerogatives.[63]

Commercial signs were generally of painted wood suspended from metal brackets anchored in the wall of the building. They often projected almost to the middle of the narrower streets and were an obvious danger to life and limb. Everyone but the merchants complained about them. They cut off light, gave offense to the moralists because of their frequent irreverences and *double-entendres* (a pious character in Molière's *Les Fâcheux* demanded police inspection of the *enseignes*), scandalized people of taste, and on windy days caused a distracting cacophony as they swung on their rusty hinges. La Reynie contemplated banning all projecting signs, but the opposition of the merchants caused him to abandon this reform. He contented himself with a decree (1669) providing that all signboards must hang 13½ feet from the pavement, measure a uniform 1½ by 2 feet in size, and extend no more than 3 feet from the wall.[64] Detailed plans were issued by the Châtelet for uniform, ornate iron brackets from which to suspend the *enseignes*. Lister, writing in 1698, was surprised how well La Reynie's orders had been obeyed. He described the signs as small, high, and unobtrusive. Either Dr Lister was a bad reporter or the Châtelet had relaxed its rules considerably by Lister's time. The overwhelming evidence is that Paris streets in the eighteenth century were as cluttered with oversized signs as they had ever been. But one should perhaps not be unduly harsh towards the merchants for their perversity. Their signs had to be large because they relied much more on painted tableaux than on the printed word.[65] A signboard artist could not be expected to do very much with the minuscule signs to which La Reynie would have limited them. All forms of publicity in the seventeenth century began with the basic premise that most people could not read, and only small and infrequent concessions were made to the slowly increasing literate public.

Public information remained the province of the town criers. There were two main kinds: one set for the dissemination of nonofficial information of interest to the public and the other set to announce laws, police regulations, news of national importance and the like. The first were organized in a guild of great antiquity which jealously guarded all the irrational prerogatives which age could bring to Parisian institutions, and it would be difficult to find one more irrational than this one. Known as the *crieurs de corps et de vin*, they derived most of their income from carrying out two strangely unrelated duties: checking on wine consumption in the taverns and serving as sole undertakers in Paris. Their police of the taverns had evolved from the medieval tavern keepers' practice of hiring criers to advertise the tapping of choice new vintages. Since excise taxes on wines were always one of the city's principal sources of income, it was natural that the Hôtel de Ville would sooner or later make use of the criers (already under its legal jurisdiction) to verify that no barrels were opened without the tax being paid thereon. However, in the seventeenth century as in the Middle Ages the *crieurs* continued to play both sides of the street by first performing the pleasant task of sampling and certifying the contents of new barrels and then advertising them by voice throughout the neighborhood.

The function of undertaker had fallen to the same guild by virtue of its long association with crying death announcements, causing the public to turn increasingly to its members for funeral arrangements in time of bereavement. Law finally caught up with custom in 1641 when a new statute gave the *crieurs* exclusive rights in this lucrative field in return for annual contributions to the care of abandoned children in Paris, too many of whom were reported to be perishing "because of lack of food." The law of 1641 in favor of the *crieurs* brought them into conflict with the parish priests and *marguilliers* (lay wardens), who naturally resented this latest secularist intrusion into their pseudo-sacred right to sell the casket to the deceased's survivors. D'Argenson wrote sorrowfully to Versailles in 1700 that hardly a week went by without a new scandal at a church funeral, where "the prayers of the church are often interrupted by . . . quarrels which sometimes lead to blows."[66] He particularly regretted the effect of these scandals on newly converted Catholics, the current object of so much official solicitude. Many, he warned, suspected that "money and vanity" had penetrated the sanctuary.

The other type of town crier was the official known as the *juré-crieur du Roi*, who came under the jurisdiction of the Châtelet rather than the Hôtel de Ville. Any time that the King wished to proclaim a new law or make any kind of official announcement, the Châtelet would call into action the *juré-crieur*. Accompanied by three royal trumpeters (*jurés-trompettes*), the *crieur* would proceed about the city, stopping at prescribed points to make his announcement. Until the sixteenth century this procedure would have sufficed to render the statute into law, but at that time the custom began of posting royal ordinances at prominent intersections, which also became the responsibility of the *juré-crieur*. Royal announcements (*les placards*) were distinguished from simple *avis* in that they were printed on special paper bearing the king's seal and were thereby ensured a fitting position on crowded wall surfaces.[67] (To cover a *placard* with an *avis* was to court trouble with the police.) Only when this had been done could the *juré-crieur* report back to the Châtelet that all legal requirements had been met and no one could henceforth plead ignorance of the law.

As in the case of the mail, this right of posting, initially reserved to the Crown and officialdom, was extended in the seventeenth century to the general public. For a small fee one could obtain permission to post a notice of any kind at an official location. Visitors to the Saint-Germain quarter were intrigued by the number of advertisements of this sort for antivenereal remedies. The registers of the Hôtel-Dieu for 1660 record a debate among the directors whether they should solicit badly needed funds through the *affiches* rather than relying, as they had, on the parish priests to make their needs known to the public.[68] The first theater posters date to the start of the seventeenth century, but not until the 1670's did they become the main means of publicity for the actors, supplanting the traditional *orateurs* who at the end of every performance had habitually given long spiels on coming attractions. Chappuzeau tells us that in the 1670's the theaters had agreed on a color scheme to distinguish their posters: red for the Hôtel de Bourgogne, green for the Guénégaud, and yellow for the Opera.[69] In the last years of the century, Dr Lister, who at times seems intent upon making variant observations on Parisian life, thought there was "very little noise in this city," and upon inquiring was shown "Printed Papers upon the Corners of Streets" offering rewards for lost objects and making announcements which presumably were made by voice in more clamorous London.

With the appearance in the first half of the seventeenth century of the first newspapers and advertising sheets, far more effective means of public communication became available than tacked announcements on overcrowded walls. Unfortunately, their potential was not realized until the following century. The seemingly simple idea of joining news reports and advertising, and making the second pay for the first, was never realized. The smallness of the reading public, the relatively high production costs, the antipathy of the authorities and merchants, the sheer dullness of the reading matter, all combined to prevent the flowering of a popular press in seventeenth-century Paris.

The first newspaper in the capital, and the object of a frequent but very shaky claim as the first of all newspapers, was the work of Théo-phraste Renaudot—talented journalist, physician (but, unfortunately for him, of the medical school of Montpellier), humanitarian, and business promoter. (He has also been called the first man in France to realize the importance of *"la publicité."*)[70] His *Gazette* was founded in 1631 and continued in publication until the Revolution. It was for the most part a dull semiofficial weekly quite content with the unexciting role of transmitting royal communiqués and narrating the unnewsworthy ac-tivities of the royal family. When Louis XIV took up residence at Ver-sailles, the page count went up from eight to twelve, but no effort was made to exploit the journalistic possibilities of the new locale. Its de-tachment from the lives of ordinary mortals was evidenced by its foun-der's aim of serving as "the journal of kings and of the powers of the world"[71]—a principle from which it rarely deviated. Martin Lister com-mented that "few people" bought it.

The third quarter of the century brought several new journals, no-tably the *Muse historique* of Loret, the *Journal des savants* (1665), and the *Mercure galant* (1672), but all three were far more literary sheets than news media. From the viewpoint of pure journalism, the most no-table publishing venture was François Colletet's attempt in 1676 at es-tablishing not only a true newspaper but a daily one at that. Its name was the *Journal de la ville de Paris* and only one issue, the first, has sur-vived. Whether more numbers were issued and what fate befell the ven-ture are not known. More than likely La Reynie's police clamped down on Colletet, despite the editor's wonderfully diplomatic statement in the first issue that Louis XIV's reign was so glorious that it deserved to be recorded not only by the year, the month, and the week, but by the day and the moment.[72]

Still another kind of medium which appeared in the seventeenth century was the *gazette à la main.* These *gazettes* were small manu-script newspapers distributed secretly to a set list of subscribers. (They were contemporaneous with and perhaps inspired by the English news letters.) One person arrested for having engaged in this business was shown to have had half a dozen scribes in his employ who ordinarily turned out 150 copies of the paper.[73] The almost psychotic fears of the authorities regarding the press were not entirely unwarranted, but the *gazettes* were more likely to contain scandalous anecdotes of the Court than politically dangerous news. This made the police no less fearful of them. So apprehensive were the King and ministers of independent public opinion that an ordinance of 1666 provided that arrested gazetteers be tried in certain lower courts without right of appeal so as to avoid the publicity of trials in the higher courts.

Paralleling in part the uncertain efforts to provide Paris with a news medium, and only slightly more successful, were the attempts of certain enterprising souls to give it an advertising organ. From 1630 on repeated efforts were made to publish printed sheets containing what American readers would recognize as classified ads but which to the seventeenth-century Parisian were known as the *petites affiches,* to differentiate them from the larger *affiches* posted at street corners. The very persistence of these efforts is indicative of the need for better methods of communication in the increasingly complex city. The sponsor of one of these early advertising sheets termed the lack of such communications a "shortcoming in the perfection of our society."[74] Another stressed the weaknesses of the system of *affichage*: there never seemed to be sufficient room on the walls set aside for this purpose, some notices were always either slipping off or being covered up by more recent arrivals. Moreover, the *honnête homme* felt ill at ease standing on a busy corner thumbing through the notices, many doubtless of a personal nature. Still another promoter of the *petites affiches* argued that they were of far more use and interest to the public than the learned *Journal des savants*.

Sensing this need for public advertising, Théophraste Renaudot pioneered in 1629, two years before he established his *Gazette*, an "ad office" adjacent to the New Market in the Cité. It was known as the Bureau d'Adresses and served as a clearing house for people trying to sell or buy "all the necessities and conveniences of life."[75] Supplementing the services of the Bureau, a printed sheet was issued periodically recapitulating the announcements held on file at the office. In order to obtain the necessary privilege for his new project, which undoubtedly was greeted with suspicion by the merchants, Renaudot had argued that the Bureau would eliminate the greatest cause of poverty and crime in Paris by enabling provincials to find employment "one hour after their arrival." Since the problems of unemployment and vagabondage were beginning at this time to assume major proportions, this was a potent argument.

Renaudot's Bureau d'Adresses and the accompanying *feuille* prospered for more than a decade but were forced out of existence by the courts in 1644 as a consequence of a lawsuit brought against Renaudot by the medical faculty, angered as usual by any success of a provincial competitor. Not only was he ordered to end the practice of medicine in the city but also to close his business activities. Only the *Gazette* was left untouched.[76] Nevertheless, the idea had taken root. In 1670, 1676, 1681, 1688, 1707, 1716, and perhaps other years as well, attempts were made to reestablish either the Bureau d'Adresses or the printed advertising sheets.[77] In his abortive daily newspaper of 1676 François Colletet tried to combine news and advertising, only to meet with almost immediate failure. A few months later he launched a small sheet containing only advertising, under the name *Journal des avis et affaires de Paris*. At least ten issues appeared before La Reynie received a ministerial letter informing him that "H.M. . . . desires that you prohibit its sale and publication."[78] In 1681 Renaudot's scheme was again revived, this time by the enterprising editor of the *Mercure galant*, Devizé, who drew up grandiose plans not only for a Bureau of Addresses and an advertising sheet but for a store as well where the goods could be displayed and sold. Once again La Reynie interfered and Devizé's plan never got off the ground. The longest-lived of these efforts was one operating from 1702 to at least 1707 from the end of the Pont Neuf, publishing in octavo for 2½ sous a list of "properties, houses, diverse things to sell or rent, new books, etc." It was said to have circulated as far as Rouen.[79]

The source of the difficulties of the bureaus of addresses and their advertising supplements is not hard to fathom. When La Reynie denied authorization to one of their promoters, he wrote that he would never give such permission, "capable as it was of overturning the entire commerce of Paris."[80] La Reynie and the Châtelet, as principal overseers of the Parisian economy, were solidly committed to the guild system, and any kind of public advertising was as much a violation of the guild philosophy as cornering sources of supply or buying outside the established markets.[81] Adding to the pressure which the powerful merchant interests of Paris must have placed on the Châtelet to halt such clear challenges to established business practices was Versailles' hostility to privately controlled communications media. This was not a soil in which journalism could take firm root, and while seventeenth-century Paris witnessed remarkable advances in physical communications, it had to await at least the undermining of the political and economic system before corresponding advances could be made in verbal communications.

CHAPTER FOUR

The theater transformed

IF the desire and ability to maintain a permanent public theater are essential criteria of a metropolis, Paris first qualified as such in the seventeenth century. In one lifetime the modern Parisian theater—professional and permanently established—was not only born but achieved full maturity. The city which could in the first years of the century provide no more than a hand-to-mouth existence for transitory Italian and French troupes was just a few decades later supporting four theatrical companies, to say nothing of the usual irregulars. In the later part of Louis XIV's reign the number was reduced to three and then to two, but the fault lay more in the monarch's penchant for consolidation and standardization than in the city's inability to support them.

For many years theater-lovers among Louis XIV's subjects were able to choose their entertainment from among approximately eight hundred representations annually, performed both summer and winter. The Comédie Française performed seven nights weekly, the Italians six, and the Opera three times. The troupes were so large and well-organized that even a command performance at Versailles or Fontainbleau caused no interruption in the usual schedule.[1] In Louis XIV's reign, close to a million livres annually was spent on theater admissions, and for the first time professional actors began to die moderately wealthy if not entirely respectable men and women. An analysis of the remuneration of the twenty or more full shareholders of the Comédie Française in the 1680's and '90's shows they earned as much as 7,000 livres each in the better years, which was a good upper-middle-class income for the times. Visitors to Paris were generally startled by the lavishness of the productions, especially the "colossal" machine plays.

At the start of the century the only theatrical structure in Paris worthy of the name was the Hôtel de Bourgogne, built in 1548 in the Saint-Denis quarter close to the Halles. It was owned by the Confrérie de la Passion, which had long enjoyed the exclusive right to present mystery plays in Paris. As this sort of entertainment declined in the sixteenth century both in popularity and in the esteem of the magistrates, the Confrérie took to renting its building to visiting provincial and foreign troupes. That the capital of the realm lagged well behind the provinces in theatrical development until well into the seventeenth century was largely due to the monopolistic and close-fisted policies of the Confrérie.[2] Not only did traveling companies find it difficult to obtain favorable terms, but even if they found a makeshift location elsewhere in the city, they were still legally bound to pay the Brotherhood a tribute for the right to produce a play in Paris.[3]

Whether performed at the Hôtel de Bourgogne or some makeshift indoor tennis court (*jeu de paume*), the city's theatrical fare at the dawn of the Grand Siècle was limited to little better than the unsavory *commedia dell'arte* of the Italian actors and equally slapstick French farces. According to Tallemant des Réaux, ladies never went to the theater before Richelieu's time so outrageous was the buffoonery seen there. Among the French *farceurs* in the early decades of the century, three actors stood out as popular favorites. Most memorable was Gros Guillaume (Robert Guérin in real life), who invariably played the stock role of the clown. So fat was he that he affected two belts, one below the navel and another high on his chest. His face was covered with flour that blew out over the stage as he grew excited. "He said almost nothing but spoke so naively and with such a pleasant face that one could not but laugh."[4] As thin as Gros Guillaume was fat was the actor who played the traditional role of the old man. He was known as Gautier-Carguille in the farces. His trademarks were a pointed beard, black cap and long, slender walking stick, and with his "lean body, long, straight and thin legs," he was able to twist like a "real marionette."[5] Finally there was the long-time favorite Turlubin, the clever and knavish valet, who always wore a mask in the style of the Italian actors along with a floppy high-brimmed hat and baggy striped pantaloons.

A brave effort to give the Parisian public something more elevating than two-belted buffoons was made at the turn of the century when an actor named Valleran le Conte staged at the Hôtel de Bourgogne tragedies and pastorals written by, among others, Alexandre Hardy. For the first time a troupe used the title of *comédiens du roi* which was to become so coveted during the seventeenth century and afterwards. But something more than a high-sounding title was apparently needed to pay salaries and expenses, for Valleran lasted only two years begore giving up his lease to a new company formed by the veteran *farceur* Gros Guillaume.[6] For more than a decade Valleran was in and out of Paris, struggling to compete with the popular favorites. He never achieved the revolution in tastes that he had hoped for and around 1613, somewhere on tour, died the frustrated death of one born before his time. Farces—characterized by a contemporary critic as works "recommendable only to ignoramuses and scum because of the rough language and vile actions which form the basis of their attraction"—continued as the popular choice.[7]

Nevertheless, Valleran had pointed the way. With a swiftness which would have gratified him, the theater public, or at least an influential part of it, began to lose interest in the vulgarities and buffoonery of the *farceurs* and Italians. More sophisticated forms of drama began to win public favor. By the 1630's Paris had become, and remained, the theatrical center of France, the provinces serving only as training grounds for ambitious young actors and playwrights.

In 1629 the long-struggling Comédiens du Roi took up their permanent abode at the already decrepit old Hôtel de Bourgogne. At almost the same time Montdory's new troupe came into existence, moving from one converted *jeu de paume* to another until finally settling in 1634 at the *jeu de paume* in the Marais from which it received its name. Works on dramatic criticism, rare at the start of the century, became increasingly common. Mairet in the 1630's adapted the Aristotelian unities of time, place, and action to French drama, and playwrights soon found they could violate them only at their peril. Patronized by great figures like Richelieu and attracting audiences concerned or professing to be concerned only with "regular" theatrical productions, the drama at last became highly respected both as a literary type and as a form of entertainment—even for ladies of delicate tastes.

While a large and discriminating theater public had come into being in Paris by the time of Louis XIV's birth in 1638, the idea of a theatrical quarter was then, and for the rest of the century, quite unknown. The five buildings which housed the leading troupes of Paris at one time or another during the second part of the seventeenth century were scattered widely about the city; only the south and southeast failed to be represented. The hall of the Palais-Royal, built by Richelieu in the 1630's as a private theater adjacent to his princely new residence and allocated in Louis XIV's time to Molière's troupe and to the Opera successively, enjoyed the most elegant location among Parisian theaters. Slightly less than one-half mile to the northeast, in a much less distinguished neighborhood in the Rue Mauconseil, stood the Hôtel de Bourgogne, which for a century and a half played a dominant role in the development of drama in the city. Still further to the east in the Rue Vieille-du-Temple, in what must surely have qualified as a low-rent district, was the Théâtre du Marais, for four decades a serious rival of the Hôtel de Bourgogne until the Sun King put it out of business in 1673 and ordered its actors to amalgamate with Molière's troupe.

All the foregoing theaters, along with the Salle du Petit-Bourbon in the Louvre—used for occasional royal spectacles and, briefly, by Molière's company—were located on the Right Bank. Not until 1674 did the theatrical world wake up to the increasingly obvious fact that much of its most important clientele was moving into the Faubourg Saint-Germain on the Left Bank. In that year Molière's company (he had died the year before) was evicted from the plush surroundings of the Palais-Royal to make room for Louis XIV's latest passion, the Opera. To the surprise of many, it chose to move across the river to the Rue Guénégaud, a fine location just a few paces removed from the south end of the Pont Neuf. In the following decade, when the best actors of Paris were amalgamated into the Comédie Française, the trend to the Left Bank was further evidenced by their choice of a site to the south of the Guénégaud in the Rue des Fossés-Saint-Germain-des-Prés.

Until the erection of the latter structure in 1688 actors and audiences

had to make do with interior theater design which showed little awareness of the amphitheaters of the ancients who inspired so much of seventeenth-century French drama. Far from taking their models from the
Greek theaters (some of which were still in ready view on French soil),
Parisian theatrical enterpreneurs chose to be inspired by the shape of the
halls used for the local *jeux de paume*. This choice rested more on economic than on functional or aesthetic considerations. While no one
knows with any degree of accuracy how many *jeux de paume* there were
at any given time in seventeenth-century Paris, it is clear that the promoters of the sport—roughly comparable to indoor tennis—had overex-
tended themselves. Many of the structures were converted into billiard
halls and covers for less innocent gaming. But for many years they were
also used as makeshift theaters by traveling troupes. The balcony which
ran along one side of the larger *jeux de paume* could easily be converted
to seating areas for the more affluent patrons of the theater, while the
ground level became a parterre for standing spectators. All that was
really needed to transform a *jeu de paume* into a modest theater was a
crude stage at one end.

Since the *jeu de paume* required a rectangular structure about
three times as long as it was wide, such became the proportions of
nearly all the seventeenth-century Parisian theaters—hardly an ideal
shape for the purpose. The Hôtel de Bourgogne, built in 1548 for the
Confrérie de la Passion, measured 102 feet in length by 36 in width.
(Although built as a theater rather than as a *jeu de paume*, there is
some speculation whether the builders were not influenced by the numerous *jeux de paume* then being erected in the city.) The company
which became known eventually as the Théâtre du Marais occupied
successively three converted *jeux de paume* in as many years before settling down in still another which became its permanent home. After
ten years' occupancy by the company of the Marais, this structure was
destroyed in 1644 in a spectacular fire. With little delay and no apparent
financial embarrassment, the company erected a new theater on the
site of the old. Again, the proportions were precisely those of a *jeu de
paume*—39 feet by 114—although it was designed from the ground up
as a theater. A generation later, when what was left of the Marais

troupe joined Molière's actors at the Guénégaud, it was again in a converted *jeu de paume*—the old Jeu de Paume de la Bouteille—that the curtain rose. Only in 1688, with the construction of the relatively luxurious Comédie Française in elliptical shape and with hall dimensions of 108 feet by 54 feet, was the old architectural tyranny of the *jeu de paume* finally broken.[8]

The interior arrangements of all these seventeenth-century theaters, like their dimensions, were basically alike. The actors looked out over the heads of—hopefully—several hundred milling standees on the perfectly flat parterres. At the Hôtel de Bourgogne the stage was at least five feet above the parterre. Adding to the sense of isolation which the parterre must have felt was a high iron grille separating the pit from the stage. It is not surprising that the footsore, macaroon-munching, wine-imbibing audiences at the feet of the actors were notorious for their unruliness and license. But troublesome as they might be, they were an economic necessity; probably half of the total receipts came from the parterre.[9]

Beyond the parterre, at the far end of the hall, was the amphitheater. These rows of shallow stone steps, on which small chairs were generally placed, were an innovation of Richelieu's Palais-Cardinal (later Palais-Royal) in the late 1630's and were copied by most of the later theaters. Queen Christina had given a certain notoriety to the *gradins* of the Palais-Royal on the occasion of her visit to Paris in 1655 when, with characteristic perversity, she chose to sit there rather than in a more befitting and comfortable loge. The newly converted and much talked about ex-monarch apparently stole the show on this occasion by her unconventional manner of sitting. One shocked spectator wrote: "Her posture was so indecent that . . . one glimpsed what even the least modest woman should keep hidden."[10]

Although the price of a seat in the amphitheater was approximately the same as that of a lower loge, it is difficult, despite such episodes, to understand their attraction. The portable stools must have been quite uncomfortable and sitting at the rear of the theater, one had to overcome all the distractions traditionally associated with the parterre. There was one obvious advantage, however. From the amphitheater one could enjoy the only good perspective in the theater; one's line of vision naturally led to the action on the stage rather than to the loges on the opposite side of the hall.

The loges at the Hôtel de Bourgogne were in two tiers; in the other Parisian theaters in three, although the Palais-Royal did not add a third until 1671. In the triple-tiered theaters one could sit or stand on the top floor for approximately the same price as the parterre. (The social prestige was also nil.) It is doubtful that these seats were even partitioned. The *premières loges* sold generally for double the price of the *secondes* and three times those of the highest tier. Members of the royal family, the older *noblesse*, and the magistracy were likely to be seen there. Each loge held eight seats and to purchase a *loge entière* for a performance was, then as now, a sure means of attracting attention. For the opening performance of Molière's *Le Malade imaginaire* at the Palais-Royal in 1671—a gala occasion for which, as was customary, seats sold *au double*—five first-tier loges were sold as units, along with 59 other seats of this type. On the same evening, 81 paid spectators were to be found in the second loges, only 23 in the third, 394 in the parterre, and 60 in the amphitheater. The total paid attendance of 682 (twenty-five sat on the stage) on this historic evening was close to capacity for the Parisian theater of those times; average attendance at the Comédie Française in its first decades averaged slightly over 400 per performance.[11]

Stage seats (the *beau monde's* revenge on the parterre for all the distractions it had to endure) were introduced around mid-century. By the 1660's Molière was finding fair game in the obnoxious marquis who considered that the parterre was honored by being allowed to watch him brush his wig, sniff tobacco, and promenade around the stage[12]— in cool disregard of the shrill whistles and shouted insults which such conduct evoked from the plebeians. At about the same time Chappuzeau described the difficulties encountered by the actors in making their way through crowds of spectators in order to arrive on the stage on cue. A seat *sur le théâtre* (as a stage seat was known) had become for certain kinds of people the most desirable seat in the house, although no more expensive than the first loges. The actors, who as owners had it within their power to forbid stage seating any time they wished, apparently were more interested in cash receipts than Art. Perhaps impelled by a well-documented incident in which a young marquis had stepped up to an actor and administered a sound *soufflet* under the mistaken impression that he had been mocked,[13] the Comédie Française late in the century erected a balustrade around its stage. The impresario of opera, Lully, vowed to discourage stage seating, so he raised the price of such seats to double that of the first loges. The result was an even greater demand to be seen in this golden area,[14] which, perhaps, was the shrewd Lully's purpose from the start.

Belatedly intervening in 1697, the King ordered the stage cleared of spectators at both the Comédie Française and the Opera. However, when Brice published the new edition of his guide the following year, he still noted stage seating at the Opera, although it had apparently disappeared at the Comédie. Shortly thereafter, the Opera made a sensible compromise between financial exigencies and the need for order by constructing raised box seats (*balcons*) on the sides and back of their stage. The right to sit there cost a patron a *louis d'or*, or close to 12 livres in the devalued currency of Louis XIV's later reign.

～ ～

What class of people attended the Parisian theater? There is abundant information in contemporary literature on the occupants of the loges, the amphitheater, and the stage seats. They ranged from royalty down through the aristocracies of birth and wealth to lesser luminaries of the church, the professions, and commerce. What is much harder to come by is precise information on the social make-up of the parterre—the economic lifeblood of the theater. There are those (for example, one of the great authorities on the seventeenth-century French stage, Henry Carrington Lancaster) who would insist on the democratic character of the audiences found there.[15] But some of the evidence makes one wonder whether representatives of the laboring class—of the 50,000 or more journeymen and apprentices who constituted the bulk of Parisian wage earners—were really to be found in significant numbers on the parterre.

In support of Lancaster's thesis of a broad-spectrum audience, one must concede that the patrons of the parterre often behaved in a most unbourgeoislike manner. If one associates the bourgeoisie with a large measure of decorum, aversion to violence, and obedience to authority, then the parterre audiences clearly were not bourgeois. Probably second in number only to the endless ordinances ordering beggars and vagabonds to leave Paris within a stated deadline were those forbidding disorderly assemblies in front of theaters, carrying arms inside the building, and causing any kind of disturbance therein. Serious riots marked the opening of the Opera in 1672, and the following year attempts were made by the parterre to set the Hôtel de Bourgogne ablaze. Chappuzeau, an eyewitness on the latter occasion, wrote of the "unparalleled brutality" with which certain elements in the audience set upon fellow spectators.[16]

The closing years of the century were another period of marked hooliganism in the Parisian theater. This time the trouble centered on a new whistling craze. It is not clear whether the whistling was produced by natural or mechanical means. One does find a contemporary theatergoer writing of "taking up his whistle,"[17] so, possibly, some of the less adept used a mechanical contrivance of some sort. But whatever the means, it became accepted practice in the theater to express one's distaste for what was taking place on the stage by emitting a shrill whistle. One modern historian of the theater of the Grand Siècle has theorized that the new custom was a natural reaction to the paucity of good theater in those years outside of the Racine-Molière-Corneille staple which was beginning to pall on audiences after endless repetition. An item in the *Mercure* in 1694 would bear this out: "People want to whistle," the article stated, "because this stirs up a commotion which one finds more entertaining than anything one might hear."[18] After receiving a *mémoire* on the subject from the unnerved actors of the Comédie Française, Versailles ordered a three-week incarceration in the Hôpital-Général for anyone convicted of whistling in the theater.[19] As was customary in such matters, La Reynie began looking around for a person to serve as an "example." After what appeared an inordinately long time, the authorities pounced upon a hapless butcher by the name of Caraque, who must have languished in the Hôpital considerably longer than three weeks since it required a letter from Pontchartrain, writing in the King's name, to free him. As the new century opened, Louis XIV was still ordering Parisian theater audiences to stop "whistling, clapping their hands, and other similar disorders."[20]

One would be very wrong, however, in assuming that such rowdyism was *prima facie* evidence of the presence of the laboring class on the parterre. The culprits were invariably such traditional disturbers of the peace as soldiers, lackeys, pages, and other livery servants, and not wage earners in the more usual sense (the above-mentioned butcher must, of course, be placed in the employer class). The worst offenders, possibly, were the King's musketeers, whose two companies were regularly quartered in Paris. Like so many other elite military units, they seemed to feel honor-bound to be in the thick of any brawl that arose—if they had not started it in the first place. It is perhaps no coincidence that the worst troubles in the theaters began in winter and in wartime (early in the Dutch War and in the 1690's) when the soldiers were in winter quarters in the capital. Some notion of the unpopularity of the military among the theatrical troupes can be derived from a still extant poster of Louis XIV's time bearing the inscription beneath the notice of a new production, "Soldiers prohibited on pain of death."[21] Chappuzeau in the early 1670's complained that so many musketeers were forcing their way without paying into Molière's theater that a small army of twelve guards commanded by a sergeant and costing 15 livres had been hired to supplement the customary one or two doorkeepers.[22]

A close second to the soldiers in giving the parterres their reputation for rowdyism were the liveried servants of *les grands*, always ready to use their insignia as an easy ticket to a performance and fully aware that if they got into trouble their masters would feel honor-bound to back them up. The police magistrates had regularly supported the theatrical troupes in their perennial conflict with the lackeys and pages. After a particularly disgraceful episode in 1674 La Reynie issued an order temporarily forbidding entrance to the theaters to all *gens de livrée* even when they were prepared to pay.[23] But it took more courage than most door attendants possessed to turn away the lackey of some great personage. The actor-owners were all too well aware of the timidity of the doorkeepers in such situations and periodically turned to the ministry for backing. Since some of the worse offenders were the lackeys of ambassadors, Pontchartrain suggested to the Secretary for Foreign Affairs that the foreign ambassadors once again be reminded that their livery, like that of the *grands seigneurs*, must pay to obtain admission to the theater.[24]

While we believe the much publicized rowdiness of the parterre should be blamed on soldiers and servants rather than on the working classes, this supposition does not in itself rule out the possibility of large representations of workers in the theater, as Lancaster assumed.[25] However, the wage earner desiring to attend the theater faced certain grave difficulties. One of the less important, admittedly, was the impractical time schedule employed by theaters. The starting time was gradually being pushed back (at the start of the century it was set by law at noon), but even in the later part of the century it was rarely past five o'clock.[26] Since the working day extended to around seven in winter and even later in summer, the working man would have been faced with a problem.

Much more inhibiting than the time conflict for any theater-minded member of the working classes must have been the matter of personal economics. One has sufficient difficulty understanding how seventeenth-century wage earners managed to keep themselves and their families alive, without picturing them patronizing the theater. Some writers may be inspired by the thought of Parisian wage earners standing engrossed on the parterres of the Comédie or the Opera, but in truth the wage earner's chances of eking out the price of a theater ticket from his meager earnings must have been very small. The theater was not cheap measured by contemporary standards. The prices cited by Brice (see the table) are the prices of an ordinary performance; theater managers were quick to double them if there was anything out of the ordinary in the performance, such as a *première*, a "machine" play, or any sort of gala.

These were not prices even the gainfully employed masses could afford. Many skilled wage earners worked from sunrise to sunset for no more than the equivalent of the cheapest ticket to the Comédie, some for less. It must also be remembered that these wages had to be stretched to cover the expenses of Sundays and the innumerable religious holidays on which the law forbade labor. Regardless of their alleged penchant for drama, few members of the populace could have been in a position to take a day or an afternoon off from their labors to patronize the theater at the cost of at least an entire day's wages.

Theater prices at the end of the seventeenth century (Brice)

Place	Comédie Française	Opera
Parterre	15 sous	30 sous
Third loge	1 livre	30 sous
Second loge	1½ livres	3 livres
First loge	3 livres	5 livres 10 sous
Amphitheater	1½ to 3 livres	5 livres 10 sous
Stage seats	3 livres	11 livres
Balcons	—	louis d'or

Another fact would tend to rule out the possibility that the patrons of the Parisian theater were a numerous group drawn from a cross-section of the city. Actually, they must have been a rather narrow fraternity. Supporting this notion is the rapidity with which plays wore out. The seventeenth-century record for consecutive performances was said to be held by Thomas Corneille's *Timocrate*, and that was a mere eighty performances.[27] Many of Molière's hits ran only for ten to twenty showings. Even the popular *Ecole des femmes*, which had the advantage of a major critical and police controversy to publicize it, was presented only seventy nonconsecutive times before Molière had to put it aside.[28] None of these figures would suggest that Parisian theaters could count on the patronage of a large percentage of the perhaps 150,000 adults in the city.

While the evidence is meager, we would be inclined to believe that seventeenth-century audiences—both seated and standing—were made up of no more than a relatively small fraction of the population, more specifically, the aristocracy and the professional and commercial middle-class, along with a small, noisy and mostly nonpaying handful from the soldiery and livery. Any wage earners attending the theater as paying spectators surely exhibited an extraordinary devotion to the arts.

ঌ   ঌ

Until the very end of the seventeenth century, the Parisian theatrical scene changed with bewildering rapidity. Troupes of actors came and went, some amalgamating, others falling out of favor or simply disappearing. But as the century drew to a close, this instability gave way to the sort of classic simplicity and permanence so dear to the heart of Louis XIV. After 1697 only two troupes of actors were permitted in the capital, that of the Comédie Française and that of the Opera, each the owner of jealously guarded monopolies over the spoken and sung theater respectively. On the stage of its lavish new home in the Rue Fossés Saint-Germain, the Comédie presented performances seven nights each week, even though it experienced somewhat the same travails in acquiring acceptable new material as a modern television producer. At the Palais-Royal, the Opera still rode the crest of popularity, taking in as much as 4,000 livres[29] (at least three or four times the receipts of the Comédie) at each of its thrice weekly performances.

In 1697 the Italian actors at last became the victims of the monarch's cultural authoritarianism. After repeated unheeded warnings, they were forced to take an extended holiday in Italy and to await a change in political climate. Before their departure, they had enjoyed the distinction of being the oldest professional group on the Parisian stage. Ever since the *Gelosi* of Henry III's time, troupes of Italian actors had followed one another in fairly close succession at various rented *jeux de paume* about the city, preserving the old tradition of the *commedia dell'arte* (traditional themes acted out more or less impromptu by stock characters) for large and appreciative audiences. The Italians' status was from the start a precarious one, for while Henry III greatly enjoyed the antics of the Italians and gave them his protection, the Parlement of Paris was unceasingly outraged by their indecencies.[30] As early as 1577 the very respectable Pierre de l'Etoile deplored the inability of the Parisian magistrates to cope with this new menace to public decency.

Despite their efforts, he wrote, the Italians continued to give performances "by the express permission and authorization of the King, the
corruption of this era being such that farce-players, buffoons, prostitutes, and mignons are in full control."[31]

Under Mazarin and during most of the personal reign of Louis XIV
the Italians enjoyed peace and prosperity. The "two young Hollanders"
went to see them on July 1, 1657, and agreed with the almost universal
verdict that while one did not understand a word, one laughed uproar-
iously. At the time the most famous actor ever produced by the Italian
theater, Scaramouche, was already the star of the company and "split-
ting the sides" of his audience with his "postures and gestures," the
Dutch visitors wrote. (Scaramouche would continue to do so until his
death in 1694, when his legacy of 100,000 *écus* to his priest-son probably
helped procure him a church funeral at Saint-Eustache, the parish that
had refused a Christian burial to Molière.[32])

From 1660 until the Revolution, except for the enforced hiatus at the
start of the eighteenth century, an Italian troupe was in permanent residence in Paris. In 1665 the Italians were accorded the status of royal actors by an appreciative Louis XIV along with an annual pension even
larger than that of the prestigious tragedians of the Hôtel de Bourgogne.[33] During the 1660's and 1670's the Italians shared theaters with
Molière's troupe (the Petit-Bourbon, the Palais-Royal, and the Guénégaud successively) and relations between the two companies of kindred
comedians were everything one would hope for. There are some experts
in the history of the seventeenth-century theater who even maintain
that it was Scaramouche who taught Molière how to act.[34]

With the consolidation of theatrical troupes and the emergence of
the Comédie Française in 1680, there was for once a surplus of theaters
in Paris, and the Italians fell heir to the Hôtel de Bourgogne. For the
more tradition-minded of Parisian theater lovers, a more distasteful
switch could hardly be imagined. For almost two generations the Hôtel
de Bourgogne had echoed to the sonorities of Corneille, Racine, and all
the other apostles of *le bon goût*, and now it was surrendered to the
earthy vulgarities and slapstick of the Italians. As if to rub salt in the
wounds of the conservatives, Scaramouche and his associates, once in

possession of the Hôtel de Bourgogne, began to act out their vulgarities in French, in apparent violation of the Comédie's legal monopoly over all theatrical performances in that tongue. (Perhaps through some sort of gentleman's agreement with Molière, as long as they had shared the same stage with his troupe they had refrained from the use of the vernacular.[35]) It is probable that the shrewd and experienced Italians had perceived that their old style of comedy had begun to pall on French audiences, and that in order to fill a large theater by their own efforts six times a week some accommodation had to be made to changing times and tastes. One of their number wrote, "If we showed only the old pieces, our theater would be poorly patronized." The "old pieces" were produced only infrequently, he added, in loyal memory of past times and "merely to preserve the real taste for comedy."[36]

The luck of the Italians finally ran out in the last years of the century. The ax fell in 1697, but for several years before this the King had become increasingly impatient with the antics which had once regaled him so. Dangeau noted in a journal entry in January 1688 that "the *comédiens Italiens* have been ordered to delete from their plays all double entendres. . . ."[37] A few years later, the Italians received another warning when they had the temerity to show a play depicting a police commissioner at the Châtelet as a "robber and forger."[38] In 1696 the minister Pontchartrain sent a letter to La Reynie expressing the King's continued concern over the indecencies of the Italians. La Reynie was ordered to call personally at the Hôtel de Bourgogne to tell the Italians that "His Majesty would break them" if there were any more "indecent postures . . . equivocal words . . . and anything contrary to modesty." Louis ordered that henceforth a police agent be secretly present at all performances to report on goings-on.[39]

A year later, however, heedless as ever of warnings and apparently convinced that they were too popular to be seriously disciplined by the police, the Italians produced a play entitled *La Fausse Prude* whose lead character was immediately recognized by the public as the unpopular and notoriously prudish morganatic wife of Louis XIV, Mme de Maintenon. After three or four performances to amazed capacity audiences, the Châtelet's police moved in. This time no threats or warnings were issued. Seals were placed on all the doors of the theater and all scripts that the police could get their hands on were seized. The actors were given one month to leave France for good. Nothing was said publicly about Mme de Maintenon, of course; the pretext was the protection of public morals. Saint-Simon, like many others, professed to be puzzled by the police action. He commented that everyone had long been in the habit of simply laughing when "impieties" and "ordures overflowed on the stage";[40] now, he wrote, everyone was a little perplexed by the sudden and unprecedented uproar.

Some of the foreign press suggested that Mme de Maintenon had possibly been only of secondary concern, and that this latest episode was simply the culmination of many such incidents which increasingly rankled a monarch grown ever more religious and strait-laced. There were even those who suggested an economic motive: by exiling the Italians the King stood to save his 15,000 livres pension,[41] and the King badly needed every livre for his latest foreign adventures. But in any event the Italians were not to be seen for the rest of the reign, and even their subsequent offers to contribute 20,000 livres annually to the Hôpital-Général if allowed to return did not move the monarch.

The Parisian theater was the poorer for their departure. Beneath their vulgarities, especially after they came under the elevating influence of the Hôtel de Bourgogne in 1680, could often be discerned a lively social conscience and a keen sense of what was ridiculous in the contemporary scene, qualities which understandably discomfited the authorities but which were sorely needed in a theatrical scene more and more dominated by "timeless" and socially sterile drama. Shortly after the demise of the Italians, Germain Brice wrote appreciatively of their efforts to correct through laughter the "corruption" of the times. They had long produced plays, he wrote, "replete with fine satire against the dissoluteness of the century, especially against the insolence of the Financiers. . . ." A final ironical note was struck when the Hôtel de Bourgogne after the departure of the "corrupting Italians" became the home of the state lottery,[42] in itself glaring evidence of the corruption of a great country's finances.

The expulsion of the Italian troupe showed Louis XIV's influence on the contemporary theater at its worst. Fortunately, he could create as well as destroy, but for this aspect of his work one must turn back to the first two decades of his personal rule—in matters theatrical as in almost every other facet of his long reign. In the early 1670's one of his finest and most enduring achievements, the Opera, made a spectacular entrance on the Parisian scene.

The new genre came to Paris from Italy via the French court. Before and after the Fronde the Queen-Mother and her friend Mazarin imported several Italian singing and dancing troupes for court entertainments, and it is doubtless from these that Louis XIV developed a strong interest in musical theater. As a young man he danced and even composed ballet for the court. Eight years before he thought of instituting an academy of music, he established a Royal Academy of the Dance. In the palace entertainments of the 1660's music and dancing often seem to outweigh the spoken theater, and some of Molière's comedy-ballets were even credited principally to the composer rather than to the author.[43] Finally, in 1669 an Abbé Perrin (one of those ubiquitous bogus *abbés* of the Old Regime) received royal permission to establish anywhere in France "academies of music for the public singing of plays, as is done in Italy, Germany, and England. . . ."[44] (Brice referred to the new creations as "Academies for Musical Opera.") Perrin took in a number of partners, including Sourdéac, the "machinist" (expert in stage machinery); Cambert, the organist at the parish of Saint-Honoré; another musician by the name of Cambon; and Champéron, the inevitable financial angel. In March 1671 they produced at the remodeled *jeu de paume* in the Rue Guénégaud the first French opera, *Pomone*, which played continuously for eight months and earned for Perrin 25,000 livres.[45]

The sources differ on the details of the ensuing events, but it is certain that the partners began squabbling over the division of the gold mine they had stumbled upon. Suits and countersuits were filed. The upshot was that Perrin not only lost his privilege but ended in prison. Apparently, his enormous financial success had been his undoing. When Louis XIV gave out the same privilege anew in 1673, he wrote with unaccustomed bluntness that Perrin had not been able to promote opera in the way he had promised. His Majesty was now giving the same opportunity to a man whose talents he was personally acquainted with.[46]

The new impresario was the Florentine Giovanni Battista Lulli, who soon became Jean-Baptiste Lully, the long-time court composer and superintendent of court music. He is generally credited with founding French opera, although Perrin obviously deserved a large share of the credit. In the general theatrical reorganization in 1673 brought on by Molière's death, Lully fell heir to the Palais-Royal, opening there at the end of the year with a great and typical hit, *The Merry Making of Love and Bacchus*, the first of innumerable successes for a man generally credited by his contemporaries as a genius of the theater. His sudden and amazing rise to power—musical and political—in the early 1670's can be explained either as the sudden uncovering of real genius or, less flatteringly, by the theory that he had obtained the backing of the current royal mistress, Mme de Montespan.[47] The only difficulty with this argument is that Lully's influence with the King remained strong even after Montespan had given way to the lady court wags referred to as "Madame de Maintenant," which would be unusual in such matters.

Whatever the explanation, Lully's position at court became unassailable. His first son, born in 1677, had no less than the King and Queen for godparents and received at baptism the survivorship rights to Lully's post as director of the Opera. (Lully had to be content at his second son's baptism in 1678 with the simple gift of an abbey.)[48] Lully was such a power at court that even Colbert backed down before him. In the contest between Perrin and Lully, Colbert had at first fought strongly for the Frenchman, but he soon realized the way the wind was blowing and changed sides. We find him writing to the president of the Parlement of Paris soliciting his "assistance and protection" on Lully's behalf in some pending lawsuits.[49]

No holder of a royal privilege fared better than Lully in protecting his rights. When a household official of the King's brother received a lucrative monopoly for the presentation of circuses, carrousels, tourneys, races, jousts, animal fights, and other such spectacles,[50] Lully objected on the ground of infringement, although the letters patent specifically disallowed the singing of music at these spectacles. The King, who was personally interested in this Royal Academy of Spectacles, gave in to Lully and ordered the plans for his new academy scrapped.[51] Even the smallest amateur plays involving music had to have ministerial approval in deference to Lully's rights. The laws prohibiting more than two singing voices in the Comédie were interpreted, on Lully's insistence, as meaning two voices belonging to regular members of the troupe. A performance was once closed by La Reynie's police on the ground that a professional singer had been hired to sing in the prologue.

Lully's reputation as a composer and producer was immense during his lifetime (he died in 1687). How much of it was deserved is debatable. As an impresario, he virtually inherited success. Europe was spiritually and psychologically ripe for opera. Not only in Paris but in other large cities—Rome, Naples, Florence, Vienna, Dresden, London—it quickly won enormous popularity.[52] But regardless of who receives the credit and how much artistry was involved (one modern critic wrote that "the opera became a sort of boil which drew away the impurities from the regular drama"[53]), opera became overnight a social phenomenon in Paris. In June 1677 the *Mercure* reported that the demand for tickets was so great that the third tier of loges at the Palais-Royal was being taken away from the livery servants and reserved for "people of quality" who now sat there "unashamed."[54] The impact made by opera on the upper classes even disturbed churchmen. Bossuet lashed out at the new art form, denying the argument that moralists need not concern themselves with the equivocations uttered by the singers since no one paid any attention to the words. That was the root of the danger, the prelate replied, for audiences became so enchanted by Lully's melodies and numbed by the marvels of the spectacle that all kinds of dangerous and unchristian sentiments insinuated their way into their hearts.[55] Visitors to Paris were as fascinated by the enthusiasm of the audiences as by the spectacle on stage. Martin Lister complained of being constantly disturbed by audience participation in the singing. At times, he wrote, it was difficult to separate the spectators from the performers.[56] Even during the melancholy last fifteen years of Louis's reign, the Opera's customary three performances weekly continued to attract large audiences.[57]

In the annals of the Parisian theater the great date is October 21, 1680, the birthday of the Comédie Française. On this day the King issued a short ordinance combining the two remaining troupes of French-speaking actors, that of the Rue Guénégaud and that of the Hôtel de Bourgogne.[58] Henceforth, only this amalgam of erstwhile bitter rivals was to have the privilege of enacting French plays in Paris. The new troupe numbered some thirty actors and actresses personally selected or approved by the King. Its organization was the informal and very democratic one which had been evolving since the start of the century among Parisian troupes. Selection of plays to be produced, distribution of roles, matters of finance, were all decided collectively; there was no director, no producer. Profits were divided into full shares or fractions thereof according to the importance of the actor or actress to the troupe. No one disputed that this handful of performers constituted the cream of the acting talent of France.

The principal source of the Comédie's greatness was the very cultural pluralism which Louis XIV so disliked, addicted as he was to the monolithic-monopolistic academy as the best way of organizing culture. The members of the Comédie represented three different theatrical traditions which, while for decades bitterly competing with one another, had each contributed something of its own to theatrical excellence. The best of each of these three historic troupes now made their way into the Comédie.

The Théâtre du Marais—one-third of the bloodline of the Comédie Française—had played an important role in the Parisian theater for at least half a century. From 1634 on it was situated in the northeast of the city, in the Rue Vieille-du-Temple, a location marred by both congestion and the presence of a malodorous open sewer "presque en face."[59] Despite these handicaps the Marais made a lasting reputation for itself, enjoying perhaps its greatest moment in 1636 or 1637 when Corneille's *Le Cid* was performed on its stage for the first time. Its fortunes then took a bad turn, and the company had to undergo the indignity of provincial tours.

About 1660, however, it perfected the "machine play," a new art form first introduced by the Italian actors,[60] and thereby earned at least another decade of prosperity and renewed prestige. The happy development consisted of elaborate mythological productions combining a seventeenth-century version of *le sexe* (or so one would judge from the titles of some of the favorites: *La Fête de Vénus, Les Amours de Vénus et d'Adonis, Les Amours du Soleil, Les Amours de Jupiter et de Sémélé,* etc.) and stage effects the like of which had never been seen before and were not to be surpassed for a long time thereafter. Audiences sat entranced as dancers, musicians, acrobats, artificial animals, satyrs, and miscellaneous divinities crossed their view. The element of suspense, seemingly, was derived not so much from the spoken word or situation, but rather from the off-chance that a wire would break and Jupiter would fall, ungodlike, from his gossamer perch. Surprisingly enough, public interest in such extravaganzas remained high long after the Marais's demise.[61] What finally defeated the Marais was not waning public support but Louis XIV's decision to give the new Opera a monopoly over machine plays. An ordinance of 1673 limited the spoken theater to six musical instruments and two singers and completely forbade their employment of dancers.[62] The Marais was thus doomed. Those actors in the troupe who had not already deserted it for the Hôtel de Bourgogne were ordered to join Molière's organization.

Molière's story is one of the best known and loved in the annals of the theater. Everyone enjoys reading of the travails of the indomitable stage-struck son of a Parisian upholsterer, who paid for his first disastrous efforts as an actor with a sojourn in debtor's prison, but who, undeterred, went back to the provinces, painfully transformed his troupe into the leading provincial actors in France, and reentered Paris in 1658 for a triumphant royal appearance at the Louvre. The delighted monarch established Molière and his actors in the hall of the Petit-Bourbon, adjacent to the Louvre, and his first great popular success, *Les Précieuses ridicules,* soon ensued. After two years at the Petit-Bourbon Molière suddenly received orders to vacate the building in order to make room for the construction of the famous east façade of the Louvre. Some have discerned in this peremptory order the long arm of the rival company of the Hôtel de Bourgogne, much nettled by the new popularity of Molière's "debased" comedy. The lofty actors of the Hôtel de

Bourgogne had been congratulating themselves, before Molière's arrival, that the hated farce had been all but removed from the theatrical
scene. In their view, it was fit only for off-days, when people of taste
could be counted to absent themselves from the theater.[63] If, however,
Molière's rivals had been instrumental in his eviction from the Petit-
Bourbon, their victory was a hollow one, because he was soon authorized by the King to move into an even better theater, the nearby Palais-
Royal.

Molière's primacy in comedy remained unchallenged, but as a theatrical producer he had one great shortcoming: he was as a rule limited
to his own dramatic creations. Partly because of his leanings to the
comic form, partly because of authors' preferences for the Hôtel de
Bourgogne, he produced only a very small number of tragedies.[64] He
was always subject to the enormous pressure of turning out a succession
of comedies to keep his theater full and his troupe intact. Of the ninety-
five presented at the Palais-Bourbon and the Palais-Royal, a third were
written by Molière himself. Some seasons were exclusively *moliéresque*,
for example, 1669-1670 and 1671-1672.[65] As long as Molière was able to
write at this frantic pace, no one, then or now, bemoaned the paucity
of new talent, but his premature death in 1673 brought the difficulties
which were to be expected. The troupe tried to remain intact without
the Master, but just as they were putting the finishing touches on a
gala performance of *Le Malade imaginaire*, four of the actors deserted
for the greener pastures of the Hôtel de Bourgogne. In view of the financial difficulties of both the Marais and Molière's old company (both
of whom were receiving annual subsidies), Louis XIV ordered a mer-
ger. The combined troupes were authorized to purchase for 30,000 livres
the old Jeu de Paume de la Bouteille in the Rue Mazarin just across the
river from the Louvre.

All in all, the future must not have seemed very bright for the new
troupe. Its location was something of a comedown from the Palais-
Royal, although not from the Marais. The competition from both the
Opera, now ensconced in the Palais-Royal, and the Hôtel de Bourgogne was severe. The actors from the Guénégaud (the theater took its
name from a side street by that name) continued to dribble to the Hôtel

de Bourgogne or to threaten to move there. The favor in which Molière's old actors were held by the monarch fell so low that the Bourgogne actors, rather than they, now received the treasured invitations to
appear at Versailles to present Molière's plays.[66] But the Guénégaud
had a few trumps left up its sleeve. One of them was its large stage,
which permitted the presentation of extravaganzas on the order of those
the Marais theater had once made famous and which the Hôtel de
Bourgogne, with its very small and antique facilities, could not match.
Some of the Guénégaud's machine plays brought good profits but also
the expected protests from the Opera that the actors were exceeding
their prerogatives.

Also very helpful to the Guénégaud was its association with a couple of popular playwrights, Thomas Corneille, the younger brother of
the great Corneille, and Donneau de Visé, who as editor of the *Mercure
galant,* the only literary journal in Paris of any consequence, was in an
excellent position to publicize his plays produced by the Guénégaud. It
was the latter enterprising young dramatist-journalist who gave the
Guénégaud its greatest hit by conceiving *La Divineresse,* written in collaboration with Thomas Corneille. Even this early, a writer showed
that a skillful and timely exploitation of a highly publicized crime made
for surefire commercial success. *La Divineresse* was the thinly disguised
story of La Voisin, the most notorious mass murderess of her generation, who was still languishing in her cell when the opening curtain
went up. Even more happily for the Guénégaud and the authors, she
was burned at the stake as a sorceress before a record audience while the
play was still running. The play made for its two authors the handsome
sum of 6,000 livres, about double the highest sum that Pierre Corneille,
Racine, or Molière ever received for one of their plays.[67] *La Divineresse*
enjoyed a fine run of consecutive performances—forty-five, or one more
than the immortal *Les Précieuses ridicules.*[68] While there is no proof
of a causal relationship, it is interesting to note that just a few months
after the public furor raised by the Voisin affair, the King decided to
amalgamate the Guénégaud with the troupe of the Hôtel de Bourgogne.

The third element which went into making the Comédie Française in 1680 was the lofty Hôtel de Bourgogne. One can easily develop a dislike of the latter, if for no other reason than its constant sniping at Molière and his romantic troupe, but one cannot minimize the contribution this company made to the French theater. If the ability and willingness to innovate are essential marks of a great theatrical company, the Hôtel de Bourgogne was far ahead of Molière's players. In the period from 1659 to 1673 the former produced more than a hundred new plays, while Molière put on only fifteen other than his own works.[69] The Hôtel played the *premières* of most of Corneille's plays and had a virtual monopoly of Racine's output. For playwrights who had a choice, no troupe was more desirable than this one.

Ever since 1629 it had performed in its cramped and antiquated theater—called by one modern authority "the least impressive theater edifice of the century"[70]—in the Rue Mauconseil northeast of the Louvre. The troupe took the same pleasure, it would appear, in its dowdy surroundings that wealthy dowagers sometimes take in affecting shabby dress. Baroque extravagance, artificial animals, stage trickery, the popular machinery, and the like, it haughtily spurned. To the Hôtel de Bourgogne flocked not only the snobs and *beau monde* but the intellectuals who expected to see a play acted according to the rules of structure, reason, and good taste. While even the Hôtel de Bourgogne had to make accommodations to public demand and show an occasional farce (especially at the time when the King himself had a strong predilection for farces), there were always ways of downgrading this genre. A favorite technique was putting on one-act farces after a Racine or Corneille opus, by which time the people whose taste counted had left the theater.

The Comédie Française fared quite well from the start, despite some annoying interference from the Dauphine, who had been given a sort of supervisory control over the new troupe and who in 1684 forced at least two members to withdraw, for reasons best known to herself.[71] To the surprise of many, internal friction was kept at a minimum; somehow, the tragedians came to terms with the comedians, and an equitable division was arrived at between the proponents of Racine and those of Molière. Another of those housing crises which were perennially affecting the theatrical profession was taken in stride. After seven years at the Guénégaud, the players of the Comédie were told they would have to move to make room for the Collège de Mazarin. Apparently, they were left to their own devices in finding new quarters. They negotiated for a large *hôtel* plus an adjacent house in the Rue Neuve des Petits-Champs, one of the new streets behind the Palais-Royal. Zoning regulations had not yet been dreamed of, but as soon as the *curé* of Saint-Eustache got wind of his new parishioners, he protested to the King that the construction of a theater in this neighborhood, "one of the most notable" in his parish, would be highly detrimental.[72] Numerous other property owners of consequence backed up the *curé* so the Comédie had to look elsewhere for a site, finally being authorized by the King to locate in the Rue des Fossés-Saint-Germain-des-Prés a short distance south of the Guénégaud. It was now the turn of the *curé* of Saint-Sulpice to become indignant. He wrote a vigorous letter of protest to the Archbishop, even offering to pay the Comédie for any expense it had incurred up to this point if it would move elsewhere.[73] But this time King and Comédie were adamant (after all, Saint-Sulpice had had to put up with a theater in this neighborhood for fifteen years or more), and the company went ahead with the construction of its new edifice.

The gala opening (*Phèdre* and *Le Médecin malgré lui*) took place on April 18, 1689, with receipts of 1,870 livres and many exclamations over the novel semielliptical shape of the seating, the first such in Paris. The tradition of fine dress for the Comédie's actresses had already begun; Brice thought this made up for a certain "avarice" on the part of the troupe in the choice of decorations.[74] But business was obviously good. The full-share actors paid 3 livres each performance into a fund to repay the 200,000 livres which the building had cost, and within five years the entire amount had been repaid.[75] Here the Comédie Française remained until 1770.

CHAPTER FIVE

The guilds linger on

THE economic life of seventeenth-century Paris still revolved around the medieval guilds (generally known contemporaneously as *communautés des arts et métiers*), although the respect, and even fondness, which we assume the thirteenth-century worker felt for the institution were clearly not shared by his more modern counterpart. Across the Channel in London and other English cities the guild was dead or dying. In Paris, however, the bourgeoisie seemed as convinced as it had ever been in medieval times of the necessity for corporate control of trade and commerce. For the bourgeois anything that smacked of economic individualism was, at least publicly, anathematized.

Equally enthusiastic about corporate organization as the main pillar of a sound economy were Louis XIV and Parisian officialdom. It is to be expected that a monarch who felt a compulsive need to uniformalize society—culture, recreation, religion, laws, and the rest—should be attracted to the guild as a means of organizing economic life. But Louis's ardor for guilds was a relatively new phenomenon among French monarchs. In medieval times the state's role in guild affairs had been minimal. The initiative in their formation had nearly always come from below; the membership had prepared corporate statutes and obtained the rather perfunctory approval of the Crown representatives.[1] Once legally approved and registered at the Châtelet, the guild had run its own affairs, inviting interference from above only in extraordinary circumstances—for example, when it became involved in a jurisdictional squabble with another guild which threatened to disturb public order.

The permissiveness once characteristic of the monarchy's relations with the guilds began to disappear in the sixteenth century as kings groped to extend their control over French society. The all-embracing but sketchy ordinances of Villers-Cotterêts, Orléans, and Moulins, called the "first codes of the nation," aimed grandiosely at subordinating all medieval autonomies, including economic ones, to the state.[2] At the end of the sixteenth century, these early efforts were capped by two comprehensive ordinances dealing specifically with economic organization. Both were national in scope and both reflected the wider ambitions of French monarchs. These ordinances, Henry III's of 1581 and Henry IV's of 1597 (the second being little more than a reaffirmation of a law issued at an inopportune time by a man with a poor record for being obeyed), attempted to universalize the regime of corporate labor throughout France.[3] Under the cover of a badly needed and long-overdue democratic reform of the guilds, but also to the undeniable fiscal and political advantage of the state, all French trades and professions were ordered either to have their statutes confirmed or to apply forthwith for corporate status.

To what extent the new laws were financially motivated, were designed to strengthen the role of the state, or were simply straightforward reform is debatable. The state undoubtedly stood to gain financially, since each guildsman under the law of 1597 was assessed, depending upon the importance of his occupation, up to one *écu*.[4] But that more was at stake than simply revenue is suggested by the very strong pro-guild statements of Henry IV's economic advisers, notably Pierre Laffemas. For the latter, unregulated commerce and industry bordered on sin. "Free labor" (i.e., labor outside the guild system), he wrote, was "the source of license and economic anarchy"—a sentiment which would be monotonously reaffirmed by all those in positions of authority in the seventeenth century. The task of dragooning all the urban workers of France into guilds, as provided by the laws of 1581 and 1597, would have strained the capacities of even a modern governmental bureaucracy. For the primitive administrative machinery of that day it was an impossibility. Outside Paris and a very few large towns the labor statutes remained dead letters. Even in the capital, since the High Middle Ages the stronghold of guilds, a surprising amount of "free labor" persisted.

This became evident in 1673 when Louis XIV, a monarch in a somewhat better position than his sixteenth-century predecessors to assure obedience, ordered every French urban worker to become affiliated immediately with a guild.[5] Clearly, a great many had not. The King's motivation this time could not be doubted. The Dutch War had just begun, and the edict on guilds was merely one of a number of revenue measures which would soon provoke serious unrest in the west of France. As evidence of the financial motivation of the edict of 1673, one may cite a schedule prepared for official scrutiny showing which trades and professions in Paris were currently unorganized and how much money could be collected from each member for the dubious privilege of receiving a royal statute. The rich potential of the booty may be judged by citing a few examples: one hundred schoolmasters were reckoned to be assessable for 30 livres each; sixty sculptors at 100 livres; three hundred tripe merchants at 20 livres; fifty cesspool cleaners at 200 livres; thirty "sellers of false diamonds" at 100 livres, and so on for some forty-odd unorganized occupations.[6]

One of the most promising occupational groups in this tabulation (at least from a financial viewpoint) was the dressmakers. Their surprising number, around 3,000, more than made up for the small tax (30 livres) which the officials hoped to extract from each. The dressmakers (long a "free" trade) and the tailors (long organized) had been waging a jurisdictional battle in Paris for generations. As Louis XIV liked to point out, a moral question was involved as well as an economic one. The ladies of Paris were often forced to have recourse to male tailors. This the king professed to disapprove. When he finally received the dressmakers' "petition" for guild status, Louis XIV expressed unctuous satisfaction that the ladies would henceforth be allowed to retain their modesty by patronizing their own sex for their clothing needs.

The edict of 1673, like those of 1581 and 1597, met lively opposition,[7] but thanks to vigorous enforcement (at least in Paris) resulted in a much higher level of guild membership as well as in a significant amount of revenue. The old, but until Louis XIV's reign, largely theoretical claim that only the king had the right to raise an occupational group to guild status now became a reality. The "foreign" doctors of

Paris (practitioners who did not possess a degree from the University of Paris) were so reminded when they made one of their perennial efforts to organize in self-protection against their University confrères.[8] The best indication of the success of the law of 1673 was the increase in the number of guilds from 60 in 1672 to 83 shortly after it went into effect and to 129 by 1691.[9]

But if anyone had any illusions about the sincerity of Louis XIV's interest in the guilds, they were removed by his policies in the closing decades of his reign. This was the period of the "creation of offices," another indication that all the bright hopes which had marked the start of Louis's reign were as dead as the minister, Colbert, in whom they had principally resided. For a quarter of a century one of the government's principal sources of revenue became the sale of offices of all kinds to almost anyone who had the price. Some of these offices promised the buyer an annual salary in return for a capital outlay, but more commonly they empowered the purchaser to collect some sort of fee from the public in order to recoup his investment. Even a partial list of offices created in commerce and industry in these years occupies more than four pages of small type, without taking into account a very large number of posts created in the financial and judicial arms of the government.[10] When even the King expressed doubts about how long this lucrative business could last, one of his ministers reassured him in words which anticipated those of a famous American showman two centuries later, "Whenever it pleases Your Majesty to create an office, God creates a fool to buy it."[11]

Having earlier succeeded in forcing the guilds onto almost all Parisian occupations, Louis proceeded to exploit them by the creation of guild-connected offices. The market areas and quays offered the richest possibilities. Here Louis created thousands of *contrôleurs, inspecteurs, mésureurs,* and the like, all legally preying on the consumer and undoubtedly contributing to the sharp rise in food prices at the end of the century. Even more alarming for the guilds was the monarch's new proclivity for interfering with their inner administration. In 1691 he transformed, or threatened to transform, the elected *jurés,* the senior guild officials, into venal officeholders, in effect making the guilds government agencies. The pretext was the familiar one of protecting the public interest by reforming the guild oligarchy. Louis's concern for the public interest, however, was immediately brought into question when he accepted the offer of the guildmasters (panicky at the prospect of suddenly becoming subordinate to officials who conceivably did not even belong to their communities) to buy back the offices. Such was doubtless the government's intention from the start. Between 1691 and 1694 the guilds paid the state some 6,000,000 livres to preserve their right to elect their own officials.[12] This was only the beginning. As the wars continued and the need for revenue grew, the government created office after office infringing in one way or another on guild administration: auditors, treasurers, examiners, archivists, and others. In every case, the guilds were given the option of buying the offices back, which they generally did as long as they had money in their treasuries, but after a couple of decades of this sort of thing there was hardly a solvent guild left in Paris. Only in 1710, when God apparently stopped "creating fools" to buy them, was the creation of offices "for the external or internal police" of the communities declared ended.[13] In the judgment of a recent economic historian Louis XIV dealt the guilds a "terrible blow" which compromised the entire system.[14] Perhaps more pertinent is whether Louis XIV and his immediate predecessors did Paris a disservice by striving to reestablish and enlarge the guilds instead of permitting them to die peaceably and naturally as in England.

Nevertheless, whatever harm Louis XIV's policies inflicted on the guilds, they remained for most seventeenth-century Parisian workers, as they had been for their thirteenth-century counterparts, the prime economic reality. A census taken shortly after Louis XIV ascended the throne showed a guild population of close to 70,000, of which close to 20,000 were masters and most of the remainder journeymen.[15] For the great majority of Parisian workers, life inescapably revolved around the ancient practices and regulations of their *communautés*.

In the seventeenth century the first rung up the economic ladder continued to be the apprenticeship. For almost every master there was an apprentice. Some guild statutes allowed two or three, but generally, in the old hope of restricting competitive growth, masters were limited to one. In Louis XIV's time the law required that a young apprentice be sponsored by a parent or guardian and have his indenture registered at the Châtelet and a copy preserved in the guild register. The indenture contract was invariably quite brief—no more than a couple of hundred words—and standardized.[16] It committed the master to teaching his trade to the apprentice, set the length of the apprenticeship (usually according to the statutes of the guild in question), spelled out the financial arrangements if any between the parties, and almost invariably concluded with a provision requiring the parent to institute a thorough search of the city for his son in case the latter fled the master's house. If the search were unsuccessful, the master was generally due an indemnification.[17]

Of no little importance were the financial terms. The guild statutes had little to say about this, so finances were a matter for the two parties to negotiate between themselves. Obviously, a young man being apprenticed to a prosperous merchant in the Cité would be expected to pay more than one apprenticed to a carder in the faubourgs. One hundred livres a year was considered adequate to cover the expenses of room and board, although some prestigious masters commanded 300 livres or more.[18] Despite the desirability of providing for a money payment to the master, many, possibly most, of the apprentice contracts made no such provision. Even in as good a neighborhood as the Cité, roughly half of such contracts signed at mid-century provided for no cash settlement.[19]

An apprentice not in a position to pay his master could expect, at the very least, to take longer than the statutory time to learn his trade. A seventeenth-century author warned that such a lad might find himself doing all sorts of extraneous chores, such as "cleaning silverware" and "walking [and] entertaining children."[20] One authority has commented that "from the seventeenth century especially, the masters occupied themselves less with teaching the trade to the apprentice than with obtaining services from him." Very sound advice was doubtless given by the writer of a manual on guild practices in 1692 when he urged apprentices to show great deference to the journeymen, "for often it is from them more than from the master that they learn their trade, and having their goodwill they hide nothing from them. . . ."[21]

The use of apprentices as silver polishers and baby-sitters was officially frowned upon by the officials at the Châtelet who watched over the training of apprentices in nearly all trades. They occasionally intervened with admonishments against the misuse of the trainees, as, for example, in a police ordinance of 1678 directed at the Parisian pastrycooks. Instead of keeping their young assistants in the kitchen learning their trade, the masters used them to hawk pastry throughout Paris, in which occupation they were allegedly "corrupted" by vagrants and cutpurses and "learned nothing of their trade."[22] The pastrycooks were threatened with 500 livres fines and confiscation of their wares if they persisted in such practices—which they doubtless did.

Intermediate between apprentice and master in the guild structure was the *compagnon* or journeyman. He was a relative newcomer on the economic scene. In the High Middle Ages an apprentice of proven skill, the statutory years of service, and sufficient financial resources to set up shop, could expect to rise with relative ease to the rank of master. If a young man did not have the capital or skill to establish his own shop, he became a *valet* or wage worker, but nothing in early guild practice or guild statutes doomed him to a lifetime as a simple worker. Unfortunately, the old economic and social fluidity gradually waned as the masters became increasingly intent on limiting their future competition. It became the custom to require years of additional labor on contract to a master after the apprenticeship had been completed. In the sixteenth century this intermediate stage of *compagnon* became almost universal. Henry III's statute of 1581 provided that, the apprenticeship completed, the worker must continue in the same shop or an equivalent shop for three years or whatever term of service the particular trade specified.[23] In the following century this might range from two to eight years or more.

In Louis XIV's time a few guilds (for example, the butchers, minters, embroiderers, gut spinners, and bird sellers) announced blatantly in their statutes that only sons of masters could aspire to that rank.

Most communities were more circumspect, the favorite method being to make the cost of becoming a master prohibitively high. Long before Louis XIV the initiation became the occasion for an endless succession of banquets, reunions, handouts to other masters and senior guild officials (as well as the royal tax collectors). Perhaps most ruinous of all was the execution of a *chef d'oeuvre* as costly as it was bizarre and impractical. The ordinance of 1581 complained of masters assigning *chefs d'oeuvre* which took more than a year to complete ("against the tenor of the ancient ordinances"), whereupon the guild inspectors might well deem them defective and order their destruction on the spot.

Many guild statutes openly proclaimed a double standard for the *chef d'oeuvre*, one for the nonprivileged journeyman and the other for sons and relatives of masters. For the privileged aspirant even the name *chef d'oeuvre* might change to *expérience*. The bakers of the Faubourg Saint-Germain-des-Prés, for example, in their statute of 1659 devoted several detailed lines to the description of the masterwork required of the ordinary aspirant. The young man was required to convert the equivalent of 36 bushels of wheat into 20-ounce units of dough which then had to bake down to precise 16-ounce loaves of white bread. Sons of masters, on the other hand, were required to make a "light *expérience*" consisting of simply converting a much smaller amount of wheat into bread.[24] Locksmiths were particularly explicit in detailing their requirements. For them there were four standards instead of the more customary two, depending upon whether the candidate was unaffiliated, the son-in-law of a master, the husband of a master's widow, or the son of a master. Each was recognizably less complicated than the preceding.

The hundred-plus Parisian guilds in the late seventeenth century existed beyond question for the benefit of the masters, but by this time various disparities were to be found even among the latter. One of the most striking tendencies in Parisian guilds under Louis XIV was the accentuation of administrative inequality at the top,[25] thanks in large part to the Crown's instinctive distrust of guild democracy. In most guilds, masters were grouped according to their years of service into *jeunes, modernes,* and *anciens.* Ten years of service usually separated each rank from the next, and only the venerable *anciens* had full-fledged rights in the community. The small inner circle (three to six) of elected masters known as the *jurés* had effective control of the community; the *jeunes* were not even allowed to participate in their election and it hardly need be said that they were ineligible to become *jurés* until achieving seniority.

The *jurés* were under oath to enforce and administer the guild statute. They assured that no other guild or individual violated the privileges of their own guild, and had recourse to the courts if such violations were discovered. Jurisdictional squabbling among Parisian guilds provided the city's lawyers with one of their surest sources of employment. It has been estimated that at the start of the eighteenth century the *communautés* were spending up to a million livres annually in such litigation.[26] The examination of the *chef d'oeuvre* and the reception of new masters, journeymen, and apprentices were all the business of the *jurés*, as was the supervision of the guild headquarters (*bureau*) if there was one. In order to avoid competition among the members most goods coming into Paris for resale were supposed to be examined for quality by the *jurés*, as they had been in the thirteenth century, and then divided by lot among the interested members of the guild. While this ancient custom was still mentioned in most seventeenth-century guild statutes and was undoubtedly widely practiced, at least one guild, the hatters, had updated their statutes in 1658 by providing that members who imported goods "at their own risk and peril" could claim exemption from the *lotissage*.[27]

Probably the most important duty of the *jurés* was visiting the shops of fellow guild members to assure that the statutory standards of production were being observed—in the language of the day to verify that goods were *bons et loyaux*, not *faux*. There were numerous exceptions but the general rule was that the visits be made four times each year, in return for which the *juré* received a fee ranging from 1 livre, 10 sous for the more important guilds to 5 sous for the least, plus a third of the fines levied for infractions of the guild statute. (The King and the Hôtel-Dieu divided the remainder.) While the possibility of fraud and collusion cannot be ruled out, the profit the *jurés* derived from these inspections probably guaranteed their performance. They were expected to be quite ruthless in exercising their office. The mercers' statute, for example, went into great detail in admonishing their *jurés* to search every nook and cranny for fraudulent merchandise and to remove it promptly, if found, to guild headquarters.

Towering far above all other masters in their affluence and importance were the aristocratic Six Corps, which from a political point of view ranked close behind Parlement, Châtelet, and Hôtel de Ville. The members of the Six Corps proudly termed themselves *maîtres marchands fabricants*, never to be confused with the lowly artisans or with the small merchants (*petit patronat*). When the hatters, for example, became members of the Six Corps, they were officially promoted from artisan status to that of merchant.[28] But what differentiated the Six Corps from lesser beings was not so much what they produced or the part they played in the productive process as the capital they had at their disposal. When we read of estimates that over 200 merchants in Paris possessed capital of more than 500,000 livres each, we can safely assume that a good majority were members of the Six Corps. Of the approximate 6,000,000 livres the guilds paid the King at the end of the reign to buy back their offices, nearly a third came from this half-dozen, comprising only about 2,500 masters and 5,000 workers, or about an eighth of the total guild population.[29]

In the later seventeenth century, the Six Corps included the drapers, grocer-apothecaries, haberdashers, furriers, hatters, and goldsmiths. The precise make-up had been constantly shifting from the fourteenth century on as some occupations went out of fashion and others grew in importance, although the drapers enjoyed continuous primacy in the Six Corps during the entire last four centuries of the Old Regime. Each of the fortunate six was assigned a rank within the Corps, which became a matter of great importance at ceremonial processions. So inordinate was the passion for precedence at such times that the financial officers of the Crown were often tempted to exploit the occasion. The haberdashers, for instance, were offered a promotion from third position to first on condition they "lend" the state 50,000 livres to help Louis XIV finance the Dutch War.[30] (Whether unusually scrupulous or temporarily short of funds, they rejected the offer.)

Some of the most memorable legal hassles of old Paris revolved around the efforts of an ambitious guild to secure a place in the Six Corps. The fish merchants had long entertained this dream, but after the butchers had finally been evicted from the Corps, the other members were apparently unwilling to admit a kindred trade. Most memorable, however, was the interminable court battle of the wine merchants to attain the Six Corps. Under Henry III in the sixteenth century they had briefly managed to gain membership, and Louis XIV had once been pressed into letting them walk in procession behind the other six as a sort of provisional seventh member of the Six Corps. (Even the *Roi Soleil* had to be mindful of the feelings of some of his largest taxpayers.) The financial strength of the wine merchants, if anyone had any doubts about it, was once again manifested in the 1690's, when they were a close second to the haberdashers in redeeming guild offices. Economically respectable as they so obviously were, the members of the aristocratic Six Corps continued to associate them with lowly tavern and cabaret keepers (which they definitely were not). Nevertheless, these pariahs stubbornly fought their case in court and out for over 300 years, finally being admitted to the Six Corps in 1776.

ﻉ   ﻉ

Highly oligarchic in character and unmindful of the interests of the workers though the guilds were, few Parisian workers could entertain any thought of evading them. The idealized image of the guild shop is one in which the master and a small, stable handful of employees worked out their lives harmoniously, with little of the tension and periodic unemployment characteristic of a later-day economy. If such a happy state had ever existed, it had not survived into the seventeenth century. Most workers undoubtedly had to cope with economic insecurity and the distinct possibility of having no employment the following day. Once a man had completed his contractual term as apprentice or journeyman, he was most likely subject for the rest of his life to being hired on a daily or, at best, a short-term basis. Employment even on piecework was regularly practiced.[31] The worker's best and perhaps only hope for employment remained the guild, all the more important of which maintained offices (*bureaux*) where a clerk received and kept on file essential information on each journeyman. Upon registering at the *bureau* the journeyman obtained a certificate without which some guilds forbade that a worker be hired.[32] Thus, he was at the mercy of the guild officials.

Le Livre commode of 1692 informs us that in a few occupations, for example, the shoemakers, locksmiths, coopers, and gunsmiths, the custom was to "arrange for one's own hiring by going in person to the shops." In the less affluent trades which did not attempt to maintain guild headquarters (notably the building trades), the unemployed "assembled," we are told by the same source, "at the Grève [in front of the Hôtel de Ville] every workday morning from four to six, where those who are needed are chosen for work."[33] One morning in 1700, for example, we are told that more than sixty journeymen carpenters were gathered here in the hope of finding a day's employment.[34] Long before the term took on its modern meaning of going on strike, *faire la grève* meant to search for work.

The existence of work markets where men presented themselves at four in the morning in the slim hope of being given the privilege of working until sunset the same day for a few sous is one token among many that the Grand Siècle had a far different meaning for the masses than it did for the habitués of Versailles. Even more revealing of the worker's lot is an analysis of daily wages and what he could hope to buy with them. From a scrutiny of real wages it is difficult to avoid the conclusion that a large part of working-class Paris was teetering constantly on the edge of starvation. Price historians have concluded that except for a brief period after the Wars of Religion, there was no time when a French laborer's wages bought less food than during the seventeenth century. D'Avenel, who compiled a number of large volumes of prices from the Middle Ages to the Revolution, drew up estimates of what a laborer's daily wage would buy in early modern times in terms of basic requirements.[35]

In terms of more specific wages and prices the same bleak picture emerges. D'Avenel's price tables for the seventeenth century show that the daily wages of a journeyman, except in a few skilled trades, did not exceed 20 sous and were generally much less. Vauban, writing at the turn of the century when all prices (including wages) took a rather sharp rise, stated that the drapers, cloth-shearers, hatters, and lock-smiths made from 15 to 30 sous; yet, he added, there were many artisans who did not even make 12 sous.[36] During the entire century wages for masons, carpenters, plasterers, roofers, and painters never exceeded 20 sous. Even in 1708 (a very bad year, it is true) a journeyman mason made only 8 sous. These, it must be remembered, were the wages of family men; apprentices, who were not allowed to marry, received nothing but room and board, and perhaps clothing and a few incidentals.

Buying power of the daily wage (D'Avenel)

Commodity	1451-1475	1501-1525	1601-1625	1701-1725
Liters of wine	5.70	8.20	4.40	3.00
Kilograms of beef	4.27	2.72	2.05	1.62
Liters of wheat	18.40	14.60	5.30	4.50

How far 10 or 15 sous would go in the seventeenth century can be judged from citing a few of D'Avenel's prices. The basic item—for many the only food item to be considered—was bread, the price of which varied enormously over the years with respect both to quality and to weight. But it was an unusual year when one could purchase a pound loaf of even low-quality bread for a sou. John Locke wrote that the price in 1677 of a 13-ounce loaf of black bread was 1 sou, which was also the price of 5 ounces of the best white bread. In the two crises of 1662 and 1693, when the King went into the bakery business personally to alleviate the lot of the poor and stave off riot and rebellion (it would be unfair to guess which was foremost in his mind), bread was sold at 2 sous 6 deniers and 2 sous, respectively, per pound.[37] These were said to be less than half the current bakery price.

The difficulty which the workingman with a family must have experienced in finding money for any kind of food or drink other than a few pounds of black bread and water, and still paying for housing, clothing, heat, taxes, and incidentals, can be imagined by glancing at a few other prices of the times: a quart of wine (1.86 liters) in 1680—4 sous; a pound of butter in 1705—7 sous; a dozen oysters in 1691—6 sous; a chicken in 1721—8 sous; a pound of beef at various times between 1649 and 1712—3 to 8 sous; a pound of veal in 1678—6 sous.[38]

The mystery of how a worker managed to support a family on a wage of considerably less than a livre a day in the face of such prices is deepened still further when one remembers that his daily wages had to stretch over Sundays and other religious holidays, days of inclement weather in the case of outdoor laborers, and of sickness and unemployment. Vauban in his *Dîme royal* reckoned the working year at 180 days. Even assuming a man was able to work every day he wished, the Church required him to refrain from labor on 103 days—51 in addition to Sundays.

This multiplicity of religious holidays had long troubled moralists (including Martin Luther), who regarded them as simply occasions for idleness, drunkenness and debauchery. At the very start of his personal reign, Louis XIV resolved to correct this old abuse. His motivation, according to the traditional story, had nothing to do with religion; he was simply dismayed by the slow progress being made on the construction of the Louvre colonnade in the early 1660's. Concluding that there was a shortage of labor in Paris, he ordered that no other building be undertaken in the city without his specific permission. When this failed to produce the desired results, the monarch decided that the workers were enjoying too many holidays and taking too long to recover from them. Louis therefore entered into negotiations with the compliant Archbishop of Paris, Hardouin de Péréfixe. The result was the ordinance of October 20, 1666, suppressing about twenty of the fifty-one religious holidays.[39] In his *Mémoires* he later wrote that he had been impelled by the "considerable prejudice to the workers" wrought by their spending great sums on these "occasions of debauchery."[40]

The popular reaction is not clear (Sauval vaguely alluded to some public "murmurs") but the Parlement of Paris showed that it was more interested in retaining the traditional calendar than in preserving working-class morality. According to a prominent parlementarian, D'Ormesson, the monarch was forced to send a *lettre de cachet* to the *parlemen-*

taires to get his new edict registered by the court. Nevertheless, D'Ormesson announced his intention to close Parlement on the customary days. The following August 16, Saint Roch's Day, one of the suppressed holidays, he wrote with evident delight in his journal that all courts had closed in Paris except those of the Châtelet.[41] A modern authority states that the reduction in the number of holidays was "rarely" obeyed among the artisans.[42] To our mind, a much more intriguing question is how the workers of Paris managed not only to take so many days off on so little money but to afford all the expensive "drink and debauchery" alleged to have characterized lower-class holiday celebrations.

ꝛ   ꝛ

Although a political and social cataclysm was finally required to destroy the guild system, numerous flaws were apparent in the structure in the seventeenth century. Among both apprentices and journeymen a number of untraditional practices developed—officially frowned upon and even actively combated by the guildmasters and their protectors at the Châtelet but continuing to grow simply because they answered to new economic realities or else promised the workers some surcease from the masters' long despotism. Among the threats to the venerable apprentice-journeyman-master relationship was the still small but growing practice of hiring *alloués* or workers who did the work of apprentices or even journeymen but had no official guild status or indenture. At best, they were boys or young men interested in learning a trade but unwilling or unable to proceed along the customary guild track. At worst, they were simply unskilled day laborers, "floaters," who provided masters with valuable help in busy seasons, limited as the employers were by guild regulations in the number of workers they could legally hire. As one would expect, a good deal of friction was engendered between the *alloués* on the one hand and certified apprentices and journeymen on the other. Many trades specifically forbade the hiring of such labor.

One of the trades which appeared to have made the widest use of the *alloués* was the printers. Beginning in the second half of the seventeenth century, the master printers hired *alloués* at such a rate that the number of apprentices in their shops declined from sixty-nine in 1666 to three in 1696.[43] In 1713 the employment of such irregular labor was legalized in the printing trade and the employers were allowed to hire as many as they wished. But as a concession to tradition, the new regulations provided that journeymen should be given the dubious right of accepting employment at the lower wage scale of the *alloués* if they preferred this humiliation to unemployment.[44] A more flagrant disregard of the old corporate spirit of the guilds can hardly be imagined. By the middle of the eighteenth century some 300 *alloués* were reported to be employed in the printshops.

The printers' guild, relatively new and less inclined to conservatism, was not really typical among the *communautés des arts et métiers* of Paris. However, the hiring of workers other than the legally indentured apprentices and journeymen was doubtless widespread and practiced under a variety of guises. The frequent references one encounters in official correspondence to "false workers" undoubtedly alluded to the *alloués* or their equivalent. For example, in the correspondence of the Controller-General for 1692 is to be found a letter from the King's Procureur at the Châtelet announcing the prosecution of some master embroiderers for hiring some *fausses ouvrières*. The Procureur explained that the masters were only allowed to employ their wives, children, daughters of impoverished masters, and their own statutory apprentices and journeymen.[45]

In the seventeenth century nothing perhaps better typified the decay of the old guild spirit than the transition that had taken place in the *confréries*. These old social and religious adjuncts of the guilds, many of which in reality antedated and had often given birth to the guilds as economic institutions, had originally included masters and workers alike. Principally in the sixteenth century a social transformation took place in the once democratic *confréries*, caused in part by the growing alienation of employers and employees but even more by the hostility (not wholly unjustified) of the political authorities. On at least four occasions during the sixteenth century they were formally condemned and prohibited.[46] But what resulted in the end was not the destruction of the *confréries* so much as the purging of the workers from them. A *Calen-*

dar of All the Confréries of Paris for 1621 still shows a *confrérie* for almost every guild in the city, dedicated as always to a patron saint and based at one or another of the city's churches. But the journeymen and apprentices were no longer members.[47] By Louis XIV's time the administration of the *confréries*, like the guilds themselves, was firmly in the hands of the most senior—and presumably politically reliable—guild officers. As Emile Levasseur wrote, "The forms of the Middle Ages were conserved [but] the democratic spirit which had once animated them had largely disappeared."[48]

Coincidental with and intimately related to the conversion of the *confréries* into organs of the mercantile and industrial aristocracy was the appearance of the exclusively journeyman organizations known as the *compagnonnages*. It is reasonable to assume that the reluctance of the masters to associate socially with their guild workers was reciprocated by the workers. As the *confréries*, along with the guilds, fell into the grip of a privileged oligarchy, the workers groped for some sort of institution which would permit them to retain their old corporate identity. The *confrérie* provided the inspiration, but the result was of a sort never contemplated by the medieval man. The new institutions—the *compagnonnages*—were far closer in spirit to the class-conscious, irreligious, and combative nineteenth-century workingman's organizations than to their thirteenth-century counterpart. Their evolution is particularly clear among the journeymen printers who, disgruntled by a seventeen-hour work day and other grievances,[49] withdrew in the sixteenth century from their *confrérie* and formed their own association under the patronage of a saint of their choosing. Their headquarters were at the Church of Saint-Jean-de-Latran on the Left Bank.

These new *compagnonnages* met with a very hostile reception. Throughout the sixteenth century admonishments against any sort of assemblage of journeymen, particularly for organizational purposes, were repeatedly issued by King, Parlement, and Châtelet. Forced by circumstances to become secret organizations, the *compagnonnages* became ever more suspect to both the authorities and employers. Possibly the first such organization to be suppressed was the one formed by the tailors' journeymen, victims of a *sentence* by the Châtelet as early as

1506.[50] Despite repression, the *compagnonnages* grew, reflecting the deterioration of relations between masters and workers so characteristic of the social history of the sixteenth century.[51]

The complaints of Henry IV's ministers were quite representative of official thinking on the social evolution taking place under their eyes. They bemoaned the new independence and belligerency of the workers, contrasting them most unfavorably with the workers of old (but never stopping to ask how the attitudes of the employers had changed as well). The workers were accused of "insubordination and irreverence towards employers," of "intolerable negligence."[52] The minister Laffemas charged that "apprentices, workers and others failed to render the honor and obedience which they owed their masters."[53] He expressed sorrow that the old "deference of workers for their employers" was no more to be seen.

The measures employed by the authorities at the start of the new century to combat this lamentable moral decay help explain why social conditions probably worsened in the seventeenth century rather than improved. Since the problem of the working man was looked upon as a moral one, the solution was likewise thought to be moral. All that was necessary to restore the old values in the worker was a crusade to root out blasphemy, concubinage, drunkenness, gambling, debauchery, and the rest. At the root of all moral laxity was reputed to be idleness, so it is not surprising to find the father of mercantilism, Laffemas, anticipating his great disciple Colbert in trying to reduce the number of religious holidays. But Laffemas made the mistake of appealing to Rome instead of to a subservient prelate of Paris, and his efforts came to naught.

The *compagnonnages* in the seventeenth century have been termed by one historian, "occult federative organizations."[54] They are difficult to pin down because of their secrecy, but clearly extended to all the larger cities of France. A new note is their condemnation by the Church. The many strange and secret rituals rumored to surround the initiation rites of the *compagnonnages* were pronounced irreligious if not sacrilegious. In 1639 the new and powerful national Catholic lay action society known as the Company of the Holy Sacrament denounced the *compagnonnages*, marking the start of an opposition so vehement and so much in the interests of the employers as to tempt one modern observer to label the Company "a genuine strike-breaking society."[55] Several other denunciations of the *compagnonnages* followed from the Officialité (the diocesan law court), but all of these were simply preliminaries to the great blast sounded by the theologians of the Sorbonne in 1655. They condemned the "impious, sacrilegious, and superstitious practices" of the journeymen, warning the faithful that "one could not join the *compagnonnages* without mortal sin." The journeymen were accused of "greatly dishonoring God, profaning all the mysteries of our religion, ruining the masters, emptying their shops of helpers . . ."[56]

The Sorbonne's pronouncement revealed the high degree of organization achieved by the journeymen of Paris and other French cities. The theologians referred to a number of elective offices, to elaborate rituals, to clandestine meetings in selected inns known as the *mères*. The latter served not only as local headquarters but as stopping-off places for out-of-town journeymen engaged in the famous *tour de France*, one of the picturesque trademarks of the *compagnonnages* by which a young man learned his trade and his country at the same time.

While the Sorbonne's action doubtless endeared it to guildmasters, the august theology faculty should not be lightly accused of having acted from economic motives. No orthodox Catholic reading the mysterious rites of the *compagnonnages* could fail to be disturbed by some of their practices and requirements—for example, the oath forbidding initiates to reveal any of the secrets of the organizations even in the confessional. Whether the "liturgy" of the *compagnonnages* was innocent superstition or intentional and blasphemous parody of Christian worship is debatable. The Church took the latter view and was probably justified in doing so. However, in assuming such hostility towards the workers—who, at the very least, deserved understanding and Christian compassion—the Church opened up a small crevice which later revolutionary events would broaden into a seemingly unbridgeable gulf. It would not be altogether rash to recognize some connection between the hostility the Church showed to the workers of the Saint-Antoine quarter in the seventeenth century and the fanatical dechristianization which occurred there during the Revolution. When one reads work regulations ordering laborers at the start of their dawn-to-dusk day to "offer their labor to God . . . , make the sign of the cross, then start work,"[57] one wonders whether Christian resignation or bitter thoughts about the seeming alliance of the Divinity and employers were uppermost in the workers' minds.

The discontent of Parisian workers with the many inequities of the guild system, the frustrations of men well qualified in point of seniority and skill who had the door to advancement slammed in their faces by their masters, were also reflected in the many sanctuaries of "free labor" to be found throughout the city. At the start of Louis XIV's reign these had numbered close to a couple of dozen, but, as we have noted, the antiseignorial law of 1674 reduced both their number and their privileges. Nevertheless, until the Revolution various abbatial and even parish churches enjoyed lucrative rents from workers assured comparative freedom from the *jurés'* inspections of merchandise and from other irksome guild regulations.

The best known of these privileged areas were the Temple (with over a hundred rental properties),[58] the cloisters and parvis of Notre-Dame, Saint-Germain-des-Prés and Saint-Jean-de-Latran, the Hôtel de Soissons, a large part of the Faubourgs Saint-Antoine, Saint-Martin-des-Champs, Saint-Benoît, and the hospitals of the Quinze-Vingts and the Trinité. In none of them could the guild officials make their inspections without the protection of the police, and even the latter complained of the "danger" of such undertakings.[59] A police raid on the enclosure of Saint-Jean-de-Latran in 1705, for example, led to the incitement of a riot apparently led by some of the resident priests bent on protecting the economic interests of their order.[60] When the officials of the Châtelet complained that 150 bankrupts were living in the Temple in perfect security, the Grand Prior's only reply was a verbose memoir detailing the historic privileges of his enclosure.[61]

Just as contemptuous of the Châtelet's authority was the Abbot of Saint-Germain-des-Prés, whose exemption from the decree of 1674 was clearly meant to apply only to the religious living within the abbey enclosure but who coolly gave shelter and complete economic immunity to hundreds of workers in rental houses around the Abbey.[62] Not only had the Abbot managed to retain his medieval autonomy, he was even expanding his domain. In the latter years of the century he constructed an additional sixty rental houses whose occupants came under his law rather than the city's.[63] Letters from Versailles to D'Argenson insisting that "the law officers exercise on the people and artisans residing in the enclosure of the abbey the same jurisdiction and authority that they would exercise if they lived in the middle of Paris" made not a whit of difference.[64] Even "in the middle of Paris" these ecclesiastical enclosures enjoyed almost as much autonomy as in feudal days. One could hardly find a more central location than the commandery of Saint-Jean-de-Latran on the Left Bank a quarter of a mile south of Notre Dame, but throughout the reign illegal manufactures were carried on here despite occasional ineffective raids and threats of "exile" to the private magistrates presiding therein.[65]

The Châtelet could always be trusted to take the side of the guilds against the privileged enclosures, but some of the other courts were openly sympathetic with the historic rights of the privileged areas. For example, in 1691 a *juré* of the mercers' guild, Sautreau by name, desended upon one Pierre Jannart, a mercer plying his trade in a privileged house owned by the powerful Knights of Malta. Charged with selling "defective goods" (i.e., not meeting guild standards), Jannart was arrested and taken to the Châtelet prison. But Jannart's influential landlords took his case to the Grand Conseil, a court superior to the Châtelet. The Grand Conseil accommodated the Knights by ordering not only Jannart's release but Sautreau's arrest. A small army of sixteen men went to Sautreau's house, from which he was "scandalously removed . . . and dragged through the streets, on foot, without hat" to a prison safe from the Châtelet's magistrates. Sautreau's reputation was saved in the nick of time by the King, who ruled personally that no *juré* could be arrested for carrying out guild visits.[66]

As the foregoing case would suggest, there was a good deal of uncertainty in official circles, up to and including the monarch, as to the legal standing of the *lieux privilégiés*. A classic example of these confusing and contradictory claims was that of the Faubourg Saint-Antoine. This neighborhood, described by Saugrain as "crowded with quantities of artisans and journeymen who work without *maîtrise*,"[67] was under the jurisdiction of the formidable Abbess of Saint-Antoine ("la Dame du Faubourg"). She was spiritual ruler of perhaps the richest convent in the Parisian area, independent of even the Archbishop of Paris, and principal legatee of the traditional economic autonomy of the surrounding faubourg. The "free" shops of Saint-Antoine were a constant thorn in the side of the town merchants and a source of frustration to the tax collectors. Finally in 1644 the faubourg's workers were ordered to join the city guilds. Needless to say, this action provoked a violent legal battle, from which the incensed Abbess emerged triumphant in 1657 when the faubourg's independence was reaffirmed.[68] Nevertheless, the King in 1675 again ordered all the workers of the faubourgs, including those of Saint-Antoine, to join the city guilds. The lawyers on both sides went back to work, but the indomitable abbesses must have at least held their own because at the end of the century they were still (to their own profit) outraging the city guildsmen by elevating Saint-Antoine journeymen to the rank of master.[69]

Trumpet as he might the right of the police to enter any "privileged area" in Paris, Louis XIV, as usual, set a bad personal example. In the three-block-long Gallery of the Louvre Louis established, to the dismay of the guilds, several dozen *ateliers* of highly skilled artisans, all completely free of guild control and having the right to automatic promotion after specified terms of service. Equally disturbing from the guilds' point of view was his habit of "giving" the *maîtrise* to any of the several hundred merchants chosen to supply the Court in its peregrinations (*marchands suivant la Cour*). These continued to remain largely free from the control of the city guilds. Since nearly all the court merchants had highly prestigious shops in the city, the possibilities for conflicts with guild members were endless.

While no one would want to equate industrial strife in Louis XIV's time with conditions in the Industrial Revolution, at least one economic historian detects a ground swell of discontent developing among the workers towards the end of the century which continued to grow until the Revolution.[70] Another researcher describes strikes and worker rebellions as becoming "very frequent" in Paris from the seventeenth century on.[71] A study of the intendants' reports at the start of Louis XIV's reign led Pierre Boissonade to describe the working classes as "agitated by the spirit of indiscipline and revolt."[72]

The frustration of journeymen unable to advance in their trades and professions is a recurring theme in the labor troubles of the period, a complaint which lends irony to the employers' charges that the *compagnonnages* were vicious contradictions of the ancient principle of economic fraternity and cooperation. One perceives this frustration at all levels. On one occasion it was evident even among the *vidangeurs* whose grim task it was to carry the filth of Paris daily to the collecting stations on the outskirts of the city. In 1670 the journeymen of this "community" grew weary of working for the masters and set out on their own account. The outraged masters seized their workers' tools and took the case to the Châtelet, which quickly (by seventeenth-century standards) ruled against the workers and forbade them under pain of prison to go about the streets of Paris crying "A curer les puits." The journeymen were advised by the magistrates "to remove themselves to the Masters of the said trade if they wished to be received to the Mastership."[73]

One also reads of the journeymen shoesmiths of the Place Maubert meeting regularly and clandestinely at the house of one Marguérite Guyot, the *mère* of the group, to plan violent reprisals against those members of the trade who refused to join them in their wage demands. Sixty of them had gathered at Mme Guyot's place at five o'clock one Sunday afternoon when a *commissaire* from the Châtelet raided the establishment and dispersed them.[74]

Still another harbinger of new labor relations was the practice of masters to resort to collective lockouts to dramatize their own economic difficulties both with labor and government. For instance, in 1708 the Controller-General wrote D'Argenson from Versailles that 800 workers in the stocking shops of Paris had marched to the palace to protest the sudden shutdown of their places of employment. The owners had apparently concluded that they could not operate at a profit; they had joined forces in shutting down the industry. D'Argenson was directed by the Controller-General to ascertain the facts from the employers. A few days later D'Argenson replied that one of the masters had "insolently" told him that the shops would remain closed since D'Argenson was not prepared to meet the payroll himself.[75]

On another occasion, the Controller-General complained to D'Argenson that "a prodigious number" of wigmakers, apparently reacting to labor troubles in the same industry at Lyons, had marched out from Paris protesting a sudden shutdown by their employers. "This has the air of the spirit of revolt," the alarmed minister wrote D'Argenson, immediately sensing collusion between the workers of Lyons and Paris.[76] The Parisian quarry workers refused to be outdone by stocking and wig workers. We find them massing in front of the house of the president of the Parlement in 1705 "in very large numbers" complaining about loss of jobs and reductions in wages.[77]

Throughout the reign, a consistent source of labor trouble was the stevedores at the various "ports" on the river front. These workers— near the bottom of the economic scale in Paris—had begun to form secret associations which set wage scales considerably at variance with the official rates long established by the Hôtel de Ville. Even more disconcerting was their habit of forcing their services on unfortunate boatowners, who were given the choice of paying the rates demanded or risking violence on themselves or their property. Not infrequently, the situation on the waterfront got so out of hand that the Hôtel de Ville had to humiliate itself by asking for police help from its hated downstream rival, the Châtelet. All in all, the economic environment of Louis XIV's Paris, despite the artificial respiration applied to the guilds of old, had taken on some strikingly modern traits.

CHAPTER SIX

Charity: old and new

PROBABLY the most troublesome social ailments afflicting Paris in the age of Louis XIV were beggary and vagabondage. Few visitors to the city failed to comment on the great number of homeless wretches deranging the Parisian street scene. A century later, Revolutionary demagogues like Barère were apt to label beggary "the leprosy of the monarchies." In truth, the problem as Barère and his contemporaries knew it was far younger than the French monarchy. Not until the last three centuries of the monarchy did it cause the authorities any real concern. Medieval society took beggars in stride, accepting them as convenient means by which Christian almsgivers could attain the grace necessary for salvation.

Medieval law was almost as indulgent towards beggars as the populace. An occasional edict ordered nonresident beggars out of Paris within a stated time on the threat of nothing worse than the pillory. (One of the earliest of these laws dates to the reign of King John in 1350.[1]) But such legislation was rare and poorly enforced. Long after the law had stiffened towards beggary, the population clung obstinately to its old attitude. When Louis XIV began treating poverty as a crime and locking up the criminals, his special "poor police" encountered great popular hostility. Several were killed by street mobs.[2] Fortunately for the monarch, by the later seventeenth century the attitude of the middle-class towards the poor had also changed. It, too, had come to regard mendicancy as a social abomination which could no longer be condoned.

The multiplicity of edicts, ordinances, and declarations against vagabonds on the streets of Paris began only with the sixteenth century.

For three centuries the deluge hardly slackened. The stiffening in official attitude was doubtless due mainly to the great increase in the number of vagrants after 1500.[3] The city magistrates found themselves no longer dealing with manageable numbers of harmless and probably physically incapacitated wretches gathered in front of cathedral doors and public buildings. Instead, they had to cope with hordes of able-bodied men and women, most of them not even natives of Paris. Only at this juncture did the authorities begin to regard the beggars as dangerous men and beggary as a serious crime. The simple punishments of the past—whippings and the pillory—gave way to more drastic penalties. In 1532 the Parlement sentenced beggars to forced labor in chains; in 1534 it warned them to get out of Paris within three days or face hanging; in 1596 the Parlement ordered all vagrants out of the city within twenty-four hours "under penalty of being hanged and strangled without benefit of trial."[4] One can assume that such extreme penalties were rarely implemented but the language itself is significant. There are no counterparts in earlier centuries.

What we are dealing with in the sixteenth and seventeenth centuries, instead of old-fashioned localized poverty, is the dislocation and pauperization of large segments of rural society in France and elsewhere in Europe. Historians write rather grandiloquently but vaguely of causes—religious conflict, the end of serfdom, the progress of capitalism, poor crops, the rise in prices, insufficient warfare to sustain the men of arms, changes in climatic conditions, and others—but no really satisfactory explanation has yet been given (perhaps none exists) as to why so many homeless and jobless individuals were moving about Europe in these centuries.

In Paris, the vagabond problem probably reached its climax in the last two decades of Louis XIII's reign and the first decades of Louis XIV's. The more immediate causes are clear. The incredibly callous financial policies Richelieu had employed to finance the Thirty Years' War, the war itself, disease and crop failures—these had helped make Richelieu's years of power among the most horrifying the French peasant had ever had to face. However great one's admiration may be for the Cardinal as a statesman and war leader, one can only deplore him from a humanitarian and social viewpoint. His ministry was punctuated by a depressing succession of rural and urban disturbances, some of surprising scope and intensity, which have recently been the subject of close study by historians, particularly by the Russian, Boris Porchnev.[5] Even though one may not agree with Porchnev's Marxist conclusions, his bulky work gives incontrovertible evidence of the miseries of the rural population. The devastating civil war known as the Fronde at mid-century can also be regarded in large part as Richelieu's legacy, but these popular uprisings did not end with the defeat of the *frondeurs*. The first fifteen years of Louis XIV's personal reign were marked by more such *émeutes*, climaxing in province-wide revolts in the southwest and in Brittany in 1675.

Thus from about 1623 to 1675 virtually all parts of France, but especially the west, were repeatedly shaken by these protests against the constituted order. The continuous ferment and economic distress in the countryside resulted in a large immigration of provincials to the capital. These the city magistrates attempted alternately to lock up, put to work, or return to their homes—succeeding on no count. In the 1650's the number of vagrants was estimated by Sauval at more than 40,000 or almost a tenth of the city's population. This sort of statistic one generally suspects to have been badly inflated. In this case succeeding events make it entirely credible. When the Hôpital-Général opened its doors in 1656, some 6,000 vagrants were quickly herded in, and as soon as additional room could be made the institution averaged 10,000 inmates or better. When one considers that nearly all these people had to be rounded up in periodic police drives, that each time such a drive was even so much as rumored a hurried evacuation of the city or mass hideout ensued, and that despite all these efforts complaints about vagrants on the streets never ceased, then Sauval's estimate of 40,000 vagrants no longer seems unreasonable.

Much as one tries to remind oneself that Paris was a city of almost half a million and that poverty was the lot of the great majority of human beings everywhere in those days, one is nevertheless appalled by what a recent historian has aptly described as the "underworld of oppression, famine, license, and revolt beyond discussion" to be found in

Paris.[6] For the historian to obtain a real conception of that world is of course impossible. All he can hope for is an occasional insight into the social and economic conditions that prevailed behind the glittering façade of the Grand Siècle. One such glimpse is provided by the statistics on infanticides. Guy Patin, a prominent physician who was in a position to know the facts, stated in 1660 that six hundred infants had been exposed that year.[7] Later in the reign, Félibien, an historian with a reputation for accuracy, set the annual figure at a minimum of five hundred. In the terrible winter of 1708-1709, undoubtedly the most depressed of the entire reign, the Controller-General was informed officially that 2,525 infants had been deposited in doorways or in front of the Hôtel-Dieu. In the month of January alone, 122 of these infants had died in the Couche, the hospital for foundlings.[8]

Another insight into the seamy side of seventeenth-century Paris can be gained from contemporary descriptions of the wards of the Hôtel-Dieu and the nightly wagonloads of corpses taken from there to the overflowing cemeteries for mass burials. Such descriptions are even more appalling when we realize they were generally written in praise of the Hôtel-Dieu rather than in criticism. Scanning the roll call of human misery in the rosters of the Hôpital-Général, the city workhouse, is likewise enlightening, especially if we bear in mind that the ten thousand or more poor listed therein were in addition to those in church-managed institutions, on parish charity rolls, or still at large. Only the poorest, the most rootless, and the less clever generally ended up in the Hôpital-Général. Police accounts of the wild scenes attending men's efforts to obtain a loaf of bread in times of grain shortage (fortunately rather infrequent) are also calculated to make one relatively satisfied with modern society.

In trying to cope with the problem of the poor in seventeenth-century Paris, the magistrates liked to distinguish between provincial vagabonds and the "honest" poor. The vagabonds, as one representative statute put it, were "those who have neither profession, nor trade, nor domicile, nor place of subsistence . . . and cannot be vouched for by people of trust."[9] On the other hand, there were many among the poor who had a trade and domicile and could be vouched for by a parish priest, yet were often reduced to a way of life difficult to distinguish from the legally defined vagabonds. The first category accounted, allegedly, for almost all the street beggars. The fiction seemed to be maintained that the others were too proud to resort to the streets, preferring to starve genteelly at home. Both groups were thought deserving of help but of a very different kind, as we shall note.

ॐ　　ॐ

Contemporary Parisian society can be criticized for inefficiency and parsimony in dealing with the poor, but not for apathy. The Christian tradition of aiding the poor remained strong, although the day was long past when the relief of the indigent was neatly centered in the Church. If anything, there were too many agencies run by too many authorities, each resentful of the others and jealously guarding its "rights." Painfully evident was the Old Regime dictum that outmoded institutions should never be destroyed but that new ones should simply be erected alongside the old.

Of the many kinds of aid extended to the Parisian poor, one of the oldest was that rendered by the monarchy itself. Such aid had never been institutionalized. The king gave to the poor simply in the capacity of almsgiver, not as head of the state. Generally, he channeled his gifts through the Church. While no one could mistake the Christian charity of Louis XIV for that of St. Louis, the Sun King was not without a measure of compassion. Once, when informed of the dire plight of the children of some workers killed in the construction of the Invalides, he personally ordered that they be admitted to the Trinité and Saint-Esprit, two of the best orphan asylums in Paris. On another occasion a private citizen lost all his worldly possessions in a fire and in accordance with tradition wrote the King for help. Louis first replied that this was a matter for private charity and that individuals must not be encouraged to appeal directly to their monarch, but apparently he had some second thoughts and a few days later ordered that the man be given a hundred francs from the royal purse.[10]

Outside of occasional alms of this sort, which he obviously did not encourage, Louis XIV assisted some 500 charities scattered throughout

136

France, a hundred or so of them in Paris. A few of these gifts ran to close to a thousand livres each (Louis IX's famous thirteenth-century refuge for the blind, the Quinze-Vingts, received 800 livres annually, for example), but most of the gifts were in the range of 100-300 livres.[11] Of more import to the needy of Paris was a new kind of annual charity of 60,000 to 80,000 livres which Louis made to the faubourgs of Paris to tide them over the winter months. The money was doled out as grants to the *curés* of some sixteen parishes whose boundaries extended beyond the city walls.[12] The King thus bypassed the lay-dominated directories which after the Fronde had been established in almost every Parisian parish to administer charity. Whether Louis chose to distribute his gifts in this way simply to spare the feelings of the parish priests, or whether he distrusted the new *charités*, as the agencies were called, we do not know, but since some of the worst miseries of Paris were to be found in the faubourgs, the gifts were extremely welcome. One of the *curés* concerned, the pastor of the parish of Saint-Sulpice, wrote the King accordingly in a letter to Versailles in 1708, saying that he had to keep alive in his parish "thirteen to fourteen thousand" poor.[13]

Louis XIV maintained the tradition of the King Bountiful in still another way, the distribution in times of serious shortage of free wheat or bread to the people of Paris. Many lives were doubtless saved thereby, but perhaps the most interesting aspect of these handouts was the woeful administrative incompetence demonstrated by the city officials placed in charge of the distribution. The fiasco was so notable that the monarch abandoned this old custom when the need was greatest.

The first King's Bread took place in 1662 when Louis had with great éclat just picked up the reins of government from Mazarin. Living as he was in the Louvre in the midst of his Parisian subjects, he was very eager to do something to alleviate the distress arising from a series of disastrous crop failures. The price of a pound loaf of bread had risen to 8 sous,[14] which represented close to a day's wage for many day laborers—if they were fortunate enough to be drawing any wages at all. The King ordered some 2,000,000 livres of wheat from Danzig and elsewhere in eastern Europe, which arrived in the ports of Paris in April 1662.[15]

The crucial question was how to distribute the grain so as to prevent profiteering and hoarding. On April 12 a conference was held on this subject in Chancellor Séguier's residence in Paris. Attending were Séguier, Colbert, the magistrates from the Châtelet, the Prévôt des Marchands, and several of the neighborhood police commissioners. They decided to distribute the newly arrived grain at reduced prices to the bourgeois and the bakers exclusively. The former were instructed to take their grain allowances to the millers to have it ground into flour for baking in their own family ovens, while the bakers were ordered to bake and display enough bread to relieve the demand of the populace. Either the bakers were the greedy rascals they were always reputed to be or someone had miscalculated the price at which they could afford to sell their bread, because while the bourgeois of Paris fared very well, few of the poor could afford the 4 or even 5 sous the bakers demanded for a very brown and coarse pound loaf.[16]

With good reason, the Parisian poor began to murmur. The police became alarmed and in the beginning of May the King gave permission to the city fathers to bake and distribute bread at the Tuileries Palace. Several openings were made in the high garden wall which then extended from a point opposite the Pont Royal west to the Porte de la Conférence, and there bread was handed out to long single files of the populace from eight in the morning starting on May 10. The numerous contemporary engravings of cripples and children reaching out hungrily to receive their quota of bread were offered as graphic proof of the King's *libéralité* towards the poor. But one is somewhat disillusioned to read in Delamare that the King's Bread was sold at 2 sous 6 deniers per pound, a price well under the market but still appreciably higher than in normal times.[17]

On only one other occasion in his reign, the near-famine of 1693, did Louis XIV attempt to undercut the operation of the grain market by selling bread at reduced prices. Faced with serious riots in the Parisian marketplaces, the King announced that distribution of the King's Bread would begin on October 20 at the Louvre, Tuileries, Bastille, Luxembourg, and several other places in Paris. The price this time was set at 6 sous for a three-pound loaf. One hundred thousand pounds daily were ordered distributed. But, again, within a few days the King received word of widespread "abuses and disorders." The wrong people were allegedly getting their hands on the bread and reselling it at higher prices. After a little more than a week Louis abandoned the effort and ordered that the daily allowance of 100,000 pounds of bread be turned over to the parish *curés* and other "charitable persons." Administrative difficulties must have been too formidable for the *curés* as well. After a couple of weeks, at their request, Louis converted the bread into a cash allowance—120,000 livres each winter month to be used by the *curés* for the poor.

The alms of the faithful, either given directly to the poor or channeled through the Church, were the traditional means of alleviating the lot of the poor. Even before Louis XIV began his reign, however, at least two kinds of new agencies for poor relief had come into use. Both originated in the reign of Francis I at the start of the sixteenth century, however difficult it may be to imagine such a pleasure-loving monarch inspiring them. But Francis I's reign was probably the first to feel the impact of the social dislocation described above. The Church was undoubtedly hard-pressed to meet the new demands of the Parisian poor, and Francis and his ministers apparently strove to fill the gap.

His first innovation was the *ateliers publics*, or work-relief projects; the second, a centralized organization known as the Grand Bureau des Pauvres to administer aid to the poor of Paris. Both institutions were in harmony with the new secular spirit of the times. They were administered entirely by the magistrates of the Hôtel de Ville and financed by the city. The King even authorized a special levy—the first Parisian poor tax—to pay the expenses of the Grand Bureau. Perhaps disturbed by secularized charity, the ecclesiastical authorities urged the faithful to supplement the tax revenues with the traditional alms. Poor boxes were provided in the parish churches as a reminder that the poor were still the concern of Christians.

Even this early, the dichotomy in the minds of the magistrates between the native poor (the deserving) and the provincial poor (the nondeserving) was very evident. The new *ateliers* were designed for vagrants picked up on the streets of Paris who had previously failed to heed orders to vacate the city. The intent, it would seem, was to make life so unpleasant for the "beneficiaries" that they would either find gainful employment or leave the capital. No dole was given; only a daily ration of brown bread.[18] What was clearly uppermost in the minds of the magistrates was the exercise of the police power over the poor in order to defend society against a class newly conceived to be dangerous to the established order.

The Grand Bureau, on the other hand, was intensely bourgeois in spirit. Its principal historian has called it a society "for the mutual assistance of the bourgeois."[19] Its principal beneficiaries were orphans of indisputably legitimate and Parisian origins and old people of sixty or over who had achieved respectability in commerce or the professions but had struck hard times in their declining years. The worker or artisan held little interest for the Grand Bureau. Individuals who had succeeded in having their names inscribed on the rolls of the Grand Bureau received weekly food allotments from its representative and a dole amounting, in the later seventeenth century, to 12 sous.

There were, however, some very unpleasant aspects about the Grand Bureau's charity. For one thing it insisted that the weekly distribution of food and alms be made publicly and with considerable fanfare, on the grounds that such public display encouraged public donations to the Grand Bureau.[20] Even more disturbing, one would imagine, to its clients was the requirement that once a person had been registered on its rolls he display the red and yellow mark of the Bureau on his right shoulder. He was forbidden to beg, was under obligation to "live Christianly," and had to declare the Bureau his legatee. A regulation of 1676 even prohibited him from leaving his parish without permission of the *commissaire des pauvres*. One apparently paid a high price for the Bureau's assistance.

Both the *atelier public* and the Grand Bureau des Pauvres were in Louis XIV's day regarded as failures. Properly administered and financed, these institutions might have rendered good service. Instead, they suffered on both counts. Small as the new poor tax was, the authorities encountered great difficulty in collecting it. The prevailing attitude was that it was not a legitimate tax and should be replaced by volun-

tary contributions. The *ateliers* continued to be resorted to intermittent-
ly, with mediocre results at best. Louis XIV made use of them on only
three occasions: 1685, 1963, and 1709. Each of these years was one of
high bread prices and serious unemployment. The King's beloved new
Hôpital-Général was crowded beyond capacity, and he probably resorted to the *atelier* out of desperation.

The *atelier* of 1709 gives us an interesting insight into political and
social conditions in Paris at the dismal end of Louis XIV's reign. It also
affords a very unflattering picture of poor-relief administrators at their
worst. The plan had been to put the unemployed to work on the long-
delayed southern rampart at the end (not inappropriately) of the Rue
d'Enfer—Hell Street.[21] A lively controversy had preceded the establishment of this *atelier*. The able Lieutenant of Police, D'Argenson, had led
the opposition to the proposal, arguing that "it is just as dangerous to
assemble all the poor as it is to leave them idle. . . ."[22] But under pressure from the nervous parlementarians and ministers at Versailles (they
had good reason to be nervous for there was more cause for revolution
in 1709 than there would be eighty years later), an Assembly of Police
voted to organize an *atelier* to give work and bread to about 2500 men.[23]
The Prévôt des Marchands' contribution to the discussion was that in
his view the threat of hard work in the *ateliers* would be the best assurance of "returning the poor to the provinces so as to work on the har-
vest and the artisans to their ordinary labors." The hat was passed
among some of the leading citizens of Paris, the First President of Parlement and the Archbishop contributing 15,000 livres between them and
the Hôtel de Ville donating an additional 15,000.[24] The opening of the
atelier was scheduled for the morning of August 20.

Precisely what ensued is difficult to piece together, but little doubt
remained when calm had been restored that D'Argenson had been
right in his reluctance to permit the unemployed to assemble. An em-
barrassed official of the Parlement wrote the Controller-General in Versailles, "All the tools [to be provided the workers] had been pilfered."
Only about two hundred out of the crowd could be assigned work.[25]
Robbed of the promise of bread, several thousand workers rioted, neces-
sitating the calling of regular troops to restore order. An aristocratic

lady accidentally caught in the riots wrote, "I do not know who directs this work, but it is very badly run." The lady went on to recount her terrifying experience: "I am half-dead. I found myself in the streets at the time of the revolt: it is a horrible thing. . . . I am not subject to fear but I swear that one can never see anything more horrifying. For God's sake, take care! It is not a thing to neglect."[26] Her words might well have been taken to heart by her fellow aristocrats.

ᴈᴡ   ᴈᴡ

One could have been fairly certain at the start of the new reign that new solutions would be sought for the old problem of Parisian beggars and vagabonds. Conditions on the streets had perhaps never been worse than they were after the Fronde. Parisians had long since lost confidence in both the *ateliers publics* and the Grand Bureau des Pauvres. New institutions for dealing with the homeless poor were obviously in order. One suspects that the reform-minded Louis XIV, with the customary collaboration of Colbert, sooner or later would have emerged with institutional innovations of one sort or another to cope with vagabondage in the capital city of France. By rather strange happenstance, however, the solutions (or what contemporaries accepted jubilantly as solutions) were provided for him while he was still in his teens and giving no thought to perplexing social problems.

Thanks to the initiative of a small group of zealous Catholics, Paris witnessed in the 1650's the creation of both the parish *charités* and the ambitious Hôpital-Général. Although laymen had a preponderant role in their formation and administration, neither could be called a secular institution. They were both by-products of the French Catholic Renaissance and of the Company of the Holy Sacrament. (This semisecret organization of Catholic Actionists was in the forefront of every kind of charitable and social work from almost the moment its founder, the Duc de Ventadour, renounced conjugal life in 1629 for the service of God until its downfall in the 1660's.) Until the Revolution, the *charités* and the Hôpital-Général were to be the principal weapons (unfortunately, the word could at times be taken literally) employed in Paris to keep the poor and poverty within bounds.

The *charité* was a new kind of parish organization for coping with the problems arising from the complexities of urban living. It could be thought of as the "aggiornamento" of seventeenth-century Parisian Catholics. Virtually all the parishes of the city were represented in the movement in very short order. Each *charité* had its own constitution, generally borrowed from or influenced by one or another of the pioneer companies of the movement, one founded in the parish of Saint-Sulpice by the famous Olier in 1651 and another in the parish of Saint-Eustache two years later.[27] The *messieurs* of each company come together in semimonthly meetings to frame general policy and decide upon specific disbursements of funds. Most of the knocking on doors, visitations of the sick, and even *descentes* into prisons, were performed by the female adjunct of the organization. The work done by the ladies often seems to loom larger among contemporaries than that of the men. Both Saint-Simon and Blégny, for example, erroneously identified the *charités* exclusively with the *dames de charité*.[28]

The *charité* was entirely separate from the ancient parish *fabrique*. The latter had traditionally watched over the temporal interests and possessions of the parish and was controlled by the lay *marguilliers* (wardens) in uneasy association with the parish *curé*. The *charités* took a much broader and more apostolic view than the *fabriques*. Instead of concerning themselves with buildings and investments, they searched the far reaches of the parish for the poverty they could alleviate, the sick they could nurse, the poor youth they could educate, the fallen women they could rescue from careers of sin, the blaspheming lips they could seal. Like the national Company of the Holy Sacrament which had inspired them, the *charités* exhibited many of the same moralistic and obtrusive tendencies which infuriated less fervent Catholics. Often the *charités* seemed more concerned with the improvement of moral conditions among the poor than with temporal relief. One constitution, that of the parish of Saint-Eustache, even reserved the right to enter an errant household "without being called." Gambling, vice, tobacco, cohabitation were specifically mentioned as coming within the province of the company. Generally the recipient of alms from the organization had to present a signed and dated certificate of confession from a priest.

A modern social worker would be disturbed by this mixture of morality and poor relief, but perhaps even more by the bourgeois bias exhibited by the *charités* in selecting aid recipients. A constant and unembarrassed distinction was made between the *mauvais pauvres* and the *pauvres honteux*. The former were the poor who were somehow held responsible for their own fate—because of immorality, laziness, drink, etc.—and thus deserved no help from parish charity. On the other hand, the *pauvres honteux*, in the words of one of the societies' constitutions, were "those who have held honorable offices or employments or who kept shops as merchants or artisans of some guild, and those who may reasonably be ashamed to ask publicly for their necessities because of their profession or birth."[29] Only the latter were thought deserving of aid from the *charités*.

To qualify for assistance, one had to be domiciled and a resident of the city for three to six months or perhaps longer, depending on the regulations of the particular society. In contrast to the Hôpital, which gathered its patrons wholesale off the streets, the *charité* moved with great deliberation, studying each case in an impersonal and professional manner. Before any aid was granted, one of the members of the society was assigned to make a full investigation at the individual's domicile. If there were any question of medical assistance, a doctor or surgeon in the employ of the *charité* made sure that the disease was not contagious and that it was curable. When all the essential information had been obtained, the case was presented to a regular session of the society (presided over by the *curé* of the parish) and a democratic decision arrived at. To avoid the importunities of the poor, such meetings were conducted in secret.[30]

Help bestowed by a *charité* on an individual or his family could take a number of forms, depending upon circumstances and the society's regulations. Some poor were given financial assistance, others furniture or clothing, still others—and by far the most common—food and medical assistance. The ladies of the parish of Saint-Laurent, for example, made their rounds daily to an approved list of beneficiaries, carrying into the homes of the sick parcels made up of a soup, half a pound of veal or lamb, all the bread that could be eaten, wine, and a bouillon for the evening. The menu of another society consisted of bouillons, a pound of meat, and bread, with the proviso that in Lent and on fast days two eggs would be served in lieu of meat. (These portions appear remarkably bountiful for the times. We perhaps should keep in mind that, being the food prescribed in the printed regulations of the societies, there may have been a good deal of window dressing involved. How much of these generous meat allowances were actually served is questionable.) The ladies of Saint-Laurent made their visits in the company of "village girls," employees of the society who were paid to administer *lavements* or whatever other unpleasant physical procedures were called for. Typically, the ladies of the Saint-Laurent *charité* were instructed to approach the sick "with a modestly gay and affable countenance" and on their return home to "meditate on the virtues they had perceived among the poor."[31] Despite the new emphasis on system and efficiency, the old idea of helping oneself spiritually by helping others was still very much in order.

As much as possible, the *charités* gave medical assistance in the homes of the ill. The Hôtel-Dieu had the reputation it deserved among the populace; Saint-Simon wrote that "home treatment was welcomed with unequivocal pleasure." The general rule was that if a poor patient did not respond to treatment in his home within three weeks, he was taken to the Hôtel-Dieu.[32] Some of the more affluent parishes boasted endowed beds there for its parishioners. In the late seventeenth century, for an endowment of 8,000 livres (the price had gone up steadily) a benefactor could ensure his surviving co-parishioners a bed and "preferential" treatment at the Hôtel-Dieu, for whatever the latter was worth.[33] In addition—and this was another innovation of the later seventeenth century—a few of the wealthier parishes had established small parish hospitals of ten beds or so for the use of their *pauvres honteux* and even of their moderately well-off parishioners. Such were the hospitals of Saint-Merry, Saint-Jacques-du-Haut-Pas, and Saint-Sulpice.

The zealous *messieurs* and *dames* of the parish *charités* would have been the first to acknowledge that their work barely touched the surface of Parisian poverty. In limiting their apostolate to a carefully screened segment of the resident poor they ruled out the crowds of vagrants who infested Paris, the great majority of them provincials. For the *charités*, imbued as they were with the moral rigorism of the Company of the Holy Sacrament, the vagabonds were a scandalous island of blasphemy and irreligion in the midst of a Christian and conformist society. Finding a remedy for this scandal was "the great aim of numerous assemblies of these charitable persons . . . from 1640 to 1649," according to a contemporary account of the founding of the Hôpital-Général.[34]

The disorders of the Fronde at mid-century interrupted this early planning but made the need for a solution all the more urgent. There was one important precedent to go by. Almost half a century earlier Henry IV had attempted to rid his capital of the homeless by locking up, or threatening to do so, every person who could not prove he had a domicile. Five *hôpitaux* had been projected for this purpose, but after a good deal of fumbling, only one had been put into operation, the Pitié. A special constabulary rounded up some beggars, but proved woefully inadequate for keeping them confined.[35] Before long, only a few little girls remained in the Pitié, and the Parlement, with characteristic blindness, charged that the "malice and corruption" of the poor were to blame.[36]

Under the leadership of the First President of the Parlement, Pomponne de Bellièvre, plans were formulated in the early 1650's for an even more ambitious lockup of the begging poor than had been projected by Henry IV. While the initiative was clearly local and inseparable from the Parisian membership of the Company of the Holy Sacrament, such an undertaking of course necessitated the King's approval and support. He, or at least his leading minister, Mazarin, enthusiastically endorsed the plans, and in April 1656 the edict appeared announcing the new Hôpital-Général. All beggars, the law proclaimed, were either to be returned to their native towns or placed in one of several workshops where they were to help support themselves. Although the King accorded some revenues to the Hôpital (wine and salt taxes, a percentage of police fines, certain investments), it soon became apparent that about half of the institution's expenses would have to come from private charity. The founding edict provided that if the various corporate groups of the city did not make voluntary contributions, they would be taxed for this purpose.[37] The prospect of being at last free from the tyranny of street beggars, some of whose methods of asking alms were hard to distinguish from outright robbery, doubtless encouraged many of the bourgeois of Paris to open their purses, although receipts from the start fell short of needs.

The King's initial contribution to the Hôpital was the grant of six buildings. According to an unsubstantiated story, he was persuaded to make this by Vincent de Paul, who at this time was very sympathetic to the idea of a municipal workshop. The more important of these units were the Salpêtrière and Bicêtre, both located in the southeast, well outside the city walls. The first had been constructed earlier in the century in response to the pleas of the residents of Faubourg Saint-Antoine that the manufacture of gunpowder be removed from the old Arsenal in their midst. (Repeated explosions had understandably made them uneasy and had caused serious damage to the building.) Bicêtre, even farther out in the country, had been originally built as a *château* in 1400, partially destroyed and then rebuilt by Louis XIII as a home for crippled soldiers. Its condition was said to reveal its age and past uses. With the help of a gift of 150,000 livres from a *dame de charité*, the largest cash donation received in the early years, the two buildings were repaired and made ready for their new occupants.[38] Salpêtrière was set aside for women, Bicêtre for men. Until the Revolution they remained among the grimmer monuments of Paris.

On Sunday morning, May 13, 1657, the day before the great lockup of the Parisian homeless was scheduled to take place, the citizens principally responsible for the founding of the Hôpital-Général met in the Chapel of the Pitié for a solemn Mass of the Holy Ghost. (This was the building that had been employed abortively half a century earlier for much the same purpose and which would now serve as headquarters for the new complex which made up the Hôpital-Général.) The founders invoked Divine aid. They had good reason to do so, for many still remembered the disorders and poor discipline which had wrecked the first Hôpital-Général. It was not happenstance that a clause in the King's edict of 1656 creating the new institution pointedly "prohibited soldiers and bourgeois from maltreating the sergeants, officers, bailiffs, etc., charged with . . . chasing after or accompanying the poor."[39] A month before the opening of the Hôpital-Général, Parlement had published an *arrêt* imposing censorship over publicity relating to the Hôpital. The action had been prompted by a rash of allegedly false stories that some unidentified individuals had been spreading on the future operations of the Hôpital-Général. Violators were threatened with the lash ("little children" with the switch) if they continued to jeopardize the Hôpital by spreading such falsehoods.[40]

The incarceration of the homeless poor began on May 14 and was carried out by the Hôpital's own *archers* with the aid, initially, of some of the King's troops. Some five thousand men and women were apprehended within a few weeks.[41] Sauval wrote exaltedly: "All Paris . . . changed face. . . . The days of salvation had arrived for the poor and Divine Providence had raised up fathers to feed them and masters to educate them."[42] According to him, the operation was carried out "without trouble," which is perhaps possible but, to judge from the later known difficulties of the *archers*, unlikely. It is possible that most of the out-of-town beggars temporarily left town in advance of the long-heralded opening of the Hôpital. The "two young Hollanders" in their journal for August 1657 asserted there was not a beggar on the streets. They told of seeing a magistrate from the Châtelet, "heavily guarded," inspecting pedestrians on the Pont Neuf.

That charity had become quite complicated by the seventeenth century and far transcended the old simple duty of dropping a coin in an outstretched hat is amply borne out by the Hôpital-Général. When Delamare prepared his *Traité de la police*, he wrote that the care and disciplining of the poor could be considered under four different headings. Perhaps in deference to his religious upbringing, he listed in first place the Christian obligation to minister to the poor. The seventeenth-century man then came in view as he proceeded to expound on the social and economic justifications for poor relief. Idleness and all the vices stemming from idleness could, Delamare argued, best be combatted by judicious poor-relief measures. Public health could be safeguarded by removing the contagion of the poor. Finally, by forcing gainful employment on the poor the economic needs of society could be met. As a police official, Delamare appeared to place more weight on the social and economic objectives than on the Christian.

Many Parisians, however, especially among the humbler folk, apparently hankered for the traditional, personal approach to the poor. To counter such views, the Hôpital-Général had the support of the very effective Jesuit propagandist Père Guévarre, who was working fervently to extend the institution to all France. Among Guévarre's writings was a pamphlet in question-and-answer form presenting, with the priest's rebuttals, various popular objections to the new approach to the poor. He cited the following complaints: unworthy cases were admitted to the Hôpital; the old system cost less; the misery and cries of the street poor were useful in exciting compassion and thus evoking alms; the right to ask alms was a "natural right" of the poor; since Jesus had said the poor would always be with us, it was futile to try to eliminate the problem.

Guévarre's rebuttals, while unappealing to the poor themselves, must have delighted the apostles of "good order." He made the customary distinction between the "poor of Jesus Christ" and the "poor of the Demon"—"the enemies of public order, sluggards, liars, drunkards, the lascivious." Under the old system, Guévarre argued, Parisians fed the worthy and the unworthy indiscriminately; now, two-thirds of the burden had been removed. He charged that anyone who maintained that the Hôpital-Général did not save the bourgeois money was simply evidencing "either that he was a very poor arithmetician or that he had not been giving alms." In support of his argument he described the thorough investigations carried out into the background of each applicant for aid, into his health, family responsibilities, his material possessions, residence, past begging record, and so on.[43] (The system of poor relief Guévarre pictured in such glowing terms was a highly rationalized one, but far more descriptive of the Hôpital-Général as originally planned than of the institution as it actually developed. After it had been in operation a few years, the "applicants" for admission to the Hôpital that the Jesuit priest alluded to were few and far between.)

Despite the Hôpital's initial success in clearing the streets and regardless of the writings of influential propagandists like Père Guévarre, there remained many doubters. Perhaps most significant was Vincent de Paul. Initially a staunch backer of the Hôpital-Général, he withdrew his support when he was unable to persuade the administrators to make the Hôpital something more than a police activity.[44] The Edict of 1656 had placed his Lazarist priests in charge of the spiritual care of the inmates, but when it became clear that the Hôpital would be provided with a private constabulary to drag the poor in, he wrote the King abruptly that his priests "had sufficient employment." Another religious order had to be substituted.

Much of the opposition to the Hôpital took a more violent form. Almost as frequent as the ordinances against the vagabonds themselves became the laws against interfering with the *archers* of the Hôpital in the prosecution of their duty.[45] Indicative of the extent of the opposition was the royal ordinance of 1669 which referred to the difficulties being experienced by the *archers* in their roundups "because of the protection given the beggars by the servants of people of quality, the bourgeois, artisans, soldiers and the lower classes." (One wonders who was left in Paris to take the side of the hapless *archers*.) The King's soldiers appeared to be the worst offenders, but much more surprising was the mention of members of the bourgeoisie as participants in these activities.

Among the many reasons for popular disaffection with the police of the Hôpital-Général was the conviction that they kidnaped boys and young girls off the streets of Paris for transport to America.[46] That human shipments for the benefit of the French colonists emanated from the Hôpital is incontestable, but the degree of coercion employed is difficult to establish. Since most of the inmates of the Hôpital were there against their will in the first place, it would have been a relatively easy matter to send them on to America without obtaining their consent. On one occasion Colbert wrote the Archbishop of Rouen asking that he find fifty or sixty robust country girls to volunteer to serve as brides of colonists, explaining that the batch sent the preceding year from the

Hôpital-Général had been unable to withstand the hard life in the Sugar Islands.[47] It is clear that the "robust villagers" requested of the Archbishop were supposed to be volunteers, but nothing was said one way or the other about their Parisian counterparts. A few years later several more consignments of girls were shipped from the Hôpital-Général. This time a number of chaperons accompanied them en route to the Islands, and Colbert insisted on a careful screening (earlier, several prostitutes had been sent in error and "had caused much disorder").[48] But again there is no way of knowing whether the girls' emigration was entirely voluntary. In any case, the populace of Paris was convinced that young people were being sent to America against their wishes, and dramatic "rescues" of potential victims from the clutches of the hated *archers* were common occurrences on the streets.

The Hôpital-Général was in one sense a considerable success. During Louis XIV's reign it maintained a population averaging around 10,000, nearly two-thirds of whom were crowded into the Salpêtrière and the Bicêtre while perhaps a thousand or more were infants mercifully farmed out to foster parents in the country.[49] Keeping such an establishment in operation was an administrative achievement for the city far surpassing any previous efforts. While one can take issue with the Draconian measures employed to get the beggars off the streets, there is something to be said, at least in principle, for rounding up the homeless, giving them housing, meals, useful employment, a future trade, and moral instruction. The philosophy of the Hôpital-Général at its best was rather close to that of a modern correctional institution. The trouble was that it never measured up to its potential. The founding Edict of 1656 provided that "the begging poor, able-bodied and invalid, of both sexes are to be shut up in the Hôpital, to be employed at ... manufactures and other labor in accordance with their ability. ..." The new institution was intended to cope only with the begging poor and, at that, with only those who by some unknown criterion could be considered Parisian; others were required to return to their places of origin in accordance with the ancient regulations.

Perhaps the Hôpital's basic difficulty was that from the start its administrators (twenty-eight in number, almost equally divided between

"King's men" and merchants of Paris, with the Archbishop added as an afterthought in 1673) either did not understand the stated objective or found it impossible to carry out. After three decades of operation, one of its directors sent a *mémoire* to the King entitled, "Means of Preserving the Hôpital-Général of Paris and of Preventing Its Failure." The author stated that ever since the hospital had opened its doors it had been burdened with all kinds of responsibilities for which it had never been intended, "the word *hôpital* having led to the belief that it would fill all public needs."[50] (Anglo-Saxons will be pleased to learn that the omnibus use of the word was equally troublesome to the seventeenth century.)

The report went on to say that because of the failure of the provinces to establish their own *hôpitaux-généraux* in sufficient quantity, Paris continued to be burdened with their poor. At that moment it was alleged that there were 1,600 of these "foreigners" in the care of the city, each costing 5 sous a day or a total of 45,675 livres per annum. To make matters worse, the Grand Bureau and other agencies had been unable to fulfill their obligations. As a result, many of the sick that should have been going elsewhere ended up instead at the Hôpital-Général. The report cited, for example, seventy-five advanced venereal cases ("their flesh rotting off in bits"); two hundred lunatics (the author expressed his willingness to accept the nonviolent cases, however); the blind (for whom the administrators of the Quinze-Vingts never seemed to find room); many hundreds of orphans, whom none of the orphanages wished to accept.

What had happened was that well before the end of the century the Hôpital-Général had been converted from a correctional workshop for the able-bodied to a hospital in the Anglo-Saxon meaning of the word. If one examines the rolls of the Hôpital in its first years, for 1662 and 1663, for example, one finds that out of a total population of slightly over 6,000, well over half were presumably able-bodied workers, neither very young nor very old and not infantile, imbecilic, pregnant, nursing, paralytic, etc.[51] But as the years passed, all the evidence indicates that the very young and the physically unfit became dominant. A law of March 1680, reorganizing the institution, acknowledged what had already become the practice: the Hôpital was henceforth declared open to boys under fifteen, girls under thirteen, oldsters over sixty, epileptics, the blind, incurably sick, venereal cases and lunatics.[52] A study of the Hôpital's population in 1713 reveals a truly sickening record of ailing and dying humanity. Of the 4,634 female inmates of the Salpêtrière, only a couple of hundred could possibly have been able-bodied young adults. The three most numerous classifications after the very young were lunatics and imbeciles (300), very old women reverted to infancy (294), and paralytics of diverse ages (268). At the Bicêtre, the male establishment, the situation was slightly better. Out of 1,385 inmates, all adults, possibly 350 could have theoretically done a day's work. Still, the largest category was 486 "aged paralytics, from 65 years to 90." One begins to appreciate the delicacy of Brice's observation on the Salpêtrière: "for the tender-hearted it is not a very agreeable thing."[53]

In the light of such figures, it is understandable that the workshops so prominent in the early planning for the Hôpital-Général were hardly in evidence at the end of the reign. Colbert had placed great store in the 1660's on the Hôpital's manufactures, envisioning the reduction of French imports, the self-liquidation of the Hôpital's expenses, and the possibility of teaching useful trades to the younger inmates. Each guild in the city had been required to furnish, when called upon, two journeymen to assist in these training duties. To give the young people an incentive they had been promised one-third of the profits from the workshop.

The most notable effort at manufacturing came in the Hôpital's first decade, when Colbert launched a carefully planned project for the production of knit stockings, then much in demand as an importation from the Channel Islands and other English sources. Skilled women were imported from the Islands to teach the women at Salpêtrière and Pitié the secrets of the trade. Arrangements were made with the somewhat apprehensive hosier's guild in Paris to furnish wool to the Hôpital, which would then be made into stockings for the guild to sell back to the public. But Colbert's experience with the kind of labor available in the Hôpital was not a happy one, and after only two years he shifted the stocking operation to a private company.[54]

Sauval wrote that all kinds of manufactures were established in the hope that the poor would be made to pay their subsistence, but all failed.[55] A "classified ad" of 1670, however, offered at the Bureau des Chapeaux of the Hôpital-Général some "excellent rainproof hats, very cheap at thirty sous completely trimmed." The President of the Parlement, and as such the chief director of the Hôpital, once proposed to Versailles that the Hôpital be given the monopoly of starch making in Paris, but the ministry turned him down on the grounds that this would cause considerable hardship among the starch-making artisans.[56] In a city where virtually every skill was jealously guarded by corporate rights, it was inevitable that every such move by the Hôpital-Général would stir up a hornet's nest of vested interests.

By the end of the reign, D'Argenson, the Lieutenant of Police, had lost all confidence in the Hôpital-Général. For one reason or another, he maintained, most beggars picked up off the streets and sent there rarely stayed. He favored sending able-bodied beggars to prison. Only the very old professional beggars or those so frail that they could not be punished "without exciting the unreasonable compassion of the populace of Paris" should in his view be sent to the Hôpital.[57] A more complete reversal of the original role of the Hôpital as envisioned by early enthusiasts like Vincent de Paul was hardly possible.

Despite the continued presence of 10,000 or more poor in the Hôpital-Général, there is little reason to think that the population of able-bodied beggars, the main preoccupation of the reformers from the start, had noticeably altered in the early eighteenth century. Large numbers of the less agile beggars—male and female—judging from the lists of inmates at the Hôpital, had been taken out of circulation, but that appears to have been about the net result. Lister, writing at the close of the seventeenth century, could see only "great multitudes of poor Wretches in all parts of this City." They were so numerous, he wrote, "that a Man in a Coach, a-foot, in the Shop, is not able to do any business for the numbers and importunities of Beggars; and to hear their Miseries is very lamentable; and if you give to one, you immediately bring a whole swarm upon you." A few years later, Nemeitz devoted an entire colorful chapter to the wiles of the beggars, who "overflow Paris to the point where one does not know how to avoid their importunities."[58] When Louis XIV paid one of his rare visits to his capital in 1700 he expressed surprise "that after all the measures that have been taken to chase the beggars out of Paris, such a large number still remain."[59] The King regretfully learned that vagrants had recently invaded the Church of Saint-Laurent and beaten up the beadle, and that bands of beggars, presumably armed, were terrorizing the environs of Paris. His Majesty gave the usual orders to pursue them "with all possible vigor and severity." Perhaps Louis XIV had discovered the only solution to the problem, namely, staying away from the city.

CHAPTER SEVEN

The police and the underworld

DESERVEDLY or not, Paris had long been reputed a city where physical security was at best precarious. Given the conditions that had prevailed long before the advent of Louis XIV and Colbert, given the large and constantly changing population, the woeful lack of professional police, the unlighted streets, divided responsibility for the maintenance of order, the ancient tradition among nobles, students, and others of autonomy from "ordinary" justice—given all this and more besides, nothing would be less surprising.

Lacking reliable and continuing crime statistics, no one can prove that Paris was relatively worse off than any other major European city in the seventeenth century. One would have no difficulty extracting from western European diaries, memoirs, and other sources of the period endless examples of mayhem committed on the streets of all large cities. Such material may make interesting reading but proves little or nothing about comparative safety. Admittedly, when one finds streets in Paris bearing such fearsome names as Rue Coupe-gorge or Rue Coupe-gueule, one is inclined to question the peacefulness of the citizens. Tradition held that these streets were so named because of the "massacres" and "brigandage" taking place there nightly.[1] However, such street nomenclature was ancient and largely limited to the University quarter. Where the dividing line lay between simple student brawling and more sophisticated criminal activity is hard to say.

Until Paris showed the way under Louis XIV, European cities had done strikingly little to organize themselves to combat crime. Quite possibly, like the problem of the poor with which it was so inextricably bound, criminal activity intensified markedly in the mid-seventeenth century, putting pressure on the magistrates to find new solutions for crime as well as for the poor. There is much evidence—unscientific to be sure—that street security in Paris sank to a nadir around mid-century. Such a conclusion is credible if one accepts a correlation between crime on the one hand and extensive foreign and civil war and economic distress on the other. As we will recall, Paris was being flooded with unprecedented numbers of beggars, vagabonds, and vagrants, a good percentage of whom we can safely assume to have been criminally inclined.

To many Parisians of the 1640's and 1650's, the bottom appeared to have dropped out of civilized society. The redoubtable Dr Guy Patin declared somberly, "Day and night, they rob and kill here. . . . We have arrived at the dregs of all the centuries."[2] Backing up his words were some statistics of murders in Paris shortly before the Fronde: 372 victims were recorded in one year, 14 being killed in one day.[3] Delamare later wrote that when Louis XIV came to the throne, the police of Paris was in a state of "almost universal disorder," that there was "no security, either in the city or in the country against robbers and assassins."[4] The Italian, Locatelli, observed that despite the execution of two or three criminals daily, street murders had become casual and even daylight affairs.[5] Visitors learned the facts of street life in Paris or did not survive to return home. The two young Dutch visitors noted in their journal for 1657 that after spending an evening at a Carnival ball, they gave their servants "pistols and muskets to escort us."[6] The editor of Louis XIV's administrative papers, Depping, concluded that in 1661 there "hardly existed what would merit the name police."[7] He cited a contemporary *mémoire* lamenting the dangers experienced by Parisians, especially in winter when the shortness of the days made it very difficult to get one's business done and still be off the streets before darkness fell. An anecdote of these grim times had a victim of a daylight robbery cry out to the thief, "Messieurs, you open shop very early today."[8] Representative of the assassins of the period was a Sieur Aubry who boasted a long string of "thrill" murders, including that of a sleeping beggar on the Pont Neuf killed, the police said, out of "gaiety of heart."[9]

157

Depending upon one's point of view and social prejudices, blame for all these disorders was placed alternately on vagabonds, soldiers, pages, and lackeys. Vagabonds had almost no defenders, of course, but the others could generally count on powerful support if the law ever caught up with them. Tradition demanded that both common soldiers and officers be turned back to their regiments for disciplining; the more elite the regiment, the more assured their protection. Other perennial trouble-makers were the servants of *les grands*, but when they got into trouble with the law, tradition and the honor of their employers demanded that the *grand seigneurs* back their flunkies. For example, the Queen-Mother, Anne of Austria, on one occasion dispatched her guard to a city prison to free forcibly two of her lackeys charged with killing a merchant.[10] Some of the great noblemen strode into the once august halls of the Parlement, swords at their sides and armed retainers following close behind, to demand their servants' release.

At the start of Louis XIV's reign, the Parlement, the highest court in France, was probably too demoralized as a result of its humiliating setback in the Fronde to protest such invasions. As one of its leading judges bitterly admitted, the Parlement was in "universal reprobation." The demoralization of the high court was symptomatic of all of official Paris. Public services were at a near standstill. Paris was "becoming a sewer" as a consequence of the failure to pay the cleaning contractors.[11]

It was to these conditions that the Conseil de Police addressed itself in 1666 and 1667. Its most important action was the creation of the office of Lieutenant of Police, probably the happiest institutional innovation in French municipal affairs during the entire Old Regime. As we have noted, the term "police" as used in the seventeenth century included every facet of municipal administration, but in practice nothing in the work of the new official seemed more important than the maintenance of street security. To think of him as a modern chief of police—the first anywhere in the Western world—is not going too far amiss.

There can be no gainsaying that La Reynie effected a striking improvement in maintaining good order in Paris. The very people—like Boileau, Patin, Sauval, the poet Robinet—who had earlier been decrying the lack of security now began to praise the new administration.

The journalist Colletet in the mid-1670's marveled at being able to cross the Pont Neuf, even after night had fallen, with perfect safety.[12] The new Lieutenant of Police's record of accomplishments in his first year in office was an enviable one by any standard. He took new measures against carrying arms on the streets, doubled the night watch and reformed its operations, led a spectacular raiding expedition into one of the inner sanctums of the underworld, and inaugurated the first street-lighting system in Paris.

There was nothing really new about the edict introduced in La Reynie's opening months in office forbidding unauthorized manufacture, storage, sale, and carrying of firearms, swords, brass knuckles, daggers, knives, and other lethal weapons.[13] Carrying arms on the streets of Paris had long been indulged in by nearly all classes. Even the bourgeois of the city claimed the right to do so by virtue of a disputed ordinance dating back to the fourteenth century,[14] and at one point the governors of the Hôtel-Dieu found it necessary to forbid its surgeons to carry swords while operating.[15] An army of policemen would have been required to enforce the sweeping new edict now announced by the Lieutenant of Police, and instead his police force was pitifully small. Almost certainly, despite the law's firm promise of "no exemptions," La Reynie intended to enforce it only against the pages and lackeys. In the general public enthusiasm which accompanied his first years in office, he doubtless managed, at least for the moment, to secure compliance. Indirect proof of this may be found in a police report of 1677 to the effect that "the lackeys begin again to carry swords during the night."[16] Nevertheless, to secure even partial compliance in as delicate a matter as disarming seventeenth-century Paris was no mean accomplishment for the new Lieutenant of Police.

Of more lasting impact was La Reynie's reorganization of the *guet*, or night watch. The authorized strength of this force, at least in the dangerous winter months, was more than trebled, from 120 to 400. The patrolmen's pay was more than doubled, from less than 4 sous to a minimum of 10. As a further morale booster, their nondescript apparel was replaced by colorful new blue uniforms. Even more important, the *guet* was ordered to cease its traditional sedentary habits. Instead of waiting for anguished citizens to seek it out, it was made to maintain continuous four- or five-man patrols from dusk to two o'clock in the morning (at which time Paris was by implication surrendered to malefactors). Evidencing laudable police sense, La Reynie ensured that the night patrols follow different routes through the streets every night so that "nothing was ever certain" to watching criminals.[17] A further illuminating provision of the law reorganizing the *guet* was the obligation placed on all citizens to come forward promptly with complaints against wrongdoers. It appears that out of fear of reprisals from organized criminal bands many citizens were failing to lodge complaints with the police.

Also within a few months of his appointment, La Reynie personally supervised the destruction of the most scandalous and pestiferous retreat of the Parisian underworld, the Cour des Miracles, known as such because of the miraculous recovery of its crippled and diseased inmates as they returned from their begging chores. For more years than anyone seemed to know, hundreds, perhaps thousands (Sauval estimated their number at 500 large families) of the "bad poor" of the city had used the area behind the thirteenth-century Convent of the Filles-Dieu in the north of Paris as a shelter from the law. When the decision had been reached during the relocation of the north wall in Louis XIII's reign to run a street through the Cour, its denizens had caused such an uproar and made things so difficult for the street contractors that they had finally been left alone.

The bourgeois of Paris were outraged by the inhabitants' philosophy of keeping nothing for the morrow and perhaps even more by their success in resisting the approach of tax-collectors. The clergy were scandalized by the godlessness of the inmates. Compounding the priests' distaste for the site and its inhabitants was the presence of a large religious statue at one end of the courtyard, stolen in the dim past from some unknown church.[18] The classic commentator on this unique landmark of Paris is the historian Sauval, who professed to have visited it shortly before it met its nemesis in the person of the new Lieutenant of Police. To him it seemed like some place "in another world," a verdict with which it is difficult to disagree. To reach the Cour, Sauval wrote, "one must often lose oneself in the narrow, wretched, stinking unfrequented streets; to enter it one must descend a long, tortuous, uneven slope. I saw there a half-buried mud hut, not even four *toises* [about 24 feet] square, tottering from old age and rottenness, where were nevertheless lodged more than fifty households encumbered with an infinity of little children—legitimate, natural, and stolen."[19]

For any reform-minded police officer, the Cour des Miracles was of particular interest and concern because it housed the equivalent of a twentieth-century city's "crime syndicate." In a day when everything had to be organized in autonomous guilds with their own officers and statutes, it was reasonable to expect that crime would follow suit. The denizens of the Cour had not one but several organizations, each with national offshoots, and the whole ruled by a grand monarch known as the Grand Coësre. They boasted hierarchies of subsidiary officials, each with a more impossible title than the next; representative assemblies ("estates") in a day when their country had mostly forgotten such things had ever existed; rules for apprentices; elaborate scales of punishments; and so on.

Of the various "guilds" represented at the Cour des Miracles, the purse cutters were the most prestigious. To be promoted from apprentice to journeyman, one had to perform two elaborate *chefs d'oeuvres*, the first a complicated test of physical dexterity and the other an actual purse snatching. Sauval related how in some busy place like the Holy Innocents Cemetery the aspirant's skill might be put to the ultimate test by having a gang member give a public and unexpected alarm so as to measure his skill in evading pursuers. While the purse cutters merited the accolade for dexterity, surely the members of the beggars' guild deserved one for ingenuity. Their forte was simulating all kinds of horrible diseases and conditions to gain the sympathy of pedestrians. They would pass themselves off as epileptics by filling their mouths with sudsy water, or as multiple amputees just returned from the wars, or as wretched victims of hydrophobia trying to gather together a few sous for a visit to a curative shrine.

The establishment of the Hôpital-Général in 1656 had somewhat demoralized the Cour des Miracles. The Grand Coësre and many of his officers and subjects disappeared into that institution as the police stepped up their efforts to rid the streets of all beggars.[20] Finally in 1667 La Reynie marched in at the head of two hundred or so armed men and with the help of a squadron of sappers borrowed from the Swiss Regiment stormed and captured the ill-famed Cour des Miracles.

The campaign to rid Paris of robbers, purse snatchers, and other thieves continued apace. In 1672 we find Colbert bravely claiming to the intendant of Poitou that robbers had been totally eliminated in Paris and twitting him for being so far behind the times in his own province.[21] The King professed to be much gratified and, perhaps prematurely, ordered a medal struck commemorating "the reestablishment of public safety."[22]

The year 1667 was memorable for much more than the elimination of the Cour des Miracles, for it was then that the new municipal street-lighting system was inaugurated and Paris finally emerged from its age-old nocturnal gloom. No longer did pedestrians have to rely desperately on moonlight, their flickering hand lanterns, or stray friendly reflections from the windows of shopkeepers and taverners. Under La Reynie's orders, up to 6,500 lanterns were strung across the streets, a number which did not increase appreciably until well along in the next reign and probably even declined at times.[23] Lister in his visit of 1698 was all praises for the new lights and thought the "near 50,000 l. Sterling" they cost to operate five months each year well worth the price.[24] He particularly admired the policy of keeping the lights burning throughout all the winter nights, contrasting this more open-handed practice with "the impertinent usage of our People at London to take away the Lights for half of the Month, as though the Moon was certain to shine and light the Streets and that there could be no Cloudy Weather in Winter."[25]

La Reynie's lanterns consisted of simple squares of glass reinforced at the edges by iron frames. They utilized quarter-pound candles made of "good and trusty tallow of Paris."[26] One unscrupulous manufacturer was once fined the enormous sum of 1,000 livres for providing candles made of butter (*sic*) and grease. Supplying these candles became "big business." At the end of the century over 200,000 pounds of candles were used annually to light the streets, and one heard occasional charges that the butchers were conspiring to corner the tallow market and drive up prices.[27]

The innovation of 1667 was by no means the first attempt to relieve the darkness of the streets. In the sixteenth century, and probably even earlier, efforts were made to persuade the citizens living on lower stories of houses to keep candles at their windows during the early evening hours. In 1588 (a more inopportune time can hardly be imagined for such experimentation), the Parlement of Paris ordered the fabrication of lanterns to be placed at the windows of householders at public expense. None of this worked. The lanterns were soon sold to pay for the cost of manufacture,[28] and nothing more was attempted until Louis XIV's time.

In 1662 an Italian *abbé* of the distinguished Caraffa family obtained a privilege for the rental of lanterns and torches on the principal streets of Paris. The *abbé*'s plan was to establish stations spaced six hundred feet apart at which one could rent a lantern for 1 sou to use from one station to the next. The torches, more expensive but giving off a great deal more light than the lanterns, were pound-and-a-half sticks of tallow inscribed with the arms of Paris and marked off into ten divisions. One paid according to the divisions one consumed.[29] Caraffa's plan was probably quite sound except that it came too late. The Paris of young Louis XIV and Colbert was ready for bolder schemes based on the principle that street lighting was the common responsibility of the bourgeois, just as street cleaning had long been recognized to be. The lighting ordinance of September 1667 provided that the relatively high cost of operating the system should be met by a new tax supplementing the old street-cleaning levy. The resulting *taxe des boues et lanternes* was destined to become very familiar for the balance of the Old Regime as the only direct levy on property owners.

While La Reynie's street lights were a marvelous novelty, the system by which they were operated was strictly traditional in its complexity and excessive decentralization of authority. The financing of the lanterns was placed in the hands of select committees of the bourgeoisie in each of the then seventeen quarters of the city; the purchase of all equipment was entrusted to the Lieutenant of Police; overall supervision of the operation was given to the latter's subordinates, the *commissaires*. The actual nightly lighting of the lanterns was the province of men quite independent of any of the foregoing. Once a year, the residents contiguous to a string of ten lanterns convened to elect from their number a *commis-allumeur* who for the next year enjoyed the unenviable (and unpaid) privilege of making his rounds before dusk each evening with his basket of fresh candles and inserting one in each lantern as it was lowered by rope and pulley from one of the second-floor windows. (In the better neighborhoods, it was customary for the nominee to hire some laborer to perform the duty of lamplighter.)

One of the great difficulties in the operation, the authorities soon discovered, was the failure of residents to lower their lanterns at the moment the *allumeur* appeared in the street below them. La Reynie therefore issued a police regulation in 1671 which called for the ringing of a bell to signal the arrival of the lamplighter on the street.[30] However, the problem was only solved when the lamp-lowering mechanism was enclosed in a locked box set at the street level, thus obviating the need to rely on the residents. These devices had become so widely used by the start of the eighteenth century that Louis XIV, by this time overlooking no possible source of revenue, imposed a sort of luxury tax on them. Indignant owners responded by tearing down their boxes by the hundreds, causing a momentary lighting crisis in the city. The Lieutenant of Police restored order only by personally walking about the streets to assure citizens that the King intended to tax only a very limited category of wealthy users.[31]

It would appear almost impossible for moderns, except possibly those who have lived in a large city under wartime conditions, to fathom the psychological impact of the new lanterns on the Parisian population. An historian of the subject has commented on the fascination which the nightly ritual exercised on the citizens, how the sound of the signal bell would cause them to gather at their windows and stop on the streets to watch the heavy lanterns descend and reascend armed with a fat candle. As night came on, the reassuring shadow of the rooster, the symbol of vigilance mounted on top the lanterns, would appear on adjacent walls.[32] If some vandal or wrongdoer did not interfere between patrols of the watch, or if wind or rain did not enter the air holes and snuff out the light, the candle burned until about two o'clock in the morning. A possible galley sentence awaited anyone convicted of breaking the lights, and Lister tells of "3 young Gentlemen of good Families who were in Prison [for months] for having done it in a Frolick."[33]

Originally, the season for street lights was limited to the worst winter months, from November 1 to February 28, but after experiencing the intoxication of illuminated streets for a few months, the citizenry manifested its readiness to finance an expanded service.[34] Consequently, the *commissaires* from the Châtelet arranged for meetings of the neighborhood oligarchies which decided such matters, and after much sounding out of opinions it was resolved to add forty days to the burning season. The new season extended from October 20 to March 31. One faction wished to save money by eliminating the candles during the full moon, but this was voted down on the grounds that criminal activity was at its peak then since the moonlight never quite reached down into the narrow, crooked streets where most crimes were committed.[35] In 1708, the service was again extended, despite the sad state of the economy, and now ran from September 1 to the end of May.[36]

Lighting an area as large as that of Paris by candlelight would seem a difficult undertaking indeed, but—especially on the busier streets where supplementary illumination could be counted on from shops, carriages, and other sources—it seems to have been quite effective. Nemeitz observed that "it was all very pretty to watch."[37] The lanterns, according to Lister, hung 20 feet above the ground and about 60 feet apart.[38] The second figure is credible and agrees with other estimates, but a height of 20 feet would appear somewhat excessive and self-defeating. Some authorities maintain so positively that they hung in the middle of the street, and others, with equal assurance, from the sides of buildings, that one is led to conclude that both methods were employed depending upon circumstances. There are also differences in the estimates of the number of lanterns on the streets of Paris ranging from 4,500 to 6,500,[39] the lower figure generally being cited for the end of the reign and the higher for La Reynie's time. However, an apparently reliable census showed 5,580 lanterns in 1715,[40] in close agreement with the figure of 5,522 shown on a map of Paris for 1715. If we accept an estimate of 5,500 and intervals of 60 feet, the result would have been the illumination, all in the early part of Louis XIV's personal reign, of some 65 miles of city streets—a very respectable civic accomplishment certainly.

Before the end of Louis XIV's reign, still another municipal service, professional fire fighting, came into being. Until that time, techniques employed to keep fires in check had changed very little since the Middle Ages. Bucket brigades manned by residents had continued to be the principal weapon against conflagrations. As soon as a fire was detected, the *commissaire* of the quarter was supposed to be notified and would take charge at the scene. If the ordinances had been obeyed, buckets, axes, and ladders were to be found stored in the houses of the *commissaire, quartenier,* or *dizainier.*

The main problem was finding a nearby water supply for the bucket brigade. For some obvious firetraps like the wooden sheds of the Saint-Germain fair, owners provided substantial nearby water reservoirs to be used if the need arose.[41] A private well on the scene was, of course, a great boon for fighting smaller fires, and La Reynie had established a 50-livre fine for householders neglecting to maintain their back-yard wells in good operating condition. Public wells were another obvious source of supply, but if an underground conduit ran close by the burning house, the *commissaire* would likely give the order to *dépaver* and tap the pipe. Often little could be done except to prevent the blaze from spreading, so it was very important for knowledgeable people like masons, carpenters, and roofers to be on hand if needed. If such nearby mechanics did not heed the tocsin, they risked the loss of their guild privileges.[42] Residents of the Saint-Honoré quarter were fortunate in having available the services of the volunteer fire fighters from the Capuchin convent in the Rue Saint-Honoré, recipients of gifts from the farsighted members of Molière's theatrical company, among others.[43]

In the last quarter of the century, hand-powered, wheeled water pumps began to make their appearance in Holland. Jan van der Heyden's device was perhaps the first to come into use there. A syringelike contraption enabled him to squirt a jet of water to the top floors of city houses.[44] It was probably his machine which furnished the model in 1699 for the *pompes à incendie* promoted by a versatile actor at the Comédie by the name of Dumourier Dupérier. They were successfully demonstrated at several fires, but because of the reluctance of the magistrates to invest in the new devices at a time when the city was on the verge of insolvency, a few years passed before they received official sanction.

A turning point in Dupérier's fortunes came in 1704 when a fire broke out in the Tuileries. Several notables happened to be present, including the Lieutenant of Police, the Superintendent of Buildings, Mansart, and the great Marshal Vauban. Someone sent out a call for "Dupérier, *comédien*, with his pumps."[45] His distinguished audience saw him dart water "wherever he wanted" and he was credited with extinguishing the fire. "*Admirable*," wrote one witness to the Controller-General at Versailles.[46] Dupérier was put in charge of the city's first fire department the following year, but his troubles were not over. In the financial disasters of the closing years of the reign, fire fighting was sacrificed on the altar of economy and Dupérier disappeared temporarily from the scene, to be recalled in the last year of the reign when the pumps were revived and fire fighting established on a permanent basis.[47] In 1716 the actor-turned-fireman was finally recognized as Directeur Général of the city's fire pumps at a salary of 6,000 livres annually. He became responsible for maintaining sixteen pumps (thirty by 1722)[48] stored in strategic locations, mainly convents, about the city. Each contraption was manned by a trained two-man crew, whose professional status was signified by *bonnets particuliers* by which they could be more easily recognized in the hubbub of a street fire.[49]

The centralization of police authority in the hands of the Lieutenant of Police, the reformation of the ancient *guet*, the illumination of the streets, and the new professionalism in fire fighting were all undoubtedly great steps forward in the proper administration of the city. Unfortunately, the constabulary itself remained as archaic as the old system of lighting streets by ordering householders to place candles on their window sills or of extinguishing dangerous blazes by improvised bucket brigades. What La Reynie and D'Argenson needed was a professional police force responsive to their orders, but what they had to settle for was a motley assortment of autonomous, venal, and self-serving office-holders. We have noted La Reynie's vigorous but only partially successful efforts to create a modern administrative tradition among his key subordinates, the forty-eight *commissaires*. No comparable effort was made to create such a tradition among the rank and file of the police. Within the latter were to be found not one but several independent "corporations," each largely unmindful of its nominal superior at the Châtelet and long accustomed to looking within its own membership for direction. The system was so time-honored that even a powerful minister like Colbert drew back at reform when faced with similar situations.

In considering the make-up of the police force of seventeenth-century Paris, one can give short shrift to the constabulary of the Hôtel de Ville (generally referred to as the *archers de la ville*). Like the institution it professed to serve, it was in full decadence in the later seventeenth century. At one point in Louis XIV's reign the Prévôt des Marchands, contemplating "the uncleanliness of many [of the members]," felt compelled to order their return to the practice of wearing uniforms.[50] The *archers* had relatively little to do with the maintenance of physical security and were much more concerned with exploiting the privileges (mainly exemption from entry taxes on wines) which they had accumulated over the centuries than with serving the public. Their numbers were not unimpressive by the standards of that day: they consisted of three companies totaling 300 rank and file, commanded by six sergeants, nine ensigns, three captains, an *aide-major*, a major lieutenant-colonel, and colonel. To keep alive a semblance of discipline, the three companies ostensibly held weekly drills with the arquebus and monthly exercises of an unspecified nature on the ramparts. Although the magistrates had reason, apparently, to complain about their everyday appearance, on ceremonial occasions they blossomed out with halberd, plumery, trumpets, and fine accouterments of all sorts. As was true of almost all the various police units, the *archers de ville* had a common treasury in which all fees and fines accruing to the members were deposited and divided periodically among them.

While the reality of power now lay in the Châtelet's hands rather than those of the Hôtel de Ville, anyone seeking the spirit of modernity in the Châtelet's police would be disappointed. It consisted of totally separate day and night components, the day unit being subdivided into three additional corps, also mutually independent. This chaotic organization was somewhat meliorated by the creation of the office of Lieutenant of Police in 1667. For the first time all four units of the constabulary were placed under unified command. But their subordination to the new magistrate was almost the only thing they had in common. In accordance with the practice of the times, and like the *archers* of the Hôtel de Ville, the police of the Châtelet were organized into "communities" very much on the same order as those of the butchers, bakers, and artisans. Each had its own officers, rules for admission, rules for remaining in good standing (with the community itself and not necessarily with the Châtelet), its own treasury, patron saint, provisions for its widows and orphans, and so on.

By something on the order of treaty agreements between sovereign powers, these four communities condescended to furnish personnel to the Châtelet for police duties. But like most treaties between sovereign authorities, these agreements were subject to contention, and the Châtelet repeatedly had to resort to the courts in order to force the communities to furnish necessary personnel.[51] The root of the trouble was that the police functionaries of the Châtelet made their living, not from salaries, but from fines and fees collected in the course of their duties.[52] All these went into a common purse (*deniers communs*), with distributions made periodically by the officers according to grade. Since some types of police duties, mainly those of a civil nature rather than criminal, paid better than others, these naturally took priority.

Peculations and malversations among the police were notorious, and it is enlightening how a person who had been bilked or blackmailed by one of them could attempt to obtain redress. That indispensable compendium of everyday information, *Le Livre commode des adresses de Paris* (1692), tells us that there were two ways one could obtain redress of grievances. If one insisted upon a fairly neutral tribunal and were not in too great haste, one could appeal to the Lieutenant Civil of the Châtelet, who held an annual session devoted to complaints against the police immediately after Trinity Sunday. But if a complainant desired a faster hearing, he could attend the weekly meetings of the community's officers any Sunday morning at its headquarters and present his grievances to that tribunal. How much satisfaction one could obtain from the confrères of the accused man was, of course, questionable.

It is very difficult to judge how many agents of the law in seventeenth-century Paris were engaged during daylight hours in maintaining good order in the city as opposed to acting as court functionaries. General law enforcement officers, leaving aside the nonentities of the Hôtel de Ville and a few other specialized and unimportant services, consisted of the forty-eight *commissaires* (residing for the most part in their respective neighborhoods); 120 *huissiers-priseurs*; 380 *huissiers à cheval*; and 240 *huissiers* or *sergents* (in the seventeenth century the two terms were synonymous), all under the command, at least on paper, of the Lieutenant of Police at the Châtelet.[53] If all these near-800 men had been engaged in law enforcement in the strict sense, Paris would have boasted a very impressive police force; but most of them were at any given moment serving instead as bailiffs or clerks of court.[54] The 120 members of the community of *huissiers-priseurs* dealt exclusively with the seizure and sale of goods ordered by court judgments and were excused from service as criminal police. The 380 *huissiers à cheval* traveled anywhere in France on court business for any magistrate of the Châtelet, although a limited number were allowed to operate in Paris. One might think that this would have provided the courts of the Châtelet with all bailiffs and messengers that they could possibly need. But apparently the requirements of the judiciary were endless: if one reads the statutes of the remaining group—the 240 *huissiers* or *sergents*—one sees that they, too, were mainly concerned with picking up odd sums here and there on court business, as, for example, 4 deniers for delivering a summons on a layman (12 on a churchman), a sou for making a court arrest, 2 sous for escorting a prisoner from the Châtelet to the Parlement, 12 deniers for affixing a seal on the property of a wrongdoer, and so on.

Nevertheless, from the company of *huissiers* was selected daily a body of men to serve as policemen (in the modern sense) under the orders of the *commissaires*, as well as a sufficient number to staff the *barrières*, or police posts, scattered about the city (the *Livre commode* lists eleven of these in 1692). The seventeenth-century equivalent of "getting a cop" was either sending for a *sergent à la première barrière*, or knocking on the door of the nearest *commissaire*.

Come nightfall in Paris, all the foregoing (except the *commissaires*) went off duty and were replaced by the *guet* or night watch, which set out from the Châtelet as dusk fell to take up its assigned patrols in the various quarters of the city. There was nothing in this organization remindful of the citizens' watch of medieval times; it was purely professional in its make-up and paid by the king rather than the municipality. (The annual cost between 1685 and 1715 ranged between 115,000 and 125,000 livres.) Colbert, as we observed, had doubled the *guet* in the 1660's, but because of financial difficulties its strength had slowly declined so that in 1698 it stood at 200 men in winter, 100 in summer, plus about 50 men on horseback.[55] About this time the *guet* was made up of twenty-four squads, sixteen of which went on duty each evening, while the other eight rested. Their armament consisted of a pocket pistol (*pistolet de poche*) and a "heavy lantern," their uniform of elegant blue jerkins laced in silver and capped by a plumed hat.

Unlike the day police the *guet* does not give the impression of being mere adjuncts of the courts. As a matter of fact, a regulation of 1688 prohibited its members from becoming involved in civil affairs, this being considered the province of the day police.[56] The business of the *guet* was gamblers, assassins, robbers, drunks, and other disturbers of the public peace, who apparently were considered mainly nocturnal problems. One of its regulations prescribed that the watchmen make their rounds diligently, listening from time to time at the street corners, and occasionally making countermarches "to more easily surprise the robbers."[57] The strategy of roving patrols introduced by La Reynie continued in use throughout the reign.

Early in the eighteenth century some of the *guet* were kept on duty until daybreak instead of being sent home when the street lanterns burned out at about two in the morning. D'Argenson reported with satisfaction to his superiors at Versailles that hardly a night went by without an arrest by the new early morning patrols, most often of tenants attempting to flee their lodgings without settling their accounts.[58] People arrested by the *guet* for minor offences were supposed to be taken to the Châtelet, although they could be placed in any nearby prison on condition that they were transferred to the Châtelet by eight the following morning.[59] (The magistrates were obviously concerned that the culprits might somehow fall out of their jurisdiction.) Serious offenders like murderers were preferably taken, even in the middle of the night, to the house of the *commissaire*, along with witnesses. The *commissaires* were urged to hold a preliminary questioning on the spot.

Supplementing both day and night police when needed were the regular royal troops garrisoned in or about the city. Ostensibly in Paris to guard royal buildings, they were far more numerous than such a pedestrian task warranted. Louis XIV, like the *grands seigneurs* with respect to their errant lackeys and pages, was very indulgent towards his troops, especially members of elite units like the musketeers. Doubtless on account of the favored treatment they had come to expect, discipline was notoriously bad among the soldiery in Paris. More often than not, they were on the side of the lawbreakers rather than lawkeepers. In the bread riots of 1692 and 1693, some members of the Gardes Françaises placed themselves at the head of the rioters. The Lieutenant of Police described these soldiers as the "terror of all the bourgeois and the sworn enemies of public order."[60] On possibly only one occasion during Louis XIV's reign did the supporters of "public order" seem eager for the presence of the troops. During the terrible winter of 1708-1709, so dangerous was the state of popular opinion and so much did the citizens fear the outbreak of civil strife that the bourgeois prevailed upon the King to station fourteen companies of the Gardes in Paris instead of the customary six.[61] Perhaps because of increased bread rations, the soldiers remained for once on the side of the law. D'Argenson wrote that without them he would have been in serious straits.[62]

Normally, Louis XIV stationed three military units in Paris—the famous Musketeers, the Cent-Suisses, and the Gardes Françaises. Since the city had long been exempted from the notorious obligation of troop quarterings, these detachments were housed either in barracks or in the faubourgs. The First Company of Musketeers (called the Greys from the color of their mounts) enjoyed after 1671 a prestigious location in the Faubourg Saint-Germain opposite the Tuileries Palace. The housing of the Black Musketeers (the Second Company) was the subject of a great deal of bickering between the King and the Hôtel de Ville. Neither side wished to absorb the cost of building suitable barracks. Finally in 1701 an arrangement was worked out whereby the Hôtel de Ville agreed to build barracks in the Faubourg Saint-Antoine, just under the shadow of the Bastille.[63] In return, the municipality was released from further obligations for building the Place Louis-le-Grand (the modern Place Vendôme), then causing its sponsors such headaches.

The perennial problem, however, was presented by the regiment of the Gardes Françaises, large and notoriously undisciplined. Like all regiments, this one had a *maréchal des logis*, responsible for assigning soldiers to individual households in the faubourgs so unfortunate as to be subject to troop quarterings. In theory, the soldiers were assigned quarters close by their company officers, so as to permit a measure of surveillance; but somehow this sensible arrangement never worked out. Dissatisfied with their assignments, the troops habitually commandeered their own quarters and lived lives of happy debauchery as far away as possible from their company officers.[64] One of the most persistent laments heard in the Paris of the Grand Siècle concerned the depravations of *les gardes*. Royal orders prohibiting guardsmen from walking on the streets of Paris in groups larger than three, or even being on the streets one hour after sunset, apparently had little effect. No one dared enforce them.

ᣚ   ᣚ

In trying to carry out their responsibilities, La Reynie and D'Argenson often lamented shortage of manpower. They were justified, of course, but perhaps more to the point would have been complaints about the crushing range of their responsibilities, completely out of proportion to the size of their commands. The municipal police were expected to enforce a multiplicity of laws most of which had nothing to do with the physical security of the city and which in time would become the province of separate municipal bureaucracies. Sanitation, the control of disease, the regulation of the water supply, building regulations, the supervision of prices, the overseeing of fairs and markets, the enforcement of a mass of sumptuary laws which reason said were unenforceable—all this and much more were piled on the backs of the forty-eight *commissaires* and their few assistants. Most laws were in a constant state of suspension for want of enforcing agents and herein probably lay the best explanation of the lighthearted attitude of the public towards the law. No matter how many times the same statute was issued and reissued and penalties stiffened, the public could not but be aware that it would remain largely unenforced simply because the authorities did not have the physical means to ensure otherwise.

Louis XIV, instead of lightening the impossible burden of the Lieutenant of Police, added immeasurably thereto by reviving many long-dormant laws, or creating new ones, pertaining to the "moral police" of his capital. Few Parisians could have missed the irony of Louis XIV's determination, after legitimatizing numerous natural offspring and engaging in double adultery for a dozen years, to convert Paris into something approaching Calvin's Geneva. The scholarly editor of the archives of the Bastille (who should have been in a position to judge) once asserted that Louis XIV was the first king of France to occupy himself with the morality of his subjects.[65] This may be too sweeping a statement, but it is well known that Louis underwent a moral transformation in the 1680's. An interesting consequence of his own moral reform was his determination to reform the moral climate of Paris. From his relationship with the pious Mme de Maintenon he gained not only a morganatic wife but a new appreciation of religion and of his duties as a Christian king. His new zeal was expressed in laws relating to the

Sabbath and Lenten regulations, to proper conduct in church, and to the equally difficult tasks of suppressing prostitution, gambling, and scandalous personal behavior of all varieties. Such activities, of course, imposed great demands on the Parisian police, although the pious and strait-laced D'Argenson, unlike La Reynie, probably found the added burden not altogether uncongenial.

Louis XIV's concern with personal conduct was concentrated on but by no means limited to the privileged classes. He took great interest in preserving the honor of distinguished families, provincial as well as Parisian. Incredible as it may seem, such matters were under constant scrutiny in the King's council[66] (along with decisions on such humdrum matters as foreign policy). His minister for Parisian affairs was under standing orders to provide him with information on the personal lives of the upper classes, such information generally coming from the most knowledgeable person in the realm on such matters, the Lieutenant of Police. In 1705, for example, Pontchartrain wrote to D'Argenson for information on the goings-on between the Chevalier de Gonzague and Mlle de la Motte (plenty, apparently). "You cannot go into too great detail," the minister wrote; "the smallest circumstances will be pleasant to know."[67] The editor of this correspondence noted that Pontchartrain requested information on the same couple no fewer than ten times and surmises the requests came from the King.

Typical of the innumerable reports the Lieutenants of Police submitted to Versailles was one concerning a well-born chevalier from Toulon and his sister living in Paris on their mother's pension. Both were heavily involved in love affairs and well on their way to exhausting the family fortune. On request from above, the police paid a call on the two, issued a warning and obtained promises from both that they would mend their ways.[68] In this case, the parties obeyed. If they had not, the usual procedure was for a royal councilor to invite the family to submit a petition (*placet*) for the King's intervention by *lettre de cachet*. This was simply a brief note from the King, countersigned by a Secretary of State and generally delivered by the Lieutenant of Police, ordering a particular individual to take such action as returning home, going into exile, or reporting to some place of incarceration. Honor being what it was among the upper classes, the recipients could always be counted on to accept the King's wishes without duress.

There was clearly a double standard of justice, and aristocratic wrongdoers could generally count on having their cases kept out of court. But such malefactors could still expect to face the King's personal justice. This could perhaps consist of nothing more than a fatherly admonition, but frequently resulted in far more severe judgments. The monarch could choose from among a number of places of confinement in Paris alone, to say nothing of the provinces. If the blue-blooded culprit was sent where there were prisoners of "regular" justice, he was supposed to be strictly segregated from the others and separate prison registers were to be kept for the King's perusal. (An ever-present hazard of seventeenth-century justice was being forgotten in prison.) The officers of the Châtelet other than the Lieutenant of Police were told quite firmly not to concern themselves with the King's prisoners, for the first consideration was maintaining secrecy so as to spare family pride.[69] However, when the King learned that families were confining relatives by falsely alleging his agreement, he relented to the extent of permitting the police at least to verify the orders for imprisonment.[70]

The most elite of all prisons in France was the Bastille. Contemporary writers spoke of its *noblesse*.[71] While the impecunious inmates of "ordinary" prisons were allowed a theoretical daily maintenance allowance of 4 sous, those at the Bastille received the munificent sum of 50 sous. Traditionally, however, jailers everywhere pocketed most of their prisoners' allowances. At the Bastille, as at all Old Regime prisons, an inmate without resources of his own was in a sad predicament; but most Bastille prisoners had such resources, and unless a man was specially tagged for rigorous treatment, life could be relatively pleasant. There were no mass dungeons as at the Châtelet. The eight large towers making up the structure had rooms for prisoners on each of four or five levels, and only the ground floor, because of its dampness and its earthen construction, was considered particularly undesirable. Some of the inmates had personal servants to do their cooking, were allowed the freedom of the battlements and courtyards, and even permitted occasional visitors. Others, however, were strictly confined to their cells and could speak to no one. Adding to the dread but not entirely deserved reputation of the place was the strict rule that even after release one was forbidden to say anything about one's experiences there under pain of rearrest.[72]

On an entirely different level from the Bastille as a place of confinement for the victims of "irregular justice" were the two largest units of the Hôpital-Général: Bicêtre for men, Salpêtrière for women and children. Rather early in its history, as we have noted, the Hôpital-Général became in part a sort of penal institution, but well-born people, at least those who had maintained a semblance of the noble way of life, were only occasionally sent there. For example, one of the letters of the Lieutenant of Police tells of the wife of a high-ranking army officer who repeatedly became *enceinte* when her husband was off at war. D'Argenson wrote Versailles for instructions on what to do with her. No convent would have her as a boarder and the Hôpital, he wrote, was not befitting a person of her rank.[73]

On the other hand, there was the case of a "gentleman from Anjou" guilty of incest—a crime, the King wrote, "well to hide from the public"—who was sent in 1704 to the Hôpital-Général for the rest of his days.[74] Why he was not sent to the Bastille where similar acts against nature were frequently punished is not clear; most likely neither his lineage nor the state of his finances earned him the honors of the state prison.

While the two main units of the Hôpital-Général infrequently saw blue-bloods, one small unit, the Refuge (also known as Sainte-Pélagie), run by nuns under the administration of the Hôpital-Général, was frequently employed by the King to confine well-born ladies bent on disgracing their families. (Statistics are lacking, but one can readily see that females were much more frequently subjected to the King's "family discipline" than males.) The Refuge was without question a *clôture honteuse*. It could be assumed that neither the inmates nor their families had the financial resources to pay board at more acceptable places of detention. If the situation became intolerable for the lady, a family council might convene to find ways of financing her board at a private institution, and a *placet* would accordingly be submitted to the King asking for permission to make the change.[75] The second wife of the famous Italian actor Scaramouche, although certainly not a noble lady, was sent to the Refuge in 1693 because of scandalous misconduct with a young man. But her estranged husband, although a notorious tightwad, took pity on her and had her transferred to a convent, promising to pay her board there.[76] A case of a different sort was that of the lady who went about publicly proclaiming that since she did not love her husband, she had the right to withhold herself from him. D'Argenson tried to scotch this dangerous doctrine by recommending to Versailles that she be sent to the Refuge for two or three months so that she would see that there were even sadder places in the world than at the side of an unloved husband. (Pontchartrain's marginal notation was, "Too harsh. Speak to her severely."[77])

The place of detention *par excellence* for aristocratic female malefactors was the convent. It was generally well disciplined, secure, dependable, and discreet. For 500 livres or so a year, paid by the family or the inmate herself, any one of a number of convents in the city (the provinces were less expensive but also less desirable even for one who could expect to remain behind convent walls) could usually be prevailed upon by the police to take in a boarder for disciplining. Because some of these high-born lodgers could be disruptive of the conventual routine, the Lieutenant of Police might be forced to put pressure on a religious superior or even appeal to the Archbishop to have one of his errant ladies admitted.[78] D'Argenson was for a number of years in conflict with the superior of the famous convent of the Madeleine, who was much more intent on her house's apostolate of aiding repentant streetwalkers than in coping with the eccentricities of *grandes dames* or their troublesome offspring. He charged her with laxity in enforcing security rules and with being less interested in the preservation of "public order" than with the "good order" of her own sisters.[79]

Probably, other convents would have liked to show the independence of the Madeleine but either could not financially afford to or did not care to show themselves uncooperative with the police. There was, for example, a Mme de Savonnière who as a young bride had been so dissolute that her husband (a high *parlementaire*) had obtained the

King's consent to relegate her to a provincial convent. Now, twenty years later, her husband dead, she was back in Paris so intent on making up for lost time with her husband's legacy that her conduct came to the attention of the King, and D'Argenson was asked to investigate. A convent was obviously in order, but her reputation was too notorious for most religious houses. D'Argenson finally persuaded one (the Bernardines), whose extreme poverty was as notorious as the lady's behavior, to accept her, "whatever it might cost their delicacy and peace."[80]

On the other hand, some convents, instead of annoying the police simply because they wished to remain convents, were perversely taken to task for their laxity. D'Argenson referred to these as "contraband convents from which one leaves at all hours and which are really only seminaries of debauchery." One of the most troublesome "religious" houses of this sort was the Convent of the Saint-Esprit in the Faubourg Saint-Germain. One of the parish priests in that neighborhood wrote to D'Argenson complaining that an adulterous woman theoretically confined to the convent was seen daily in carriage promenades with her lover. "The sisters and their boarders," D'Argenson wrote disgustedly, "live in nearly equal liberty."[81] When a well-born girl guilty of incest could not be placed in any convent but one of this character, D'Argenson ordered that she be allowed instead to remain with her mother.[82]

While a dozen or more convents are mentioned repeatedly in D'Argenson's reports to Versailles as quasi-prisons for well-born ladies whose misconduct reached the ears of the King, only two male counterparts can be discerned—Charenton and Saint-Lazare. Discipline in both was strict, but neither entailed the notoriety incurred by a sentence to the Bastille or the Hôpital-Général. Like the convents and other places of detention, they were supervised by the Lieutenant of Police, who tried his best with the limited resources at his command to ensure that inmates were not forgotten.[83] Saint-Lazare, the old leprosarium in the northern outskirts of the city turned over to Vincent de Paul's Congregation of the Mission after leprosy began to fade out of existence, specialized in young delinquents of good family. For five or six hundred livres annually, the priests were so successful in rehabilitation that Sauval maintained that "children are almost never sent elsewhere." Male adults were likely to be sent to either Saint-Lazare or Charenton when the monarch wished, for the sake of their families, to keep their adventures out of public view. Of three young men charged with homosexuality, whose fathers held high posts in the magistracy, one was sent to the Bastille, another to the provinces, and the third, in response to a *placet* from his parents, to Charenton, where they promised to keep him "a long time."[84] Another parlementarian was spared the disgrace of a *mésalliance* in his family by petitioning the King to send his son to Saint-Lazare and the girl to a convent.[85] When the King consented to do so, D'Argenson sent the head of the family his felicitations for the "kindness the King has done."

Louis XIV's striking concern with upper-class behavior and family honor was no more than one facet of his "moral police" in the latter part of his reign. Seignelay told La Reynie in 1688 that "His Majesty intends to establish order in Paris in all kinds of matters." Inevitably he was allured by the prospect of cleaning Paris of two of its worst social scandals—prostitution and gambling.

When Louis XIV began his personal reign in 1661, legal prostitution had been absent from the Parisian scene for almost exactly a century. The early 1560's saw the closing of the 300-year-old center of Parisian vice, a short distance southeast of the Cour des Miracles, known as the Huleu. The name was derived from the Rue du Grand-Hurleur which traversed it and which had in turn received its name from the neighbors' inclination to greet emerging patrons with howls of derision.[86] The Huleu and the Rue de Glatigny in the Cité had been perhaps the only areas where houses of ill fame were allowed; prostitutes caught practicing their trade elsewhere were liable to be rudely returned to their legal quarters sitting backwards astride a mule.

Needless to say, the closing of the old legal centers of vice had resulted only in scattering their inmates about the city. Probably the best authority for the state of Parisian prostitution at the start of Louis XIV's personal reign was the very respectable bourgeois historian Henri Sauval. Unwilling to shock the readers of his large three-volume history of the city with the seamier aspects of Parisian life, he wrote a separate chapter entitled *La Chronique scandaleuse de Paris*. Writing in the 1660's, Sauval conjectured that prostitution had increased since it had been prohibited a century earlier. (Even more lamentable, if true, was his assertion that the professionals were constantly complaining that "their trade was worth nothing since honest women had gotten mixed up in it.")[87] "If we wish to listen to scandalous . . . sayings," the author primly told his readers, prostitutes were scattered about the Right Bank along half a dozen or more streets, the majority in the Saint-Martin quarter not far from the notorious district from which they had been chased a century earlier.[88] (Unfortunately, Sauval had nothing to say about the Left Bank.)

In the century after the abolition of legal prostitution the magistrates had carried on a two-pronged but manifestly unenthusiastic campaign against prostitution; one aspect directed against the practitioners, the other against their landlords. The latest of these ordinances had been issued in 1644. Its provisions were quite sensible and urbane. If the prostitutes were quiet and no neighbors complained, nothing was to be done to them. But if they committed a nuisance and were the object of a complaint, they were to be hauled before a magistrate at the Châtelet by a *commissaire* and given twenty-four hours to vacate, or if a previous offender, ordered to leave the city. The landlords of convicted prostitutes were subject to more severe punishments than their tenants, culminating in the boarding-up of their properties for six months to a year.

The ordinance of 1644 remained official policy on prostitutes until the 1680's—no fines, no imprisonment, only the threat of exile to which probably no one paid any attention. Then the new Louis XIV appeared, the man who had finally put aside (reluctantly, to be sure) Mme de Montespan and married Mme de Maintenon, and who proceeded to demonstrate his orthodoxy by revoking his grandfather's edict of religious toleration. In 1684 the King announced the opening of a separate Maison de Force at the Salpêtrière, the female unit of the Hôpital-Général. Henceforth, the magistrates were to send all convicted prostitutes to this new prison. How long they remained was left to the discretion of the directors of the institution, which meant that many of the prostitutes would simply be forgotten there. They were to be given bread, water, and a *potage* for nourishment and "worked as long hours and at the hardest tasks which their strength would permit them. . . ."[89] Fifteen minutes morning and evening they would receive catechism lessons and throughout their labors be made to read "books of piety." More startling and surely unprecedented was an accompanying edict which decreed the same punishment (but in the workshop proper rather than the Maison de Force) for the daughters of Parisian artisans or laborers under twenty-five years of age who "had been debauched or . . . were in evident peril of being."[90]

Louis XIV's new mood was not a passing thing. One reads a letter written three years later from a minister, Seignelay, to La Reynie enclosing a long list of alleged prostitutes which the monarch wished to incarcerate in the Maison de Force. Seignelay mentioned in the letter that he had suggested to Louis that "seven or eight" would serve as an adequate example to the others, but that the King had insisted "that all be locked up."[91] It was then that Seignelay repeated the Monarch's avowed intention to reform Paris in "all matters." A few months later an ecclesiastical journal commenting on the imprisonment of a noted procuress in the Bastille, no less, remarked that "every day they pick up women by order of the King to lock them up"; in recent days eighty women "of bad reputation" had been imprisoned.[92]

How long Louis XIV took to become discouraged about the possibility of ridding Paris of prostitutes is not clear. Nothing in the statutes, of course, suggests that he ever acknowledged defeat, nor does any contemporary testimony evidence that Louis XIV's Maison de Force and other Draconian measures had an appreciable effect on the volume of Parisian prostitution. In commenting on the extraordinary number of the *filles de joie* he observed on the streets at the close of the reign, Nemeitz wrote: "[In Paris] a poor girl will do anything in the world rather than die of hunger."[93] Perhaps the ladies obtained a measure of revenge for their harsh treatment by making royal property—the Louvre courtyard and the Tuileries gardens—their two favorite hunting-grounds in Paris.[94]

The King's double standard of morality was also glaringly apparent in his treatment of gamblers. Although he had calmly watched Mme de Montespan and members of his family lose or gain enough in the course of an evening to finance the Hôtel-Dieu for a year, he had been from the start of his reign adamantly opposed to far more modest gambling operations in Paris. No sudden hardening of his views on the subject was apparent as in the case of prostitution. French kings from the earliest times had followed the precepts of the Church on gambling, to wit, while there was nothing morally reprehensible in games of chance, they were immoral for those who could not afford to lose. (Logically, Louis could not be accused of following a double standard, since he clearly could afford to lose.) It should be recognized that he lived at a time when gambling had taken an extraordinary and socially dangerous hold on nearly all classes.

His moral problem as Most Christian King became one of drawing the line between those who could afford to lose, and hence be permitted to gamble, and those whose losses would ruin their families, wreck commerce, fill the jails, and generally disrupt the good order of the realm. New games of chance—and during Louis XIV's reign they were introduced in bewildering number and variety—had a tendency to start at the top of the social pyramid and quickly spread down into its base. La Reynie expressed this truth clearly when he heard that the notorious game of *hocca* was taking hold among the courtiers: "If *hocca* becomes popular at court," he wrote, "it is certain that it will be taken up by the bourgeois, merchants, and artisans of Paris. . . . Just the rumor that it will become fashionable has already led to a great number of these games."[95]

The top brackets of Parisian society always assumed that they had the same license as the courtiers of Versailles, but the King frequently confounded them. In 1682, for example, Colbert wrote La Reynie expressing the King's approval of some rather harsh fines that the police had recently imposed on several social luminaries for gambling. His Majesty, Colbert assured him, hoped that "even more distinguished" ladies might receive the same treatment so as to serve as examples to the rest.[96] In much the same vein was a letter from Pontchartrain to D'Argenson passing on to the latter the indignant protests the Minister had received from a noble lady whose house had been raided by the neighborhood *commissaire* as a common gambling den. Mlle de Beaufrémont, the fuming victim of what she termed a "signal affront," claimed that "this has never been the practice with regard to people of her quality." The angry lady argued that in the past they had simply been discreetly informed of the King's disapproval by the Lieutenant of Police or some agent from Versailles.[97] But D'Argenson was by no means reprimanded for his temerity. Versailles backed him up, although it is an interesting commentary on the relations between officialdom and the high nobility that D'Argenson was asked his opinion on what should be done "for form's sake" in order to placate the indignant Mlle de Beaufrémont.

Coping with the seventeenth-century craze for gambling must have been almost as discouraging a task for the police as converting ladies of the night to Christian living. In an era addicted to the construction of town houses and country residences on a scale never before known, to gilded carriages and lavish new standards of house furnishings and dress, gambling provided still another symbol of opulence and status. One pernicious threat to social order after another took the public fancy—dice, *trictrac*, *lansquenet*, *barbacolle*, *bassette*, and, worst of all in the eyes of the magistrates, *hocca*, recently imported from Italy whence it had been banned by Popes Urban VIII and Innocent X.[98]

Inevitably, the response of Versailles and the Parisian police was the usual succession of ordinances, each a little sterner than the preceding and apparently equally ineffective. But to the credit of King and magistrates should be marked one brave attempt—perhaps unique in police annals—at a positive solution for gambling. A new non-gambling game was officially introduced to Parisian society. Allegedly, it was so stimulating and entertaining that the old gambling favorites would simply fall out of public favor. In 1673 a man by the name of Desmartins was given a thirty-year national monopoly for the promotion of this game, known as the *jeu de lignes* or *jeu de fortification*. According to the letters patent it was not only educational (in that it would serve as an introduction to military geometry), but even more important, "would distract most of our Subjects from their too great attachment . . . to illicit games."99

The *jeu de lignes* was a noble effort but a dismal failure. La Reynie had doubts about the new venture from the start and tried to limit the Parisian franchise to two locations, thereby incurring the displeasure of both the promoter and the King.100 The public refused to be sold on geometry as entertainment. Worse still, unscrupulous individuals began to use the new game as a subterfuge for other more popular—and more profitable—operations. In 1680 the disillusioned King finally outlawed the *jeux de lignes*. Violators were threatened with an exorbitant fine of 3000 livres, which put this once-innocuous game of soldiers in the same select category as *hocca* and a few others.

The social and economic elite of Paris gambled in their residences (some of the most blue-blooded aristocrats sponsored semipublic gambling in their *hôtels*) and occasionally in full-time gambling houses. Those farther down the economic ladder had to be content with losing their money in less plush surroundings, generally the back rooms of *jeux de paume* and coffeehouses. The first, faced with a steadily declining market and a superfluity of space, were always prime suspects as gambling dens. Shortly after the Fronde the operators of the *jeux de paumes* had been forbidden even to have billiard tables in their establishments but had appealed to the courts and won on the ground that billiards were a game of skill. The *Livre commode des adresses* for 1692 noted that nearly all the *jeux de paume* also featured billiards. Delamare told with obvious relish of a police raid on a *jeu de paume* by three *commissaires* who found billiard players busily engaged at the sport, but, not deceived by this innocuous scene or perhaps well briefed by an informer, they looked into a back room and there interrupted thirty players concentrated around six *trictrac* tables. Since this was only 1670, the owner got by with a 500-livre fine, one-sixth of what he would have paid under the law a decade later when *trictrac* really got out of hand.101

Coffeehouses were a new phenomenon in Paris. The beverage itself had only become popular among the upper classes in the 1660's when a new Turkish ambassador showed how a bit of sugar could be employed to counteract its bitter taste. The first coffeehouses appeared in the same decade, and by the end of the century their number was estimated at around 300.[102] But almost from the start they were *lieux suspects* and *lieux de débauche* in the eyes of the police, perhaps for no other reason than that the latter by nature suspected any kind of idle assembly or conversation. The police were constantly attempting to advance the closing hours of the *cafetiers*. If they had had their way, these establishments would have closed at nine in the summer and five in the winter, but public opinion generally prevailed against the rather understandable but antiquated desire of the police to get everyone off the streets before dark. By the start of the new century the coffeehouses were legally allowed to remain open until ten in the summer and eight in the winter and were notorious cheaters in observing even these hours.

While there doubtless was a marked improvement in the police of Paris during the last third of the century under La Reynie, it is equally certain that a decline had set in even before his departure in 1697. By all conceivable criteria, the last decade or two of Louis XIV's reign were a period of decadence, and the police of the capital was no exception. The reign ended on the same ominous notes on which it had begun in 1643—war, civil discontent, financial and administrative mismanagement, insufficiency of funds, and universal lack of confidence in the men charged with affairs of state. One seems to have turned back the pages of history to the unruly period of the Fronde when one reads angry letters from the Controller-General denouncing the *guet* for its inability to prevent robbers from breaking into his *hôtel* three or four times each year.[103] If one of the most powerful political figures in the state could not receive adequate protection, the lot of less eminent men must have indeed been a dismal one. These were the years when the King was liable to receive anonymous letters reminding him that "there are still Ravaillacs" (Ravaillac had killed Henry IV) in Paris, when Saint-Simon referred to the "inundation of the most audacious placards" against the person of the King, when the statues of Louis XIV at the Place des Victoires and the Place Vendôme were "insulted" time and time again, when the regular troops stationed in the faubourgs were doubled despite the needs of war.[104]

Even D'Argenson, an exceptionally humane official who was repeatedly charged by his enemies with being too easy with the hungry populace, was not entirely free from the anger of the mob. In 1709 a large demonstration was held outside his residence by a bread-hungry crowd and his carriage was stoned.[105] Perhaps the most terrible commentary on conditions in Paris in these years—terrible in its prescience —was made by D'Argenson himself as he observed the misery and discontent around him: "I foresee that the fires will be lighted soon in this capital and I fear that they will be very difficult to extinguish."[106]

CHAPTER EIGHT

Out of the mud

IN the summer of 1676 the nursing sisters of the small Hôpital of the Miséricorde complained to the Châtelet about the unpleasant odors wafting their way from the burial grounds of the Hôtel-Dieu slightly more than a quarter mile distant. As was customary in such matters, a member of the Bureau, or administrative board, of the Hôtel-Dieu was assigned to investigate the grievances. In the entry for June 3 of the proceedings of the Bureau we read the gist of his report. It is one of those innumerable bits of evidence suggesting that those who think great cities became unpleasant places to live in only with nineteenth-century industrialization are either unhistorical or incurably romantic.

As one would expect, the Hôtel-Dieu's inspecting officer denied the hospital's cemetery was the cause of the unpleasantness (although there is abundant evidence that it was). Instead he placed the blame on several other malodorous spots in the immediate neighborhood. Leading his list was the Bièvre, a small stream running sluggishly to the Seine between the complainant and the cemetery. No one could deny that it served as both neighborhood sewer and drainage ditch for all the objectionable wastes of the flourishing Gobelins Works. Another suspect was a nearby pig farm, the legality of which was very questionable despite the fact it may have been a shade outside the city limits. Also mentioned by the Hôtel-Dieu's inspector were a neighborhood tanner and a starch maker, as well as the slaughterhouse of the Maison de Scipion where the meat for the 10,000 or so inmates of the Hôpital-Général was prepared. Blood was reported flowing in the street in front of the Scipion in clear violation of laws dating back to at least the thirteenth century.[1]

Nothing is said in the *registres* of the Hôtel-Dieu about how this particular case was resolved, but thirty-seven years later, in 1713, the same complaint of bad odors emanating from the same cemetery reappears in the minutes. (In the Old Regime, decades often passed like years, centuries like decades.) The Bureau dutifully dispatched another investigator who acknowledged that while the Bièvre was again full of malodorous sewage, the Hôtel-Dieu's cemetery was partly to blame. It seems that the gravediggers had thrown insufficient earth on top of the corpses buried in the mass graves of the cemetery.[2]

Although the Bureau's clear intention was again to brush off responsibility, it met its nemesis in the person of the Lieutenant of Police D'Argenson, a long-time crusader for cleaner city air. He became interested in the case, paid a personal visit to the cemetery, and on August 5 appeared before the administrators to lay down the law. He charged that 13,000 bodies had been thrown in a mass grave originally designed for 10,000 to 12,000 and that still more were being added daily. Furthermore, another old grave containing 18,000 corpses had become partially uncovered. D'Argenson demanded liberal applications of quick lime and a cover of four hundred cartloads of dirt. He laid down new regulations for the mass burials of the Parisian poor. Henceforth, an excavation 10 feet deep, 9 feet wide, and 48 feet long would be considered adequate for no more than 500 bodies placed in six or seven layers. To all these demands the Bureau meekly assented.[3]

The cemetery with such distressingly slipshod procedures was known as the Clamart. Located in the southeast, not far from the much-visited Jardin des Plantes, it had been acquired by the Hôtel-Dieu after the middle of the seventeenth century in an effort to cope with the expanding population of Paris. Most of the poor who died in Louis XIV's time at the Hôtel-Dieu were taken there.

Still functioning but much curtailed in its operations was the Cemetery of the Holy Innocents adjacent to the Halles, perhaps the most famous and fearsome place of interment in Europe. It was founded probably in the eleventh century, when the state of culture was relatively low but the sound Roman practice of burying the dead outside the walls was still in vogue. Holy Innocents became *intra muros* when

Philip Augustus at the end of the twelfth century built his new wall
before departing for the Holy Land to fight the infidels. During the
seven centuries or so of its existence (the decision to abandon it preceded
the Revolution of 1789 by only a few years) an estimated 1,200,000 persons were buried there[4]—in an area considerably smaller than an American football field. One has no difficulty understanding the growth of
the ancient legend attributing to the soil of Holy Innocents the ability
to consume a corpse within twenty-four hours. When "the two young
Hollanders" visited the cemetery in 1657, walking from their hotel "just
twenty paces" distant, they reported seeing a great many bones in the
charnel houses (located on three sides of the cemetery) but no evidence
of any miraculous soil absorbency.[5]

The poor buried at Holy Innocents were generally laid in open pits
but these were much smaller (1,500 bodies or so) than the Clamart had
been wont to employ before D'Argenson's intervention. Burial was by
no means limited to the poor, since some twenty of the city's parishes
that did not have their own churchyard cemeteries had burial rights at
Holy Innocents.[6] The *charniers* were filled with innumerable tombs
and epitaphs of the privileged classes. Brice tells of seeing the obsequies
of the famous historian Mézeray at Holy Innocents in 1683.[7] In truth,
even if one enjoyed the right to use one of the parish cemeteries, the
chances of preserving one's identity in death were still pretty slim, for
space was as lacking there as at Holy Innocents. For example, the tiny
churchyard of Saint-Laurent Parish counted an average of close to a
thousand burials annually at the end of the seventeenth century.[8]

In the reign of Louis XIV the pressure of urban growth was finally
challenging the right of Holy Innocents to operate a cemetery in one of
the most valuable and congested areas in Paris. One of the earliest street
projects approved by the King (1669) called for straightening and
widening the Rue de la Ferronerie,[9] which ran along the south side of
the Holy Innocents and constituted a key link in the east-west crossing
of the city. In an interesting blend of old and new, entire responsibility
for this street modernization was placed in the hands of the *seigneur* of
the neighborhood, the Chapter of the nearby Church of Saint-Germain-
l'Auxerrois. (The antiseignorial law of 1674 which ended this sort of

private authority over the streets was still a number of years off.) The Chapter was authorized to tear down both the charnel house abutting on the Rue de la Ferronerie and the numerous little shops and scriveners' stalls which lay in its shadow. In their place was to be erected a row of well-aligned and symmetrical houses (future valuable rental property for the Chapter) facing on a street newly straightened and widened to 31 feet.[10]

A modern note of sorts was struck by the provision that a new charnel house should be constructed by the Chapter *under* the houses and that the tombs, bones, epitaphs, and so on from the old should be carefully transferred to it.[11] The project must have been an economic success because a few years later the minutes of the administrators of the Hôtel-Dieu mention an offer from "some private individuals" to duplicate on the west side of the cemetery what had been achieved in 1669 on the south. But the directors of the Hôtel-Dieu were apparently not interested in further whittling down the cemetery. The secretary curtly noted, "The Company did not wish to listen."[12]

ɔʊ ɔʊ

The proper disposal of the human dead falls into a hygienic category of its own, but virtually all other aspects of sanitation in Old Regime Paris were directly related to the ancient problem of an adequate water supply. The story of Paris water has never been written but would provide a fascinating chapter in the history of urban development, to say nothing of Parisian and even national politics. How much of the dirt of the old city was due to inbred attitudes and habits and how much to the difficulty of obtaining water for cleaning, no one can say. In defense of the Parisians, it is difficult to imagine cleanliness where a requirement as basic as water was in such short supply. Colbert showed an awareness of the problem when he declared in 1666 that in order to have water to supply private needs adequately and still have enough left over to clean the streets at monthly intervals, almost three times as many public fountains would be needed.[13] But even given such an increase, the Parisian housewife would have remained the object of mixed pity and wonderment for her modern counterpart.

To appreciate the difficulties of life in Paris in the seventeenth century (and for a long time thereafter, since demand always seemed to remain ahead of increased sources of supply) requires a short lesson in contemporary hydraulics. Water being a terribly scarce commodity, it was measured out with the care and precision befitting more traditional French beverages. The standard of measure was the *pouce d'eau*, defined as the amount of water flowing through an aperture approximately one inch in diameter, the surface of the water behind the aperture being maintained at one-twelfth of an inch above its top rim. Experience had shown that such a flow amounted to approximately 19,300 *pintes de Paris* during a twenty-four hour period,[14] equivalent to almost 4,000 gallons. All water concessions to privileged individuals and institutions were made on the basis of the *pouce d'eau* or, much more likely, on the fraction thereof known as the *ligne d'eau*, that is, the water which would flow through an aperture approximately one-twelfth of an inch in diameter.

One of the great status symbols of the Old Regime was one's water privileges. For example, each Prévôt des Marchands upon retirement was granted a concession of 4 *lignes* for use in his domicile.[15] To encourage the sale of lots at the Place Louis-le-Grand (Place Vendôme), which for a time was meeting with considerable resistance, the Hôtel de Ville offered the magnificent concession of 10 *lignes* to buyers. In the latter case, the water was to be obtained from the nearby street fountain of Saint-Ovide—from its "upper level" where the fortunate few collected their water concessions while the common herd used the spigot on the street level.[16] The really important *seigneurs* in Paris did not even have to bother with sending their servants to the public fountains. Their concessions were too large to make portage practicable, so water pipes equipped with the authorized apertures were run off the nearest street conduit into the yards of their *hôtels*. However, only great political figures qualified for such treatment.

At the start of the seventeenth century the total municipal water supply available at the public fountains amounted to 28 *pouces* brought in two lines from the springs of Belleville and Pré-Saint-Gervais a few miles to the north of Paris. This water serviced the Right Bank exclusively; the Left was dependent upon wells and potted water carried from the Seine. However, the Left Bank made some progress during the first half of the century, thanks to Marie de Médecis' determination to obtain water for her beloved new Luxembourg Palace. She built a new aqueduct to carry water from the springs of Arcueil to the south, paralleling, incidentally, the ruins of the old Roman aqueduct. By the time Louis XIV began his personal rule the southern aqueduct was bringing into the city 83 *pouces*, which, added to the 28 from the northern sources, gave Paris a total of 111.[17]

Unfortunately, only a small part of this water served the needs of the ordinary people of Paris. The Arcueil water, having been tapped at royal rather than municipal expense, was considered the property of the Crown and 60 of its 83 *pouces* were allocated to the royal houses and favorites of the King. Probably another 15 *pouces* or so were allocated by the Hôtel de Ville to institutional users like the Hôtel-Dieu or to political favorites. After all these priorities had been met, the inhabitants of Paris were left with an average daily supply, obtainable in some twenty-six public fountains, of about 35 *pouces*, or roughly 1 quart per person.

Even this niggardly amount assumes the proper functioning of the water system, an assumption no experienced inhabitant of Paris would have made. Breakdowns were notorious. Brice, in describing the architectural beauty of the fountain at the Holy Innocents Cemetery, lamented the "criminal negligence" which was causing its ruin.[18] At the close of the War of Spanish Succession the King was forced to grant a special appropriation to the city for large-scale repairs, the Prévôt des Marchands having complained to Versailles that "everything was in such disorder that almost a total reconstruction [is] necessary."[19]

In the 1660's, when change and reform were so much the order of the day, the possibility of enlarging the water supply inevitably came under discussion. The alternatives were either to bring more spring water into the city by means of new wells and aqueducts—a costly and uncertain procedure—or to utilize the cheapest and surest source of supply, the Seine. The advocates of economy over quality won out (not that they could have been made to put the issue in those terms). Few seventeenth-century Parisians saw anything wrong with drinking water from the Seine; some attached positive virtues thereto. The natives, Germain Brice asserted, boasted that the river water was the "best and healthiest which could be drunk."[20] Michel de Marolles wrote that "there is no river water better to drink than that of the Seine." But Brice, Neimitz, Lister, and others all attested to the stomach ailments that plagued visitors to Paris, which they were inclined to blame on the effect of river water on unconditioned intestines.[21] Nicolas Delamare, consistently solicitous of the public health, professed to see nothing wrong in utilizing the Seine for drinking purposes but sensibly recommended that its water be drawn from upstream (something the authorities had been vainly attempting to enforce for hundreds of years) and filtered through sand to improve its "clarity."[22]

In drawing up plans for pumping water from the river, the Hôtel de Ville fortunately had at hand a successful prototype. Ever since Henry IV's time, the Samaritaine, a water-driven pump at the north end of the Pont Neuf designed by the Flemish engineer, Jean Lintlaer, had been successfully providing water for the Louvre and Tuileries. Virtually copying the construction of the Samaritaine, a new pump was erected in 1671 on a water mill alongside the Pont Notre-Dame. This location was a quarter of a mile upstream from the Samaritaine, but the cause of pure water could hardly be said to have gained a notable victory in view of the proximity of some of the busiest dock areas in Paris. The King's engineer, Sieur de Jolly, provided the technical skill for the mechanism, while the city bore most of the expense. The results were so encouraging that the Hôtel de Ville shortly afterwards authorized a second and more modern pump at the same location.

The two contrivances produced some 80 *pouces*, thus more than doubling the Parisian municipal water supply.[23] From the reservoirs inside a house on the Pont Notre-Dame, the water flowed both north and south through two 6-inch pipes to the street fountains, a dozen or so new ones having been built in the 1660's and 1670's. The Bullet-Blondell map of 1676 clearly shows that no effort was made to keep the river water separate from the spring water. The two systems were entirely compatible, in itself a source of pride to the city fathers. The legend on a map of the Parisian water system in the *Traité de la police* even boasted of this compatibility on the ground that it guaranteed flexibility in meeting water requirements.[24]

The thirty to forty street fountains serving Paris in the reign of Louis XIV were the source of public water, but there were at least two other ways of obtaining a private supply if one cared to obtain it and could afford the expense. One of these was private wells, which were quite common in at least the better neighborhoods. There was never any question of making wells mandatory, but the Châtelet was constantly ordering their owners to keep them clean and to maintain the pulleys and rope in good repair. They became very important when there was a fire where no public fountain or underground water pipe was available.[25] (If the latter was at hand, fire fighters, as we have noted, customarily ripped up the street surface and tapped the pipe.) In the poorer neighborhoods one judges that private wells were very much the exception. For example, a police ordinance dated 1697 deplored that in the neighborhood of the Montagne Saint-Hilaire, described as forming a "considerable part" of the Place Maubert quarter, only three wells were to be found in private domiciles.[26] This was undoubtedly a very run-down neighborhood as the absence of private wells itself indicates.

That most Parisians did not have the use of private wells can be implied also from the great numbers of professional water carriers. Shortly before mid-seventeenth century, Sauval counted some 600. (A century later a seemingly reliable source estimated an incredible 20,000.[27]) They obtained the water they sold either at the public fountains or at the river, emptying the contents of their jugs, worth about a sou, into the large copper receptacles which almost every household maintained.[28]

If the water carriers filled their jugs at a city fountain, they were required by a host of police regulations, dating back at least to 1369, to give precedence at the spigot to the bourgeois of the city, their children and domestics. They were supposed to use no more than two jugs at a time and forbidden to lay aside private stores of water for resale. But seventeenth-century "water racketeers" recognized their opportunity. A police *ordonnance* of July 1698 took note of the complaint that a group of water carriers had literally taken possession of certain Left Bank fountains, chasing away all good bourgeois who dared approach and forcing the latter to obtain their water from the carriers at inflated rates.[29] These same unprincipled individuals were also known to hoard jugs of water in their domiciles in expectation of periods of short supply and higher prices, again in clear violation of ancient laws.

If the water carriers utilized the Seine instead of the public fountains to fill their jugs, the police could likewise expect trouble. (Like the lackeys and soldiers, the water porters were traditional troublemakers for law enforcement officers.) They had to be reminded continually to fill their jugs in the "full current" of the river. In order to avoid long walks with their heavy jugs, the porters liked to use the "canal of the Seine," the narrow channel south of the Cité which carried off all the impurities of the Hôtel-Dieu along with much other filth.

The authorities never ceased cautioning the water carriers that the approved location for filling water jugs was the north channel of the Seine. After the new pumps were built at the Pont Notre-Dame, the Châtelet intensified its efforts to keep that part of the stream relatively free of contamination. The main offenders had long been the tanners and dyers from the nearby Rue de la Tannerie on the Right Bank. Letters patent of 1673 (reiterating laws of 1577 and 1623) ordered them to move to the outskirts of Paris.[30] While a good many were prevailed upon to move, they went in the wrong direction, moving upstream to the not-too-distant Faubourg Saint-Marcel on the Left Bank. They continued to use the banks of the Seine for their objectionable industrial processes, and when further legal efforts were made to stop them, they had recourse to the Parlement and were upheld in 1697. About this time even the water carriers were complaining to the Châtelet about the "greasiness" of the water, thanks to the tanners' use of the river.[31]

۞   ۞

One of the most basic requirements for a city worthy of the grandeur of Louis XIV and the new role of Paris in European affairs was clean streets. The attainment of this elusive goal was partly related to the difficulty of obtaining water for cleaning and flushing purposes but much more to the slowness in hard-surfacing the streets. Until this had been achieved, water was more likely to be a hindrance than a help in maintaining street cleanliness. Philip Augustus had concluded in the late twelfth century, as he put his head out of his palace window (the palace on the Cité that later became the Palais de Justice) and smelled the mud of the streets, the only solution was to pave the streets.[32] He made a beginning, but almost half a millennium later we are told that the kings of France frequently absented themselves from the city simply to avoid the unpleasant street odors.[33]

Parisians of the Old Regime took a certain perverse pride in the wondrous qualities of their mud. At very much the same time that Louis XIV was issuing a commemorative medal to celebrate the new cleanliness of the city (along with medals to honor the new lighting, the new police, and other achievements) Sauval wrote his classic description of Parisian mud. He termed it "black, stinking, of an intolerable odor to strangers." According to him, it could be smelled at "three or four leagues" distance, and if some got on one's clothes, one appreciated the truth of the old Parisian saying, "It clings like the mud of Paris."[34] Neimitz, among many others, bore out Sauval, warning that one must be especially careful if dressed in scarlet because the stains were impossible to remove. Boileau consecrated verses to this unlikely subject.[35] Generally, the strong odor was attributed to the mud's high sulfur content, which Sauval thought all to the good since the sulfur helped purify the air and guard against contagion.[36]

At the start of the seventeenth century, four hundred years after Philip Augustus inaugurated the paving of Parisian streets, we are told that citizens were still coping with seas of mud after every rain. Social callers arrived with spare footgear in hand and were expected to change before entering a lady's salon. Parlementarians were using mules to get to their chambers in the Cité.

Nevertheless, Paris was far from being a dirt town as the new century began. An official survey of the streets made in 1604 revealed the existence of 178,728 square *toises* of public pavement (a *toise* was slightly over 6 feet). Of the total, 33,260 square *toises* "belonged" to the king, 32,860 to the municipality, and 112,608 to private individuals.[37] The crown was responsible for the areas around royal edifices; the Hôtel de

Ville for quays, bridges, and the Grande Croisée (the north-south, east-west crossing); and property owners for the pavements facing their properties. If one eliminates the king's pavement and can trust the statistics, Paris thus boasted the equivalent of a paved strip somewhat over 50 miles long and 18 feet wide—a not inconsiderable amount of pavement, considering that the era of the carriage had not even dawned.

The condition of the pavement was clearly another matter. In 1600 Paris had recently emerged from forty years of civil strife during which one can assume the streets had been neglected. But more basic in accounting for street decay was the traditional system of maintenance. Each property owner was responsible not only for paving in front of his house but for maintaining the paving blocks in good repair. Unless one dwelled on heavily frequented streets, one was quite free to decide when and how to pave and repair. One result of this administrative permissiveness was that after a good rain the paved sections of a street might literally disappear under the mud washed down from the frontage of adjacent less civic-minded neighbors. We read of magistrates setting out to investigate such complaints and finding that the pavement had become so covered with "earth, mud, and filth" that passage was impossible. The order might then be given to the hapless property owner to "reestablish" the old pavement.[38]

Henry IV resolved to place the care of the streets of Paris on a more modern footing, and it was in preparation for this long-overdue action that he conducted the aforementioned street census. In the same year, 1604, he issued the first general contract (*bail*) for the maintenance of the streets—all streets. No longer were they to be solely the responsibility of individual property owners. A paving entrepreneur named Sieur Claude Voysin contracted to repair and maintain the badly run-down pavements for 18 deniers per square *toise*, or a total of something over 13,000 livres for the 178,778 *toises* in the city.[39] From this time until the Revolution and beyond the *bail* system remained in force. Each successive contract provided for the specifications of the stone blocks to be used (7 or 8 inches in all dimensions on new work), the quarries near Paris which could be utilized, the thickness and quality of sand used as a base, the maximum space allowed between blocks (generally one-third of an inch), and so on.[40] On paper each contract ran for a considerable length of time, but more often than not it was broken by the Conseil d'État or the Trésoriers de France long before the expiration date. Voysin's contract, for example, legally ran for thirty years, but within five the government decided that more advantageous terms could be obtained from another *entrepreneur*. The government's informality was often reciprocated by the contractor: if he found himself losing money, he did not hesitate to request a contract modification.

Despite inevitable difficulties,[41] the *bail* system worked reasonably well and was an immeasurable improvement over the administrative anarchy which had preceded it. The annual expenditures on repairs and maintenance of the streets rose steadily almost every decade in the seventeenth century. From an average outlay of 13,400 livres the first five years, expenditures mounted to around 50,000 livres in the middle of the century and to a range of 100,000 to 150,000 during Louis XIV's personal reign, or a tenfold increase or better in the course of the century.[42]

The money paid to the general paving contractor was almost entirely devoted to existing pavements. Defective paving blocks were supposed to be replaced and where necessary old surfaces taken up and new sand foundations put down before re-laying the stone. However, much progress was also made in the seventeenth century in new construction. A great advance in the conversion of dirt streets into paved thoroughfares was made by a decree of 1639.[43] Up until that time property owners had been issued little more than invitations to pave their frontages in accordance with the ancient principle of the *premier pavé*. Henceforth, orders were issued by the Council of State for the paving of specific streets, and if the owners did not comply within a stated time limit, the paving contractor was directed to do the work at a cost to the owner of 6 livres 10 sous for each square *toise*. Failure to pay these charges made the property owner subject to having his furniture or his rents seized. In the following few years the new regulations were instrumental in getting some hundred streets paved.[44] Typical was the *arrêt* of the Conseil in 1656 ordering the residents of half a dozen contiguous streets in the Marais quarter to pave forthwith in front of their properties. Many had already done so, but there remained numerous lacunae where the accumulated mud and filth, the decree read, had caused "such stench and infection that the bourgeois . . . are on the verge of deserting and abandoning their residences. . . ."[45] The afflicted citizens, residents of a very good neighborhood, had organized to present a petition to the Conseil and were apparently finally getting some satisfaction.

Perhaps even more important in hard-surfacing Paris was the practice begun by Louis XIV in 1662 of making annual subsidies to the city's paving program. Between 1662 and 1707, Louis gave 2,449,505 livres for this purpose, or an average of over 50,000 livres each year.[46] This money went into either major repairs or new pavement and preferably was allocated to through streets. If one calculates the cost of a square *toise* of new pavement at 10 livres (a liberal estimate for the later seventeenth century), the King's subsidies alone could have financed almost 250,000 *toises* of pavement—more by far than Paris had boasted at the start of the century.

Somewhat prematurely, to be sure, by 1667 the King felt enough progress had been made to commemorate with a medal the transformation of his capital. On one side of the piece was to be found, of course, the monarch's effigy. On the reverse side was the figure of a lady holding a level in one hand to suggest the improvement in street grades and drainage, and in the other hand a wheel symbolizing the new ease of circulation. The legend read, *Urbs novo lapide strata.* That much had been accomplished but perhaps even more remained to be done was evidenced in Sauval's comment written at much the same time that the King was issuing commemorative medals. The historian declared in one breath that no city in the world was better paved than Paris and in the next that none was muddier or dirtier.[47] On the other hand, Dr Lister at the end of the century was favorably impressed with the cleanliness of Paris, commenting that the "avenues to the city and all the Streets are paved."[48] We can suspect the English physician of overstating his case a bit.

ع   ع

Paved streets, desirable as they were as a means of facilitating communications, were from the viewpoint of sanitation only a means to an end. With increasingly large sums of money being expended on pavements and their maintenance, the need was all the more apparent for a well-organized street-cleaning system. The same Conseil de Police of 1666 and 1667 which established the street-lighting system and created the office of Lieutenant of Police placed this subject high on its agenda.

For centuries Parisian street cleaning had involved little more than the principle that each householder should sweep in front of his own property and carry the accumulated mud and filth (*les boues et les immondices* always formed one phrase) to the nearby fields. As a practical matter neighbors had often combined to hire a tumbril to cart away the dirt, but in either case, no public authority had been involved. According to the *Traité de la police*, not until 1348 was an ordinance enacted which even provided a penalty for failure to clean one's housefront.[49] A major change came in 1506 with the creation by the Parlement of the first street-cleaning tax, levied on real property by small neighborhood committees of prominent bourgeois and collected by their representatives. Each of the sixteen *quartiers* of Paris acted autonomously in financing its cleaning operations and hiring the necessary tumbrils and crews, the conviction long being held by the citizens that the most efficient way to achieve such tasks was by neighborhood action. Promising on paper, the new scheme never worked satisfactorily. The "great," both lay and ecclesiastical, refused to demean themselves by paying the tax, and, as was so often the case, the "majority of the bourgeois" followed their example.[50]

After a century during which Paris must have been a very malodorous place, Henry IV resolved in 1608 to do for street cleaning what he had done a few years earlier for the repair and upkeep of the pavements. The upper classes were freed from the burden of the much resented and ill-paid property tax, and street cleaning was placed under a general contract paid by the state with the help of a new levy of 15 sous on each *muid* of wine entering the city.[51] But on this occasion the victory of centralized administration over neighborhood autonomy was short-lived. After twenty years Richelieu, hard-pressed as ever for money to finance the Thirty Years' War, abandoned the responsibility for keeping Parisian streets in proper order. Management was returned to the committees of neighborhood bourgeois as of old,[52] although one may be certain that the government retained Henry IV's excise tax for its own use. From 1637 until the early 1660's no system of street cleaning worthy of the name existed in Paris. The *Traité de la police* referred to the streets as "sewers," and the author excused himself from even citing the succession of empty laws which followed one on the other.[53]

The first decade of Louis XIV's personal reign brought notable improvement, climaxed by the activities of the Conseil de Police of 1666-1667. The irascible Dr Guy Patin, who a few years earlier had been making scathing remarks about the condition of the streets and rarely said anything good about anything, wrote at the end of 1666, "They are working diligently to clean the streets of Paris, which have never been so fine."[54] The King, still living in his capital, took a personal interest in the campaign, sending word to the Conseil de Police that he intended to walk the streets to assure himself they were at long last clean.[55] Apparently, he was satisfied with the results because he ordered the minting of still another commemorative medal, this one to celebrate the new cleanliness of the streets.

The relative effectiveness of the street-cleaning measures in the 1660's and thereafter must be ascribed to the indefatigable La Reynie and his reinvigorated *commissaires* from the Châtelet because the system employed was basically one of neighborhood control that had been employed off and on since the start of the sixteenth century. Despite all the difficulties experienced for 160 years with property taxes, these were retained along with the "elected," spare-time, unpaid tax assessors and collectors (forbidden by law to refuse the appointments). The task of the tax collectors was made all the more difficult by the creation of a supplementary levy for the operation of the street lanterns, forming the already noted *taxe des boues et lanternes.*

The system may have been old, but a great deal of new enthusiasm and determination appear to have been injected into the "nettoyment des rues" by the new regime. This fact probably spelled the difference

between the old failure and the new success. The continuator of Delamare's *Traité de la police* writes with some pride that street cleaning
"appeared of such importance for the beauty of the city, the convenience of its citizens, the ease of commerce, and especially for health,
that the principal magistrates wanted to take part. . . ."[56] To the aston-
ishment of many contemporaries, the Chancellor of the realm, the first
presidents of the Parlement and the Chambre des Comptes, and many
other august magistrates volunteered to become *chefs des directions de
quartier* in the neighborhoods.[57] These officials became responsible for
arranging for cleaning contractors in their respective quarters, each of
whom was required to furnish a certain number of tumbrils of specified
design drawn by two horses and staffed by two workmen apiece. From
seven to noon and two to six in the winter months and from six to
eleven and three to seven in the summer, the entrepreneur's tumbrils,
each costing the taxpayers 2,000 livres annually, made their scheduled
routes through the various neighborhoods, announcing their coming by
means of small bells which the drivers were enjoined to ring continuously on penalty of 100 livres fine.[58] The police ordinances enjoined
every householder to sweep every evening in front of his house; thus,
hopefully, the *boues et immondices* were neatly gathered against the
front of the house (or better still, deposited in baskets) in expectation
of the arrival of the tumbril.[59]

Along with the street sweepings the tumbril operators were also required to pick up the human filth from within the house, carried out
to them in baskets, buckets, or other containers. The law was quite in-
sistent about this, all the more so because many of the cleaning contractors had been reluctant to comply. One of La Reynie's police ordinances of 1668 took note of this fact, citing the great harm done to
public health especially in the warm months by the retention of such
matter inside one's domicile. (The more traditional solution was, of
course, disposition in the streets.) The Lieutenant of Police ordered the
cleaning contractor in each quarter to provide special high-sided wagons "to remove the ordure which at the sound of the bell will be taken
out to them from the houses of the inhabitants."[60]

Theoretically, at least, the tumbril operators should have separated the contents of their wagons in order to satisfy the regulations of the *voiries*, or dumping areas, where they unloaded their carts. These dumps were of two kinds; one to receive the *boues et immondices*, the other "all that is corrupted or subject to corruption."[61] A *voirie* of the former variety was to be found just outside most of the city gates. Contemporary maps generally show them quite clearly (there was one just a few hundred yards north of the bustling Saint-Antoine gate, for example). Before feudal justice was abolished in 1674, it was the responsibility of the *seigneurs* to provide adequate *voiries* of this sort for their respective jurisdictions. After 1674 the king's magistrates at the Châtelet assumed the burden.

The second category of *voirie* was, for obvious reasons, located much farther out from the walls of the city. The *Traité de la police* refers hopefully to plans for a "model" *voirie* for night soil, carcasses, dead animals, and such, which would serve the needs of the entire city and be completely enclosed by a "thick wall seven to eight feet high" to keep in the odors and keep out the neighboring farmers who were forever invading such precincts in search of free fertilizer.[62] However, such an establishment remained just a dream of a few of the city fathers. Meanwhile, they had to content themselves with simple ditches. The needs of the Right Bank were met by such a ditch located near the famous medieval execution site of Montfaucon, but what site was available to residents of the Left Bank is not clear. One document dated 1727 referred vaguely to a ditch outside the Faubourg Saint-Germain,[63] but no details were given.

It is abundantly clear that the distinction between "corruptible" and "noncorruptible" matter was a very tenuous one. Human wastes were "corruptibles" and were supposed to go to the *voiries* reserved for such. The cleaning contractors justified their reluctance to handle them on the disputed ground that they were required to handle only noncorruptible items. About the great quantities of animal excreta swept up on the streets, there was no debate. These were "noncorruptibles." Valuable fertilizer was obtained from both kinds of *voiries*. Lister described the excellent "forced mushrooms" grown throughout the winter months in the faubourgs of Paris thanks to artificial beds with "Horse Dung 2 or 3 foot thick." We are assured that the *boues et immondices* emanating from the street cleaners' tumbrils did not remain long in the *voiries*, for "the farmers generally remove them as they are brought there."[64] Human excreta gave the authorities pause even in those days. Experience had shown that its use as fertilizer had "produced only bad grain and vegetables injurious to good health,"[65] so the rule had come into being that it must lie on the ground for three years before use by the farmers. There is no reason, however, to think that this regulation was any better observed than other regulations. Nothing prevented a farmer from helping himself at the *voirie* to whatever quantity of raw fertilizer he cared to pick up. One case is on record of a farmer who arranged with a cart operator to dump his freshly collected cargo in front of his farm so as to save him the trouble of a trip to the *voirie*.

The separation of human from animal matter was made virtually impossible by the time-honored practice of throwing the contents of family chamber pots into the streets. The authorities had been inveighing against this pernicious custom at least since March 29, 1372, when they revoked the permission to throw liquids out of one's window on condition one shouted the warning cry, "Gare l'eau!" three times to passers-by below.[66] The *Traité de la police* at the start of the eighteenth century placed this prohibition at the head of a list of "The Obligations of the Bourgeois and Inhabitants of Paris Regarding Street Cleaning," along with the requirement that every property owner provide a latrine for his house and sweep at the designated hour.[67] Delamare's continuator, in commenting that "there was no aspect of the Police which is contravened more often than this one," noted that it was a rare session at the Châtelet that did not include such a case. D'Argenson's correspondence tells of a man who, walking along a city street in the company of a lady, had been drenched by liquids carelessly thrown from overhead. Understandably, the pedestrian remonstrated. His assailant, aptly described in the report as "bad-tempered," came raging into the street, sword in hand. But this turned out to be a fatal mistake because the agile pedestrian, unarmed, seized his opponent's sword, broke it in three, and used the stump to kill its owner.[68]

Despite the endless prohibitions, householders continued to use their streets as sewers. The great difficulty for the police was that the practice was carried on at night mainly, "at a time when one cannot readily see from what spot came the contravention." With a large number of families dwelling in a four- or five-story house, one can only sympathize with the police. Nor was the problem limited to the poorer neighborhoods where latrines were probably in short supply and often out of operation for lack of upkeep. One of the most fashionable residential areas in Paris was the Place Royale (Place des Vosges). In 1670 the police were compelled to issue a police ordinance enjoining the proprietors against dumping their ordure in the courtyard, presumably at the feet of the famous equestrian statue of Louis XIII.[69] A small garden existed at this spot at the time, so it may be that the aristocratic tenants, like the simple farmers in the faubourgs, were simply trying to fertilize their plants with readily available manure. (The same ordinance disparages the practice of drying clothes on the decrepit wooden balustrade which then enclosed the area, suggesting something other than the tidy formal garden one sees in drawings later in the reign.)

Beginning with the early sixteenth century the city magistrates had tried to cope with the unsanitary habits of Parisians by requiring the construction of a latrine behind every house, although, until they could persuade householders to make the long trek down many flights of stairs, even this was no solution. The latest of a long succession of ordinances on the subject was the *règlement général* of 1663. How many householders had actually built latrines is, as always, questionable. The *Traité de la police* leaves the impression that all houses except a few in the faubourgs had complied, but in 1668 the *commissaires* of the Châtelet declared that "in most of the quarters, the proprietors have dispensed themselves from making pits and latrines."[70] What is to be strongly suspected is that, in addition to the houses that had no latrines at all, there were many others where they were inoperable, giving the tenants a welcome excuse not to avail themselves of these noisome facilities.

The best reason for concluding that most houses did not possess working privies was the striking paucity of laborers empowered to maintain them. Not only sanitary trenches but all wells and storm sewers were in the care of one small corporation of workers, the *maîtres des basses-oeuvres*, more familiarly known as the *maîtres Fi-Fi*. It was one of the smallest of the trades, numbering at the start of the eighteenth century only thirty-six masters.[71] The number of apprentices and journeymen is not known, but unless the *maîtres Fi-Fi* were different in organization from all other corporations, there could have been no more than 200 men all told engaged in this profession. Considering the amount of manual labor involved and the regulation that all such cleaning take place only during the night hours, one can hardly imagine how a few dozen masters and their assistants could have coped with the nearly 25,000 latrines which Paris theoretically boasted. The very high cost of this operation—30 to 40 livres depending on the proximity of the *voirie*—suggests the man-hours involved and the unlikelihood that it could be a regular procedure in the poorer neighborhoods. We are inclined to fall back on Alfred Franklin's opinion that "at Paris as everywhere, the inhabitants did not yet know any system other than that of 'everything in the street.' "[72]

It is not surprising that the epoch which gave birth to such modern public conveniences as street lighting, an intracity postal system, and buses should also have conceived the idea of public latrines, although its implementation dates to a somewhat later period. One of the items in the Delamare manuscript collection (by far the largest part of which was never incorporated in his *Traité de la police*) is a petition dated around 1680 to the King from an enterprising bourgeois of the city asking permission to establish public closets in the Louvre, the Palais de Justice, the royal houses and other well-frequented spots around the city and faubourgs.[73] According to the petitioner, everywhere one went in the city, "one sees a thousand ordures, one smells a thousand intolerable stenches. . . ." To prevent all this he proposed the establishment of portable *chaises percées* made in a "seemly fashion and not looking like what they will be; those who will make use of them will be comfortable and sheltered, without being seen." Users, the inventor explained delicately, would pay for the service by means of "a little remembrance which they will give amiably to those who will attend the said chairs."

"Persons who could not afford to give would give nothing," he added in the spirit of either charity or of democracy rare for the times.

There is no evidence, however, of the adoption of this forward-looking project in the seventeenth century either in Paris or at Versailles, where the King was by this time residing and where, judging from the testimony of Saint-Simon and others, such a service was as badly needed as in any obscure Parisian alley. A few decades later the author of the *Traité de la police*, who doubtless remembered this rejected proposal, sadly compared conditions on the Parisian streets with those of ancient Rome, which he credited with no fewer than 144 public latrines, "contributing greatly to the cleanliness of the city and to the salubrity of the air."[74] In this respect at least, no one would quarrel with Delamare's inclination to look backward rather than to the future for his model.

CHAPTER NINE

The world of medicine

SOME intuitive souls like D'Argenson and Delamare were aware of
the difficulty of improving public health while public hygiene remained so primitive. Nevertheless, the authorities could congratulate
themselves on having apparently vanquished two of the greatest health
menaces of earlier times. By the late seventeenth century both leprosy
and the plague belonged to history for Parisians, and at least some members of the medical profession were convinced that medical progress deserved the credit. Notable among these self-satisfied practitioners was
the redoubtable Dr Guy Patin, who railed superiorly at the "barbarity"
of earlier generations of his profession. There must have been others,
especially laymen, more inclined to credit Divine Providence or continuing good fortune, but the happy fact remains that at the end of the
seventeenth century few Parisian adults knew anything about either
leprosy or the plague other than what they had read in books.

Leprosy had become a legal rather than a medical problem. As the
dread disease disappeared, all manner of people attempted to fall heir
to the great wealth of the defunct leprosariums. The scramble became
so scandalous that the kings of France felt compelled to intervene.[1] In
1632 Louis XIII handed over the great medieval leper hospital of Saint-
Lazare, north of the city walls, to Vincent de Paul's Congregation for
the Missions for its own use, with the understanding that the new owners would receive any leper who presented himself for admission. When
the future saint took possession, he wrote that only one leper remained
in the establishment.[2]

Louis XIV professed to be equally disturbed by the sight of so much
ill-used property. He charged that leper hospitals in France had become

such attractive institutions that beggars had taken to rubbing their skins with certain drugs to simulate the disease and thus gain admittance. In 1672 he decreed, rather ineffectively to be sure, that the inmates of all leprosariums in France be concentrated in the one hospital of Saint-Mesmin near Orléans. For several decades the Order of Saint-Lazare, which still had enormous holdings in leper hospitals, fought in the courts to retain its nationwide property, but finally in 1693 a long-awaited edict placed its hospitals in the hands of royal agents "for the benefit of the poor."[3]

While few people in Louis XIV's time were any longer concerned about leprosy except as an isolated phenomenon, the same could not be said about the plague—the dreaded *peste*. Parisians of his day would have been vastly relieved to know that they were not destined to witness a single outbreak. In marked contrast to the fate of London, which in the plague year of 1665 alone lost 68,596 people from the plague (according to that inveterate critic of Parisian health standards, Sir William Petty), Paris was completely spared in the second half of the century. To be sure, some adult Parisians at the start of Louis XIV's reign must have had bad memories of the *peste*. Elderly citizens undoubtedly recalled the great outbreak of 1580 when 30,000 citizens were reputed to have perished, and younger adults could hardly have been unaware that in the early seventeenth century hardly a decade passed in Paris without at least a minor epidemic.[4]

The fear of the plague was real enough to have led to the establishment of two large isolation hospitals in the opening years of the seventeenth century—Saint-Louis in the northern faubourgs and Sainte-Anne to the south. Both were under the direction of the Hôtel-Dieu and were meant to be opened only when the plague threatened. Unlike the Hôtel-Dieu, the two new hospitals boasted private facilities for their more affluent patients. Hitherto, the authorities had experienced understandable difficulty persuading such patients that they owed it to the common good to retreat to the horrors of the great central hospital.

To cope with the *peste* should the dreaded alarum sound, generations of magistrates had worked out carefully detailed procedures. Many of them were patently absurd, but founded as they were on the very sound principles of isolation and sanitation no one can quarrel with the program's fundamental soundness. As soon as a case of the plague was detected in a provincial city, all human intercourse with the infected area was supposed to cease. Letters therefrom were deposited on the ground at a point two leagues distant from the walls of Paris, and after the courier had safely retreated (having made his presence known by the sound of a trumpet), men from the city were sent out to retrieve the messages with long iron hooks. Even then, the letters had to be exposed to cannon powder before being admitted into the city.[5]

Meanwhile, inside Paris a major clean-up was theoretically under way. Citizens long monumentally indifferent to civic cleanliness were urged to clean the streets, flush out accumulated ordure, and drive hogs, rabbits, pigeons, and stray dogs outside the walls. The moldy prohibitions against throwing refuse out of windows, against slaughtering animals in the center of the city, against dumping the contents of latrines in forbidden places, were probably briefly obeyed out of sheer fright. Citizens were advised not to work too hard, to avoid exciting themselves, and, above all, to remain continent.

As soon as a house in Paris was suspected of harboring the plague it was subject to rigorous fumigation. Professionals known a *parfumeurs* carefully swept and dusted the premises, spread earth in the center of each room, and set ablaze small clumps of hay set on earthern insulation, each clump having first been impregnated with one or another of a variety of disinfectants depending on the nature of the object being fumigated—clothing, furniture, humans, and so on. The necessity for preserving social distinctions being what it was, there was one kind of "perfume" for poor people and another for *personnes de condition*. The chemical employed to disinfect the latter was not harmful even after half an hour's exposure, but the poor were cautioned to limit their exposure to no longer than it takes to recite a *paternoster*.[6] Assuming a conflagration was not started, the *parfumeurs* proceeded from cellar to attic, and then, the task completed, betook themselves to a designated place of isolation. If, after nine days, they were still hale and hearty, they were allowed to rejoin society. Considering the demands made on them, it is not surprising that when there was an outbreak of the plague in Amiens in 1668, *parfumeurs* were in such short supply that an urgent call had to go out to Paris for volunteers.[7]

In the 1660's, Paris was in a very nervous state as it received reports of outbreaks of the plague on all sides and of the catastrophe which had befallen London in 1665. As early as 1664, the Parlement of Paris limited commerce with certain Dutch cities and two years later with Dunkirk and Cologne. In 1668 the noose seemed to tighten as word was received of heavy mortality in Amiens, Soissons, and Rouen—five hundred in Rouen alone.[8] Goods arriving in Paris from these cities were placed on a forty-two day quarantine or in some cases totally interdicted if thought especially susceptible to the disease. The statutory restrictions on mail deliveries from plague cities were enforced, although the Parlement relented to the extent of permitting messengers from the affected cities to deposit mail in the "last house" in certain faubourgs of Paris instead of two leagues out in the open country as the regulations required. Fairs were, of course, suspended.[9]

Despite such vigorous preventive measures, a case of the plague was diagnosed in Paris in the summer of 1668. A merchant from Amiens residing in an inn in the south of the city (his presence there must have been an embarrassment for the police) died of a suspicious ailment. His valet, taken immediately to the Hôtel-Dieu, was found by the horrified doctors to have the *peste*. La Reynie and the *parlementaires* having been informed of the development, orders were promptly given for the valet's transfer to the remote Saint-Louis Hospital, along with the doctor and surgeon who had attended him and even the nursing sister who had changed his bed.[10] All the guests at the inn where the merchant and his servant had been staying were sent to the country to "air off." Fortunately, the plague went no further. Perhaps it would not be wholly amiss to credit La Reynie and his somewhat Draconian regulations for avoiding a calamity such as Paris had known in the past and London had experienced only three years earlier.

As the traditional scourges receded into memory, new ones took their place. In the opinion of some doctors, syphilis was only leprosy in a new form.[11] The ravages of and possible cures for *la grosse maladie* were the subject of endless discussion; "it was the great business of the

Town." Martin Lister in his journal of 1698 commented that "everyone here . . . meddles with the Cure of this Disease: Apothecaries, Barbers, Women and Monks."[12] But he noted with some surprise that despite the innumerable "Quack Bills Printed in great Uncial Letters," particularly in the Faubourg Saint-Germain, there still remained a certain reticence "even among the French" about revealing that one had contracted the ailment. This understandable modesty, Lister wrote, had had the same results as in England: "little Contemptible Animals of all sorts" (the quacks) had gained a near monopoly of the field and by the private treatment of venereal diseases gained "Riches beyond any of the Physicians."[13] A few years earlier, another Englishman, the yet unknown John Locke, also commented on the wall placards he saw all over Paris. He was particularly struck by one *affiche* offering a medication (for which no less a personage than the Duke of Bouillon had the privilege) guaranteed to remove all "vermin" from the body "without mercury."[14]

꒰ꞏ꒱   ꒰ꞏ꒱

A Parisian of the later seventeenth century in need of medical attention could, depending on the state of his pocketbook and his solicitude for the statutes, call on the services of a representative of one or another of four main groups of healers: the medical doctors of the University of Paris, the surgeons of the Collège de Saint-Côme, the barber-surgeons, and the apothecaries. (We shall disregard the *empiriques*, or quacks.) If he were a citizen of unusual substance, he might be visited by a "team" consisting of representatives of all four groups. Such might well be the case if a bleeding were deemed in order. The august member of the Faculty would be in overall command, the Saint-Côme surgeon would direct the more menial barber-surgeon in drawing the blood, and the apothecary would stand by to provide whatever resuscitative drugs the doctor might order. Few could afford such extravagance, of course.

At the apex of the Parisian professions stood the medical graduates of the University. Their great prestige was perhaps related to their paucity—never more than 110 in the reign of Louis XIV, or about 1 for every 5,000 Parisians. Rarely were more than four or five graduated annually from the medical school of the University, and some of these left Paris upon receiving their degrees.[15] A young man's four years or so of unsystematic medical education, on top of what passed in those days for a Master of Arts degree, gave him an absolute minimum of clinical training. Towards the end of his reign, when Louis XIV attempted to improve medical education, he criticized the medical degree as an empty title "better calculated to deceive the public than to merit confidence."[16] What his professional education often best qualified a young doctor to do was to expound, in the incomparable pidgin Latin immortalized by Molière, on such theses as, "Does libertinage bring baldness?" "Is the female more lascivious than the male?" "Are Parisians subject to the cough when the wind is from the north?" etc.[17] Once a member of the elite group of a hundred or so medical doctors, his future was assured. He could expect an income of at least 12,000 livres annually, the high regard of his fellow citizens, and the protection of the state (never very effective to be sure) against interlopers from any of several directions—surgeons, provincial and foreign doctors, and *les empiriques.*

If, as has been said, a doctor's fee in the later seventeenth century for a home visit was 3 livres,[18] a poor man could rarely have afforded his services. However, Paris in the seventeenth century saw the beginnings of organized and gratuitous medical clinics for the indigent. The doctor to be credited with this innovation was none other than Théophraste Renaudot, the remarkable physician from Montpellier who was also, we will recall, responsible for starting the first Parisian newspaper in 1631 as well as the unique clearinghouse for miscellaneous public information and goods known as the Bureau d'Adresses. In the same busy house in the Cité where he ran his other commercial enterprises, he began in the 1630's free medical consultations for the poor, motivated, as far as we can tell, mainly by humanitarian impulses. By 1640 he had fifteen doctors, all from provincial faculties, assisting him.[19]

Inevitably, Renaudot's puzzling activities drew the attention and hostility of the Faculty of Paris, which sporadically contested the right of provincial doctors to practice in Paris. A lawsuit forced Renaudot and his associates to halt the practice of medicine. He reluctantly complied and turned back to the publication of his *Gazette*, but the resulting publicity for Renaudot's activities on behalf of the poor apparently shamed the Faculty into organizing a similar service. On Easter Sunday 1641, announcements were made from all the pulpits of the city that free consultations would begin at the medical college, Rue de la Bucherie, each Saturday morning from ten until midday. This service became a permanent part of the Parisian medical scene, or so we would judge from an edict appearing sixty-six years later, in 1707, enjoining the doctors to continue to provide four of their fellows each Saturday at the same time and place, along with a "capable and experienced surgeon."[20]

For three centuries, thanks mainly to Molière, seventeenth-century Parisian doctors have remained emblems of pedantry, ignorance, and obscurantism. Whether the playwright was directing laughter at a few practitioners or at the medical profession as a whole is open to discussion. It is interesting, and perhaps significant, that the proud doctors who were the butt of Molière's laughter never really replied to him. The fiercely partisan physician who was probably the most logical respondent, Guy Patin, has only five isolated and unexcited comments about Molière in his voluminous correspondence.[21] Perhaps Patin and his colleagues thought the playwright's indictment unworthy of a reply. That at least some of the physicians were not the buffoons Molière made them out to be is suggested by his close friendship with several members of the Faculty, one of whom may have furnished the playwright with many of the shafts he directed against their colleagues. Molière himself was a constant patient of the doctors he was wont to ridicule and, of course, has even been suspected of hypochondria.

To our knowledge, no one has ever suggested that as a result of Molière's plays the medical profession of Paris suffered a decline in his day. Perhaps no greater testimony could be cited for the high public esteem the profession continued to enjoy than the enormous popularity of phlebotomy in Molière's time. The doctors' insistence that every conceivable ailment could be cured by drawing varying amounts of supposedly "impure" blood from any of three dozen or more veins went virtually unchallenged among the natives of Paris. Age made no difference, nor did the state of one's health. The way to stay well, as well as to get well, was through regular bleedings. Even in nunneries it was as much part of the routine as prayer. For the doctors to be able to continue, generation after generation, to convince their patients of the benefits to be derived from such a painful and even hazardous operation was indeed high tribute to the public confidence they commanded.

Parisian doctors could not legitimately maintain that they were simply following a universal practice, for phlebotomy on the scale they practiced it was something of a trademark of Paris and the University physicians. Many foreign doctors and even the graduates of some French provincial schools were opposed to it. When John Evelyn visited the city in 1652 he criticized the mania for bleeding and asserted that he would prefer to entrust his life to one English doctor than "to a whole college of these French leeches."[22] The Sicilian Marana wrote of the incredulity of French doctors when he told them he had never been bled in his entire lifetime. To convince them of the fact he had to strip naked for their inspection.

The "ignorance" of foreigners like Lister and Marana was understandable. However, relatively few Parisians (especially of the upper classes) seemed to have qualms. Even Molière submitted docilely. The King, who generally set the pattern for the public in medical matters, had as a young man been the victim of a near-fatal bleeding and consequently had long been quite hostile to phlebotomy.[23] Under the influence of Mme de Maintenon he eventually made his peace with his importunate doctors and from 1703 on never once evaded his regular spring prophylactic bleeding. As a matter of fact, he became such an ardent advocate of the practice for his entire family that he once threatened to have his recalcitrant brother bled by force.[24] In the last year of the reign, decades after Molière's death, Nemeitz complained that the traditional treatment still prevailed among Parisian doctors: first the enema, followed by the bleeding, and finally the purgative, or according to the famous moliéresque formula, *clysterium donare, postea signare, ensuita purgare.* Also a generation after Molière, the noted surgeon Dionis acknowledged without a qualm that patients were bled "more in France, and particularly in Paris, than in any other place in the universe."[25] According to him (Guy Patin had said precisely the same thing in 1659), the rich eating habits of Parisians, their proclivity for *nouveaux ragoûts* to excite the appetite, had forced phlebotomy on the medical profession. Patin had termed it the "debauchery" of Parisian life.

Farther down the ladder, whose rungs perhaps symbolize social prestige rather than medical knowledge, were the surgeons of Saint-Côme and the barber-surgeons. The history of Paris has no more bewildering tale to tell than the relations of these two groups with one another, to say nothing of their quarrels with the medical doctors above them and the simple barbers below. For three or four centuries a bewildering succession of ambiguous, contradictory, and meaningless statutes followed one on the other, professing to rearrange the relationships among these groups. By the end of the seventeenth century, however, a degree of stability was finally achieved in the affairs of surgeons and barber-surgeons, as we shall explain.

Towards the close of his reign, in 1637, Louis XIII created a special corporation of simple barbers (*barbiers-barbants*) authorized to do nothing except cut hair and give baths. Barber-surgeons, who had been in the habit of cutting hair along with limbs, at first protested, until they realized that this new creation helped their cause by implicitly recognizing their old claims as surgeons.[26] But this unintentional upgrading of the barber-surgeons caused new friction between the latter and the surgeons of Saint-Côme, who had for centuries claimed to be the only true surgeons in Paris. The men of Saint-Côme regarded themselves as in no way comparable to those crude mechanics, the barber-surgeons. They had acquired a building which they called a Collegium and were constantly pressing for recognition as an integral part of the University with the right to give public lectures, dissect, grant degrees, and so on. Such pretensions in turn brought blood to the eyes of the medical doctors of the Faculty, for whom the men of Saint-Côme, no matter how much they tried to spout Latin and leave the worst gore to the barber-surgeons, were simply ignorant subordinates.

In still another royal effort to tidy up an impossible situation, the Saint-Côme group and their bitter enemies the barber-surgeons were ordered amalgamated in 1655. The former fought this humiliation with all their resources, but after five years the courts upheld the union. Even worse than their forced association with tradesmen, the surgeons of Saint-Côme found themselves stripped of all their old claims as a teaching faculty. A more clear-cut victory for the Faculty cannot be imagined. To show their gratitude to the Parlement, the doctors promised the chief magistrate and his family free medical treatment for life. The dean of the Faculty, accompanied by a baliff, removed the offensive word "Collegium" from the portals of Saint-Côme, only to have it replaced by the surgeons, who went out of their way to show that for them nothing had changed. There matters stood for the rest of the reign of Louis XIV. Legally, the surgeons—both the Saint-Côme variety and the barber-surgeons (who were not barbers at all)—remained members of the same working-class corporation.

But appearance and reality did not always coincide in Old Regime France. In the last decades of the seventeenth century, Parisian surgeons, particularly the more unpretentious and adventuresome barber-surgeons, made spectacular advances, earning for themselves a leadership in the Western world which would continue far into the next century. (It became a common saying that "England had the best doctors, France the best surgeons, and Germany the best apothecaries.")[27] The turning point in the fortunes of the surgical profession came halfway through Louis XIV's reign when the King contracted an anal fistula and after great hesitation decided to allow Felix, his *premier chirurgien*, to perform the dangerous operation to remove it.[28] With the help of four apothecaries whose awesome task it was to pin down the Roi Soleil and a specially perfected silver bistoury (*le bistouri à la Royale*), Felix gave two strokes which cleared up both the King's troubles and most of those of the Parisian surgeons. The latter's prestige rose meteorically. A visible mark of their new prosperity was the erection in 1691 of a fine new building, equipped with a large amphitheater where anatomical demonstrations were held without benefit of an attending doctor, in clear violation of the statutes.

For many, especially the poor and those wary of bleeding doctors and surgeons, recourse in illness was to neither of these types of practitioners but rather to the neighborhood apothecary. Despite many legal prohibitions, apothecaries made house calls of their own in addition to tending shop. They were as restless under the tutelage of the doctors as were the surgeons and staunchly opposed the treatment closest to the hearts of their superiors—phlebotomy. In the seventeenth century their own particular nostrum was antimony, the pros and cons of which provided a medical controversy only slightly less heated than whether blood circulated. The Faculty thought the issue had been settled back in the sixteenth century when under its proddings a parlementary decree had outlawed the use of the metal as a drug. Its advocates, centered in the faculty of the medical college of Montpellier, historic enemies of the Paris faculty, found that the law could be successfully evaded by prescribing white wine administered from cups of antimony.[29] This became the *vin émétique* so famous in the literature of Louis XIV's time. Its patronage by the apothecaries of Paris earned them the wrath of the doctors, who had long labeled antimony a poison.

In retaliation, the doctors began a campaign, thoroughly justified, to be sure, against the ridiculously complicated and exotic compounds of the apothecaries. They argued that all the drugs necessary for good health (and in view of their emphasis on bleedings, enemas, and purgatives, these were very few) could be purchased at the nearest grocer.[30] One of their members gave substance to such assertions by writing a small book on the cheap self-care of illnesses. This little volume turned out to be one of the best-sellers of the century. It was entitled, in part, *The Charitable Doctor, teaching how to make and prepare at home, with ease and little expense, the remedies suitable for all sorts of sicknesses.* . . . That most choleric of all seventeenth-century Parisian doctors of whom we have knowledge, Guy Patin, wrote in 1649 that "[with this book] we have ruined the apothecaries of Paris." He thought the future so dim for their profession that he recommended they not even be allowed to accept apprentices.[31] One is led to speculate why this sort of book (it had many imitators) did not work to the economic disadvantage of the medical practitioners as well as of the apothecaries. Perhaps the social and economic groups interested in such home treatments were not normally among the clientele of the doctors, or perhaps there were so few doctors in Paris they could afford to show such concern for public health.

Unbeknown to Patin the apothecaries, far from being ruined, were at mid-century on the verge of a great rehabilitation. Once again, Louis XIV's ill health worked against the doctors of Paris. In 1658 the King fell seriously ill, and Cardinal Mazarin despairingly, and to the dismay of the royal physicians, consented to the administration of one ounce of antimony in white wine, which was then followed by twenty-two purgations. To the further humiliation of the doctors, the entire procedure was entrusted to an *empirique*.[32] The King recovered nicely from both disease and treatment, and antimony was, of course, given the credit. The Parlement, obviously unwilling to be on record as condemning a remedy which had saved the life of the King, quickly reversed its old prohibition against the use of antimony. Even among the Faculty the *vin émétique* was reluctantly accepted by all but a few die-hards, although it never replaced bleeding as their favorite panacea.

Regardless of who administered the treatment—doctor, surgeon, barber-surgeon, apothecary, *empirique*, or a member of one's own family —the chances were, unless one were very poor or homeless, that the ministrations would take place at home. The greater one's wealth, the more likely this became, whether one lived in Paris or any other seventeenth-century European city. Sir William Petty in his essays comparing London and Paris could find no better way of demonstrating the greater poverty of Paris than by asserting that "the number of those at London who chuse to lie sick in Hospitals rather than in their own Houses are to the like People of Paris as one to twenty."[33] The proportion, like many of Petty's statistics, is questionable but not the basic premise that hospitals were for the poor.

The dozens of *hôpitaux, hospices,* and *refuges* which one finds listed in any seventeenth-century Paris guide were rarely the equivalent of modern hospitals. Most were simply shelters run by one or another of the innumerable religious orders to alleviate some special kind of human misery. One of the oldest and most famous was the Quinze-Vingts in the Rue Saint-Honoré, founded in 1254 by Louis IX for 300 indigent blind who for centuries enjoyed the legal right to beg on the streets of Paris. Others were orphan asylums, homes for the aged, lunatic asylums or perhaps temporary shelters for young provincial girls adrift in Paris.

The only hospital in Paris which we might recognize as modern, in that it was relatively large (150 beds) and clean, well-staffed, solicitous of the welfare of its patients, entered voluntarily by both paying and charity patients and in the spirit of hope rather than despair or resignation, was La Charité. Established in the early years of the seventeenth century in the Faubourg Saint-Germain by the Brothers of St. John, this institution never failed to draw compliments from visitors. When one of the servants of "the two young Hollanders" fell ill in 1657 with an abscess, they sent him there for treatment and were apparently delighted. "Such ills," they enthused, "are marvelously well treated at La Charité."[34] John Evelyn, who as we have noted went on record as preferring any English doctor to the aggregate of the French medical profession, said that "the Charité gave me great satisfaction, in seeing how decently and Christianly the sick people are attended, even to delicacy. . . . They have gardens, walks, and fountains." Naturally, people tried to get admitted to the Charité in preference to the Hôtel-Dieu. The regulations for the conduct of the charity schools, for example, provided that if a child became ill and his parents were too poor to treat him at home, efforts were to be made to get him admitted to the Charité, "otherwise to the Hôtel-Dieu."[35] One can easily sense the animosity of the latter to its modern and much lauded rival. For years the Hôtel-Dieu fought a running battle to impose a measure of public control over the Charité, charging that the Brothers were siphoning off alms to Italy.[36]

One of the many notable features of La Charité was its strict policy of one patient–one bed, in contrast to the Hôtel-Dieu's seeming reluctance to permit the smallest part of a mattress to remain unoccupied by human flesh. Equally commendable was the medical care assured the patients. Daily, a house doctor, accompanied by surgeon, apothecary, and hospital attendants, saw every patient. Day or night, trained brothers were on hand for both temporal and spiritual service, and there was

even available a small convalescent home with twelve beds on the outskirts of the faubourg where certain patients could be sent for a few
days "to get fresh air and reestablish themselves."[37]

The environment at La Charité was so obviously superior to that of
the Hôtel-Dieu that one surmises that Nature there at least had a fighting chance of overcoming the butcheries of the medical practitioners.
Although the two institutions had separate professional staffs, in training and experience the staffs were very much alike. Any differences in
mortality rates could probably not be credited to the varying skills of
attending doctors and surgeons. Petty cited some figures which, based
as they were on the official bills of mortality, are probably reliable and
certainly bear out what we would expect. He tells us that in 1678 and
1679 a total of 5,765 people were admitted to La Charité, of whom 790
died, while in the same period 50,126 were admitted to the Hôtel-Dieu,
of whom 14,027 died, many leaving by way of the nightly cemetery-
bound wagons. In percentages this works out to a 14 percent death rate
at La Charité compared with 28 percent at Hôtel-Dieu. (It might be
added that Petty compared mortality at La Charité with that at St.
Bartholomew and St. Thomas Hospitals in London, arriving at the conclusion that, by a very narrow margin, "out of the most poor and
wretched hospitals of London there died fewer in proportion than out
of the best in Paris."[38])

A small bit of evidence supporting the case for the relative salubri-
ousness of La Charité is given by Martin Lister in his account of his
visit to Paris in 1698. He tells us that Père Jacques (also known as
Frère Jacques), one of the most notorious charlatans of the age and the
inventor of a new technique for the removal of the stone, had recently
been allowed to demonstrate (on live patients) at both La Charité and
the Hôtel-Dieu. Lister gives the grisly mortality figures. Since we are
dealing with the same operation, performed by the same man within
the same year, we may be permitted to attribute the difference to the
much greater danger of infection at Hôtel-Dieu. Of Père Jacques' forty-
five victims at Hôtel-Dieu, twenty-nine, or 64 percent, died, while of
his nineteen patients at Charité, eight, or 42 percent, died. To the further
credit of La Charité, it may be added that one of the staff surgeons

there, Maréchal, a highly respected name to this day in the annals of surgery, had recognized Jacques for what he was and had "harangued against him before the Governors."[39] Unfortunately, Maréchal did not have his way. By this time (1698), Louis XIV had imposed a lay board composed of magistrates and merchants on the religious who had once operated the hospital with complete freedom. These laymen were by now exercising a dictatorial rule over all phases of the institution's administration, including surgical procedures.

La Charité, with all its obvious shortcomings, at least suggested a better tradition of hospital administration. Looming far larger on the local scene, however, was the oldest Parisian institution after the Church from which it had sprung—the Hôtel-Dieu. Its great bulk clung precariously to the bank of the Cité a few feet south of Notre-Dame Cathedral, inspiring alternate pride and horror in the hearts of the citizenry. For a millennium well-intentioned people had taken pious pleasure in its existence, rarely suspecting that even poor beggars picked up off the streets would often have been better off left where they lay. Sir William Petty observed with a good deal of logic that over 3,000 people died there annually not "by natural necessity but by the evil administration of that Hospital."[40] He arrived at this figure by postulating the mortality rate at La Charité as a norm one could expect under good hospital management and applying this percentage to the admissions at the Hôtel-Dieu.

John Locke stated at this time that about 20,000 people died annually in Paris.[41] Thus, if we accept Petty's mortality figures for the Hôtel-Dieu, about a third of all the people who died in Paris around 1680 breathed their last in this ancient institution. By far the greatest part of this mortality was among the very poor. Few people able to obtain treatment at home would have consented to being sent to the Hôtel-Dieu. Small wonder that one of the hospital's historians, Rondonneau, later called it the "most extensive, the largest, the richest, and the most frightful of . . . hospitals."[42]

Getting admitted to the Hôtel-Dieu was an easy matter, doubtless the most painless aspect of a sick person's relations with the institution. It had remained admirably faithful to its ancient policy of turning no one away from its doors, regardless of race, nationality, or religion. Infidels and Protestants, who could not legally be buried with Catholics, were allowed the privilege of dying with them. In recent years, it is true, certain categories of contagious and other diseases had been turned away from the Hôtel-Dieu on the ground that specialized hospitals had been erected to shelter such cases. People with venereal diseases (unless pregnant), scurvy (thought to be contagious), mental disorders deemed incurable, foundlings, and chronically ill oldsters were supposed to be sent elsewhere.[43]

At the front entrance of the Hôtel-Dieu was always stationed one of the twelve journeyman surgeons attached to the hospital. His duty was to examine the patient, determine his ailment and eligibility for admission, and then turn him over to a chaplain who recorded simple biographical information and attached a little slip of paper on the patient's right arm for identification in case of necessity. The newly admitted patient was then escorted to one of the nineteen wards, assigned, theoretically, according to sex and the nature of the disease but more likely according to where a vacant bed, or fraction of a bed, could be found.

Many incredible statements have been made, then and now, about multiple occupancy of the Hôtel-Dieu beds. As careful an historian as Félibien maintained that in the dreadful winter of 1709 there were up to twelve in a bed. The registers of the Board of Administrators contain an entry for 1679 to the effect that five or six adults or up to ten children were jammed in some beds. In 1694 the same source raised the figure to eight adults, and in 1709 we read that the sick were being "put on the testers of the beds."[44]

Some simple mathematics may cause us to question these much-quoted assertions. Rondonneau tells us that the *grands lits* of the Hôtel-Dieu were 4 feet 4 inches wide and designed originally for two adults. He does not give their length, but judging from the many contemporary drawings it is certain that they were no longer than a moderately tall male. In view of the manifest impossibility of sleeping adults crossways in a bed measuring only 4⅓ feet in width, it is difficult to give credence to the accounts of more than four adults to a bed unless one accepts the even more unlikely hypothesis of multiple layers of humans in each bed. As for the account of patients reclining on the canopies of the great four-poster beds (these came into use in the seventeenth century), the authenticity of the assertion is undeniable, but its credibility is another matter. No one has ever been able to find any corroborating evidence for the statement.[45] It was made by one of the hospital's administrators in 1709 in the midst of one of the worst crises Paris and the Hôtel-Dieu ever experienced. Our guess is that it was a simple hyperbole never meant to be taken seriously or to be recorded by a secretary for posterity to puzzle over.

The number of patients in the Hôtel-Dieu at one time is, like the count per bed, subject to much exaggeration. Unfortunately, the registers of the hospital's board of administrators do not shed much light on this problem. They give, towards the end of the reign, annual admissions but not daily averages. The generally reliable eighteenth-century historian of the hospital, Rondonneau, claimed that in the peak year of 1709 some 9,000 patients were present. Saugrain speaks more vaguely of 8,000. Numerous contemporaries refer to 6,000 to 8,000 sick without specifying dates. For 1678 and 1679, Sir William Petty set the average population of the Hôtel-Dieu at 4,197.[46] Quite possibly, all these figures are correct for the dates specified, but there are also available some police statistics for 1713 and 1714 which support Alfred Franklin's estimate of a "mere" 2,500 as the average number of patients.[47] For January 1713 there were listed 2,189 patients, and a little more than a year later D'Argenson fixed the number in a letter to Pontchartrain at 2,002, even breaking this down by wards.

For the patient the matter of greatest moment was how much medical attention he could expect to receive—assuming he had enough confidence in the doctors to wish to see one. The following personnel was available for his care: six part-time doctors, one master surgeon assisted by thirteen resident journeymen, approximately forty-five extern journeyman surgeons, forty-one nursing sisters, six apothecaries or apprentices, twenty-four garçons, fourteen filles, and ten chaplains to give spiritual solace.[48] According to long-standing regulations, the six staff doctors were supposed to make the rounds of the wards accompanied by their subordinate surgeons and apothecaries each morning at eight in summer and nine in winter. The rounds lasted one hour, which is to say that each of the six doctors theoretically looked at about 400 patients in that time, a good many more if the hospital was undergoing one of its busy periods. According to regulations, one of the six doctors was required to be on duty at night, but in the afternoon no doctor was required to be on the premises.

In 1661, according to the registers of the Bureau, one of the administrators tried to lengthen the doctors' visits to two hours daily, thereby allowing the surgeons and apothecaries at least enough time to record the doctors' orders. The same conscientious individual also attempted to get a ruling that one doctor was to remain on the premises each afternoon.[49] Rising in indignant protest to the first proposal was a certain Dr Moreau who argued that if he were made to devote two hours daily to hospital rounds "it would be necessary to abandon the largest part of his city practice, which no doctor of repute would do, so the Hôtel-Dieu would be left with only the least experienced persons to take care of the sick."

Dr Moreau's colleagues were obviously in full agreement. They apparently concluded that the best defense against the demands of the administrators was to launch an attack on certain practices of the hospital completely irrelevant to the matter at hand. They decried the nursing sisters' irrational insistence on moving patients from one bed to another ("this has caused the death of several thousand people"[50]), and their equally stubborn refusal to group patients according to special dietary requirements. The tactic apparently worked. The forces of reform on the hospital's board were beaten down and the doctors continued to limit their morning visits to one hour and to make themselves unavailable in the afternoons. In the board meetings of May 2, 1687, and March 17, 1691, both matters were again brought up, but with the same results.

It is clear that a patient at the Hôtel-Dieu did not see very much of the medical doctors, but it was otherwise with surgeons and their journeymen. These, if anything, were too much in view. They made their presence painfully felt by performing all surgical operations in the wards proper, in full view of the survivors of the previous day's ordeal and of the next day's victims. Not even a curtain hid the grisly sights.[51] The Hôtel-Dieu had one chief surgeon, who was a master in the city's guild of surgeons, one chief journeyman, who could expect to be received as master upon completion of his six years of service, twelve full-time resident journeymen, who stood relatively little chance of ever gaining the mastership, and a large number (at one time set at forty-five) of journeymen from the city, who worked part-time at the Hôtel-Dieu gaining experience.

The main function of these journeymen—resident or extern—was bleeding, which is understandable in view of the acceptance of the current dogma on frequent, even daily, bloodlettings. The more difficult of the bleeding procedures (the regulations of 1666 mentioned "extraordinary bleedings like the jugular, the *salvatelle*, the artery, and others of this nature") were forbidden to the externs.[52] No surgical operation, however, was closed to the resident journeymen as long as it was approved and observed by medical superiors. The constant subordination of surgeons to doctors is visible at every turn: the surgeons were forbidden to perform any serious operation, like an amputation or trepan, without the consent of three doctors, one of whom had to be actually present. Even the time of surgery could not be set without the approval of the attending physician.

For many wretched souls, the spiritual consolation to be received at the Hôtel-Dieu was more important than medical attention. The establishment's tradition was of course solidly Catholic. For many centuries the Bishop of Paris and the Chapter of Notre-Dame had ruled uncontested over the affairs of the nearby hospital. But in the century of Louis XIV this clerical control was a thing of the past. The Archbishop retained only a face-saving role among the lay administrators, while the cathedral chapter was reduced to the supervision, not without much gratuitous assistance, of the spiritual life of the hospital.[53] Bad feeling between lay and clerical groups was constantly manifesting itself. There was nothing doctrinal or philosophical apparent in this friction. More than anything else it was grounded in the obvious impatience of lay administrators—successful professional men or merchants that they were

—with the way the religious operated the hospital. For the clerics, on the other hand, their subordination on all hands to the lay administrators was obviously galling.

We see, for example, members of the Bureau complaining on one occasion that the soft-hearted sisters were endangering lives by admitting syphilitics to the hospital. The sisters replied that the men in question (fifteen in as many days in this particular instance) had been picked up off the streets, and since they could be admitted to the regular hospital for venereal cases only twice a week, Christian charity demanded that they be given temporary shelter.[54] On another occasion, the Bureau complained of the great disorder caused by crowds of boys congregating at the doors in search of odd jobs customarily assigned by the sisters. Even more vexing to the governors than the noise stirred up was that the sisters often did not have the money to pay such workers and were forced to bring them into the hospital to pay them off in meals. This, too, the Bureau complained, violated the rules.[55]

The nursing sisters of Hôtel-Dieu are generally conceded to have been one of the most hard-working and heroic groups of women in the history of Paris. But members of the board did not always seem to agree. They alleged that only the "daughters of good homes" upon payment of dowries of 1,500 livres were being accepted as sisters, and that such girls had none of the old tradition of selfless service to the poor. It would be well, one Bureau member declared, to remind the novice sisters that they had come to the hospital to help the sick and not "to practice all these private devotions."[56]

In the 1670's and 1680's, one of the main complaints of the Bureau was the alleged failure of the chaplains to give spiritual aid to the dying —the *agonisants*. Ten chaplains were assigned to this work, but only two, it was charged, were on duty at any one time and the rest were said to be unavailable when needed. At night none was to be found. The priests replied with some heat that in order for them to answer sick calls at night the hospital doors would have to be left unlocked. This they termed very imprudent.

The religious did not always remain on the defensive. For example, we find a representative of the Cathedral Chapter, the *pénitencier*, lash-ing back at the Bureau for issuing a set of regulations for the maternity ward so disliked by one of the sisters that she had ripped it off the wall, to the wrath of the lay administrators. Defending her conduct before the Bureau, the *pénitencier* asserted that the former had no authority whatsoever over the hospital's operations and were simply "administrators of revenue." The battle of the maternity ward raged a long time. The Bureau's regulations having been reaffixed to the wall, the sisters countered by covering them with a crucifix. Still later notices were covered with mud or charcoal. Tempers became so inflamed that the wife of the President of the Parlement (by the nature of her husband's office a sort of First Lady of Paris) offered her house for a peace conference between the Bureau and *messieurs du spirituel*.

The overall administration of the Hôtel-Dieu had been transferred early in the sixteenth century from the Chapter of Notre-Dame to a board of eight (later twelve) lay members appointed for life by the king. Until the middle of the seventeenth century, the Hôtel de Ville had retained a strong voice in the hospital's management, but its influence began to weaken quite perceptibly after the unpleasantness of the Fronde. A list of seventeenth-century administrators shows almost solid ranks of parlementarians, royal councillors, and assorted King's men.[57]

In 1690 Louis XIV combined the administration of all Parisian hospitals, including the infirmaries of the Hôpital-Général, in a blue-ribbon board composed of the Archbishop of Paris, the First Presidents of the three principal sovereign courts, the Procureur-Général of Parlement, the Prévôt des Marchands, and the Lieutenant of Police at the Châtelet. This was the Grand Bureau which met every three months until the Revolution to discuss matters of higher policy affecting all the city's hospitals. Although the Archbishop of Paris was titular head of the Grand Bureau, he was at best a minority of one, and effective power lay in the hands of the President of Parlement. It was he to whom appeal was made when real crises developed. In the lay-spiritual troubles to which we have alluded, the Premier Président, and not the Archbishop, was constantly being urged by his colleagues to discipline the sisters and their clerical defenders.

Beneath the Grand Bureau lay a second body of administrators immediately responsible for the good order of the Hôtel-Dieu. For all those concerned with that hospital, this group was known simply as "le Bureau." It was composed of sixteen men of substance—all laymen—who met every Wednesday and Saturday to discuss the details of the hospital's operations. The greatest misjudgment one could make about the Bureau of the Hôtel-Dieu is to think of it as a group of well-intentioned and unobtrusive lay trustees who gathered for perfunctory reviews of the temporal welfare of the institution. In truth, the Bureau exercised as absolute a control over the Hôtel-Dieu as the King did over France and doubtless a more effective one. Doctors, surgeons, nursing sisters, chaplains, *garçons*, were all equally under the thumb of the sixteen administrators, not one of whom had any medical training.

The interference of the nonprofessionals with the doctors and surgeons was by no means always a bad thing. The laymen frequently displayed an intuitiveness, diligence, and open-mindedness about things medical which put them at an advantage over the professionals. One heard, for example, complaints in the Bureau of the laxity of the examinations administered to the incoming surgical assistants by the doctors. Consequently, the governors insisted that some of their number sit in on the sessions. Then there were the constant efforts of the administrators to convince the nursing sisters that seriously ill patients should not be taken to the *salle basse*, a low-lying room which was subject to seepage from the Seine and was notoriously *malsain*. On still another occasion the Bureau also conveyed its "special wish" that the doctors emerging from the smallpox ward refrain from visiting the children's room.[58] It is curious to find these laymen often showing a much keener appreciation of the dangers of infection than the doctors.

We have noted the furor caused among the Hôtel-Dieu's sisters by the Bureau's arbitrary promulgation of new regulations for maternity cases. That body sometimes exercised an equally strong hand over the hospital's surgical staff. A notable example was the Bureau's preparation of a new set of rules for the "stone ward," one of the busiest surgical areas of the hospital. (Parisians were peculiarly susceptible to kidney stone.) Again, the Bureau consulted neither doctors nor surgeons. At its meeting of May 4, 1659, one of the administrators charged with preparing the new regulations was asked to read his handiwork to the members. After this had been done, the six house doctors were called in and the new rules communicated to them. While agreeing that new regulations were needed, they asked for more time for consideration. Nothing more was heard from that quarter, but a month later a journeyman named Lanier, who acted as chief stone remover at the hospital (referred to as *opérateur*, never as *chirurgien*), stormed into the meeting room of the Bureau and said he understood that new regulations for his ward had been prepared. Since he had not been consulted in their preparation, he demanded to see them. The Bureau heard him out, but informed him that he would see the statutes only when they were put in effect. After he left, a motion was adopted that Sieur Gouin perform the stone operation the following day in place of Sieur Lanier.[59]

Members of the Bureau were also frequently to be found at operating tables evaluating the skill of one or another of the surgical journeymen. A year before the aforementioned incident, the same Sieur Lanier had been the object of a visitation by a Bureau member, M. Perrichon, to observe Lanier's employment of a new instrument on live patients. M. Perrichon reported his findings to the Bureau the following day. Lanier, he said, had used the new invention first on two old men and the operations had not gone too smoothly. Both old men had been kept on the "bench" half an hour each, much longer than was customary, and one died shortly after. A child was next in line and M. Perrichon and the attending doctors had argued for the return to the old instrument but had not suceeded in convincing Lanier. The child too died shortly. The Bureau summoned Lanier for an accounting, but he stoutly defended his instrument and blamed the boy's death on the *disposition du corps*.[60]

"Le Bureau" was theoretically responsible for the finances of the Hôtel-Dieu, but in actual practice money matters cropped up rather rarely in its registers. They appear to have been reserved for the sessions of the Grand Bureau. The public never caught so much as a glimpse of the hospital's finances, which did not prevent it from being bombarded by constant reminders of its dire needs. Its wealth was reputed to be enormous. Over the centuries it had been one of the favorite benefactions of the rich and had come into ownership of a vast amount of landed property in Paris and elsewhere. The hospital also enjoyed a great assortment of revenues other than from real estate. Some were quaintly medieval, like the right to inherit the bed of a deceased or resigned canon of the Cathedral Chapter. Insignificant as this may seem, the administrators were still in Louis XIV's time religiously collecting their due whenever a canon died. In 1683 they even brought suit against the Chapter when the latter allegedly tried to palm off a bed so rickety that no one believed the deceased had ever slept in it.

Fortunately, other sources of revenue were more lucrative. The hospital enjoyed the right to hold special collections in both Parisian and provincial churches, to conduct special house-to-house appeals, and to sell certain indulgences—its prized Seven Pardons. One of its best sources of income was a percentage (generally a third) of judicial fines imposed on a long list of offenders. Convicted duellists had the choice of either spending six months in jail or paying 1,500 livres to the Hôtel-Dieu, a law which made the administrators undoubtedly the most assiduous prosecutors of duellists in the land. The hospital also enjoyed certain monopolies, like the right to sell meat in Lent to all those dispensed from fasting. Some people thought its income far outstripped its expenses. The Archbishop of Sens, for example, refused to permit agents of the Hôtel-Dieu to dispose of its Seven Pardons in his archdiocese on the grounds that the hospital was "too rich."[61]

But unless the Bureau was playing tricks with its books, the Archbishop was being grossly unfair to the Hôtel-Dieu. In Louis XIV's time it was in sad straits financially, constantly being forced to dip into its capital in order to meet its obligations and once even selling the organ from the hospital church. At a session of the Bureau in 1662 one official declared that the hospital had dipped into its capital in 1658 and 1659 to the amount of 180,000 livres.[62] Income was rising, but expenses were mounting even faster. Among the few seemingly reliable figures available are those given by Rondonneau showing income and expenses for three years in the mid-seventeenth century.[63] What was undoubtedly happening was that the Hôtel-Dieu was showing the effects of the great influx of the very poor and homeless from the provinces, the same phenomenon as forced the establishment of the Hôpital-Général in 1656. A report of the Bureau in 1663 lamented "the prodigious number of the sick, who formerly numbered only eight to nine hundred [and now] mounts to more than 2500. . . ."[64] The same writer complained that charitable contributions had declined sharply. Nothing was said of this openly, but it was doubtless true that the Hôpital-Général was making

The Hôtel-Dieu in the Seventeenth Century: Receipts and Expenditures (Rondonneau)

Year	Receipts	Expenditures
1640	197,758 livres	229,376 livres
1651	258,313 livres	325,624 livres
1663	360,098 livres	588,102 livres

heavy inroads into the bequests traditionally made to the Hôtel-Dieu. Legacies were described as rare and "very mediocre.[65] Church collections, judging from Rondonneau's figures, had become a scandal—1,750 livres in 1640, 1,800 in 1651 and 1663. While in the later seventeenth century, the Hôtel-Dieu remained far more representative of the old tradition of living off the alms of the faithful than the Hôpital-Général (which was constantly turning to the state for revenue), secularism had seriously disrupted both its finances and its administration. Fortunately for the ancient institution, it could still fall back on the accumulated generosities of countless earlier generations of pious Christians.

CHAPTER TEN

The stomach of Paris

A few hundred yards northeast of the Louvre an unwary visitor to old Paris was quickly ensnared in the worst crush of human beings, animals, and vehicles to be found anywhere in the city. The most popular guidebook of the times, that of Germain Brice, termed it a "place which one should avoid."[1] Saugrain in his description of the area cautioned his readers that he was not recommending they visit it but rather was simply acquainting them with its usefulness "in case of need." Sauval deplored the congestion which made it "very difficult to move" and the high, crowded, decrepit houses shutting off badly needed light.[2]

This was the area of the Halles, a sprawling, formless complex of open-air and covered markets—wholesale and retail—catering to every conceivable human need from foodstuffs and silverware to enough old clothing, Sauval wrote, "for entire armies." The triangular-shaped grain market, largest building in the area, and half a dozen irregular rows of shabby old buildings and stalls all loosely enclosed by lines of porticoed houses known as Les Piliers constituted what Emile Zola later called the "stomach of Paris." To the northeast was the only open area, punctuated by the notorious revolving octagonal pillory where for centuries malefactors, notably merchants and peddlars accused of giving incorrect weights or otherwise fleecing their customers, were exposed to public ridicule and mudslinging (anything short of rocks).[3] On market days the open area would disappear beneath the wares of hundreds of small vendors, particularly of bread. The ostensible limits of the Halles had long ceased to suffice, and by Louis XIV's time the market unofficially extended for blocks to the south, making access to the market proper that much more difficult.

From its beginnings in the twelfth century as a small fair outside the walls of Paris the Halles had been essentially "the King's market." The monarchs collected increasingly lucrative rental fees from the merchants using its stalls, in addition to the customary taxes on all goods sold therein. Like all his successors—royal and commoner—for the next three centuries, Louis XIV was well aware of the inadequacies of the Halles. The Council of State in 1663 expressed its "distress that [the market] was not in keeping with the present grandeur of Paris and its faubourgs."[4] A few years later Louis XIV vaguely proposed to transfer one of the most crowded markets at the Halles to a new location in view of the "inconvenience" which often made it impossible for the merchants to approach the site, but nothing came of this and many similar proposals.[5] Only on the eve of the Revolution did the Hôtel de Ville finally lose patience and dig into its own coffers to make some long-needed improvements in the Halles.[6]

The character of the market in the seventeenth century was quite different from what it had been in the Middle Ages. At one time it had been the custom, as well as the law, for Parisian merchants of all descriptions to take their wares twice weekly (Wednesdays and Saturdays) to the Halles for public display and sale. In the fifteenth and sixteenth centuries, however, many local merchants found it more advantageous to conduct their commerce from shops, thereby escaping the annoying and costly regulatory mechanism of the Halles. In the seventeenth century the only merchants still bound by the ancient obligation to exhibit at the Halles on designated market days were the pork butchers and the candlemakers, and the former, at least, were waging a continuous court battle against what they rightfully considered discrimination against their trade.[7]

On the other hand, out-of-town merchants, particularly of foodstuffs, found the stalls at the Halles convenient and profitable, so the ancient marketplace became increasingly an alimentary market for these *forains*.[8] They sold on a wholesale basis to Parisian merchants very early in the morning, subsequently turning into retailers and thereby incurring the resentment of local merchants. The officials at the Châtelet responsible for providing adequate foodstocks for the population of Paris recognized the vital role of these "foreigners" in "bringing abundance" and urged that they be accorded fair treatment so that still more would be attracted to Paris.[9] The magistrates of Paris much preferred to attract farmers with their wagonloads of wares to the city markets than to have city middlemen scour the countryside and thereby, they were convinced, add greatly to the prices the consumers would ultimately have to pay.

By eight o'clock in the morning most wholesale food merchants had completed their transactions at the Halles. From that time on, buyers made use either of the Halles' retailers or of one of the neighborhood markets.[10] At the end of the seventeenth century there were better than a dozen of these *petits marchés* scattered throughout the city,[11] dispensing a fairly well-rounded line of foodstuffs, although never matching the variety of foods the Halles offered. Some were quite ancient (like the markets of the Rue Notre-Dame, the Place Maubert, and the Saint-Jean Cemetery), but most were of rather recent foundation. The growing population of the city and the mounting congestion at the central Halles naturally created a demand for neighborhood markets for the purchase of such staples as bread, vegetables, fish, meat, and butter.

There was no question, of course, of enterprising individuals establishing such markets purely on their own initiative. As with almost any large business enterprise, one had to be authorized by the Crown. The rents which a market entrepreneur could charge for stallage were carefully prescribed by the Council, presumably in consultation with the Châtelet, whose police function included the supervision of all markets. In the early years of the eighteenth century a baker wishing to sell his wares in one of the neighborhood markets paid a rent of 12 sous per week for an open-air area 4 feet in depth, and 3 feet (the size of his basket) in width. If the same area were covered, his rent would go up to 20 sous. Rents charged to vendors of meat, eggs, cheese, and fruit were much the same. The police were much stricter in enforcing the ancient market regulations at the neighborhood markets than at the Halles. While, for example, one was likely to find some sort of trading at the central market any day except Sunday, the smaller markets were strictly limited to the traditional Wednesdays and Saturdays.[12] Abbeys such as the Temple, Saint-Germain, and Saint-Antoine had been quick to obtain permission to operate lucrative marketplaces on their properties. Noble names do not appear among the participants in such enterprises, but parlementarians and other well-connected middle-class Parisians were obviously involved.[13]

Of even greater importance than the Halles in providing the city with its needs were the two dozen or so *quais* or *ports* (the words were used more or less interchangeably) stretching from the west end of the Tuileries Gardens to the Bastille. Sales off the multitudinous river boats tied up here were almost entirely of a wholesale nature, so these goods generally reached the Halles and other markets for subsequent sale. It has been estimated that around the year 1700 two-thirds to three-quarters of the most vital of all commodities, grain, reached Paris by water, and the percentage had doubtless been even larger in earlier times.[14] Wine was waterborne to an even greater extent. Vital wood and coal also arrived mainly by water. Roads had of course greatly improved in the course of the century, and the increasing amounts of grain, wine, and other goods arriving overland reflected the improvement. However, overland transportation was still far costlier and less convenient than river boats when the latter were available. The ministers at Versailles tended to concentrate highway construction in areas where water routes were either poor or unavailable; it appeared to them rather foolish to expend funds merely to facilitate the passage of an occasional stagecoach if the needs of commerce could be met by river boats.[15] One string of boats with a six-man crew and fourteen horses could transport as much cargo as 400 horses driven by 200 men.[16]

The size of the shallow-draft, flat-bottomed river boats varied greatly, of course. The leviathans of the river traffic were the grain boats which made the upstream journey from as far as Rouen. They were pulled by twenty to twenty-four horses (by law a 25-foot path along both banks had to be kept clear of all obstructions[17]) and took from four to six weeks to transport cargoes comparable to ocean tonnages.[18] These must have been the boats that Brice described as measuring up to 33 *toises* in length (over 200 feet) and unique to the Seine basin.[19] The English visitor Richard Ferrier asserted they had rudders 25 feet long

and capacities of up to 700 tons.²⁰ Such giants could not pass under the
bridges of the Cité, so they unloaded at the Quai de l'École, opposite the
Louvre, which served as the downstream grain port, while the Grève in
front of the Hôtel de Ville accommodated the upstream commerce.

Making the passage of the bridges of the Cité was an experience
which all but the smallest boats avoided. The heavy river traffic in this
restricted area, the low bridge arches (several obstructed by the massive
machinery employed to pump city water), the nine watermills along
the Quai de la Mégisserie (the site of a flourishing market in birds, flow-
ers, and plants quite incongruous in such hubbub²¹), to say nothing of
the expense of the *maîtres des ponts* who had to be hired to pass a boat
under a bridge—all these considerations assured that the island of the
Cité effectively bisected river commerce. The eastern, or upstream, ports
were, as one would expect, clearly the busier of the two.

Besides the central and neighborhood markets, the shops, and, to a
minor extent, the river boats, Parisians could fall back for their everyday table needs on the hordes of street peddlers whose distinctive cries
added as much to the color of the capital as they disturbed its peace. For
centuries they had circulated in the streets of Paris, always to the annoy-
ance of the more sedentary merchants who not only had to pay rents
but also cope with guild and police regulations which the street hawk-
ers generally managed to evade. The peddlers were among the very few
merchants in Paris who had consistently remained unorganized (outside the guild system), and there was deep resentment of the fact
among guildsmen. (Perhaps the only exceptions were the fruit peddlers,
who were required to serve six years of apprenticeship and then pass a
guild examination before becoming qualified to peddle their wares.)²²
In the eyes of the respectable gentlemen of the guilds any kind of street
selling was shameful. By relying on street cries, tantamount to advertising and implying competition, peddlers violated basic guild precepts.²³
Furthermore, by selling away from the marketplace the street peddler
evaded inspection of his wares and committed the unpardonable sin of
regrating. But much as peddling was disapproved, no one had ever been
able to stop the practice. Apparently, as long as householders were willing to pay a small premium for the convenience, the authorities were

helpless. They insisted, however, that guildsmen, at least, refrain from street selling. Quite common were arrests such as the one we read of in the *Traité de la police* of a baker apprehended for merely selling a loaf of bread to a passerby while en route to the legal marketplace.[24]

꒰ ꒰

Whatever the channel by which goods reached the consumer, their sale was organized and regulated under the same philosophy of scarcity that underlay the entire Parisian economy. The magistrates responsible for maintaining an adequate flow of foodstuffs into the city were haunted even in times of plenty by the realization that any year might bring disaster. (Their fears materialized on at least three occasions during the reign of Louis XIV.) Probably because the city lived on the constant edge of scarcity or worse, a chronic state of tension existed between the merchant community and the populace. The complex system of market regulations which had developed over the centuries was based on the unvarying principle of protecting the buyer from the chicaneries of the men of commerce.[25] La Reynie once remarked that "liberty was the soul of commerce," and even Colbert wrote several times of the uselessness of economic policies which restrained the freedom of merchants,[26] but few of their actions suggested that they placed any faith in these words. Far more in character was D'Argenson's assessment of bakers and grain merchants as the "cruellest enemies of the people."[27]

The populace of Paris customarily looked to the city magistrates for the proper regulation of the marketplace. In times of marked distress it was towards the peak of the pyramid—the King himself— that their eyes turned. He was the "national baker." (It was as such that the people of Paris forced his return to the capital during the October Days of 1789.) In truth, the role of Great Provider was one which Louis XIV found rather congenial. After he had helped to ease the wheat shortage of 1662, he wrote in his *Mémoires*, "I appeared to all my subjects like a veritable father of the family who . . . equitably divides his children's and servants' food."[28]

Nothing was dearer to the hearts of economic traditionalists (and both La Reynie and D'Argenson fitted squarely in this category) than

239

amassing the greatest possible volume of food and merchandise in the public markets. Such abundance, created on a regular semiweekly schedule and visible to all eyes, was thought to be the most effective guarantee of fair prices and the surest weapon against hoarders and monopolists. The conservatives bemoaned the decline of the old custom of requiring Parisian merchants to close their shops on market days and forcing them to display their wares at the marketplace.[29] For example, Delamare criticized the recent permission given to the fish merchants to sell their cargoes on the river banks rather than to take them to the fish market at the Halles where they would be in sight of all. "Such is the present state of this commerce," he sadly concluded, "which apparently will be tolerated until it pleases God . . . that the old ordinances and regulations be reinstated.[30] (The same authors on another occasion wrote that "all novelties in matters of police and government are to be feared.")[31]

The time-tested method for assuring abundance at the marketplace —assuming a reasonable degree of cooperation from Nature— was to establish concentric circles around the city for different types of commodities, forbidding local merchants to buy their needs within the area of the circle which applied to their trade. In the seventeenth century, for example, city grain merchants were forbidden to buy in the countryside within a radius of 8 leagues from the city (a Parisian league was about 2.4 miles), wine merchants within 20 leagues, butchers within 7 leagues, chicken merchants within 2 leagues, and so on.[32] For most commodities the distances were set so as to cause the out-of-town producer to lose no more than two days on his trip to market: one day to get to Paris (a journey of 8 leagues in a loaded wagon was about the limit for one day) and another to dispose of his wares in the early hours and make his return journey. It was all to the good if the farmer felt pressed for time, since he might be led to sell at a lower price.[33]

All kinds of benefits were alleged for this system: regional farmers were almost forced to come into Paris since they could not expect anyone to go out to them; the hated middleman was eliminated, since goods had to be carted in by the producer himself or members of his family; the Parisian merchants who could not buy all they required at the Halles were compelled to go out into the countryside a far greater distance than they would have ordinarily expected to go. To force local merchants to obtain their needs in distant markets, their legal purchases at the Halles were often restricted.[34] The same philosophy underlay the innumerable and very ancient prohibitions—still very much a part of the official doctrine—against intercepting a farmer on his way to market and buying the wares off his wagon. The simple logic was that since such merchandise was obviously destined for the Parisian market, it was far more desirable to force the merchants to hunt out food supplies which might otherwise go to rival markets.

Once foodstuffs had reached the Halles in the hoped-for quantities, all kinds of regulations went into effect, ostensibly to guarantee fairness to both buyer and seller. The Lieutenant of Police and his *commissaires* from the Châtelet were responsible for all operations at the Halles and the numerous *petits marchés*, but they worked closely with the officials of the various guilds (the *jurés*) in implementing these market regulations. If, for example, a *juré* determined upon inspection of a batch of merchandise that the quality did not come up to guild regulations, the *commissaire* was called upon to impose the prescribed penalty, in flagrant cases the destruction of the goods. The jurisdiction of the *jurés* extended to all articles offered for sale in the Parisian markets—hence, an obvious source of endless friction with the faubourg and "foreign" merchants.

A vital matter like the determination of prices was rarely left to the vagaries of economic laws. The suspicion was always strong in the minds of the magistrates that when prices underwent unusual fluctuations, sinister manipulators and monopolists must be at work. While a good deal of economic freedom was permitted in the determination of the initial price of a wagonload or boatload of a particular commodity at the start of the market day, from that moment on only downward modifications were permitted. At no time could the opening price be exceeded. Even the opening price was subject to questioning by the authorities if it appeared to be out of line with the prices of similar wares coming from a comparable distance. The first price was supposed to represent no more than cost plus a fair profit, and the average of all opening prices at the Halles, as determined by the *commissaire* on the scene, became the maximum price for that commodity in all the local and even many of the regional markets.[35] Bread and certain other perishables which were still unsold at the end of the market day could not be withdrawn to a storehouse without the specific permission of the *commissaire*. Generally, this official ordered that the price on such perishables be progressively reduced until the goods were sold. This was the moment the poor anxiously awaited. Other types of foodstuffs could be stored overnight and reexhibited the following day and perhaps even the day after that. At no time, however, could the opening price on a batch of goods be exceeded. Grain had to be marked down on the third market day after its arrival if still unsold.

The regulations pertaining to nonalimentary goods were less rigid but operated on much the same principles. Wood and coal prices were established by the authorities (in this case the Hôtel de Ville) in consultation with the merchants as soon as these commodities reached the ports of the city. For three days the price remained the same, then was lowered slightly for another three-day period, and so on until the wares had been sold.[36] Certain kinds of cloth however, could remain on the market for six weeks, but then had to be stored away for a month before being reexhibited—apparently without any price reduction.

Price and market regulations varied greatly from one commodity to the next, usually according to the importance of the item in the overall provisioning of the city. One of the most favored items—in the sense of being the least regulated—was meat. The butchers were the acknowledged aristocrats of the alimentary trades, particularly those fortunate practitioners who owned stalls at the Grande Boucherie located opposite the Châtelet since the days of Louis the Fat (d. 1137). For centuries only they had been admitted to the butchers' guild. During the social and political turmoil of the late fourteenth and early fifteenth centuries (in which butchers played a leading role), the oligarchy of the Grande Boucherie was suppressed at least twice, and in 1416 its *halle* was destroyed. However, the butchers proved as durable as some of their wares. In short order, the Grande Boucherie was rebuilt, the oligarchy's privileges restored, and most of its competitors suppressed. The prized stalls at the Grande Boucherie continued to pass from father to son (the Salic Law prevailed among them), and the Châtelet showed its good will towards the dynasty by forbidding the rental of these stalls to outsiders. In 1637 letters patent of Louis XIII confirmed (in return for a contribution of 90,000 livres to Richelieu's hard-pressed treasury[37]) the rights and privileges of four remaining families of the ancient clan, by name, D'Auvergne, De Saintyon, Thibert, and De Ladéhors. The first-named finally expired in the course of the century, leading to an interminable lawsuit between the three surviving families and, among others, the mistress of Louis XIV, Mme de Montespan, one of the claimants to the property. By the time a judgment was rendered in 1686, the lady had gone the way of most mistresses, a departure that doubtless contributed to a verdict unfavorable to her interests.[38]

While the "Bourbons" of the Grande Boucherie still loomed large in the meat trade in the era of Louis XIV, their historic strangle hold had been loosened considerably. In 1650, over their bitter objections, they had been forced into a city-wide guild of butchers. The Grande Boucherie de la Porte de Paris (which had ceased to be a *porte* for half a millenium) remained with its twenty-nine stalls the most prestigious butcher shop in the city, but a great many competitors had sprung up in every neighborhood. By the end of Louis XIV's reign there were almost half a hundred, some containing only one or two stalls, others, particularly in the *petits marchés,* ten or more.[39] The Boucherie de Beauvais in the Halles with its twenty-eight stalls was the largest of the Grande Boucherie's competitors. All these meat markets were established by royal grant. Their owners were well-placed individuals, neighboring churches, or abbeys, whose only connection with the butcher trade, generally, was collecting rents from the professionals who operated the stalls (a stall at the Grande Boucherie at the end of the century brought a handsome rent of 950 livres annually, doubtless the highest sum collected on butcher stalls in the city).

The butcher trade was relatively free of price regulation. The reason is obvious. The more basic a food item was in the diet of the populace, the greater the political danger resulting from a breakdown in its supply; hence the more stringent the market regulations were likely to be. While bread riots were constantly recurring events in the history of Paris, there was yet to be recorded an *émeute* caused by high meat prices. Meat was simply not a staple of the Parisian masses. Few wage earners could have afforded more than a rare taste of meat. John Locke gave the prices of a pound of various kinds of meat in Paris in 1677. The cheapest, beef, sold for 3 sous. At the end of the century, the price of the same amount of beef had more than doubled.[40] A man making a daily wage of 10 or 15 sous was not likely to eat much beef at such prices. Even as late as 1703, D'Argenson calculated the sale of cattle in the Parisian markets at a mere 20,000 heads, and at that, this figure represented a considerable increase over earlier years.[41]

Although meat was not a critical item for the magistrates, economic traditionalists at the start of the eighteenth century were bemoaning the decay (which mainly meant modernization) of the trade in recent times. Nicolas Delamare expressed indignation over the new "indiscipline" and callous disregard of the public interest on the part of the butchers. At one time, he wrote, the authorities had permitted only trusted and experienced families to work at the meat trade, but as most of these expired the "vicious" practice had been introduced of permitting the rental of butcher stalls to unqualified outsiders solely for profit. Although the police had attempted to hold down prices by regulating the rents that could be charged for the stalls, the influx of "inexperienced, lazy young apprentice butchers" had led to all manner of trouble in the meat markets. At the end of the seventeenth century, Delamare went on, even the remnants of the old butcher aristocracy were trying to worm out from under what remained of "that ancient discipline" that Delamare admired so much. They seemed to be interested only in obtaining authorization for still further increases in their stall rents, regardless of the cost to the public.[42]

Practically all the animals butchered in Paris were procured from the new animal markets south of the city, Poissy and Sceaux. The latter was founded in 1667 on the newly acquired baronial estate of none other than Jean-Baptiste Colbert, who apparently was more interested in collecting the lucrative market fees (conveniently set under his eyes in the Conseil) than in preserving a rural atmosphere on his new barony. The law, again based on the conviction that all middlemen were enemies of society, required Parisian butchers either to appear in person or to send a member of their family to purchase animals for slaughter. Likewise, the seller could not be represented by an agent, since agents were alleged to be under no pressure to close a sale and return to the provinces. If the butcher after purchasing some animals was not quite ready to slaughter them, he could invoke the medieval right of pasturage in the outskirts of the city. However, most of the pasture lands had become heavily populated, and we are told there was likely to be a good deal of opposition, involving even "violence," to such a procedure.[43]

Eventually, however, the newly acquired animals would be driven into the city for slaughter. Delamare tells of constant complaints, not from outraged citizens—they took cattle-drives on the streets of Paris for granted—but rather from the cattle merchants who objected to the harsh treatment accorded the animals on the way from Sceaux to Paris. Since the sellers had to guarantee that the cattle they sold would live at least nine days after purchase, they nervously complained to the Châtelet that the butchers rounded up too many head of cattle at one time, that "this multitude made it impossible to give the animals the care they needed," and that once in Paris they were put in dirty, open stalls, causing "the sudden death of some animals"—and, presumably, lawsuits.[44]

Slaughtering was performed either in the back of the butcher shops or in some nearby location almost certain to be within the city limits. The Grande Boucherie employed a *tuerie et écorcherie* a few hundred yards upstream adjacent to the veal market.[45] The six-stall Boucherie de la Montagne, which belonged to the Church of Sainte-Geneviève, had been forced in the fourteenth century after long litigation to move its slaughterhouse further to the outskirts, but by the seventeenth century this location was, of course, once again in a heavily populated area. When the new Collège Mazarin was erected on the Left Bank in the 1660's, there was much talk of moving a nearby slaughterhouse farther downstream until it was realized that this would place it opposite the Tuileries Palace. Parisian sensibilities appeared to be unruffled by the sight of blood and entrails in the street gutters. Some enterprising subjects of Louis XIV offered to erect new slaughterhouses outside the city limits in return for a fee on each animal slaughtered, but either official indifference or conflicting interests caused these promising plans to come to naught. Public apathy in such matters was so great that Delamare—always the good Roman convinced that such abominations would never have been tolerated in the city of the Caesars—included in his *Traité de la police* an elementary question-and-answer dialogue to expose the speciousness of the objections to reforms,[46] as if they were not already abundantly clear to anyone who walked the streets.

Fish, highly important in a Catholic city like Paris and much prized by the gourmets, formed a commerce entirely unrelated to meat. Its sale was centered in two markets at the Halles: ocean fish in the Marée at the north end of the enclosure and fresh-water fish in a converted house in the Rue de la Cossonerie just to the east. The latter product was provided by the guild of local fishermen which since the early thirteenth century had enjoyed the monopoly of fishing the King's Water extending a short distance upstream from the tip of the Ile Notre-Dame.[47] Carp was easily the most common of a variety of fish caught in these waters. Dr Lister alluded to the "incredible quantity" of this "well-tasted" species consumed during Lent (in contrast to John Locke's comment a few years earlier that "the observation of Lent at Paris is come almost to noe-thing"[48]).

There was nothing very distinctive about the operations of the market for fresh-water fish, but the Marée, the salt-water-fish market, was from several points of view unique. Its operations have been described by a recent historian of the Halles as "completely original" and "astonishing" in their modernity.[49] Even more astonishing, we might add, is the fact that although this "first modern market at the Halles" was already in being at the time of the Crusades, it had been able over all these centuries to exercise so little modernizing influence on its neighbors at the Halles. Of course, the Marée operated under exceptional conditions which forced it to adopt different methods of operation.

Given the transportation facilities of those days, a more hazardous product than fresh ocean fish can hardly be imagined. The nature of the product was such as to make inevitable the separation of producer and seller. A middleman had of necessity to be called upon to carry out the function of transport, and thus the fundamental concept of the market as a place where producer and buyer could be brought into direct contact had long gone by the board.

This intermediary at the Marée between producer and buyer bore the colorful title of *chasse-marée*. Generally he was an inhabitant of one of the coastal fishing villages who purchased fish on his own account from the fishing boats and proceeded to make a wild dash with them by relays of horses or carts to the Halles. Delamare wrote that such men took two days to get to market. A modern authority asserts they made the trip from the Channel ports in less than a day, improbable as this would seem.[50] (In any case, air temperature would in large part determine their speed.) Special roads were set aside for the use of the *chasse-marée*, and the Parlement of Paris, which had overall supervision of this commerce, was constantly urging the *seigneurs* along the routes to improve their road maintenance.[51] Anyone impeding the progress of the *chasse-marées* could count on incurring the displeasure of the *parlementaires*, who we can safely assume took a personal, as well as a professional, interest in the procurement of fresh mackerel, oysters, and other delicacies for the tables of the rich.

On his arrival at the Halles, before daylight if all had gone well and no barrier officer had tried to hold him up for some free fish, the *chasse-marée* was met by a variety of market officials. Their functions were quite ancient, but Louis XIV had not only greatly augmented their numbers but transformed them (for a price) into royal officials, along with small armies of other market and port functionaries. The *déchargeurs-competeurs* were responsible for unloading the fish from the special baskets in which they had been carried to market, making certain there was no more than one kind in each basket, and establishing a count for the benefit of the future buyer. For these services they were paid a small fee deducted from the purchase price according to a prescribed schedule, thereby justifying the price they had paid the King for their offices. Next, the *jurés-vendeurs,* or auctioneers (there were ten of these at the Marée), took over, making the rounds of the market, stopping at each pile of fish and accepting the highest bid offered from the buyers clustered before him. The money received from the sale was immediately handed to the *chasse-marée* so that he could turn homeward, but 12 deniers were first deducted from each pound of fish sold, 10 of the 12 going to the auctioneer and the remainder into a unique insurance fund designed to reimburse any unlucky *chasse-marée* who lost a wheel or a horse on the road, was robbed, or had his fish spoil for any other reason.[52]

The Marée was strictly a wholesale market. It had been the first such market at the Halles and in the seventeenth century continued almost alone in its careful separation of wholesale and retail trade, hopelessly confused in most of the other markets. To buy a small quantity of fish, one went to one of the stalls just outside the Marée proper, to one of the eleven fish markets licensed to operate in Paris, or if one were not too discriminating, to the carts of the fishmongers. The latter were very numerous and in the seventeenth century, unlike earlier times, exclusively female and of a notoriously low social status. The true measure of the social and economic insignificance of the *poissonnières* or *harengères* (in reality they also sold other kinds of fish than herring) was that the authorities had never bothered to organize them—like nearly all the street peddlers, they remained among the rare "free" occupations. Delamare distrusted the quality of their wares, expressing the hope that some day they would come under proper police supervision and be made to cull out their spoiled fish.

Second only to grain in importance among the commodities entering Paris, and from the point of view of tax revenues second to none, was wine. Year in and year out towards the close of the seventeenth century some 200,000 *muids* of wine arrived in Paris by water or by land. Only truly catastrophic economic conditions such as those that occurred in 1708 and 1709 had any visible effect on imports.[53] The liquid capacity of a *muid* at any particular period in the Old Regime is a sub-

ject of endless confusion, but probably the lowest estimate of its equivalent English measure is to be found in Cotgrave's seventeenth-century
dictionary. According to that source, the *muid* would be equivalent to
about 60 gallons, which would make yearly wine imports amount to
some 12,000,000 gallons, or a per capita consumption of roughly 25 gallons. It has been held that wine was too expensive for the masses and
that they drank cheap cider from Normandy.[54] However, the official
lists of Parisian imports for the later seventeenth century show only an
insignificant quantity of cider arriving in the capital (about 1 percent of
the wine[55]), so the populace must have consumed either cheap wine or
water. Despite the usual difficulty of seeing how they could afford it,
one feels compelled to declare for the wine.

Parisian wine merchants were required to travel a record 20 leagues
or more out of the city to obtain their supplies. Only the producer or
members of his family could bring into the city wine made within the
20-league circle. The time and capital necessary for such long-range
commerce partly explain the domination of a small group of wholesalers over the Paris market. These were the wealthy *marchands en
gros* who during most of the Old Regime sought so impassionately to
gain admittance to the Six Corps, the inner sanctum of the merchant
oligarchy. Despite their affluence the guildsmen who had already attained the heights always associated wine merchants with such unsavory professions as the *gargotiers, cabaretiers, taverniers,* and *hôteliers.*
Legally, all these wine merchants were thrown together in an unusual
catchall guild (*les marchands de vin en gros–taverniers–cabaretiers–
hôteliers*) whose members had little in common other than that they
all sold wine in one way or another.[56]

Only the *marchands en gros* enjoyed the right to act as combined
wholesalers and retailers. They all owned their own retail shops in Paris
and when their wine casks rolled off their barges took them there to be
bottled or sold *à pot.* Obviously, the arrangement would have meant
danger from monopolists and price fixers had not some safeguards been
built into the system. For one thing, the *marchands en gros* were compelled to set aside at least one-third of their imports for the small merchants' wholesale market known as L'Etape located in front of the Hô-

tel de Ville. Furthermore, in wine commerce as in all the others the magistrates generally did everything they could to encourage small producers to come to Paris with their wares. In Louis XIV's time a new market especially designed for these *forains* was opened opposite the Place de Grève. Small taverners and cabaret owners could obtain their stocks either at L'Etape or this new market and thus were able to compete with the *marchands en gros.*

Time-honored methods of dispensing alcoholic beverages were changing in the later seventeenth century. Since the Middle Ages wine merchants had been forbidden to allow drinking on their premises. However, they had been allowed to sell *à huis coupés et pot renversé,* which meant that one passed a flacon through an exterior grille, had it returned full, and consumed its contents off the premises. This inconvenient old rule was being increasingly disregarded in Louis XIV's day.[57] Many of the merchants had opened adjoining rooms where one could sit down and drink wine as long as no food was served. Likewise, the medieval distinction between the *tavernier* and the *cabaretier* was crumbling. Traditionally, the *tavernier* could only sell wine *à pot,* unaccompanied by food. But workingmen had gotten into the habit of taking bread to the taverns, and in 1680 a law finally permitted the tavern keeper to furnish "napkins and plates" and certain kinds[58] of simple foods (*ragoûts* excluded) not requiring the services of a cook. The right to serve full-course meals along with wine had from the start been reserved for the *cabaretier.*

The *taverne,* even when it began using napkins, continued to be identified with the *menu peuple.* The *cabaret* attracted a somewhat better class of patrons, at least from an economic point of view, but it is doubtful whether the police and the moralists made any distinction between them. Delamare described *cabarets* as "odious" places of "debauchery." Their reputation was so bad that some of the *cabaretiers* were at the end of the seventeenth century beginning to call themselves *traiteurs* (*restaurant* would not come into use until well into the eighteenth century). For example, in a play presented at the Comédie in 1687 the virtuous heroine is asked to have supper "chez Lamy." She professes to be shocked that a lady of honor like herself should be asked to enter a cabaret, to which the hero replies, "Please, Lamy is not a *cabaret*, it's a *traiteur* of good repute."[59]

❧   ❧

Far and away the most vital requirement of the Parisian market was grain. Because it was so important to the populace, whose diet rested primarily on bread, it was the constant preoccupation of the authorities, from *commissaires* to monarch. The rising of the Parisian *frondeurs* at mid-century made such a psychological impact on young Louis XIV that he never ceased to fear a repetition. A simple police matter like the posting of a seditious placard by a demented peasant would lead to investigations, personally ordered and directed by the King, all out of proportion to the importance of the case. As the editor of the archives of the Bastille observed, "The slightest stirrings [in Paris] put Louis XIV in a state of inexpressible alarm."[60]

The accepted key to the preservation of order in the capital was an abundance of grain. At both the Châtelet and the Hôtel de Ville (between which the supervision of grain imports was regrettably divided according to whether they arrived by land or by water), nothing took priority over this objective. Any time a grain shortage was threatened, the magistrates, with the backing of the ministers, sought to bleed the surrounding countryside of its supply, on the sound principle that the peasant and villager were much less to be feared politically than the city dweller.[61] The irony was that the hungry peasants naturally followed the grain into the city, causing the authorities to thunder out once again with the hoary ordinances against vagabonds.

If one seeks an explanation of the traditional antipathy of Paris and countryside, a good place to begin is the old assumption that the rural areas must feed the capital regardless of consequences to the former. Parisian merchants generally could offer higher prices in the regional markets, and while they often had to cope with protests and even violence from the villagers as the local grain floated away towards the hungry capital, they knew they could count on the support of the intendant and the ministers. Besides, there were all sorts of ways of hiding the grain's true destination; one of the commonest was to allege that it was destined for the army.[62]

In ordinary times, the city magistrates worked through the grain merchants in provisioning the city, but in emergencies this reliance would cease. Commissioners would instead be dispatched by both the Châtelet and the Hôtel de Ville into the surrounding wheat-growing regions to check into real and imagined contraventions of the ordinances (all prepared under urban auspices) and literally pry away grain hoards from local granaries. Delamare proudly claimed that such dramatic "descentes sur les provinces" by the Châtelet commissioners had broken the 1694 famine and had forced down the price of wheat in the Parisian markets from 54 livres per *setier* to 15.[63] At such times, too, the government might well be impelled to import grain at great expense from distant countries: in 1662, for example, from Poland; in 1709-1710 from as far away as the Levant, despite the British naval blockade.[64]

The grain markets of Paris were, at least officially, the most tradition-bound in the city. There were more restrictions, it has been said, on the commerce of grain in the seventeenth century than in the Middle Ages,[65] all aimed at holding down prices and preventing monopoly. At every turn one encountered the medieval conviction that every merchant was a potential enemy of society and the almost universal assurance that human legislation could outmatch their trickeries. Parisian grain merchants were forbidden to buy inside an eight-league zone (extended to ten at the end of the century); they were required to buy in the local markets, never in the farmers' fields; their grain purchases could not be stored in the country, and on arrival in Paris had to be put up for sale immediately in the merchants' boats; they could charge for any part of a boatload of wheat no more than the first price they received; they had to give priority to bourgeois buyers and limit their sales to bakers; they could not employ intermediaries in arranging the sales contract without incurring at least the suspicion of the authorities ... on and on it went. All these regulations were based on experience, and each had doubtless made sense at one time or another. But the idea of changing laws to meet changing market conditions seemed completely foreign to the magistrates. The *anciennes ordonnances* cast a sort of mystical spell on magistrates and public alike.

No voice of economic progressivism was to be heard at either the Châtelet or the Hôtel de Ville. Nicolas Delamare wrote in his *Traité de la police* that the tricks employed by the grain merchants were so numerous that "to detail them would take too long" (although he proceeded to list some common ones). No official was more single-minded and traditionalist in enforcing the grain laws than his superior, La Reynie, who climaxed a lifetime vendetta against the grain merchants by his harsh prosecution in 1694 of the most noted grain merchant in Paris, Jean Roger. (On appeal Roger was later found innocent of La Reynie's accusations.[66]) Typical of La Reynie's economic thinking was a letter he wrote to the Controller-General at Versailles opposing the grain merchants' request for a long-needed roof over the open-air grain market at the Halles. La Reynie's thinking was that if the merchants did not have to fear the rain they would be in no hurry to sell and prices would inevitably rise.[67] (This from the man who in so many other respects showed himself the great advocate of progress.) D'Argenson could be just as hostile towards the grain merchants as his predecessor, as witness the following scolding: "There is present in the commerce of wheat . . . in this city an inexcusable malice, but the large number of accomplices and their closeness . . . make it impossible to penetrate this mystery of iniquity." He went on to rebuke the "criminal collusion" among "farmers, bakers, and merchants."[68]

Such official outbursts had long been a familiar part of the Parisian scene. They were entirely politic on the occasions when the elements and antiquated marketing methods combined to create grain shortages, but given the very limited financial resources of the Parisian grain merchants at this time and the great diffusion of the grain trade among hosts of very small "farmers, bakers, and merchants," such talk of widespread "collusion" was naïve at best. How much of this the magistrates sincerely believed and how much was red herring to distract public opinion is difficult to say.

While the economic thinking of men like La Reynie and D'Argenson was entirely traditional, the growth of Paris in the seventeenth century was creating pressures and changes which they were helpless to prevent and could only deplore. In the view of one authority on the French grain trade, Abbott Payson Usher, the old marketing system for grains began to crumble in the second quarter of the seventeenth century.[69] Up until then the grain supply in the region of Paris had been so bountiful in relation to the demand that the most primitive marketing methods sufficed. But as the reign of the Roi Soleil commenced, the growth of the Parisian market caused a development, Usher wrote, "which carries us rapidly from conditions that are purely medieval to conditions that are almost modern."[70] The capital began to dominate the regional markets in a manner the government had always striven to prevent but which to the modern mind seems a natural and inevitable result of the growth of the city.

Usher's thesis is that instead of grain being taken by the regional producers to innumerable small local markets, allowed to find its price, and being retained, at least in part, to meet the just demands of the locality, the long-forbidden practice of "country buying" by Parisian merchants came into practice. Both within the restricted zone and beyond it, eager buyers (merchants, bakers, and agents of all sorts) from Paris began to scour the countryside, contacting producers directly instead of in the marketplace, and even committing the worst of all sins—contracting for crops still green in the fields. Some of these purchases found their way immediately to Paris, but more were stored in rural granaries—again illegally. As a consequence, the small regional markets began to dry up, and the only meaningful grain prices became those of Paris. The competition of the urban giant, in earlier times feared only in times of scarcity, became perennial. For example, the once flourishing market of Lagny, seven leagues to the east of Paris, was described by an inhabitant in 1699 as "quite deserted for eighteen or twenty years."[71]

From the viewpoint of a La Reynie or a Delamare, the most deplorable part of these new developments was that a great deal of grain, having been illegally acquired in the first place, was never taken to the legal marketplaces in Paris, making it impossible to ascertain the quantities held by the bakers. Since, in turn, the regulation of bread prices was very much dependent on knowledge of the supplies of grain in the possession of the bakers, one can understand the anguish of the magistrates. When really bad crop years like those of 1694, 1698, or 1708 materialized and the price of bread skyrocketed, economic conservatives pointed knowingly to the disregard of the revered ordinances as the cause of all the trouble. The growth of "country buying" was only one of many sins they could point to. Grain merchants could also be accused of playing fast and loose with regulations such as those limiting the period of sale for a shipment to three days, prohibiting price increases during the market period, and barring the employment of agents to consummate sales, among others.[72] Regardless of what one reads in the statutes and market regulations, the Parisian grain market at the end of the seventeenth century was a much different piece of economic machinery from what it had been at the start of that century.

Grain, of course, was only a means to an end. "The Diet of the Parisians," Dr Lister observed, "consists chiefly of Bread and Herbs";[73] it was the responsibility of the magistrates at the Châtelet to assure adequate grain for that bread. Bread-eating habits of the natives being what they were, a quantity of grain was needed which would surely have supplied modern cities several times the size of seventeenth-century Paris. One can only sympathize with the magistrates as they walked a tightrope between popular unrest and the alienation of some or all of the people connected with the production and distribution of bread in Paris. Many things conspired to make their task a difficult one. The real value of wages had been sinking generation by generation for several centuries. As we have noted, price historians estimate that a day laborer's wage expressed in the amount of wheat it would buy was at the start of the eighteenth century about a quarter of what it had been around 1450. The marked rise in the population of seventeenth-century Paris undoubtedly contributed to this long-term inflationary process. Archaic market regulations, which officialdom stubbornly refused to recognize as archaic, compounded difficulties.

Also detrimental to the cause of social tranquillity was the effect of increased upper-class opulence on long-established consumer habits. Along with the demand for carriages, theater tickets, ever-finer dining places, and other hitherto undreamed-of amenities of life, the new affluence of the middle and aristocratic classes demanded not only more store-bought bread but a much better variety and quality. Delamare referred to this new trend as "voluptuousness . . . in the manner of bread."[74] Striking a note familiar to later generations of Americans, he deplored the popular demand for still "more whiteness, more softness," greater "delicacy." All kinds of new and expensive store breads, employing milk, barm, and the like, came on the market: *pain à la Reine, pain à la Montoron, pain mollet, pain façon de Gonnesse, pain cornu, pain de Sigovie, pain blême, pain à la citrouille,* to name only the more important ones.

Such innovations were most upsetting to police officials who equated change with trouble. Nothing had appeared more safely unchanging than the bread industry; the statutes of the bakers' guild for 1719 were remarkably similar, at least on paper, to those of 1319.[75] Only three grades of bread could be legally sold by the city bakers until almost the dawn of the seventeenth century, at which time a fourth made its appearance, named *pain du chapitre* because it emanated from the bake ovens of the Chapter of Notre-Dame. This was a fine white bread which utilized a dough so heavy it had to be kneaded by foot—"after carefully washing them in hot water." The Châtelet was finally persuaded to sanction the new bread, but tried valiantly during the entire seventeenth century to hold the line at four grades. An ordinance of 1635 and subsequent laws restricted bakers to the display of the four official varieties, although permitting them to bake the more exotic breads on special order and on condition they be shelved in the "back room or . . . out of view."[76]

During the great bread shortages at the turn of the century, D'Argenson waged an intensive campaign against what he considered excessive pampering of the popular tastes. In his view, the greater the variety of breads the more difficult became the Châtelet's task of setting and enforcing the weekly prices of those breads. After repeated appeals to the Controller-General he managed to have Parlement exhume an ordinance dating back to 1436, reducing the number of allowable breads to two: brown-white and brown, thus excluding the two varieties of white bread (*chapitre* and *challis*) most in demand by the bourgeois clientele.[77] As evidence of the social sensitivity of the Châtelet in times of bread shortage, Delamare's words may be cited: ". . . we will see no more of that enormous difference in the nourishment of the rich and that of the poor which gave birth to envy and caused murmurings." During the crisis *commissaires* from the Châtelet were required to visit all Parisian bakeries twice weekly to ensure that they baked *le pain bis* —the rye bread which was the only kind the poor could afford. At that, the reluctant bakers had to be promised indemnification if they lost money on the trade.[78] D'Argenson, something of a Spartan, referred contemptuously to the "delicacy of a few bourgeois who insist absolutely on eating white bread despite the prohibitions."[79] As he feared, the traffic in such bootleg bread continued at the Halles, but one sees why D'Argenson was such a favorite among the Parisian poor.

Not only were the bakers told in good times and bad the quality of bread they were allowed to sell; they also had their prices and profits carefully regulated by the Châtelet, which worked hand-in-hand with the bakers' guild to maintain "order" in the trade. For centuries there had been bitter arguments among the magistrates on how best to control bread prices (the principle itself was never disputed). Some had called for varying the price of a loaf fixed in weight, others for varying the weight and maintaining the price—in either case, of course, according to the fluctuations of grain prices. Both systems had been tried repeatedly without a consensus having been reached. In the later seventeenth century the advocates of the fixed price–variable weight school were in the ascendancy. The price for the basic loaf (double and half sizes were also available) was 1 sou, but the amount of bread one received for one's money varied sharply according to the price of grain and the quality of the loaf. When John Locke was in Paris in 1677, he wrote that for 1 sou he could buy a five-ounce loaf of *pain mollet*, seven ounces of *pain de Challis*, ten of the intermediate grade, and thirteen of the *pain noir*.[80] Some idea of the price squeeze consumers had to face in the seventeenth century can be gained from the comparison of the quantity of the best white bread one received for 1 sou in the course of the century: in 1635, ten ounces; in 1677, five; in 1700, three.[81]

In order to arrive at what constituted a fair margin of profit for the trade, it became necessary for the *commissaires* of the Châtelet to turn bakers themselves periodically. In company with a trusted retired baker, senior members of the guild, and other officials, they would buy different kinds of grain on the local market, supervise their milling, and then retire to a neutral arena (the Hôtel-Dieu bakery generally) to find out how many loaves of bread could be produced from a given quantity of flour. From these experiments would come tariffs of prices the city bakers were allowed to charge.[82]

Ironically, while all these regulations designed to protect the less opulent consumers applied only to the city bakeries, the latter were of relatively little import to the lower classes except possibly in times of crisis. Bakeries were mainly for the bourgeoisie. From them came the bourgeois *petit pain*, which is to say any loaf less than three pounds in weight (generally a good deal less) and usually made with white flour. Such delicacies were beyond the reach of the working man. He patronized, not the city bake shops, but rather the semiweekly (Wednesdays and Saturdays) bread markets held at the Halles and the *petits marchés* scattered about the city. The bakers found there were mainly the *forains*, village bakers who carted into Paris semiweekly loads of *gros pain* from as far distant, La Reynie wrote, as fifteen leagues.[83] Such loaves weighed at least three pounds, were dark in color, heavy in consistency, and a good deal cheaper than anything the city bakers had for sale. The latter were allowed to sell in the public markets only the *petit pain* of less than three pounds. However, like so many other city merchants in the seventeenth century, bakers were making only minor use of the traditional markets. When La Reynie was asked once by a minister how the city bakers could be made to lower their prices, he replied that the bakers were not worth bothering about, since they were few in number and "sent no bread to the public markets."[84] Most Parisians would have been in dire straits had they had to depend on local bakers alone. Sauval (from whom Delamare apparently borrowed his statistics in this instance) listed 1524 bread vendors in the public markets, of whom no more than five or six hundred came from the city and faubourgs.[85]

The *forains* must have made a colorful sight as they crowded by the hundreds into the tiny plots the Châtelet assigned them in the public markets. Just how limited they were in elbow room can be judged from the 342 stalls assigned to the *forains* in the small northeast area of the Halles between the famous pillory and the salt-water fish market, to say nothing of 158 in the even more restricted market of the Cimetière Saint-Jean and 159 in the Place Maubert.[86] To encourage them to keep returning to the city (and in bad times the long trip through the hungry countryside followed by a sojourn in a disorderly marketplace could be hazardous indeed), the *forains* were exempt from the usual regulations regarding price and weight. However, they were required to sell all their bread during the market day, reducing their prices after four o'clock if any loaves remained unsold. Especially when grain prices were high, the police enforced this rule with "rigor" amidst the protestations of the bread merchants but the paeans of the masses.[87] Nothing, however, except the law of supply and demand prevented the *forains* from asking any price they wished for their bread before four o'clock and baking it however they pleased. All the Châtelet had ever been able to do in this regard was to require them to stamp weights on their loaves. These out-of-town bakers played such a vital role in feeding the Parisian masses that apparently even the most inveterate traditionalist trod softly in their presence.

Life becomes difficult for the Grand Chantre

LIKE so much else in the Paris of the Grand Siècle, education, at least below the university level, was a fascinating battleground of the old and the new. That the same could not be said of university education was due to the astonishing success of its directors in assuring that the battle was never joined and the *status quo* was maintained. In the words of a great historian of the University of Paris, while all other cultural institutions were flowering, "it was isolating itself more and more from the rest of society."[1] For its absurd attachment to superannuated traditions, the University had had to pay a heavy price. Its prestige among the progressive intellectuals of Europe probably hit an all-time low by the end of the seventeenth century. Its student body declined so disastrously that of the forty-three *collèges* which made up the University at the start of the century, at least nine had closed their doors a hundred years later. Its arts faculty became caricatured in contemporary literature as solemn imbeciles, the medical faculty attained dubious immortality in Molière's lampoons as the slaves of Aristotle, and the entire law faculty at one point sank to a total of one.[2]

However, we are not much concerned with the University of Paris as an institution of higher learning. As such it belonged not to Paris so much as to all France and, in a better day, all Europe. What does concern us is what is today neatly categorized as primary and secondary education, although it never would have occurred to seventeenth-century educators to make such a distinction. In this area the conflict between the old and the new was abundantly evident. Here the dynamism so badly lacking at the top of the educational ladder made the history of seventeenth-century Parisian education as fruitful as it was bewildering in its complexity.

Historically and legally, the responsibility for teaching seventeenth-century Parisian children to read, write, and reckon rested incontestably in the hands of the Grand Chantre of the Cathedral Chapter of Notre-Dame. This official's control over primary education constituted one of the most ancient privileges in the city, resting as it did on his connection with the school which Notre-Dame, like all cathedrals, had once provided for the training of its choir boys. On occasion, the Grands Chantres had been known to trace back their alleged educational rights a full millennium to the start of the Christian era, although one of the most noted of their number, Claude Joly (d. 1700), in defending the rights of the Grands Chantres against a growing list of challengers wisely made no claims anterior to the twelfth century.[3] By natural progression, however, the bailiwick of the Grand Chantre had slowly expanded from the cathedral school to all Paris and its outskirts. Proudly bearing the title Collateur, Juge, et Directeur des Ecoles de Grammaire, he claimed exclusive jurisdiction over the whole of the *petites écoles*, or grammar schools, of the city.

Precisely how many of these *petites écoles* there were at any one time in seventeenth-century Paris is very difficult to say. Around 1620 the city and faubourgs were districted for school purposes into 166 zones—104 on the River Bank, 51 on the Left, and 11 in the Cité.[4] In each of these 166 zones, two *petites écoles*, one for boys and another for girls, were supposed to be available. That the authorities had once again confused the desirable with the actual state of things is to be strongly suspected. The number of schools should have, if anything, increased considerably in the course of the century; but when Louis XIV in 1673 imposed a special tax on the *maîtres d'écoles*, he was informed that the schoolmasters of the *petites écoles* numbered only about a hundred.[5] (Their economic status, incidentally, was evidenced by their inclusion in virtually the lowest tax bracket in a long list of occupations.) However, the stagnation or even decline in the number of the *petites écoles* does not necessarily mean that total school enrollments were suffering, since there is much evidence, including the alarmed outbursts of the Grand Chantre, that new and different kinds of schools were taking up the slack.[6]

The *petites écoles* were tuition-supported grammar schools meeting six days each week from eight to eleven and two to five, with Thursday afternoon off. School buildings were nil; the master or mistress generally used a ground-floor room in his or her own dwelling as a classroom. Prohibitions against the mixing of sexes were almost as frequent as enjoinders against heresy. In one of the Grand Chantre's pronouncements on the subject (1655) he alluded to the "depravity of the present century" and the alarming fact that six-year-olds now knew as much as adults.[7] Nevertheless, the very wording and repetitiousness of these prohibitions suggest that teachers and parents were less concerned about the precociousness of the children than the Grand Chantre and that a good deal of coeducation must have been practiced. Seriousness of purpose characterized every aspect of the work of the grammar schools. To try to stir up interest in the learning process was not apparently the teacher's function, and a schoolmaster who dared employ a *roman* in his classroom might well find himself in jail.[8]

As remuneration, a member of the teachers' guild received around 300 to 400 livres depending on sex. Considering that he or she had to hand over 32 livres annually to the Grand Chantre for renewal of license,[9] the teacher's lot must have been a hard one. Whether some masters were worth even this pittance is questionable. A satirical pamphlet prepared by some of the many enemies of Claude Joly accused him of employing as teachers a motley collection of "cooks, wigmakers, puppeteers, and even lackeys for whom neither name nor address can be given."[10] Perhaps a fairer judgment can be reached by reading between the lines of Joly's ardent defense of the *petites écoles*. He acknowledged that there were schoolmasters "who had not studied," which, coming from this source, was an admission that the *petites écoles* sometimes dragged the bottom of the barrel for teachers. But he went on to say that "there are very capable ones among them, some being priests, others masters of arts, and still others without degrees who have nonetheless studied a good deal."[11] Striking a rare nonpolemical note, he admitted that the qualifications of his teachers varied from one school to the next, often according to the wealth of the neighborhood, which is doubtless as close as one will ever come to a correct appraisal of the teachers of the *petites écoles*.

Whatever the quality of his teachers, the Grand Chantre remained the absolute monarch of primary education. He governed according to statutes unchanged except in trifling details since the Middle Ages. According to Félibien, an "uprising" of the teachers against the Grand Chantre's authority had (predictably) taken place in 1626, but, even more predictably, the Parlement had backed up the voice of authority and the teachers probably emerged in a worse position than ever. No person could legally teach in a lower school without being personally screened by the Grand Chantre for both professional competence and, perhaps more important, orthodoxy.[12] (However, formal religious instruction was not allotted disproportionate time at the *petites écoles*; the statutes required catechism lessons only on parts of Wednesday and Saturday afternoons.) Licenses to teach were good for one year only. In his book on the *petites écoles*, Joly noted with obvious satisfaction that the teacher did not enjoy an "office" but rather a "commission" which could be revoked any time the Grand Chantre was displeased.[13]

Since the school was generally held in the teacher's domicile, the statutes forbade him to change residence without an inspection of the new premises by the Grand Chantre's agents and his formal approval. Unauthorized meetings of the schoolmasters and collection of funds for community use without permission were sternly forbidden in terms very much like those applied to clandestine organizations of journeymen. As befitted an absolute ruler, the Grand Chantre sat as judge each Thursday afternoon (the traditional free time) at three o'clock to pass on all *contestations* involving teachers or schools.[14] Appeals from his rulings went directly to Parlement, bypassing the Châtelet—in itself a good indication of his power.

One of the most surprising features of the Grand Chantre's long domination of primary education was that he had managed to crowd out the parish priests from any voice in the educational process, which one would assume would be one of their principal responsibilities. The *curés* had no say in any grammar school that the Grand Chantre chose to license in their parishes. The selection of books, teachers, curricula, in short, the total administration of the schools lay outside the province of the *curés*. If the parish priest wished to establish a school within his parish, he could do so only with the approval of the Grand Chantre, and how much voice he would be allowed in its administration was for the Grand Chantre to decide.[15] Backing up his vicegerent, the Archbishop of Paris in 1666 issued an order cautioning laymen and priests alike against meddling in the affairs of the *petites écoles*, the former under penalty of excommunication, the latter of suspension from their priestly office.[16] However, as we shall see, the day was not far off when Grand Chantre and *curés* would meet in acrimonious legal battle and when even archbishops would be "protecting [the *curés*] with all their power" against the tyranny of the Grand Chantre.[17]

According to the letter of the law (in this case the revised University statutes of 1600), a young man finishing a *petite école* at the age of about nine could continue his education in one of the *collèges* affiliated with the University.[18] He could choose from among almost forty of these on the Left Bank. All these institutions attracted students from both Paris and the provinces. Many were ancient foundations established by some wealthy lay or clerical patron out of sympathy for the poor homeless provincial students. Each college provided living quarters and to favored students small *bourses* amounting to 50 to 150 livres annually. The recipients (*boursiers*) could count on this aid until they had attained the degree of *maître ès arts*. Frequently, the donor had provided that these foundation scholars emanate from specific towns or provinces. For example, the Collège de Hubant in the Rue de la Montagne-Sainte-Geneviève was supposed to admit three *boursiers* from the village of Hubant or the surrounding region. In making his annual visitation in 1696 the University Rector was disgruntled to find that all three *boursiers* from this college were Parisians. Apparently, its revenues were no longer sufficient to cover the expenses of students from distant parts of France.

Many of these colleges were on the verge of physical and moral bankruptcy. Still reflecting the clerical orientation of medieval education, they resembled cloisters (sometimes prisons) far more than university residence halls. The members theoretically lived a community life. All doors were locked at nine every evening and the keys deposited with the principal. For many of the teachers, sons of poor villagers and miserably paid, the semimonastic existence offered no difficulties, and there is even one well-authenticated case of a teacher never setting foot outside of the high walls surrounding his college over a ten-year period.[19] The visitation records for Louis XIV's day too often provided a catalog of miseries and shortcomings affecting both teachers and students. They allude to "great disorders," "the need to restore discipline," the failure of college principals to render financial accounting "since twelve years," insufficient revenues to maintain a student body, the rental of living quarters to commercial warehouses for the sake of a few livres, and the like.[20] There were exceptions, of course. For example, the Rector lauded the "rigorously observed" discipline of the Collège de Montaigu, except "for three *boursiers* who having come into money have fallen into the corruption and contagion of riches."[21]

The University colleges were of two sorts: *grands* and *petits*. The latter were particularly apt to be decadent and the source of constant trouble for the authorities. Little or no teaching was done in them. The revenues which had been bestowed on them at the time of their foundation had, because of the constant rise in prices, become very inadequate. Consequently, the principals and the *boursiers* often made ends meet by renting out rooms or giving lessons. The *grands collèges* were somewhat more prosperous. After Mazarin's elegant new Collège des Quatre Nations became affiliated with the University in 1688, there were ten of these *grands collèges*, also known as *collèges de plein exercice*. These were residence halls like the others, the great difference being that the *grands collèges* were teaching institutions as well. Each normally offered eight grades, from the sixth up, culminating in two years of "philosophy." Thus, what we would today term secondary education merged imperceptibly into higher education. As soon as a student had completed his two years of philosophy, he was eligible to take his examination for the bachelor's degree. He was supposed to have studied at a University college since the age of nine or ten, which, if the University statutes had been strictly enforced, would have barred the graduates of the popular Jesuit and other religious schools from a University degree. But in actual practice, this rule was not observed, and the two years of philosophy at a University college generally sufficed for the *baccalauréat*. The *license* and *maîtrise ès arts* followed in quick succession.[22]

The teachers at these colleges, known as *régents*, all had M.A. degrees, were members of the University's Faculty of Arts and products of the educational system in which they were now teaching. Poorly esteemed by contemporary society, they eked out miserable existences from the pittances passed on to them from the profits of the *messageries* (the long-distance messenger service the University had operated since the time of the Crusades), small student fees, and tutorial income. None was a specialist. Each taught in its entirety one or another of the eight grades his college offered. None had ever been exposed to mathematical or scientific studies, and if he touched on such matters in his classes it was at the expense of the official curriculum.

The *régents* of the Arts faculty were still legally bound to celibacy, although their colleagues on both the law and medical faculties had by this time been permitted to marry. Violations of the rules of celibacy were frequent and more or less condoned, but a strong faction among the Arts faculty was always ready to argue that marriage should at least bar a *régent* from the higher administrative and honorific offices. In the 1670's a prominent professor's marriage provided a *cause célèbre* in the course of which "sonnets of the married *régents* against celibacy" were presented to the chancellor and Louis XIV.[23] Although the latter should certainly have been very receptive to the theme, he discreetly dodged the issue, and celibacy remained a legal obligation for the Arts faculty. Not surprisingly, the seventeenth century witnessed something of a crisis among these *régents*. Their ranks were barely being replenished, thanks largely to the understandable attraction for both parents and students of the more lucrative and glamorous professional careers, particularly law. The University helped matters not a whit by stubbornly refusing to recognize any but its own Arts graduates as worthy of an academic position in the colleges.[24]

Students in the colleges were broadly classified as *boursiers*, board-ers, and day students. Some well-to-do Parisians were willing to pay 300 to 500 livres to board their sons at one or another of the colleges, but most Parisian students went to the University schools as *externes*, at-tending one of the nine or ten *collèges de plein exercice*. The principals and teachers had little regard for these *externes* and complained of see-ing them only when they paid their fees or presented themselves for a degree. The daily contact of the footloose day students with the regula-tion-ridden boarders and the "envy" stirred up among the latter for more freedom were never-ending sources of trouble for the University officials.

꙳   ꙳

The historic division of Parisian education between the Grand Chan-tre and the University, with the line of demarcation drawn about at nine-year-olds, had worked relatively well until the seventeenth century. There had been inevitable conflicts and occasional invasions of one or another's jurisdictions by third parties, but the public had generally ac-cepted the arrangement. Perhaps even more important, the law courts had always strongly defended the *status quo*. On both these counts— public and legal opinion—the old order changed radically in the seven-teenth century. The public showed its impatience with both Grand Chantre and University by patronizing a surprising number of schools new not only in name but in pedagogy, and the Parlement, generally so conservative, rendered a number of decisions sharply opposed to the Grand Chantre. The latter spent a large part of the seventeenth century in litigation. In 1661, it is said that he had nineteen suits pending in the Parlement with the scriveners alone, only one of his many compet-itors.[25] The extent of his legal entanglements can be seen in the sharp increases in the dues which the Grand Chantre assessed on the teachers of the *petites écoles*. At the start of the seventeenth century the teachers paid only a few sous tribute; in the 1670's 32 livres (some authorities say 50) were demanded of the impoverished teachers.[26] The increase was justified by the extraordinary number of lawsuits the Grand Chantre felt obliged to wage to defend the interests of the *petites écoles*.

That the old order was at last changing can hardly cause surprise. While reliable statistics on school enrollments during the century are almost nonexistent, one can reasonably surmise that the known increases in population and wealth in Paris in the seventeenth century resulted in a demand for more and better education. Furthermore, we know that the great Catholic renaissance of the first half of the century made itself felt in education. One of the principal forms taken by the religious renaissance was the revitalization of old teaching orders and the establishment of new ones. The education of young females was the main gainer as new orders like the Ursulines, the Daughters of the Congregation of Notre Dame, the Daughters of the Cross, and many others began establishing convent schools thought by many to be superior to anything available for boys.[27] The religious revival also led to a strong movement to educate the poor. Since none of the existing schools could perform this function, the *école de charité* had to be created, leading to half a century of bitter litigation with the Grand Chantre. Finally, it should be obvious that a society which produced and in good part accepted unorthodox geniuses like Descartes and Pascal would not be altogether tolerant of the obscurantism of the *petites écoles* and the *collèges* of the University.

By the time Louis XIV died, the once simple educational structure of Paris had been replaced by a jumble of church, lay, and mixed schools controlled by a number of conflicting authorities. Oddly enough, Louis had kept hands off. The monarch who made almost a fetish of tidying institutional jumbles apparently drew back from tampering with entrenched interests such as these. Late in Louis XIV's reign, when financiers and others were exploiting the state's desperate need for money, an offer of 150,000 livres was made for the exclusive right to manage Parisian education below the University level. D'Argenson, asked his opinion by Versailles, wrote back to the Controller-General that while it would be highly "desirable" to end all this "confusion" and place all schoolteachers under the same superior, he doubted if the money offered "was worth the difficulties which would have to be surmounted."[28] Nothing came of the offer, of course.

The incessant wrangling and furor which characterized the Parisian educational scene in the seventeenth century possibly reached their height in the 1670's. Finding himself attacked from all sides, Claude Joly, the Grand Chantre, marshaled all his counterarguments and published in 1678 a classic diatribe of nearly six hundred pages "against the machinations of those who threatened the ancient and Canonical order which must be maintained for the proper education and instruction of the young" (conveniently known as Joly's *Traitté historique*). In his Preface, Joly ascribed the educational unrest of the times to two simple causes: the appearance of pedagogical fortune-hunters as a consequence of the recent growth of the city, and ignorance of the historical origins of the Grand Chantre's rights. He announced his intention to clarify the second in order to foil the machinations of the first. Like many people born for combat, however, instead of simply defending a fixed position he proceeded to extend it into enemy territory.

Joly was unwilling to concede that the age of nine was the proper breakoff point between his schools and the University's. He wished to remove the latter from all education below the two years of Philosophy which led directly to the bachelor's degree,[29] a proposal which appears quite sensible to an American mind but was anathema to a *universitaire*. In his view, his *petites écoles* were and had been from the earliest times "the true Grammar Schools without reservation." Furthermore, "grammar" he associated with the humanities. He strongly supported an assertion he ascribed to Erasmus that young men should receive a humanistic education to the age of eighteen, imparted, in the Parisian area, at least, in Joly's *petites écoles*. Most of the confusion over education had developed, he argued, from taking too literally the word *petites* and thinking of these schools as places where small children simply learned to read, write, and reckon. Just how far he was prepared to stretch his interpretation of "grammar" can be judged by his ensnarement of even Oriental languages for his schools on the ground that "there is no language which is not learned by Grammar." He acknowledged the argument was rather pointless since there existed neither a demand for such languages nor masters to teach them, but if both conditions were met he insisted that Oriental languages be taught only in his *petites écoles*.[30]

Some months before the appearance of Joly's *Traitté historique* the author found himself summoned before Parlement as co-defendant along with the teachers of the *petites écoles* in a suit brought by the Faculty of Arts of the University. The charge was that the defendants had flagrantly violated Article X of the University Statutes forbidding the *petites écoles* to take students over the age of nine. This suit was only one phase of an intensive campaign waged by the University against its junior rivals. To the immense indignation of the Grand Chantre, the University Rector placed posters "in all the public places and streets" of the city informing the public that henceforth teachers or pupils affiliated with any *petite école* accepting students over the age of nine were declared "incapable of acquiring any degree or privilege in the [University] and forfeited any which they might have acquired earlier."[31]

It goes without saying that both parties to the dispute were playing the same game. While the Grand Chantre was making irresponsible demands that secondary education be vested in his hands, the University was moving downward into his bailiwick. There is probably some truth to Joly's charge that some of the *collèges* were even conducting classes in reading. It was no secret that young Parisian children often either boarded at these *collèges* or were given lessons by the *régents* in preference to being sent to a *petite école*. D'Argenson once wrote to the Controller-General of the economic importance of such work, especially to clerical students at the *collèges*: "How many clerics attain the highest degrees ... only by means of the lessons which they give at their houses or ... at those of the bourgeois!"[32] The minutes of the directors of the Hôtel-Dieu contain frequent denunciations of the University masters of arts by schoolmasters for accepting primary grade students in defiance of the law. (The hospital's interest in such cases lay in the percentage of the fines they received upon conviction.) Parlement had several times accommodated the Grand Chantre by ruling that no master of arts affiliated with the University could give lessons in the *ville* proper.[33] When Blégny prepared his city directory in the early 1690's, this law was apparently being observed. He stated that numerous masters of arts were available in the University Quarter and faubourgs to teach the young, but he mentioned none in the *ville*.[34]

While the Grand Chantre and the University were waiting interminably for the courts to settle their differences, the acrimony between them raged as fiercely as ever. One of Joly's most notable antagonists was a certain Pourchot, at the time *régent* of the Collège des Grassins but who went on later to become Rector of the University. The two men exchanged such unacademic compliments as *parricide, factieux,* and *rapace.* Pourchot repeatedly and publicly charged that the Grand Chantre, thanks to his sale of teachers' licenses and the court fees he collected in his Thursday afternoon sessions, had built up a fine racket worth four to five thousand livres annually.[35] Joly, in his turn, charged that Pourchot was simply trying to extend and enrich his own domain. The charge was quite credible, since the marked interest which the university personnel were showing in primary education in the later part of the century[36] could hardly have been without economic motivation. However, equally clear was the fact that for many Parisian parents the *petites écoles* of the Grand Chantre were not filling educational needs.

Of all the battles the Grand Chantre waged in the later seventeenth century in defense of the medieval *status quo,* the one which probably went worst for him was with the orders of teaching sisters. From the earliest times convent schools had formed part of the educational scene in Paris, but their main function had always been the education of girls intended for the religious life. The appearance in the Catholic revival of the early seventeenth century of many new religious orders dedicated to the Christian education of young females irrespective of their future intentions in life not only changed the character of the convent schools but also the hitherto tolerant attitude of the Grand Chantre. As day schools for the education of the daughters of the Parisian bourgeoisie, they now posed a serious threat to the *petites écoles.* When Claude Joly accused the sisters of illegally accepting children whose parents were able to pay tuition at the *petites écoles,* one replied: "If others than poor girls slip in, it would be against public liberty and charity to prevent [them] from choosing the education which seems to them the best and most convenient. . . ."[37]

In defense of their right to maintain lay schools the sisters cited names that would have silenced a lesser antagonist. They claimed authorization from bishops, archbishops, and the Parlement; the Ursulines went to the top of the hierarchy and claimed papal support. None of these, however, intimidated Joly. "Neither the Pope nor *messieurs les archevêques*," he wrote, "intended to diminish in the least the rights of the *chantre* of Paris."[38] He termed the sisters' arguments "specious" and brought suit against them in the Parlement. Doubtless to his great sorrow, the verdict when finally rendered was a sweeping victory for the sisters, upholding their right to maintain tuition schools for girls in Paris in competition with the *petites écoles*. It has been suggested that the Parlement was at last becoming cognizant of the insufficiency of the *petites écoles* and wished to show its approval of educational innovations regardless of how they conflicted with traditional rights.[39] This may be unduly flattering to the hidebound conservatives in the Parlement, but one can hardly question the public's growing impatience with the Grand Chantre's educational autocracy. The convent schools continued to grow in the second half of the century at a rate which by the Grand Chantre's own admission "astonished" him.

A more manageable *bête noire* for the Grands Chantres in the seventeenth century than the teaching sisters was the scriveners' schools. The scriveners—*écrivains*—had once been copyists but were understandably shaken by the invention of printing in the fifteenth century and had accommodated themselves to a new world by becoming teachers of penmanship. In 1570 they obtained royal authorization to form a scriveners' guild, thus coming under the protection of the Châtelet, which supervised all the *communautés des arts et métiers*. They gradually broadened out from the teaching of penmanship to basic education, thereby undoubtedly qualifying as some of the pedagogical fortune-hunters Joly claimed had sprung up with the recent expansion of Paris. With the Châtelet's backing the scriveners were by the early seventeenth century not only running full-fledged primary schools but boldly challenging the right of the *petites écoles* to teach penmanship. Inevitably, litigation began between the Grand Chantre and the scriveners. Throughout much of the seventeenth century highly unprofessional conflict raged between the rival schoolmasters, the Châtelet backing the scriveners and the Parlement the *petites écoles*. On behalf of the scriveners the Châtelet's police repeatedly invaded the classrooms of the *petites écoles* and seized any sort of teaching device that suggested that penmanship was being taught therein, while the Parlement in a sort of reflex action to their traditional foes at the Châtelet staged counterraids on the schools of the writing masters on behalf of the *petites écoles*.

Early in Louis XIV's personal reign the Parlement handed down a verdict on the old conflict between the *petites écoles* and the scriveners which again suggests that the court had for some reason ended its role of protector of the educational establishment. The victory of the scriveners was as complete as that of the sisters in their earlier battle with the Grand Chantre. The scriveners were authorized by the parlementarians to teach virtually all subjects and skills essential to primary instruction. Perhaps even more galling to the Grand Chantre was the court's injunction against the teaching of anything but the most rudimentary writing in the *petites écoles*, reserving the very elaborate penmanship of the times to the masters of the scriveners' schools. The *petites écoles* were told they could no longer display in their classrooms handwriting samples executed by anyone but the teacher personally. Joly rebutted with his customary brusqueness that penmanship was an essential part of grammar and that it went without saying that only the masters of the *petites écoles* were qualified grammarians. Using arguments adduced from fifteen hundred years of Western history the Grand Chantre sought to demonstrate that a good handwriting was more than something simply pleasing to the eye. Even the finest professional handwriting, Joly insisted, was "often difficult to read because of inattention to the proper shaping of the characters. . . ."[40] (How Joly could accuse the writing masters of the seventeenth century of carelessness in shaping their characters remains a mystery only he could unravel.)

During the balance of the century the schools of the scriveners were second in number only to the *petites écoles*. How much attention the Grand Chantre's schoolmasters paid to the ruling of 1661 limiting their teaching of writing is impossible to say. Blégny's directory of city addresses in 1692 suggests that some, at least, heeded the court's admonitions. Blégny wrote that in each quarter of the city there was a *petite école* "instituted by M. le Chantre de Paris" whose purpose it was "to teach both sexes Catechism, Christian prayers, the reading of Latin and French books, and the principles of Grammar, Writing, and Arithmetic."[41] He went on to describe the schools of the writing masters, "who taught young people who have already passed through the *petites Écoles* to perfect Writing, Orthography and Arithmetic."[42] Blégny was probably simplifying a confused situation in passing off the writing schools as quasi-finishing schools undertaken only upon completion of the *petites écoles*, for there is nothing in Joly's writings suggesting that the two were not direct competitors. Nevertheless, judging by Blégny, at least some of the *petites écoles* had accepted the somewhat limited role assigned to them by the Parlement.

When the disastrous verdict of 1661 had been announced by the Parlement, the Grand Chantre had appealed directly to the Conseil d'Etat for a reversal. The long-awaited decision was not given until 1719, four years after the Sun King had passed to his reward.[43] It represented a minor victory for the *petites écoles* but hardly one which would have elated Claude Joly had he still been alive. The right of the *petites écoles* to teach even the most complicated and flowery penmanship was restored after a lapse of fifty-nine years, but the scriveners were left undisturbed as teachers of the complete elementary curriculum. So remained relations between the two until the end of the Old Regime.

ॐ   ॐ

Convent schools, scriveners' schools, the lower grades of the University, the *petites écoles*—all were basically tuition-supported institutions. Out of the Catholic revival of the early seventeenth century and its many-faceted efforts at social amelioration, there inevitably emerged various projects to educate the children of the poor. Giving rudimentary education to the poor was, of course, as old as Parisian Christianity. But the approach to the problem had been different in medieval times. Medieval society had been quite casual and unself-conscious in such matters. Poor children had been thrown in with children of the wealthy, and education was regarded as something apart from social classes.[44] Such had once been the tradition of the *petites écoles*; those who could pay paid, while the children of the worthy poor (presumably on the recommendation of the parish *curé*) were admitted without charge.[45] When around mid-seventeenth century new schools were created specifically for poor children, defenders of the old order like Claude Joly professed to be annoyed by the "pretense" and "affectation" of the new endeavor, arguing that the needs of society had always been met by the admission of charity students to the paying schools.

What was novel in the seventeenth-century approach was the segregation of the poor into special "charity" schools. Perhaps the comparison is unfair, but one is reminded immediately of the treatment the same society accorded the adult poor—figuratively branding them and confining them to the Hôpital-Général for the crime of destitution. It is difficult to say how much of this educational segregation was due to well-meant efforts to achieve greater system and efficiency in the difficult task of educating the poor and how much it was another indication of the growing social alienation characteristic of the seventeenth-century scene. (One anonymous contemporary justified separation of rich and poor on the simple need for sparing rich children, "ordinarily clean," from the "vermin inseparable from the poor."[46]) In poor parishes, especially, there were obvious advantages to concentrating all the poor in special schools rather than finding places for them in scarce *petites écoles*. On the other hand, one of the historians who has occupied himself most with the problem of the Parisian poor in the Old Regime concluded that the new schools were primarily social organs designed to teach morality to the children of the poor and hence dangerous classes.[47] As with that other new institution of the same period, the Hôpital-Général, police, social and religious objectives were strikingly intertwined.

Whatever the motive, the apostolate of educating the children of the poor came as naturally to the Catholic activists of the century as the home care of the aged sick, visits to the pestilent wards of the Hôtel-Dieu or the even more repulsive dungeons of the Châtelet, and so many other good works. As in almost every phase of Parisian charity in this era, the giant figure of Vincent de Paul dominated here too, and behind him the long and mysterious arm of the Company of the Holy Sacrament, the lay Catholic organization so prominent in the formation of the Hôpital-Général. Their offspring—the *écoles de charité*—were basic education in the fullest sense. Each school had two divisions, one for children under seven, the other for those over seven, a year generally being spent in each. Hours were from 8:30 to 11:00 and 2:30 to 4:00 or 5:00. Hopefully, the children learned the elements of reading, writing, and reckoning plus their catechism. Upon completion, efforts were made to place at least the more meritorious in apprenticeship.

The first such school was probably founded in the Parish of Saint-Séverin in 1636. Three years later De Paul, "wishing to have instructed a few poor children of both sexes," founded at his own expense a similar school in Saint-Laurent Parish. But not until after the Fronde, when the problem of the poor and homeless seems to have struck so hard in Paris, did the *écoles de charité* catch on. They became especially common in large parishes like Saint-Sulpice, Saint-Laurent, Saint-Eustache, and Saint-Paul.[48] Within one year, 1654, the parishioners of Saint-Paul Parish, which encompassed the industrial Saint-Antoine quarter, established five such schools in their parish, and three more followed soon thereafter. Before he died in 1656, the noted pastor and founder of the Sulpician Seminary, Olier, organized seven charity schools in his sprawling parish (it included the Faubourg Saint-Germain and more).[49] The movement became so successful that one generation after the first foundation Claude Joly was lamenting that "there are almost no children" in the *petites écoles* of certain parishes.[50]

Vincent de Paul, being the soul of charity, prudence, and diplomacy, had in establishing the first charity schools carefully obtained clearance from the Grand Chantre, recognizing the latter's rights over all primary education in Paris. The Grand Chantre was promised quarterly lists of students and official certification of their indigence so that he could assure himself of their inability to pay tuition at one of the *petites écoles*. He was also promised that signs would be hung outside the front doors identifying the establishments as charity schools. With this understanding, the Grand Chantre had sanctioned the project. But before long, Joly charged, the "spirit of independence" so overcame the *curés* that they found it unnecessary to ask anyone's permission to establish new *écoles de charité*, least of all, that of the Grand Chantre. In truth, the parish priests had reason to show "independence" because the new schools gave them their first opportunity to gain control over the education of their parish children. When the Parish of Saint-Paul founded its first five charity schools in 1654, the *curé* allegedly uttered not a word to either the Archbishop or the Grand Chantre.[51]

After the Fronde the parish priests obtained powerful support (as well as potential rivals) from the new *charités*, the highly efficient lay action organizations that sprang up in every parish from 1651 on. It will be recalled that behind this movement, too, was the Company of the Holy Sacrament,[52] notorious for the manner it coolly bypassed ecclesiastical authority. The new *charités* undoubtedly seconded the *curés* in the latter's determination to evade the Grand Chantre, but the price many of the parish priests had to pay was a greater measure of lay control over the new parish schools. For the rest of the Old Regime control of the charity schools was divided among the *curés*, the *charités*, and the *marguilliers* (church wardens) in varying proportions. The vital matter of teacher appointments, for example, might rest in the hands of any one of these authorities.

In parishes in which the *charités* were strongly entrenched and took the initiative in the formation of the charity schools, the *curés* were possibly no better off than under the Grand Chantre. The *charités*, also in the spirit of their parent organization, the Company of the Holy Sacrament, kept their funds in lay hands completely apart from the parish treasury (*fabrique*) controlled by the *marguilliers*. A case in point was that of the Parish of Saint-Laurent, where one of the first charity schools was started and which long remained a leader in the movement. A complete list of all benefactions made to this important parish has been published.[53] A scrutiny of these donations shows the niggardly support parish benefactors were giving the charity schools through the traditional parish *fabriques*. Large gifts were flowing in to the latter, but nearly always earmarked for other purposes. One does not encounter any donation to the parish's charity schools until 1665, ten years after the first *écoles de charité* had been established in this parish. In that year an annuity of 15 livres annually on behalf of the "priest of the charity school" was received. In 1673 an annuity of 100 livres was given to the girl's school and in 1680 a capital gift of 454 livres. Not until 1712 does one encounter a substantial gift for the schools: 1600 livres of annuities for the establishment of four *écoles de charité*. (Since teachers in the charity schools received about 400 livres, the donor was none too generous.)

However, the list of published benefactions to the Parish of Saint-Laurent gives us an interesting insight into the philanthropic habits of well-to-do seventeenth-century Parisians (Saint-Laurent was a wealthy church). The parish was engaged in a great deal of social work, but funds and effort for it were clearly being channeled through the lay-dominated *charité*. Most gifts bestowed on the parish were of a devotional and traditional type. They were calculated to keep a large staff of priests busy saying Masses and conducting other services for the deceased, but had little social value. The long-time favorite of pious Catholics at the Parish of Saint-Laurent, or any other contemporary parish, was what was known as the *service complet*, an institution dating back to the fifteenth century. This consisted of three High Masses for one's intention preceded by vigils and lauds. (Sometimes the bequest further provided that after the Masses the priest would retire to the churchyard to recite the *De Profundis* on the tomb of the deceased.) Like everything else the cost of the *service complet* mounted steadily in the course of the seventeenth century: in 1608 to assure such a service for perpetuity required a capital gift of 300 livres, in 1636 of 400 livres, and in 1680 of 450 livres. The embarrassment of being committed in perpetuity to provide services entirely out of proportion to current yields on capital can be readily perceived; hence the frequent anguished petitions by the *curés* to the Archbishop for a reduction in solemn commitments made to benefactors generations earlier.[54]

Enough has been said of the disposition of the Grand Chantre to cause us to suspect he would not take easily to the charity schools. Nor did he. Joly's argument was that the charity schools were bogus affairs —"alleged" charity schools, he termed them—designed to evade the Grand Chantre's ancient privileges. "It is not," he wrote with heavy sarcasm, "that we wish to say that *Messieurs les Curés* derive any profit from their schools; they are too virtuous and too disinterested for such business." Nevertheless, he devoted a large part of his adult life assuring himself that the *curés* would not stray from the path of virtue. Litigation began early. In 1666 he obtained a ruling from the Parlement that the new schools could only instruct the "truly poor." Determined to enforce this ruling, the Grand Chantre began to make personal inspections to verify that "the filth and tatters of the wretched poor," as certified by the parish priests, were truly in evidence in the *écoles de charité*. He professed not to find them. In a visit to a girl's charity school in the Faubourg Saint-Germain, he found the pupils so clean and neat that he remonstrated with the schoolmistress, who curtly retorted that he could not judge their needs from their appearance. Joly's position was that "it is axiomatic that whenever anything is free, all the world comes running, both rich and poor."[55]

In his book written in 1678 Joly mentioned a pending suit which his predecessor had brought in 1656 to close down altogether the charity schools. The years dragged by and no decision ensued. The Archbishop tried in 1684 to arbitrate the case out of court, but suceeded only in outraging both sides to the dispute. Finally, in 1699, forty-three years after it had all begun, the parties, "animated," as an unknown third party charitably described them, "by the spirit of peace and good understanding so proper between people of their character," came together at the Châtelet and signed a peace treaty, or, as it was called, *transaction.*[56] The Grand Chantre was allowed to save face, but victory clearly belonged to the *curés*. They were left in complete control of the *écoles de charité* within their respective parishes, although required to obtain a perfunctory authorization, at no cost to themselves, from the Cathedral Chapter. The *curés* were held responsible for maintaining an up-to-date register of all the children in the charity schools, certifying them to be without exception "truly poor." The masters and mistresses of the *petites écoles,* who apparently had long been causing trouble even of a physical nature to the teachers of the charity schools, were enjoined to stay away from their rivals. Finally, reverting to the days of Vincent de Paul and to avoid ambiguity, the charity schools agreed once again to hang signs above their doors reading, "Charity School for the Poor of the Parish."

༂ᴥ   ༂ᴥ

The *transaction* of 1699 between the Grand Chantre and the *curés* brought welcome peace to the educational scene in Paris except for one last emotional and particularly unfortunate episode. It was obvious that the agreement was only as good as the *curés'* willingness and ability to keep bourgeois children out of the charity schools. By and large they were prepared to do so; after fifty years the controversy had, one would think, begun to pall on them. But in the closing decade of the seventeenth century, a new religious order of primary school teachers appeared in Paris, still very few in number but destined to grow one day into the largest educational organization in the world. This was the Brothers of the Christian Schools.

Responding to the invitation of the *curé* of Saint-Sulpice, the founder of the new order of teaching brothers, Jean-Baptiste de La Salle, arrived in Paris in 1688 with two companions. Their mission was to revitalize one of the charity schools founded by Olier a generation earlier— moribund, like so many of these schools at the end of the century, because of the shortage of teachers. The Brothers performed their task with great credit. By 1699 they were staffing five charity schools in the sprawling parish of Saint-Sulpice and shortly after branched out into the parishes of Saint-Hippolyte and Saint-Paul. At Saint-Hippolyte, De La Salle also founded a normal school to help meet the chronic shortage of teachers, an idea as sensible as it was novel.[57] The excellent training of De La Salle's teachers, the good order evidenced in his schools, and his novel pedagogy (notably his pioneering decision not to introduce Latin until the pupils had learned to read French[58]) made his schools increasingly popular and influential. On one occasion we even find the King's wife, Mme de Maintenon, soliciting the aid of the president of the Parlement for De La Salle's schools. "There have never been," she wrote, "more useful or more disinterested ones."[59]

The Grand Chantre and the teachers of the *petites écoles* had reason to be alarmed by the growing reputation and success of De La Salle's schools, most of all because he clung to the old ideal of Christian social democracy and eschewed the separation of rich and poor children in the classroom. While his main interest was educating the children of the poor, he welcomed—free of charge—the offspring of bourgeois parents attracted by the superiority of his methods. For support he counted on the contributions of all who could afford to give. After the parish priests and the Grand Chantre arrived at their *transaction* of 1699, however, he was obviously headed for trouble. De La Salle's failure to certify the indigence of his pupils led his enemies to prepare their own lists purporting to show that among his pupils were sons of surgeons, wine merchants, goldsmiths, "proprietors of two houses," and others known to be "very well off."[60]

Forgetting long generations of bitter rivalry and countless lawsuits, the Grand Chantre joined forces with the scriveners, who had belatedly become aware of the challenge posed by the excellent calligraphers among De La Salle's brothers. The scriveners struck first. They obtained an order halting the teaching of calligraphy at De La Salle's newest school in the Faubourg Saint-Antoine. In early February 1704 two *commissaires* from the Châtelet swooped down with their cohorts to confiscate such unlikely items as pens, inkwells, tablets, and handwriting samples. A week or so later, the Grand Chantre contributed his bit by ordering the closing of all the Christian Brothers' schools in Paris. De La Salle of course appealed to the Parlement, but his earlier good luck in the courts seems to have vanished. While the appeal was pending, his enemies repeatedly raided his schools in search of sons of the bourgeois, whom they doubtless had little trouble finding. In the summer of 1706 the Parlement confirmed the earlier rulings of both the Châtelet and the Grand Chantre. The status of neither *école de charité* nor *petite école* was conceded to the Christian Brothers. Apparently the Parlement deemed their schools "neither flesh nor fowl" and ordered them out of the city. The Brothers obediently dismantled what the police had left of their schools and withdrew. They would return, but only on the terms laid down by the Grand Chantre. The Old Order in education had at least one solid victory to show in an age in which things had generally gone rather badly.

Conclusion

I F one were asked for an opinion on when Paris evolved from "medieval" to "modern" city, a likely response would be the era of Napoleon III and Haussmann. In less than two decades—the 1850's and
1860's—these two men directed a program of urban renewal so immense
in scope as to stagger the imagination even in a day when one is left un-
moved by far vaster projects. The latest historian of this unique urban
transformation refers at the start of his book to the "overgrown medieval city" which faced the Emperor and his prefect in 1850 and whose
inadequacies provoked them to their drastic urban facelifting.[1] Presumably, the author is of the opinion that "modern" Paris emerged from all
the dust and rubble of Haussmann's demolitions.

The foregoing chapters have attempted to put the history of Paris in
somewhat larger perspective. Long before Napoleon III and Haussmann, even before the Industrial Revolution made its impact on the
city, other forces were shaping Paris in a way which can only be termed
modern, despite numerous and obvious medieval survivals. Napoleon
III and Haussmann, far from marking the transition from medieval to
modern Paris are in reality links in a chain which stretches back to the
seventeenth century and forward to present-day urbanists. The problems
confronting Colbert and La Reynie in the seventeenth century were
minuscule compared with those of today's urban planner. But they were
the same kinds of problems—of circulation, physical security,
health, pollution of the environment, education, urban aesthetics, and
so on. In the seventeenth century, for the first time at least since ancient
times, urban administrators became aware of these problems in something more than a haphazard way and began to attempt rational solutions. Haussmann simply continued in this tradition, on a grander
scale than his predecessors, of course.

Likewise, Haussmann's projects were prompted by the same force which acted on Colbert in the seventeenth century and causes modern urbanists often to despair of the future of the city, namely, the pressure of population growth. The problems of Louis XIV's Paris can nearly all be traced to the recent sharp climb in the city's population. As a result, seventeenth-century French monarchs attempted to set arbitrary limits on their capital, and not the least reason for Louis XIV's construction of Versailles was his hope that Paris would suffer in size and importance by his move to that unlikely locale. Haussmann's basic problem was also a superfluity of people. The population of Paris had doubled in the first half of the nineteenth century. Paris was not only building outward but using the inner city ever more intensively. It has been estimated that the population of the small Marais quarter today would have to be reduced by 20,000 inhabitants, or 25 percent, to make the neighborhood as livable as it was in the eighteenth century.[2]

From the seventeenth century on, European urbanists abound.[3] Mainly architects by profession, they differed from the older "urban embellishers" by taking the city as a whole as their frame of reference. They strove for not only a beautiful city but one able to supply the basic needs of its inhabitants. In Louis XIV's time, Colbert and La Reynie, although neither was a professional architect, both earned the right to the later appellation. The first overall plan for the "modernization" of the city was that drawn up in 1676 by two of the King's architects, Pierre Bullet and François Blondell. The letters patent which commissioned this work specified that the King wished to see depicted not only Paris as it stood but all the projects the architects planned for the improvement of the quays and public fountains, the widening of streets, etc. The lifelong interest which Bullet, especially, took in matters of public welfare, in addition to aesthetics, is noteworthy. At one point this concern led him to invent a machine guaranteed to remove bad odors from cesspools and water closets. A 24-page pamphlet described in Bullet's own words the ill effects of such odors. [4]

Behind the urbanizers of Louis XIV's day lay the unrelenting pressure of a growing population. As we have noted, the population of Paris, relatively stable in the medieval and sixteenth centuries, began to mount sharply in the seventeenth. Precisely how large this increase was is a moot question, since not until 1801 was there a census of Paris. One can make some sort of case for the growth of Paris from around 250,000 at the start of the seventeenth century to double that at its end. Such statistics are generally based on the number of houses in the city, something which is known rather accurately from tax records, but the weakness of the method lies in setting more or less arbitrary coefficients for the number of people dwelling in an average Parisian house. Since dwellings varied from single-family residences to multi-story apartments sometimes housing several families on each floor, the rashness of such estimates is obvious.

A far more satisfactory manner of judging the seventeenth-century growth of Paris is to examine the maps of the city, which in the Grand Siècle appear in almost geometric progression—itself a significant fact. For the early part of the century, the Mathieu Mérian (1615) and Tavernier (1630) *plans* are especially useful; for the turn of the century, those of Nicolas de Fer (1697), Jean de la Caille (1709), and Jaillot (1713).[5] One would estimate from comparing these maps that the built-up areas of the city had easily trebled in the course of the century. The old walls had mostly disappeared in the later maps—entirely so on the Right Bank—and Paris was now an open city, confidently entrusting its fate to Vauban's chain of fortresses many leagues to the north and northeast. Beyond the new promenades of Louis XIV, built on the rubble of the old walls, new construction was visible in almost every direction. On the Left Bank it was especially heavy in the faubourgs Saint-Marceau and Saint-Germain. In the latter faubourg the city had reached the Invalides, which a generation earlier Louis XIV had confidently placed in a purely rural setting. On the Right Bank the faubourgs Saint-Antoine, du Temple, Saint-Denis, and Saint-Honoré reached far out into the countryside. Towns which had once been completely set apart from the city, like Les Porcherons, La Nouvelle France, and Ville l'Evêque, and even the heights of Montmartre, had been or were in the process of being engulfed by the encroaching city.

How can one account for the exceptional growth of seventeenth-century Paris? Because of the paucity of quantitative data one can make only tentative replies to why so many more people lived in the city at the end of the century than at its start. One historic attraction of the city—the University—we can rather quickly rule out, since it is doubtful whether that venerable institution even managed to keep up its enrollment as the century advanced. We can also rule out the possibility of a natural growth of the city's population. There is no reason to think that life expectancy and infant mortality had improved sufficiently in the seventeenth century to occasion any significant rise in population.

Clearly, more people were choosing to move to Paris from the provinces—hardly a new phenomenon, only the numbers were new. Much of this movement is tied in with the poorly understood seventeenth-century depopulation of the countryside. It is a moot point whether country people were coming to Paris because of the attractions of the city or because life was becoming intolerable in the provinces. But the fact of their coming is indisputable. Seventeenth-century Parisians were much struck by this influx of provincials. The older residents, we can be certain, did not welcome the new arrivals and liked to characterize them as soldiers, robbers, strangers, and just plain "little people."[6] Many provincials undoubtedly quickly became cases for the police and the *archers* of the Hôpital-Général, but recent studies have shown their importance for the growing economy of the capital. Utilizing notarial archives, one of these studies analyzed the apprenticeship contracts negotiated at mid-century by the guildmasters of the Cité quarter. Of eighty contracts examined, thirty-eight were entered into by boys and young men born in Paris, while a majority—forty-two—involved non-Parisians.[7]

That the new arrivals were a constant concern of the magistrates is evidenced by the arguments advanced by Théophraste Renaudot when he sought to obtain authorization in the 1630's for his pioneer informational clearing house known as the Bureau d'Adresses. Knowing how the authorities associated provincials with vagabondage and lawbreaking, the shrewd Renaudot argued that the institution he proposed to establish would enable them to obtain employment "one hour after their arrival." The prime cause of crime in Paris, he maintained, would thus be eliminated.

At the same time that Paris was witnessing the arrival of a stream of country people—mostly impoverished and destined to become, at least initially, lackeys, apprentices, servants, laborers, and the like—the city was receiving a large influx of a totally different sort. Inseparable from the seventeenth-century expansion of Paris was the augmentation of the power and the functions of the state. Government became a large enterprise in the course of the century, especially with Louis XIV, and the city inevitably grew with it. As Professor Mousnier has cautioned, we must not assume that when the King changed his permanent abode from Paris to Versailles, the lifeblood went out of Paris as a political center.[8] Paris remained the capital, and the maze of administrative and judicial organs centered in the Palais de Justice on the Cité was little concerned with the King's move to Versailles. These institutions only grew in size as more and more state work was demanded of them. Ministers and other important officials were expected to be seen at Versailles; but most of them divided their time between Paris and Versailles, had houses in both cities, and probably thought of the two as one.

La Reynie and D'Argenson, the two most important Parisian magistrates of the seventeenth century, were both provincials who had come to the attention of Louis XIV's ministers and had received offers to come to Paris to fill the new post of Lieutenant of Police. They were thus both beneficiaries of an expanding government. Had the King and his ministers not seen the necessity for reorganizing the administration of Paris, both men would probably have lived out their lives on their country estates. There must have been many others who moved to Paris in the hope of obtaining political employment. Some of the impact of the expanded state on the city can be seen in the ambitious initial plans (sadly abortive) for the Place Louis-le-Grand—the modern Place Vendôme—which would have created the first administrative and cultural center in the city, or anywhere else.

In assessing the importance of Louis XIV's massive state apparatus in the burgeoning of the capital, one must also take into account the role of the financiers. The exploitation of the environs of Paris for the benefit of Parisian stomachs was as nothing compared with the plundering of France by the tax farmers and their agents. The system of tax farming antedated the seventeenth century but reached hitherto undreamed-of peaks with Richelieu and Louis XIV. The many provincial uprisings of the seventeenth century were mainly protests against the exploitation of the provinces by the men of Versailles and Paris. As one provincial said after the 1656 peasant uprising in Saintonge, "the name 'Parisian' is held in such hatred and horror . . . that simply to describe oneself as such is cause enough to be set upon."

The directors and beneficiaries of the tax-farming system were all centered in Paris and emerge in Louis XIV's reign as an extremely wealthy, well-knit, and potent little fraternity. For the balance of the Old Regime, the Bourbon monarchs would too often be at their mercy. In the elegant new neighborhoods, at first to the north and west of the Palais-Royal and later scattered throughout the west of Paris, the financiers held forth in town houses on a par with anything the aristocrats could boast. When one starts adding up the small armies of servants each such household entailed, along with its economic and cultural requirements, the importance of such wealth in the overall development of the city is evident.

The accelerated flow of provincials to Paris was undoubtedly tied in with improvements in transportation and communications. Paris must have seemed relatively close to country people who, for the first time, could ride into the city from almost any part of the realm, or who could easily be advised by a relative or fellow-townsman of the delights of city living. The new ease of communications could only have encouraged the flow to Paris.

For many and varied reasons, then, the population of Paris increased sharply in the seventeenth century. In our view, it is this upturn in the population curve which, coming as it did after several centuries of minimal growth, was responsible for changing Paris from a "medieval" to a "modern" city. The many changes and evolutions described in the foregoing pages can all be traced back to the presence in Paris of far more people than the city had ever known. The community which had for so long served the needs of a stable population was suddenly found wanting. Streets were no longer adequate for the new wheeled vehicles; municipal administration was found archaic; unlighted streets became intolerable in view of the thousands of questionable characters crowding into the city; water supplies were insufficient; schools outdated; cultural facilities, such as the theaters, unworthy of larger, wealthier, and more sophisticated audiences; old methods of coping with the poor no longer satisfactory; and so on. The urban crisis which faced Paris at the start of Louis XIV's personal reign and caused the formation of the high-level Conseil de Police of 1666 is analogous to the crisis that faced the city in 1850 after the population had doubled in half a century, as well as to the situation urbanists are wrestling with today after the far more spectacular population rises of recent years.

By the end of the seventeenth century, Paris must be accounted a more attractive, livable, and rationally administered community. In the person of the Lieutenant of Police it had obtained for the first time a modern administrator. More streets had been paved in one lifetime than probably in the entire previous history of the city. The widening and straightening of medieval streets had begun. To facilitate travel at night, the first municipal lighting system had come into being, and to safeguard property the first municipal fire fighters. The water available at the public fountains had more than doubled. The opening of the first public squares worthy of the name admitted a little light into the city. Paris had ceased to be the self-contained and relatively isolated community characteristic of medieval times. The razing of the walls and gates aptly symbolized the new openness, as did the ability to clamber aboard a stagecoach bound for almost any part of France, to say nothing of the intoxication which must have come from being able to drop a message in a street box and have it delivered to addresses hundreds of leagues distant. Economically, Paris had begun to dominate a large peripheral region, traditionally autonomous but which now seemed to exist only to serve the needs of the insatiable capital. Even in the world of culture, the rest of France began to bow low to Paris in the course of the century. At the start of Louis XIII's reign, the capital's theater was reputed inferior in both quality and quantity to that of several other French cities. One lifetime later, French actors and actresses could dream no finer dream than being accepted by the audiences of Paris.

Aesthetically, too, Paris "emerged" in Louis XIV's time. The most characteristic features of the inner city of today—the part best known to visitors—were implanted on Paris in the seventeenth century. The urban aesthetic which guided the great undertakings of Napoleon III and Haussmann was, of course, borrowed from the French seventeenth century, which in turn had borrowed it from Renaissance Italy. The most characteristic feature of this aesthetic was the wide tree-lined boulevard artfully laid out for an eye-filling perspective. Henry IV and Marie de Médicis had embellished the city with two such promenades at the start of the century, and both became immensely popular and influential in later planning. Alongside the Arsenal on the eastern edge of the city, Henry IV executed the Mail with its four rows of elms. The site became a favorite for playing the croquetlike game which gave the place its name. At the other end of the city, Marie built the Cours-la-Reine, the most popular promenade in the city in the seventeenth century for the fashionable world.

The success of the Mail and the Cours-la-Reine encouraged far more grandiose projects of this sort early in Louis XIV's reign. Le Nôtre reterraced and redesigned the Tuileries Gardens in the form known today, so pleasing Colbert thereby that the latter argued (unsuccessfully) that only the royal family should have access thereto. At the same time Le Nôtre extended the perspective of the Tuileries Gardens by conceiving what was later to receive the name Champs-Elysées. The new promenade stopped approximately at the present Rond-Point, which was tied in with the landscaping of the Invalides when Louis XIV began work on his famous old soldiers' home in the 1670's. From the Rond-Point, then, the strolling Parisian was given two superb perspectives: looking eastward down the later Champs-Elysées, his eyes followed past the Tuileries Gardens to the Palace; looking to the right, his view traveled along equally magnificent promenades across the river to the new Invalides.

Admirers of urban beauty were given even more to cheer about in the last quarter of the seventeenth century as work slowly progressed (Haussmann would not have been patient) on the conversion of the old walls into the same sort of tree-lined promenade. On the Right Bank, where the walls of Charles V and Louis XIII had stood, the new *boulevards* (the term was military in origin) were laid out. They were completed by 1705, although poorly utilized until the second half of the century.

After the unlamented death of the Sun King, the plan he had laid down in broad outline was slowly filled in. The Champs-Elysées was extended to Chaillot (the present Place de l'Etoile) in 1724, and fifty years later to Neuilly. By this time half a dozen promenades radiated from the site of Napoleon's later triumphal arch. In the third quarter of the eighteenth century a great square honoring Louis XV was laid out between the Tuileries Gardens and the starting point of the Champs-Elysées. Completed in time to serve as the site of the murderous panic which accompanied the marriage festivities of the Dauphin and Marie-Antoinette, it was later the execution place for the groom and in calmer days became the Place de la Concorde. Mme de Pompadour interested herself in the construction of the Ecole Militaire further downstream, in front of which her architect, Gabriel, laid out the Champs-de-Mars, all undoubtedly inspired by the magnificent setting of the earlier Invalides. At much the same time, the *remparts* (the later *grands boulevards*) of the Sun King came into their own as fashionable gathering places and for the first time were paved and lighted.

The Revolution of 1789 had little time for or interest in urban embellishments. Napoleon, insofar as he concerned himself at all with the city, acted simply as executor of the Bourbon monarchs. His most memorable achievement was the Arc de Triomphe, ordered shortly after the great victory on the field of Austerlitz. (For fifty years a lively debate had gone on concerning the best way to adorn this site; a gigantic bronze elephant complete with several levels of chambers had been seriously considered.) After being laid aside by the restored Bourbons, Napoleon's gigantic arch was completed by Louis-Philippe just in time for the passage of Napoleon's ashes in 1840, newly returned from St. Helena.

It has been said that Paris has known only two great periods of innovation: the classical monarchy and that of Haussmann.[9] Even a summary account of the latter's achievements does not lie within the scope of the present book, but it would be well to stress the obvious continuity between the work of Napoleon III's prefect and that of the pioneer urbanists of the age of Louis XIV. Much of Haussmann's work lay beyond the limits of Louis XIV's Paris and was carried out on a scale inconceivable for the seventeenth century, but Colbert and La Reynie would have been, we think, very much at home with Haussmann and would have approved the results. (They probably would have been amused by the trouble Haussmann encountered, preparatory to laying out the Avenue de l'Opéra, in leveling the area west of the Palais-Royal; the developers of the Quartier Richelieu in the 1660's had the same dificulty with the old *buttes*.)

Haussmann's conception of urban beauty was precisely that of the seventeenth century: wide streets lavishly planted with trees, monumental vistas, maximum uniformity of façades, plenty of free space. He inherited a conception like the Etoile with relish and proceeded to extend it. Seven new spokes were added to the existing hub, making the present total of twelve stately avenues. In the same grand manner, he put the final touches on the *grands boulevards*, erecting new *places* (*l'Opéra, la République*) along their length, into which grand avenues debouched.

One of the projects to which Napoleon III gave maximum priority was the long-dreamed-of east-west passage on the Right Bank connecting the Champs-Elysées and Vincennes. In Louis XIV's day the city planners were far more inclined to stress the entrance from the east than from the west. We have noted how Perrault actually began an immense triumphal arch between Vincennes and the Bastille which would have oriented the city in an opposite direction from today. It was eventually abandoned, however, and all that Louis XIV left behind in this area was a magisterial promenade leading to Vincennes. The continuation of this avenue all the way to the Tuileries was much discussed in the eighteenth century. From about the Hôtel de Ville to the Tuileries, one was caught up in a medieval maze which made movement extremely difficult. Napoleon I helped matters by building the Rue de Rivoli, but, unfortunately, extended it no further to the east than the modern Place du Palais-Royal. It was left to Haussmann to realize the dream of centuries by continuing the Rue de Rivoli into the Saint-Antoine quarter.

As had begun to be true of urbanists from Louis XIV's day on,

Haussmann was not content with simply achieving a beautiful city. Considerations of traffic, hygiene, water supply, health, and breathing space loomed as large in his mind as promenades. He probably took as much pride in his four great collector sewers—veritable underground canals—and in the fact that for the first time virtually every house in Paris was provided with fresh water as he did in the Etoile and the new boulevards. Good urbanist that he was, his view was that of the whole city and its needs.

The tragedy of Haussmann—shared with most of the urbanists of the Western world from the seventeenth century to now—is that he was, unbeknown to himself, defeated by the very force which had brought his talents into play. In the period between 1851 and 1870 when he was laboring so prodigiously to correct conditions mostly due to the doubling of Paris's population in the preceding fifty years, the population of the city again very nearly doubled.[10] His improvements made possible, even encouraged, an ever greater flow of newcomers to the capital. Complicating matters further, within a decade of Haussmann's death the automobile appeared on the streets of the city, eventually destined to make a mockery of the *étoiles* and system of circulation he had so confidently conceived. The prefect probably would have derived little comfort from the knowledge that his successors would one day draw up plans for costly six- and eight-lane routes into Paris—only to find them inadequate to carry the traffic which materialized in the long course of construction.

The annual reception of the King
at the Hotel de Ville.

The new use of urban space: the Place Royale—the modern
Place des Vosges—early in the reign of Louis XIII.

Vüe et Perspective de la Place des Victoires

The Place des Victoires. The defeated powers sit
in chains at the feet of Louis XIV.

Finishing touches being given to Claude Perrault's Colonnade of the Louvre (1677). The record weight of the columns called for special machines to lift the sections into place.

River scene. The just rebuilt (1647) Pont au Change is seen from the Pont Neuf. Right, the Conciergerie; left, the Châtelet and the Tour St.-Jacques.

Jean-Baptiste Colbert

Jules Hardouin-Mansart

Marc-René de Voyer d'Argenson

Nicolas de la Reynie

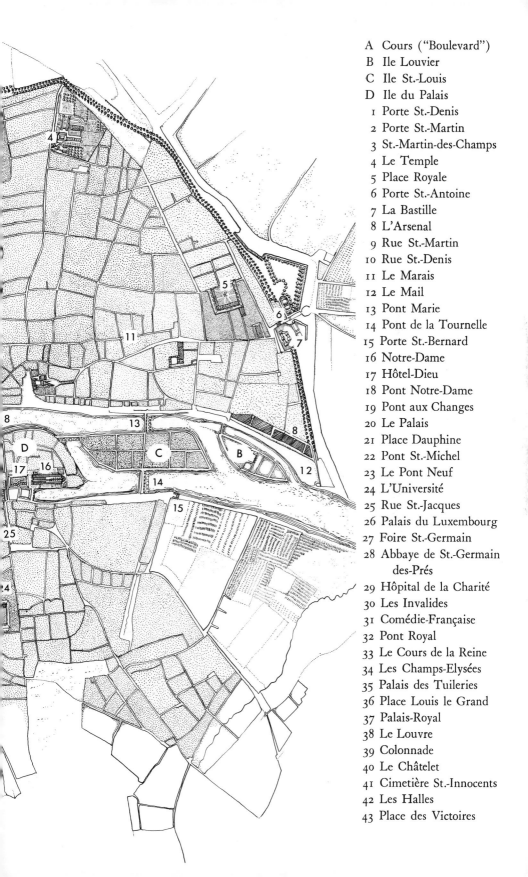

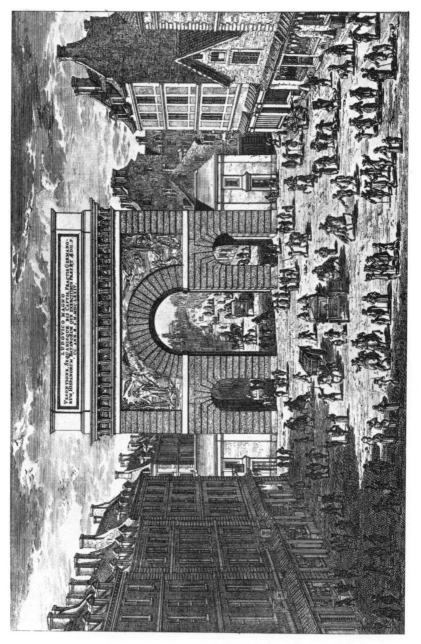

The new openness of Paris: the Porte St.-Martin (1674).

DEPART DES COMEDIENS ITALIENS EN 1697   ITALORUM COMEDORUM DISCESSUS ANNO M.DC.XCVII.

The Italian actors banished, 1697—their reward for
impolitic treatment of Mme de Maintenon.

Holy Innocents Cemetery, for six centuries the burial place of Parisians.
Charnel houses are on both sides of the church.

Holy Innocents Fountain, one of many fountains established in
Louis XIV's time to ease a chronic shortage of water.

The Bureau d'Adresse, the meeting ground of buyers
and sellers of all sorts of wares and services.

Upper-class ladies, properly accompanied,
handing out alms in a prison.

Home treatment for the sick: "le clystère."

Treatment for the sick in the model
hospital of La Charité.

Distribution du Pain du Roy au Louure

Distribution of the King's Bread
at the Louvre in a year
of grain shortage.

Le Vomitif des Marchands de Bled

Profiteering grain merchants
forced to disgorge their
excessive gains.

REFERENCES

Full titles are to be found in the Bibliography

PREFACE

1 Eric E. Lampard, "Urbanization and Social Change: On Broadening the Scope and Relevance of Urban History," in Handlin and Burchard, *Historian and the City*, p. 239.
2 John Burchard, "Some Afterthoughts," ibid., p. 261.

CHAPTER ONE

1 Delamare, *Traité*, 4:397.
2 Ibid.
3 Chappuzeau, *Théâtre français*, p. 152.
4 Lister, *Journey*, p. 17.
5 Voltaire, *Louis XIV*, p. 323.
6 Pillement, *Les hôtels de Paris*, Introduction.
7 Lister, *Journey*, p. 9.
8 Marana, *Lettre d'un Sicilien*, p. 17.
9 Sauval, *Histoire*, 1:626.
10 Mousnier, *Paris*, 1:2; Boislisle, *Mémoires des intendants*, 21:656.
11 Dumolin, "L'hôtel de la reine Marguérite," *Etudes de topographie*, 1:146-48.
12 Mathorez, *Les étrangers*, 1:3; Delamare, *Traité*, 1:97.
13 Lavedan, *Histoire de l'urbanisme*, 2:145, 341-42.
14 Dumolin, *Etudes de topographie*, 1:139.
15 Ibid., p. 129.
16 Ibid., p. 160.
17 Dumolin, "L'enceinte des Fossés-jaunes et la formation du Quartier Richelieu," *Etudes de topographie*, 2:111.
18 Ibid., 2:120.
19 Deville and Hochéreau, *Recueil*, 1:1-2.
20 Lavedan, *Histoire de l'urbanisme*, 2:342.
21 Dumolin, *Etudes de topographie*, 2:154-55, 334.
22 Ibid., p. 111.
23 Clément, *Lettres de Colbert*, 5:269.
24 Boislisle, "Notices historiques," 1 n.
25 Clément, *Lettres de Colbert*, 5:xxxiv-xxxvi.
26 Guiffrey, *Comptes des bâtiments*, 1:xxix.
27 Ibid., 1:111.
28 Félibien, *Histoire de Paris*, 5:228.
29 Lavedan, *Histoire de l'urbanisme*, 2:198.
30 Mousnier, *Paris*, p. 8.
31 Félibien, *Histoire de Paris*, 3:1514.
32 Sauval, *Histoire*, 1:671; Félibien, *Histoire de Paris*, 5:318.
33 Félibien, *Histoire de Paris*, 5:271.
34 Sauval, *Histoire*, 1:106.
35 Lister, *Journey*, p. 38.
36 Clément, *Lettres de Colbert*, 5:xlix.
37 Brice, *Description de Paris*, 1:349-50.
38 Félibien, *Histoire de Paris*, 5:271, 274.
39 Brice, *Description de Paris*, 1:138, 346; Félibien, *Histoire de Paris*, 5:414.
40 Boislisle, "Notices historiques," p. 107.
41 Sauval, *Histoire*, 1:618.
42 Christian, *Etudes*, p. 193.
43 Sauval, *Histoire*, 1:618.
44 Lavedan, *Histoire de l'urbanisme*, 2:277.
45 Deville and Hochéreau, *Recueil*, p. 1.
46 Dumolin, "Les propriétaires," pp. 276-77.
47 Lambeau, *Place Royale*, pp. 65-66.
48 Poete, *La Promenade*, p. 68.
49 Lavedan, *Histoire de l'urbanisme*, 2:280.
50 Boislisle, "Notices historiques," p. 107.
51 Sellier, *Anciens hôtels*, p 142.

52 Félibien, *Histoire de Paris*, 5:274 n.
53 Sauval, *Histoire*, 1:626.
54 Brice, *Description de Paris*, 1:170.
55 Depping, *Correspondance*, 1:882.
56 Saugrain, *Curiosités de Paris*, p. 58.
57 Depping, *Correspondance*, 1:882.
58 Brice, *Description de Paris*, 1:170.
59 Saint-Germain, *Les financiers*, p. 194.
60 Boislisle, "Notices historiques," p. 107.
61 Saint-Germain, *Les financiers*, p. 194.
62 Ibid.; Boislisle, "Notices historiques," p. 108.
63 Sauval, *Histoire*, 1:627-28.
64 Boislisle, "Notices historiques," pp. 6-8.
65 Deville and Hochéreau, *Recueil*, p. 14.
66 Boislisle, *Mémoires de Saint-Simon*, 1:364.
67 Saint-Germain, *Les financiers*, p. 192.
68 Delamare, *Traité*, 4:400, 401, 406.
69 Mousnier, *Paris*, p. 148.
70 Pradel, *Livre commode*.
71 Saint-Germain, *Les financiers*, pp. 200-203.
72 Sauval, *Histoire*, 1:26.
73 Brice, *Description de Paris*, 2:197.
74 Lister, *Journey*, p. 11.
75 Nemeitz, *Séjour*, p. 315.
76 Delamare, *Traité*, 4:464.
77 Lemonnier, *Procès-verbaux*, 1:xxiv.
78 Blondell, *Cours d'architecture*, pp. 603-4.
79 Lavedan, *Histoire de l'urbanisme*, 2:197.
80 Lemonnier, *Procès-verbaux*, 1:iv.

CHAPTER TWO

1 Kleindienst, "Topographie," passim; Isambert et al., *Recueil*, 13:63-64.
2 Deville and Hochéreau, *Recueil*, p. 12.
3 Ibid., p. 14.
4 Clément, *Lettres de Colbert*, 5:539.
5 Ibid., pp. 537-38.
6 Marion, *Dictionnaire*, p. 441.
7 Villers, *Journal*, p. 303.
8 Picot, "Recherches," pp. 134, 145-46, 157.
9 Ibid.
10 Pradel, *Livre commode*, 2:366.
11 Le Roux de Lincy, *Histoire de l'Hôtel de Ville*, Introduction, iii.
12 Lefevre d'Ormesson, *Journal*, 2:540.
13 Clément, *Lettres de Colbert*, 5:537-38.

14 Isambert et al., *Recueil*, 20:362-63.
15 Delamare, *Traité*, 1:197.
16 Tanon, *Histoire des justices*, p. 227.
17 Villers, *Journal*, pp. 34, 41.
18 Sauval, *Histoire*, 2:425.
19 Lespinasse, *Les métiers*, 1:210-14.
20 Mousnier, *Paris*, p. 185.
21 Lespinasse, *Les métiers*, 1:195-96.
22 Delamare, *Traité*, 2:197.
23 Herlaut, "L'éclairage," p. 139.
24 Delamare, *Traité*, 4:229.
25 Ibid.
26 Saint-Germain, *La Reynie*, p. 25.
27 Mousnier, *Paris*, p. 107.
28 Delamare, *Traité*, 1:143.
29 Chassaigne, *Lieutenance générale*, pp. 95, 127.
30 Depping, *Correspondance*, 2:xliv.
31 Saint-Germain, *La Reynie*, p. 338.
32 Boislisle, *Mémoires de Saint-Simon*, 4:10-12.
33 Voltaire, *Louis XIV*, p. 325.
34 Depping, *Correspondance*, 2:818, 821-22, 827.
35 Ibid., p. 827.
36 Chassaigne, *Lieutenance générale*, p. 54; Argenson, *Notes*, pp. ix, x.
37 Herlaut, "La disette," pp. 72-73.
38 Ibid., p. 33.
39 Argenson, *Notes*, p. xii.
40 Ibid.
41 Delamare, *Traité*, 1:147.
42 Ibid., p. 219.
43 Desmaze, *Châtelet de Paris*, p. 184.
44 Delamare, *Traité*, 1:220.
45 Saint-Germain, *La Reynie*, p. 40.
46 Delamare, *Traité*, 1:143.
47 Ibid., p. 124.
48 Lehoux, "La cour de St. Germain-des-Prés," p. 90 n.
49 Marion, *Dictionnaire*, p. 421.
50 Guérout, "La taille," p. 190.
51 Sauval, *Histoire*, 2:408.
52 Boislisle, *Mémoires des intendants*, p. 494.
53 Saugrain, *Curiosités de Paris*, p. 64.
54 Félibien, *Histoire de Paris*, 5:428.
55 Isambert et al., *Recueil*, 19:277.
56 Delamare, *Traité*, 4:272.

57 Sauval, *Histoire*, 1:207.
58 Despierres, "Construction du Pont-Royal," p. 192.
59 Félibien, *Histoire de Paris*, 5:271-72.
60 Ibid., p. 426; Boislisle, *Correspondance des Contrôleurs-Généraux*, 3, no. 129.
61 Félibien, *Histoire de Paris*, 3:148r.
62 Pasturier, *L'Assistance à Paris*, p. 99.
63 Herlaut, "La disette," pp. 77-78.
64 Daguesseau to Controller-General, Aug. 3 and Sept. 4, 1709, Boislisle, *Correspondance des Contrôleurs-Généraux*, 3, no. 543.
65 Pasturier, *L'Assistance à Paris*, p. 89.
66 Cahen, "Les idées charitables," p. 67; Boislisle, *Correspondance des Contrôleurs-Généraux*, 3, no. 543.
67 Delamare, *Traité*, 4:231.
68 Ibid., pp. 237-39.
69 Ibid., p. 233.

CHAPTER THREE

1 Delamare, *Traité*, 4:437.
2 Ibid., p. 436.
3 Sauval, *Histoire*, 1:191.
4 Franklin, *Dictionnaire des arts*, p. 127.
5 Sauval, *Histoire*, 1:26.
6 Villers, *Journal*, p. 70.
7 Voltaire, *Louis XIV*, p. 326.
8 Brice, *Description de Paris*, 1:348.
9 Delamare, *Traité*, 4:144.
10 Lister, *Journey*, p. 12.
11 Delamare, *Traité*, 1:431-58.
12 Brice, *Description de Paris*, 1:12.
13 Nemeitz, *Séjour*, pp. 243, 250.
14 Poete, *La Promenade*, p. 177.
15 Villefose, *Histoire gourmande*, p. 36, citing Evelyn's *Diary*.
16 Villers, *Journal*, p. 228.
17 Poete, *La Promenade*, p. 294.
18 Lister, *Journey*, pp. 11, 178.
19 Nemeitz, *Séjour*, p. 96.
20 Ibid.
21 Delamare, *Traité*, 4:437.
22 Ibid., p. 449.
23 Ibid., p. 451.
24 Ibid.
25 Brice, *Description de Paris*, 1:13.
26 Sauval, *Histoire*, 1:194.
27 Nemeitz, *Séjour*, p. 218.
28 Boislisle, *Correspondance des Contrôleurs-Généraux*, 2:130.
29 Lister, *Journey*, p. 13.
30 Marana, *Lettre d'un Sicilien*, p. 11.
31 Nemeitz, *Séjour*, p. 221.
32 Ibid., p. 222.
33 Lister, *Journey*, p. 13.
34 Sauval, *Histoire*, 1:193.
35 Isambert et al., *Recueil*, 18:16-17.
36 Franklin, *Dictionnaire des arts*, p. 425.
37 Sauval, *Histoire*, 1:192.
38 Franklin, *Dictionnaire des arts*, p. 425.
39 Hénard, *La Rue Saint-Honoré*, p. 341.
40 Sauval, *Histoire*, 1:192.
41 Delamare, *Traité*, 4:464.
42 Ibid., p. 10.
43 Deville and Hochéreau, *Recueil*.
44 Delamare, *Traité*, 4:11.
45 Ibid.
46 Ibid., 4:624.
47 Franklin, *Dictionnaire des arts*, pp. 772-74.
48 Ibid., p. 705.
49 Lough, *Locke's Travels*, p. 49.
50 Franklin, *Dictionnaire des arts*, p. 706.
51 Avenel, *L'Evolution*, p. 71.
52 Delamare, *Traité*, 4:571.
53 Brunel, *La Poste*, pp. 2-4; Delamare, *Traité*, 4:581.
54 Delamare, *Traité*, 4:582 ff.
55 "Mémoire de M. le Pelletier, député de la ville de Paris . . . ," April 8, 1701, Boislisle, *Correspondance des Contrôleurs-Généraux*, 2:500-501.
56 Saugrain, *Curiosités de Paris*, p. 76; Delamare, *Traité*, 4:595.
57 Isambert et al., *Recueil*, 18:308.
58 Brunel, *La Poste*, p. 8.
59 Ibid., p. 26; Crousaz-Crétet, *Paris sous Louis XIV*, 2:362.
60 Sauval, *Histoire*, 1:106-67; Saugrain, *Curiosités de Paris*, pp. 367-81.
61 Friedmann, *Paris*, p. 332.
62 Fournier, *Histoire des enseignes*, p. 38.
63 Boislisle, *Mémoires de Saint-Simon*, 3:75-77.
64 Delamare, *Traité*, 4:336-37.

65 Fournier, *Histoire des enseignes*, p. 79.
66 Argenson, *Notes*, p. 31.
67 Pradel, *Livre commode*, p. 357 n.
68 Brièle, *Collection de documents*, 1:144.
69 Wiley, *Early Public Theater*, p. 219.
70 Raynaud, *Les médecins*, p. 246.
71 Hatin, *Histoire de la presse*, 1:148.
72 Ibid., 2:7-8.
73 Mathorez, *Les étrangers*, 2:125.
74 Hatin, *Histoire de la presse*, 2:64.
75 Pradel, *Livre commode*, 1:xx.
76 Raynaud, *Les médecins*, p. 271.
77 Pradel, *Livre commode*, 1:xxx-xli.
78 Depping, *Correspondance*, 2:569.
79 Hatin, *Histoire de la presse*, 2:98-99.
80 Pradel, *Livre commode*, 1:xl.
81 Franklin, *L'Annonce et la réclame*, pp. 111-12.

CHAPTER FOUR

1 Lancaster, *The Comédie Française, 1701-1774*, p. 19.
2 Lancaster, *History of French Dramatic Literature*, 1 (2):709.
3 Wiley, *Early Public Theater*, pp. 41-42.
4 Lancaster, *History of French Dramatic Literature*, 1 (2):732.
5 Wiley, *Early Public Theater*, p. 63.
6 Ibid., pp. 49, 51.
7 Abbé d'Aubignac as cited by Wiley, ibid., p. 57.
8. Lancaster, *History of French Dramatic Literature*, 4 (1):42.
9 Lawrenson, *French Stage*, pp. 164-65.
10 Ibid., pp. 171-72.
11 Despois, *Théâtre français*, p. 363; Lancaster, *The Comédie Française, 1680-1701*, passim.
12 Molière, *Les fâcheux*, act 1, scene 1.
13 Dulaure, *Histoire physique*, 3:258.
14 Mélèse, *Théâtre à Paris*, p. 212.
15 Lancaster, *History of French Dramatic Literature*, 4 (1):43; 5:5.
16 Chappuzeau, *Théâtre français*, p. 124.
17 Mélèse, *Théâtre à Paris*, p. 218.
18 Despois, *Théâtre français*, p. 121; Mélèse, *Théâtre à Paris*, p. 217.
19 Depping, *Correspondance*, 2:711.

20 Ibid., p. 775.
21 Mélèse, *Théâtre à Paris*, p. 237.
22 Chappuzeau, *Théâtre français*, pp. 155-56.
23 Delamare, *Traité*, 1:475.
24 Depping, *Correspondance*, 2:764.
25 Lancaster, *History of French Dramatic Literature*, 4 (1):43; 5:5.
26 Delamare, *Traité*, 1:472; Franklin, *Dictionnaire des arts*, p. 264.
27 Despois, *Théâtre français*, p. 14.
28 Bray, *Molière*, pp. 130-31.
29 Brice, *Description de Paris*, 1:117-18.
30 Félibien, *Histoire de Paris*, 3:1251.
31 Pierre de l'Estoile, *Mémoires-Journaux*, as cited by Wiley, *Early Public Theatre*, p. 3.
32 Despois, *Théâtre français*, p. 321.
33 Brenner, *The Théâtre Italien*, p. 1; Mélèse, *Théâtre à Paris*, p. 53.
34 Lancaster, *History of French Dramatic Literature*, 3 (1):35-36.
35 Ibid., 4 (2):599.
36 Mélèse, *Théâtre à Paris*, p. 51 n.
37 Cited by Mélèse, ibid.
38 Ibid., p. 51.
39 Depping, *Correspondance*, 2:711.
40 Boislisle, *Mémoires de Saint-Simon*, 4:124.
41 Mélèse, *Théâtre à Paris*, p. 53.
42 Brice, *Description de Paris*, 1:227; Saugrain, *Curiosités de Paris*, p. 84.
43 Despois, *Théâtre français*, p. 329; Bray, *Molière*, p. 130.
44 Clément, *Lettres de Colbert*, 5:536.
45 Boislisle, "Les debuts de l'Opéra," p. 179.
46 Clément, *Lettres de Colbert*, 5:536.
47 Despois, *Théâtre français*, p. 81.
48 Ibid., pp. 323-24.
49 Clément, *Lettres de Colbert*, 5:lxxiv.
50 Ibid., 5:551.
51 Ibid., p. lxxv.
52 Hazard, *European Mind*, pp. 381-82.
53 Lawrenson, *French Stage*, pp. 154-55.
54 Mélèse, *Théâtre à Paris*, p. 42.
55 Urbain and Levesque, *Correspondance de Bossuet*, 6:257 n.
56 Lister, *Journey*, p. 171.
57 Mélèse, *Théâtre à Paris*, p. 58.

58 Isambert et al., *Recueil*, 19:253.
59 Chappuzeau, *Théâtre français*, p. 159.
60 Ibid., p. 42.
61 Lancaster, *History of French Dramatic Literature*, 4 (2):924.
62 Isambert et al., *Recueil*, 19:110.
63 Despois, *Théâtre français*, p. 277.
64 Lancaster, *History of French Dramatic Literature*, 3 (1):31-32.
65 Bray, *Molière*, p. 146.
66 Despois, *Théâtre français*, p. 40.
67 Ibid., p. 46.
68 Mélèse, *Théâtre à Paris*, p. 282 n.
69 Despois, *Théâtre français*, p. 6.
70 Lawrenson, *French Stage*, p. xxv.
71 Lancaster, *The Comédie Française, 1680-1701*, pp. 9-12.
72 Depping, *Correspondance*, 2:578.
73 Mélèse, *Théâtre à Paris*, p. 50.
74 Brice, *Description de Paris*, 2:275-76.
75 Lancaster, *The Comédie Française, 1680-1701*, p. 13.

CHAPTER FIVE

1 Lespinasse, *Les métiers*, 1:2, 318; Delamare, *Traité*, 2:127.
2 Levasseur, *Histoire des classes ouvrières*, 2:125-26.
3 Lespinasse, *Les métiers*, 1:84-110.
4 Ibid., p. 101.
5 Ibid., pp. 117-19.
6 Franklin, *Dictionnaire des arts*, p. 291.
7 Clément, *Lettres de Colbert*, 2:324, 325 n., 328.
8 Félibien, *Histoire de Paris*, 5:234.
9 Boissonnade, *Le Socialisme d'état*, p. 284.
10 Levasseur, *Histoire des classes ouvrières*, 2:362-66.
11 Ibid., p. 355.
12 Bouvier-Ajam, *Histoire du travail*, p. 572.
13 Lespinasse, *Les métiers*, 1:145.
14 Bouvier-Ajam, *Histoire du travail*, p. 572.
15 Sauval, *Histoire*, 1:26.
16 Franklin, *Comment on devenait patron*, p. 267; idem, *Dictionnaire des arts*, p. 30.

17 Franklin, *Dictionnaire des arts*, p. 29.
18 Bourgeon, "L'Ile de la Cité," p. 90.
19 Ibid., p. 107.
20 Audiger, "La maison réglée," in Franklin, *Vie de Paris sous Louis XIV: Tenue de maison et domesticité*, p. 130.
21 Ibid., p. 129.
22 Delamare, *Traité*, 3:476.
23 Bouvier-Ajam, *Histoire du travail*, p. 456; Lespinasse, *Les métiers*, 1:89.
24 Lespinasse, *Les métiers*, 1:211-12.
25 Coornaert, *Les corporations en France*, p. 218; Bouvier-Ajam, *Histoire du travail*, p. 574.
26 Bouvier-Ajam, *Histoire du travail*, p. 578.
27 Franklin, *L'Annonce et la réclame*, pp. 81-82.
28 Vidal and Duru, *Histoire des marchands merciers*, p. 39.
29 Sauval, *Histoire*, 1:26.
30 Vidal and Duru, *Histoire des marchands merciers*, pp. 38-39.
31 Coornaert, *Les corporations en France*, pp. 271-73.
32 Franklin, *Dictionnaire des arts*, p. 113.
33 Pradel, *Livre commode*, 2:51.
34 Coornaert, *Les corporations en France*, p. 271.
35 Levasseur, *Histoire des classes ouvrières*, 2:401.
36 Ibid., p. 394.
37 Lough, *Locke's Travels*, p. 71; Delamare, *Traité*, 2:389.
38 Avenel, *Histoire économique*, passim.
39 Clément, *Lettres de Colbert*, 6:433-35.
40 Grimoard and Grouvelle, *Oeuvres de Louis XIV*, 2:238.
41 Ormesson, *Journal*, 2:517.
42 Bouvier-Ajam, *Histoire du travail*, p. 596.
43 Pottinger, *The French Book Trade*, p. 243.
44 Ibid., p. 242.
45 Robert to Controller-General, April 4, 1692, Boislisle, *Correspondance des Contrôleurs-Généraux*, 1:283.
46 Le Masson, *Calendrier des confréries*, p. xxviii.

47 Coornaert, *Les corporations en France*, p. 280.

48 Levasseur, *Histoire des classes ouvrières*, 2:414.

49 Ibid., pp. 389-93; Boissonnade, *Le Socialisme d'état*, p. 301.

50 Martin Saint-Léon, *Le Compagnonnage*, p. 39.

51 Boissonnade, *Le Socialisme d'état*, p. 302.

52 Ibid., p. 300.

53 Coornaert, *Les corporations en France*, p. 141.

54 Martin Saint-Léon, *Le Compagnonnage*, p. 39.

55 Pottinger, *The French Book Trade*, p. 262.

56 Martin Saint-Léon, *Le Compagnonnage*, p. 40.

57 Levasseur, *Histoire des classes ouvrières*, 2:423.

58 Saugrain, *Curiosités de Paris*, p. 104.

59 Officials of the *grenier à sel* to the Controller-General, June 21, 1698, Boislisle, *Correspondance des Contrôleurs-Généraux*, 1:482.

60 D'Argenson to the Controller-General, Nov. 8, 1705, ibid., p. 283.

61 Le Camus to the Controller-General, Oct. 1701, ibid., p. 288.

62 Delamare, *Traité*, 1:162; Lehoux, "La cour de Saint-Germain-des-Prés," p. 92.

63 Lehoux, ibid., p. 92 n.

64 Depping, *Correspondance*, 2:741.

65 D'Argenson to the Controller-General, Nov. 8, 1705, Boislisle, *Correspondance des Contrôleurs-Généraux*, 2:283.

66 Vidal and Duru, *Histoire des marchands merciers*, p. 206.

67 Saugrain, *Curiosités de Paris*, p. 132.

68 Félibien, *Histoire de Paris*, 3:1392.

69 Lespinasse, *Les métiers*, 1:121 n.

70 Coornaert, *Les corporations en France*, p. 167.

71 Franklin, *Dictionnaire des arts*, p. 372.

72 Boissonnade, *Le Socialisme d'état*, p. 309.

73 Delamare, *Traité*, 4:287.

74 Levasseur, *Histoire des classes ouvrières*, 2:392 n.

75 Controller-General to D'Argenson, Oct. 31, 1708; D'Argenson to the Controller-General, Nov. 7, 1708, Boislisle, *Correspondance des Contrôleurs-Généraux*, 3, no. 212.

76 Desmaretz to D'Argenson, May 18, 1706, ibid., 2, no. 1050.

77 Harlay to Pontchartrain, July 29, 1705, Depping, *Correspondance*, 2:847.

CHAPTER SIX

1 *Recueil pour l'établissement de l'Hôpital général*, p. 71.

2 Isambert et al., *Recueil,* 18: passim, and 19:232-35.

3 Paultre, *Répression du vagabondage*, p. 56.

4 Boucher, *La Salpêtrière*, pp. 20-21; Bru, *Histoire de Bicêtre*, p. 19.

5 Porchnev, *Les soulèvements populaires en France*.

6 Chill, "Religion and Mendicity in Seventeenth Century France," p. 424.

7 Franklin, *Variétés chirurgicales*, p. 70.

8 Daguesseau to the Controller-General, Feb. 10, 1711, Boislisle, *Correspondance des Contrôleurs-Généraux*, 3:974.

9 Paultre, *Répression du vagabondage*, p. 318, citing the Law of August 27, 1701.

10 Depping, *Correspondance*, 2:823.

11 Boislisle, *Correspondance des Contrôleurs-Généraux*, 3, appendix:667-72.

12 Boislisle, *Mémoires des intendants*, pp. 418-20.

13 Boislisle, *Correspondance des Contrôleurs-Généraux*, 3, no. 3.

14 Delamare, *Traité*, 2:384.

15 Ibid.

16 Ibid., p. 389.

17 Ibid.

18 Herlaut, "La disette," pp. 62-63.

19 Cahen, "Les idées charitables à Paris," p. 27.

20 Pasturier, *L'Assistance à Paris*, pp. 108-9.

21 Herlaut, "La disette," p. 63.

22 Ibid., p. 30.

23 Daguesseau to the Controller-General,

April 29, 1709, Boislisle, *Correspondance des Contrôleurs-Généraux*, 3, no. 384.

24 Herlaut, "La disette," pp. 62-63; Bignon to the Controller-General. Aug. 3, 1709, Boislisle, *Correspondance des Contrôleurs-Généraux*, 3, no. 522.

25 Robert to the Controller-General, Aug. 20, 1709, ibid.

26 Comtesse de Séberville to the Controller-General, ibid.

27 Chill, "Company of the Holy Sacrament," p. 121.

28 Boislisle, *Mémoires de Saint-Simon*, 3: 167; Pradel, *Livre commode*, 1:24.

29 Chill, "Company of the Holy Sacrament," p. 121.

30 Brochard, *Histoire de l'Eglise Saint-Laurent*, pp. 367-77.

31 Ibid.

32 Pasturier, *L'Assistance à Paris*, p. 187.

33 Brièle, Documents pour l'histoire des hôpitaux, 1:229.

34 *Recueil pour l'établissement de l'Hôpital général*, p. 2.

35 Félibien, *Histoire de Paris*, 3:1459.

36 Cole, *Colbert*, 1:134-35.

37 Félibien, *Histoire de Paris*, 3:1481.

38 *Recueil pour l'établissement de l'Hôpital général*, p. 4.

39 Ibid., art. 20.

40 Ibid., p. 73.

41 Lallemand, *Histoire de la charité*, 4 (1):259.

42 Sauval, *Histoire*, 1:526-27.

43 As quoted by Lallemand, *Histoire de la charité*, 4 (1):216-19.

44 Pasturier, *L'Assistance à Paris*, p. 127.

45 Sauval, *Histoire*, 1:535-36.

46 Félibien, *Histoire de Paris*, 3:1487.

47 Clément, *Lettres de Colbert*, 3 (2):476.

48 Depping, *Correspondance*, 2:593-94.

49 Boislisle, *Mémoires des intendants*, pp. 419-20.

50 Ibid., p. 415.

51 Cole, *Colbert*, 2:477; Pasturier, *L'Assistance à Paris*, p. 180.

52 *Recueil pour l'établissement de l'Hôpital général*, supplement.

53 Brice, *Description de Paris*, 2:18-19.

54 Cole, *Colbert*, 2:217-37.

55 Sauval, *Histoire*, 1:528.

56 Depping, *Correspondance*, 2:759.

57 Paultre, *Répression du vagabondage*, p. 315.

58 Nemeitz, *Séjour*, p. 231.

59 Depping, *Correspondance*, 2:735.

CHAPTER SEVEN

1 Sauval, *Histoire*, 1:169.

2 Chassaigne, *Lieutenance générale*, p. 34.

3 Marion *Dictionnaire*, p. 441.

4 Delamare, *Traité*, vol. 1, Epitre.

5 Marion, *Dictionnaire*, p. 441.

6 Villers, *Journal*, p. 71.

7 Depping, *Correspondance*, 2:xli.

8 Hénard, *La Rue Saint-Honoré*, 1:335.

9 Desmaze, *Le Châtelet*, p. 360.

10 Dulaure, *Histoire de Paris*, 3:267.

11 Delamare, *Traité*, 4:229.

12 Saint-Germain, *La Reynie*, p. 68.

13 Delamare, *Traité*, 1:144-46.

14 Félibien, *Histoire de Paris*, 3:1502.

15 Brièle, *Documents pour l'histoire des hôpitaux*, 1:251.

16 Depping, *Correspondance*, 2:570.

17 Saint-Germain, *La Reynie*, p. 63.

18 Sauval, *Histoire*, 1:512.

19 Ibid., p. 511.

20 Ibid., p. 514.

21 Clément, *Lettres de Colbert*, 4:80.

22 Ibid., 5:585.

23 Herlaut, "L'éclairage," p. 164.

24 Lister, *Journey*, p. 24.

25 Ibid., p. 23.

26 Herlaut, "L'éclairage," p. 162.

27 Ibid., p. 173

28 Franklin, *Dictionnaire des arts*, p. 422.

29 Félibien, *Histoire de Paris*, 3:1477.

30 Herlaut, "L'éclairage," p. 184.

31 Robert to the Controller-General, Sept. and Oct. 1702, Boislisle, *Correspondance des Contrôleurs-Généraux*, 2:119, 123.

32 Fournier, *Les lanternes*, p. 25.

33 Lister, *Journey*, p. 33.

34 Félibien, *Histoire de Paris*, 6:213.

35 Ibid.

36 Herlaut, "L'éclairage," p. 165.
37 Nemeitz, *Séjour*, p. 57.
38 Lister, *Journey*, p. 23.
39 Boislisle, *Correspondance des Contrôleurs-Généraux*, 2:119.
40 Herlaut, "L'éclairage," p. 157.
41 Levy, *Unpublished Plays of Carolet*, p. 42.
42 Delamare, *Traité*, 4:153.
43 Young and Young, *Registre de Lagrange*, 1:35, 57, 67, 71.
44 Saint-Germain, *La Reynie*, p. 248.
45 Robert to the Controller-General, March 26, 1704, in "Variétés," *Bulletin de la Société de l'histoire de Paris* 11 (1884): 29-30.
46 Robert to the Controller-General, March 26, 1704, Boislisle, *Correspondance des Contrôleurs-Généraux*, 2:173.
47 Bignon, Prévôt des Marchands, to the Controller-General, March 29, 1715, ibid., 3, no. 1639.
48 Delamare, *Traité*, 4:157.
49 Félibien, *Histoire de Paris*, 5:450-52.
50 Le Roux de Lincy, *L'Hôtel de Ville*, p. 207.
51 Chassaigne, *Lieutenance générale*, p. 181.
52 Desmaze, *Le Châtelet*, pp. 212-19.
53 Pradel, *Livre commode*, 1:100; Boislisle, *Mémoires des intendants*, pp. 173-211.
54 Desmaze, *Le Châtelet*, p. 212.
55 Boislisle, *Mémoires des intendants*, p. 202.
56 Félibien, *Histoire de Paris*, 5:286.
57 Ibid.
58 Argenson, *Notes*, p. 63.
59 Delamare, *Traité*, 1:266.
60 Argenson, *Notes*, p. 64.
61 Boislisle, *Mémoires de Saint-Simon*, 17: 394 n.; Herlaut, "La disette," p. 39.
62 Argenson, *Rapports inédits*, p. xc.
63 Boislisle, "Notices historiques," p. 139.
64 Boislisle, *Mémoires des intendants*, appendix, p. 466.
65 Ravaisson, *Archives de la Bastille*, 10: iv.
66 Mousnier, *Paris*, p. 66.
67 Depping, *Correspondance*, p. 818.

68 Argenson, *Rapports inédits*, pp. 229-32.
69 Depping, *Correspondance*, 2:282, 835.
70 Ibid., p. 322.
71 Funck-Brentano, "La Bastille," p. 48.
72 Mousnier, *Paris*, p. 73.
73 Argenson, *Rapports inédits*, p. 210.
74 Depping, *Correspondance*, 2:409.
75 Argenson, *Rapports inédits*, p. 174.
76 Longnon, "La vieillesse de Scaramouche," p. 107.
77 Argenson, *Notes*, pp. 111-12.
78 Fosseyeux, "Cardinal de Noailles," p. 283.
79 Argenson, *Rapports inédits*, p. 28.
80 Ibid., p. 292.
81 Ibid., pp. 45-49.
82 Ibid., pp. 59-60.
83 Depping, *Correspondance*, 2:834.
84 Argenson, *Rapports inédits*, pp. 72-74.
85 Depping, *Correspondance*, 2:832.
86 Delamare, *Traité*, 1:525.
87 Sauval, *Chronique scandaleuse*, p. 114.
88 Ibid., p. 71.
89 Delamare, *Traité*, 1:529.
90 Ibid.
91 Depping, *Correspondance*, 2:577.
92 Ravaisson, *Archives de la Bastille*, 9:38 n.
93 Nemeitz, *Séjour*, p. 233.
94 Depping, *Correspondance*, 2:791; Nemeitz, *Séjour*, p. 233.
95 Saint-Germain, *La Reynie*, p. 133.
96 Clément, *Lettres de Colbert*, 6:77 n.
97 Depping, *Correspondance*, 2:742.
98 Delamare, *Traité*, 1:492.
99 Ibid., p. 496.
100 Clément, *Lettres de Colbert*, 6:50.
101 Delamare, *Traité*, 1:495, 497.
102 Ibid., p. 63.
103 D'Argenson to the Controller-General, Jan. 11, 1704, Boislisle, *Correspondance des Contrôleurs-Généraux*, 2:166.
104 Boislisle, *Mémoires de Saint-Simon*, 17: 394-97.
105 Prévôt des Marchands to the Controller-General, Aug. 3, 1709, Boislisle, *Correspondance des Contrôleurs-Généraux*, 3, no. 522.
106 Herlaut, "La disette," p. 30.

CHAPTER EIGHT

1 Brièle, *Documents pour l'histoire des hôpitaux*, 1:204-5.
2 Ibid., p. 267.
3 Ibid., p. 268.
4 Fosseyeux, *L'Hôtel-Dieu*, p. 248.
5 Villers, *Journal*, pp. 49-50.
6 Fosseyeux, *L'Hôtel-Dieu*, p. 248.
7 Brice, *Description de Paris*, 1:234.
8 Brochard, *La Paroisse Saint-Laurent*, p. 143.
9 Deville and Hochéreau, *Recueil*, p. 6.
10 Ibid.
11 Ibid., p. 11.
12 Brièle, *Documents pour l'histoire des hôpitaux*, 1:196.
13 Crousaz-Crétet, *Paris sous Louis XIV*, 2:311.
14 *Encyclopédie*, 13:186b; suppl. 4:375b, 519b.
15 Dulaure, *Histoire physique*, 2:243.
16 Félibien, *Histoire de Paris*, 5:319.
17 Delamare, *Traité*, 1:581.
18 Brice, *Description de Paris*, 1:235.
19 Prévôt des Marchands to the Controller-General, Feb. 17, 1715, Boislisle, *Correspondance des Contrôleurs-Généraux*, 3, no. 1790.
20 Brice, *Description de Paris*, 2:5.
21 Ibid., 4; Lister, *Journey*, p. 169; Nemeitz, *Séjour*, p. 263.
22 Delamare, *Traité*, 1:576.
23 Sauval, *Histoire*, 1:211.
24 Delamare, *Traité*, vol. 4.
25 Ibid., 155-56.
26 Ibid.
27 Franklin, *Dictionnaire des arts*, p. 589.
28 Bourgeon, "L'Ile de la Cité," p. 50.
29 Delamare, *Traité*, 1:582-83.
30 Ibid., p. 587.
31 Franklin, *Magasins de nouveautés*, pp. 101-2.
32 Sauval, *Histoire*, 1:185.
33 Kauler, "Un projet d'assainissement," pp. 41-43.
34 Sauval, *Histoire*, 1:186.
35 Franklin, *L'Hygiène*, pp. 131-32.
36 Sauval, *Histoire*, 1:186.

37 Dupain, *Le pavé de Paris*, p. 60.
38 Delamare, *Traité*, 4:199.
39 Dupain, *Le pavé de Paris*, pp. 54 ff.
40 Delamare, *Traité*, 4:179-80.
41 Dupain, *Le pavé de Paris*, pp. 54 ff.
42 Ibid., p. 162.
43 Ibid., pp. 169-70.
44 Ibid., p. 170.
45 Ibid., p. 171.
46 Ibid., p. 106.
47 Sauval, *Histoire*, 1:186.
48 Lister, *Journey*, p. 24.
49 Delamare, *Traité*, 4:201.
50 Ibid., p. 214.
51 Ibid., p. 215.
52 Ibid., p. 217.
53 Ibid., pp. 225, 229.
54 Franklin, *L'Hygiène*, p. 122.
55 Delamare, *Traité*, 4:229.
56 Ibid., p. 230.
57 Ibid.
58 Ibid., pp. 226, 242.
59 Ibid., p. 227.
60 Ibid., p. 262.
61 Ibid., p. 279.
62 Ibid., p. 283.
63 Ibid., p. 286.
64 Ibid., p. 281.
65 Ibid., p. 285.
66 Ibid., p. 253.
67 Ibid., p. 252.
68 Argenson, *Notes*, p. 47.
69 Delamare, *Traité*, 4:395.
70 Franklin, *Dictionnaire des arts*, p. 729.
71 Ibid., p. 730.
72 Ibid., p. 728.
73 Ibid., pp. 426-27.
74 Delamare, *Traité*, 1:568.

CHAPTER NINE

1 Delamare, *Traité*, 1:639.
2 Bizard and Chapon, *Histoire de la prison St. Lazare*, p. 69.
3 Delamare, *Traité*, 1:640-42.
4 Ibid., p. 650; Mathorez, *Les étrangers*, 1:32.
5 Delamare, *Traité*, 1:723.
6 Ibid., pp. 666-67.

7 Clément, *Lettres de Colbert*, 2 (2):443.
8 Mathorez, *Les étrangers*, 1:32.
9 Delamare, *Traité*, 1:669-73.
10 Brièle, *Documents pour l'histoire des hôpitaux*, 1:182-83.
11 Franklin, *L'Hygiène*, p. 105.
12 Lister, *Journey*, p. 238.
13 Ibid., p. 236.
14 Lough, *Locke's Travels*, p. 268.
15 Raynaud, *Les médecins*, p. 20.
16 Isambert et al., *Recueil*, 20:508.
17 Franklin, *Les médicins*, pp. 107-8.
18 Saint-Germain, *La Reynie*, p. 41.
19 Raynaud, *Les médecins*, p. 259.
20 Isambert et al., *Recueil*, 20:517.
21 Raynaud, *Les médecins*, p. 409.
22 Marana, *Lettre d'un Sicilien*, p. 5.
23 Bernard, "Medicine at the Court of Louis XIV," p. 23.
24 Soulié et al., *Journal du Marquis de Dangeau*, 8:119.
25 Franklin, *Variétés chirurgicales*, pp. 20-21.
26 Ibid., p. 85.
27 Marion, *Dictionnaire*, p. 92.
28 Bernard, "Medicine at the Court of Louis XIV," p. 206.
29 Mettler, *History of Medicine*, p. 203.
30 Raynaud, *Les médecins*, pp. 248-49.
31 Franklin, *Les médicaments*, pp. 28-29.
32 Raynaud, *Les médecins*, p. 206.
33 Hull, *Economic Writings of Sir William Petty*, 2:508.
34 Villers, *Journal*, p. 245.
35 Fosseyeux, "Les écoles de charité," p. 294.
36 Brièle, *Documents pour l'histoire des hôpitaux*, 1:161, 181.
37 Félibien, *Histoire de Paris*, 5:1265; Saugrain, *Curiosités de Paris*, p. 259.
38 Hull, *Economic Writings of Sir William Petty*, 2:511.
39 Lister, *Journey*, p. 233.
40 Hull, *Economic Writings of Sir William Petty*, 2:511.
41 Lough, *Locke's Travels*, p. 256.
42 Rondonneau, *Essai historique sur l'Hôtel-Dieu*, p. 20.
43 Ibid., p. 86.

44 Brièle, *Documents pour l'histoire des hôpitaux*, 1:213, 246, 262.
45 Lallemand, *Histoire de la charité*, 4 (1): 502 n.
46 Hull, *Economic Writings of Sir William Petty*, 2:512.
47 Franklin, *Variétés chirurgicales*, p. 233.
48 Brièle, *Documents pour l'histoire des hôpitaux*, 1:253.
49 Ibid., p. 147.
50 Ibid.
51 Rondonneau, *Essai historique sur l'Hôtel-Dieu*, p. 241.
52 Brièle, *Documents pour l'histoire des hôpitaux*, 1:230.
53 Fosseyeux, *L'Hôtel-Dieu*, pp. 1-2.
54 Brièle, *Documents pour l'histoire des hôpitaux*, 1:230.
55 Ibid., p. 292.
56 Ibid., p. 123.
57 Fosseyeux, *L'Hôtel-Dieu*, pp. 2, 394.
58 Brièle, *Documents pour l'histoire des hôpitaux*, 1:149.
59 Ibid., pp. 135-36.
60 Ibid., p. 160.
61 Fosseyeux, *L'Hôtel-Dieu*, pp. 95-97; Rondonneau, *Essai historique sur l'Hôtel-Dieu*, p. 165; Brièle, *Documents pour l'histoire des hôpitaux*, 1:193-94.
62 Brièle, *Documents pour l'histoire des hôpitaux*, 1:153.
63 Rondonneau, *Essai historique sur l'Hôtel-Dieu*, p. 124.
64 Ibid., p. 127.
65 Ibid., p. 126.

CHAPTER TEN

1 Brice, *Description de Paris*, 1:226.
2 Sauval, *Histoire*, 1:651-52.
3 Hillairet, *Evocation du vieux Paris*, 1: 100.
4 Saint-Germain, *La Reynie*, p. 286.
5 Clément, *Lettres de Colbert*, 5:537-40; Biollay, "Les Halles," p. 342.
6 Martineau, *Les Halles*, pp. 166-68.
7 Delamare, *Traité*, 2:698-99.
8 Martineau, *Les Halles*, p. 213; Levasseur, *Histoire des classes ouvrières*, 2: 370.

9 Delamare, *Traité*, 2:240.
10 Pradel, *Livre commode*, 1:299.
11 Boislisle, *Mémoires des intendants*, pp. 669-72.
12 Bourgeon, "L'Ile de la Cité," p. 43; Brice, *Description de Paris*, 2:53.
13 Delamare, *Traité*, 4:376-78; Clément, *Lettres de Colbert*, 6:80.
14 Usher, *History of the Grain Trade*, p. 72.
15 Clément, *Lettres de Colbert*, 4:518.
16 Bouvier-Ajam, *Histoire du travail*, p. 567 n.
17 Isambert et al., *Recueil*, 19:26.
18 Meuvret, "Le commerce des grains," p. 172.
19 Brice, *Description de Paris*, 2:2.
20 Ferrier, *Journal*, p. 25.
21 Saugrain, *Curiosités de Paris*, p. 77.
22 Lespinasse, *Les métiers*, 1:474.
23 Franklin, *L'Annonce et la réclame*, p. 80.
24 Delamare, *Traité*, 2:243-44.
25 Martineau, *Les Halles*, p. 229.
26 Coornaert, *Les corporations en France*, p. 143.
27 Boislisle, *Correspondance des Contrôleurs-Généraux*, 3, no. 636.
28 Grimoard and Grouvelle, *Oeuvres de Louis XIV*, 1:153.
29 Delamare, *Traité*, 2:697.
30 Ibid., 3:320.
31 Ibid., 2:584.
32 Ibid., 1:138-39.
33 Ibid., 2:67.
34 Martineau, *Les Halles*, p. 230.
35 Ibid., p. 185.
36 Delamare, *Traité*, 3:933.
37 Lespinasse, *Les métiers*, 1:287-88.
38 Ibid., 1:261 n.
39 Sauval, *Histoire*, 1:624; Delamare, *Traité*, 2:566.
40 Avenel, *Histoire économique de la propriété*, 5:140-41.
41 Boislisle, *Correspondance des Contrôleurs-Généraux*, 2:160.
42 Delamare, *Traité*, 2:590-91.
43 Ibid., 2:607-8.
44 Ibid., 2:534-35.
45 Sauval, *Histoire*, 1:636.

46 Delamare, *Traité*, 2:624-26.
47 Lespinasse, *Les métiers*, 1:465.
48 Lough, *Locke's Travels*, p. 255.
49 Martineau, *Les Halles*, pp. 107-25.
50 Ibid., p. 112; Delamare, *Traité*, 3:82.
51 Delamare, *Traité*, 3:82.
52 Ibid., p. 86.
53 Boislisle, *Mémoires des intendants*, p. 501.
54 Saint-Germain, *La Reynie*, p. 283.
55 Boislisle, *Mémoires des intendants*, p. 501.
56 Lespinasse, *Les métiers*, 1:670.
57 Franklin, *Dictionnaire des arts*, p. 732.
58 Delamare, *Traité*, 3:724.
59 Gherardi, *Le Banqueroutier*, as cited by Pradel, *Livre commode*, 1:313 n.
60 Ravaisson, *Archives de la Bastille*, 10 (3):12-16.
61. Bonnemère, *Histoire des paysans*, 2:116.
62 Boislisle, *Correspondance des Contrôleurs-Généraux*, 1:304; 2:4, 7; Usher, *History of the Grain Trade*, p. 310.
63 Delamare, *Traité*, 2:406-7.
64 Herlaut, "La disette," pp. 98-99.
65 Levasseur, *Histoire des classes ouvrières*, 2:371.
66 Meuvret, "Les commerces des grains," pp. 200-201.
67 Boislisle, *Correspondance des Contrôleurs-Généraux*, 1:433.
68 Ibid., 1:467.
69 Usher, *History of the Grain Trade*, p. 82.
70 Ibid.
71 Ibid., p. 119.
72 Saint-Germain, *La Reynie*, p. 262.
73 Lister, *Journey*, p. 146.
74 Delamare, *Traité*, 2:246.
75 Lespinasse, *Les métiers*, 1:195.
76 Delamare, *Traité*, 2:263.
77 Ibid., 2, suppl.:5.
78 Herlaut, "La disette," p. 19.
79 Boislisle, *Correspondance des Contrôleurs-Généraux*, 3, no. 426.
80 Lough, *Locke's Travels*, p. 171.
81 Ibid.; Delamare, *Traité*, 2:263, 423, 434.
82 Delamare, *Traité*, pp. 423-35.
83 La Reynie to Harlay, June 7, 1693, Depping, *Correspondance*, 2:644.

84 Ibid.
85 Sauval, *Histoire*, 1:656.
86 Ibid.; Martineau, *Les Halles*, p. 162.
87 La Reynie to Harlay, Dec. 19, 1693, Depping, *Correspondance*, 2:670.

CHAPTER ELEVEN

1 Jourdain, *Histoire de l'Université*, 1:149.
2 Targe, *Professeurs et régents*, p. 34; Mousnier, *Paris*, p. 306.
3 Joly, *Traitté historique*, p. 265.
4 Poete, *Une vie de cité*, 3:564.
5 Franklin, *Dictionnaire des arts*, p. 291.
6 D'Argenson to the Controller General, Sept. 21, 1702, Boislisle, *Correspondance des Contrôleurs-Généraux*, 2:121-22.
7 Jourdain, *Histoire de l'Université*, Pièces justificatives, p. 97.
8 Brièle, *Documents pour l'histoire des hôpitaux*, 1:167.
9 Ferté, *Rollin*, p. 139 n.
10 Ibid., p. 243.
11 Joly, *Traitté historique*, pp. 481-82.
12 Félibien, *Histoire de Paris*, 4:455.
13 Joly, *Traitté historique*, p. 286.
14 Pradel, *Livre commode*, p. 18.
15 Félibien, *Histoire de Paris*, 4:447-48.
16 Ibid., p. 461.
17 Boislisle, *Correspondance des Contrôleurs-Généraux*, 2:121-22.
18 Targe, *Professeurs et régents*, p. 53 n.
19 Mousnier, *Paris*, p. 306.
20 Ferté, *Rollin*, pp. 397-412.
21 Ibid., p. 410.
22 Targe, *Professeurs et régents*, pp. 59-60.
23 Ferté, *Rollin*, pp. 477-78.
24 Targe, *Professeurs et régents*, pp. 56-58.
25 Franklin, *Ecoles et collèges*, p. 191.
26 Ferté, *Rollin*, p. 139 n.
27 Rigault, *Histoire des Frères*, 1:31.
28 Boislisle, *Correspondance des Contrôleurs-Généraux*, 2:121-22.
29 Joly, *Traitté historique*, pp. 327-28.
30 Ibid., p. 498.
31 Ibid., p. 362.
32 Boislisle, *Correspondance des Contrôleurs-Généraux*, 2:121-22.
33 Félibien, *Histoire de Paris*, 4:461.

34 Pradel, *Livre commode*, 1:250.
35 Tisserand, "Une querelle scolaire," p. 76.
36 Ferté, *Rollin*, p. 244.
37 Joly, *Traitté historique*, p. 448.
38 Ibid., p. 447.
39 Franklin, *Ecoles et collèges*, p. 201.
40 Joly, *Traitté historique*, p. 469.
41 Pradel, *Livre commode*, p. 248.
42 Ibid., p. 249.
43 Félibien, *Histoire de Paris*, 4:468-70.
44 Rigault, *Histoire des Frères*, 1:38.
45 Fosseyeux, "Les écoles de charité," p. 251.
46 Babeau, *La Ville sous l'ancien régime*, p. 485.
47 Fosseyeux, "Les écoles de charité," p. 364.
48 Ibid., p. 250.
49 Rigault, *Histoire des Frères*, 1:191.
50 Joly, *Traitté historique*, p. 420.
51 Fosseyeux, "Les écoles de charité," p. 258.
52 Chill, "Company of the Holy Sacrament," pp. 121 ff.
53 Brochard, *La Paroisse Saint-Laurent*, pp. 220 ff.
54 Ibid., p. 232.
55 Joly, *Traitté historique*, pp. 424-26.
56 Félibien, *Histoire de Paris*, 4:465-68.
57 Gaston, *Saint-Hippolyte*, p. 84.
58 Rigault, *Histoire des Frères*, 1:585-86.
59 Depping, *Correspondance*, 4:181.
60 Rigault, *Histoire des Frères*, 1:241.

CONCLUSION

1 Pinkney, *Napoleon III and the Rebuilding of Paris*, p. 24.
2 *Le Monde*, Jan. 12-13, 1969, p. 10.
3 Lavedan, *Histoire de l'urbanisme*, 2:193 f.
4 [Bullet] "Observations sur la nature . . . de la mauvaise odeur. . . ."
5 *Atlas des anciens plans de Paris*.
6 Bourgeon, "L'Ile de la Cité," p. 59.
7 Ibid.
8 Mousnier, *Paris*, pp. 15-17.
9 Lavedan, *Histoire de l'urbanisme*, 2:333.
10 Pinkney, *Napoleon III and the Rebuilding of Paris*, p. 151.

BIBLIOGRAPHY

Allier, Raoul. *La Cabale des dévôts, 1627-1666*. Paris, 1902.

Alphand, Michaux, Tisserand, eds. *Atlas des anciens plans de Paris*. Paris, 1880.

André, Louis, and Emile Bourgeois, eds. *Les sources de l'histoire de France: XVIIe siècle (1610-1715)*. 8 vols. Paris, 1913-1935.

Argenson, Marc René de Voyer d'. *Notes de René d'Argenson intéressantes pour l'histoire des moeurs et de la police de Paris à la fin du règne de Louis XIV*. Paris: L. Larchey and E. Mabille, 1866.

———. *Rapports inédits du Lieutenant de Police René d'Argenson (1697-1715)*. Paris: Pierre Cottin, 1891.

Avenel, Georges d'. *Histoire économique de la propriété, des salaires, des denrées, et de tous les prix en général, depuis l'an 1200 jusqu'en l'an 1800*. 2d ed.; 7 vols. Paris, 1913.

———. *Les évêques et archevêques de Paris depuis Saint Denis jusqu'à nos jours, avec des documents inédits*. 2 vols. Paris, 1878.

———. *L'Evolution des moyens de transport*. Paris, 1919.

Babeau, Albert. *La Ville sous l'ancien régime*. Paris, 1880.

Bardet, Gaston. *Naissance et méconnaissance de l'urbanisme: Paris*. Paris, 1951.

Batiffol, Louis. *La Vie de Paris sous Louis XIII*. Paris, 1932.

Battersby, W. J. *De La Salle: A Pioneer of Modern Education*. London, 1949.

Belloc, Alexis. *Les postes françaises*. Paris, 1886.

Bernard, Leon. "French Society and Popular Uprisings Under Louis XIV," *French Historical Studies* 3 (1964), no. 4: 454-74.

———. "Medicine at the Court of Louis XIV," *Medical History* 6 (1962): 201-13.

Berty, Adolph. *Topographie historique du vieux Paris*. 6 vols. Paris, 1866-1897.

Biencourt, Armand de, ed. *Institutions et règlements de charité aux XVIe et XVIIIe siècles*. Paris, 1903.

Biollay, Léon. "Les Halles," *Mémoires de la Société de l'histoire de Paris* 3 (1876): 293-355.

Bizard, L., and J. Chapon. *Histoire de la prison St. Lazard du Moyen-Âge à nos jours*. Paris, 1925.

Blégny, Nicolas de. *See* Pradel, Abraham de.

Blondell, François. *Cours d'architecture enseigné dans l'Académie royale d'Architecture*. Paris, 1675-1683.

Boislisle, A. M. de, ed. *Correspondance des Contrôleurs-Généraux des finances avec les intendants des provinces, 1683-1715*. 3 vols. Paris, 1874-1897.

———. "Les débuts de l'Opéra français à Paris," *Mémoires de la Société de l'histoire de Paris* 2 (1875): 172-86.

———. "Les intendants de la généralité de Paris," *Mémoires de la Société de l'histoire de Paris* 7 (1880): 271-98.

———, ed. *Mémoires de Saint-Simon*. Les Grands Écrivains de la France. 41 vols. Paris, 1879-1915.

———, ed. *Mémoires des intendants sur l'état des généralités, dressés pour l'instruction du Duc de Bourgogne: Tome I. Paris*. Paris, 1881.

———. "Notices historiques sur la Place des Victoires et sur la Place de Vendôme," *Mémoires de la Société de l'histoire de Paris et de l'Ile de France* 15 (1888): 1-272.

Boissonnade, Pierre. *Le Socialisme d'état, l'industrie et les classes industrielles en France . . . 1453-1661*. Paris, 1927.

Bonnasieux, P., ed. *Conseil du commerce et bureau du commerce, 1700-1791: inventaire analytique des procès-verbaux*. Paris, 1900.

———. "La police à Paris," *Bulletin de la Société de l'histoire de Paris* 21 (1894): 187-92.

Bonnemère, Eugène. *Histoire des paysans*. Paris, 1856.

Bossuet. *See* Urbain.

Boucher, Louis. *La Salpêtrière: son histoire de 1656 à 1790*. Paris, 1883.

Boulainvilliers, Comte de. *État de la France*. 3 vols. London, 1727.

Bourgeon, Jean-Louis. "L'Ile de la Cité pendant la Fronde: structure sociale," *Mémoires de la Fédération des Sociétés historiques et archéologiques de Paris et de l'Ile-de-France* 13 (1962): 23-144.

Bouvier-Ajam, Maurice. *Histoire du travail en France*. Paris, 1957.

Bray, René. *Molière, homme de théâtre*. Paris, 1944.

Brenner, Clarence D. *The Théâtre Italien: Its Repertory, 1716-1797*. Berkeley, 1961.

Bretez, Louis, *Paris au XVIIIe siècle: plan de Paris en 20 planches*. Paris, 1910.

Brice, Germain. *Description nouvelle de ce qu'il y a de plus remarquable dans la ville de Paris*. 2 vols. Paris, 1698.

Brièle, Léon, ed. *Collection de documents pour servir à l'histoire des hôpitaux de Paris*. 4 vols. Paris, 1881-1887.

Brochard, Louis. *Histoire de la paroisse et de l'Eglise Saint-Laurent à Paris*. Paris, 1923.

Bru, P. *Histoire de Bicêtre*. Paris, 1890.

Brunel, Georges. *La Poste à Paris depuis sa création jusqu'à nos jours*. Amiens, 1920.

[Bullet, Pierre]. "Observations sur la nature et les effets de la mauvaise odeur des lieux. . ." etc. Paris, 1695.

Cahen, Louis. *Le Grand Bureau des pauvres de Paris, au milieu du XVIIIe siècle*. Paris, 1904.

——. "Les idées charitables à Paris au XVIIe et au XVIIIe siècles d'après les règlements des compagnies paroissiales," *Revue d'histoire moderne* 2 (1900-1901): 5-32.

Chappuzeau, Samuel. *Le Théâtre français*. Reprint of 1674 edition. Paris, 1876.

Chassaigne, Marc. *La Lieutenance Générale de police de Paris*. Paris, 1906.

Chénon, Émile. *Histoire générale du droit français public et privé des origines à 1815*. 2 vols. Paris, 1929.

Chevalier, A. "Le Grand Thomas," *Mémoires de la Société de l'histoire de Paris* 7 (1880): 61-78.

Chill, Emmanuel Stanley. "The Company of the Holy Sacrament (1630-1666): Social Aspects of the French Counter-Reformation." Ph.D. dissertation, History Department, Columbia University, 1960.

——. "Religion and Mendicity in Seventeenth Century France," *International Review of Social History* 7 (1962), pt. 3: 400-427.

Christian, Arthur. *Études sur le Paris d'autrefois: les demeures royales: les demeures aristocratiques*. Paris, 1905.

Clément, Pierre, ed. *Lettres, instructions et mémoires de Colbert*. 7 vols. Paris, 1861-1882.

——. *La Police sous Louis XIV*. Paris, 1866.

Coetlogon, Comte A. de, and L. M. Tisserand. *Les armoiries de la ville de Paris*. *Histoire Générale de Paris*. 2 vols. Paris, 1874-1875.

Cole, C. W. *Colbert and a Century of French Mercantilism*. 2 vols. New York, 1939.

Coornaert, Emile. *Les corporations en France avant 1789*. Paris, 1941.

Cotgrave, Randle. *A Dictionarie of the French and English Tongues*. Reproduced with an introduction by William S. Woods. Columbia, S. C., 1950.

Cousin, Victor. *La Société française au XVIIᵉ siècle, d'après le Grand Cyrus de Mlle de Scudéry*. Paris, 1858.

Crousaz-Crétet, Paul de. *Paris sous Louis XIV*. 2 vols. Paris, 1922.

De Lacke. *See* Villers.

Delamare, Nicolas. *Traité de la police, où l'on trouvera l'histoire de son établissement, les fonctions et les prérogatives de ses magistrats, toutes les lois et les règlements qui la concernent*. 2d ed. 4 vols. Paris, 1722-1738.

Denière, G. *La Jurisdiction consulaire de Paris, 1563-1792*. Paris, 1872.

Depping, G. B., ed. *Correspondance administrative sous le règne de Louis XIV*. Paris, 1850-1855.

Desmaze, Charles. *Le Châtelet de Paris*. Paris, 1854.

Despierres, G. "Construction du Pont-Royal de Paris (1685-1688)," *Mémoires de la Société de l'Histoire de Paris et de l'Ile-de-France* 22 (1895): 179-224.

Despois, Eugène. *Le Théâtre français sous Louis XIV*. Paris, 1874.

Deville, A., and M. Hochéreau, eds. *Recueil des lettres patentes, ordonnances royales . . . concernant les voies publiques de la ville de Paris*. 2 vols. Paris, 1886, 1902.

Dufour, Valentin, ed. *Collection des anciennes descriptions de Paris*. 10 vols. Paris, 1878-1883.

Dulaure, Jacques Antoine. *Histoire physique, civile et morale de Paris*. 4 vols. Paris, 1842.

Dumolin, Maurice. *Etudes de topographie parisienne*. 3 vols. Paris, 1929-1931.

———. "Les propriétaires de la Place Royale (1605-1789)," *La Cité* 17 (1924-1925): 273-316; 18 (1926-1927) 1-30.

———. "Notes sur les vieux guides de Paris," *Mémoires de la Société de l'histoire de Paris* 47 (1924): 209-85.

Dupain, S. *Notice historique sur le pavé de Paris*. Paris, 1881.

Encyclopédie, ou Dictionnaire raisonné des sciences, des arts et des métiers . . . par m. Diderot . . . et m. d'Alembert. 17 vols. Paris, 1751-1765. Supplement, 4 vols., Amsterdam, 1776-1777.

Esmein, Adhémar. *A History of Continental Criminal Procedure, with Special Reference to France*. Trans. John Simpson. Boston, 1913.

Evelyn, John. *Diary and Correspondence . . .* 4 vols. London, 1682.

Fegdal, Charles. *Les vieilles enseignes de Paris*. 3d ed. Paris, 1923.

Félibien, Michel. *Histoire de la ville de Paris*. 7 vols. Paris, 1725.

Ferrier, Richard. *The Journal of Richard Ferrier.* Camden Miscellany, 9 (1895).

Ferté, H. *Rollin, sa vie, ses oeuvres et l'Université de son temps.* Paris, 1902.

Fontenay, Michel. "Paysans et marchands ruraux de la vallée de l'Essonne dans la seconde moitié du XVIIᵉ siècle," *Mémoires de la Fédération des Sociétés historiques et archéologiques de Paris et de l'Ile-de-France* 9 (1957-1958) : 157-282.

Forbonnais, Véron de. *Recherches et considérations sur les finances de France depuis l'année 1595 jusqu'à l'année 1721.* 3 vols. Paris, 1758.

Fosseyeux, Marcel. "L'Assistance aux prisonniers à Paris sous l'ancien régime," *Mémoires de la Société de l'histoire de Paris* 48 (1925) : 110-29.

———. "Le Cardinal de Noailles et l'administration du diocèse de Paris (1695-1729)," *Revue historique* 114 (1913) : 261-84; 115 (1914) : 34-54.

———. "Les écoles de charité," *Mémoires de la Société de l'histoire de Paris* 39 (1912) : 249-366.

———. *L'Hôtel-Dieu au XVIIᵉ et au XVIIIᵉ siècles.* Paris, 1912.

Fournel, Victor. *Les rues du vieux Paris.* Paris, 1879.

Fournier, Edouard. *Histoire des enseignes de Paris.* Paris, 1884.

———. *Histoire du Pont Neuf.* 2 vols. Paris, 1862.

———. *Les lanternes, histoire de l'éclairage de Paris.* Paris, 1854.

——— and F. X. Michel. *Histoire des hôtelleries, cabarets . . . restaurants et cafés.* 2 vols. Paris, 1851.

Franklin, Alfred. *Les anciens plans de Paris; notices historiques et topographiques.* 2 vols. bound in one. Paris, 1878-1880.

———. *Dictionnaire historique des arts, métiers et professions exercés dans Paris depuis le treizième siècle.* 1 vol. in two parts. Paris, 1905-1906.

———. *La Vie privée d'autrefois: l'Annonce et la réclame.* Paris, 1887.

———. *La Vie privée d'autrefois:Comment on devenait patron: Histoire des corporations.* Paris, 1889.

———. *La Vie privée d'autrefois: Écoles et collèges.* Paris, 1892.

———. *La Vie privée d'autrefois: les Chirurgiens.* Paris, 1893.

———. *La Vie privée d'autrefois: les Magasins de nouveautés.* Paris, 1896.

———. *La Vie privée d'autrefois: les Médecins.* Paris, 1892.

———. *La Vie privée d'autrefois: les Médicaments.* Paris, 1891.

———. *La Vie privée d'autrefois: l'Hygiène.* Paris, 1890.

———. *La Vie privée d'autrefois: Variétés chirurgicales.* Paris, 1894.

———. *La Vie privée d'autrefois: Vie de Paris sous Louis XIV: Tenue de maison et domesticité.* Paris, 1898.

Friedmann, Abbé Adrien. *Paris, ses rues, ses paroisses du Moyen Âge à la Révolution: Origine et évolution des circonscriptions paroissiales.* Paris, 1959.

Funck-Brentano, F. "La Bastille d'après ses archives," *Revue historique* 42 (1890): 38-73, 278-316.

Furetière, A. *Dictionnaire universel.* 3 vols. The Hague and Rotterdam, 1701.

Galland, Antoine. "Journal parisien (1708-1715)," *Mémoires de la Société de l'histoire de Paris* 46 (1919): 1-156.

Gannal, F. "Une page de l'histoire de l'Hôtel-Dieu," *Bulletin de la Société de l'histoire de Paris* 19 (1892), 60-62.

Gaston, Abbé Jean. *Une paroisse parisienne avant la Révolution: Saint-Hippolyte.* Paris, 1908.

Gourdon de Genouillac, Henri. *Paris à travers les siècles.* 5 vols. Paris, 1881-1889.

Grente, J. *Une paroisse de Paris sous l'ancien régime: Saint-Jacques-du-Haut-Pas, 1566-1793.* Paris, 1897.

Grimoard, Philippe Henri, Comte de, and P. A. Grouvelle, eds. *Oeuvres de Louis XIV.* 6 vols. Paris, 1806.

Grouchy, Vicomte de. "Les carrosses à cinq sols," *Bulletin de la Société de l'histoire de Paris* 20 (1893): 167-70.

Guérout, Jean. "La taille dans la région parisienne au XVIIIe siècle," *Mémoires de la Fédération des Sociétés historiques et archéologiques de Paris et de l'Ile-de-France* 13 (1962): 145-358.

Guiffrey, Jules. *Comptes des bâtiments du roi sous le règne de Louis XIV.* 5 vols. Paris, 1881-1901.

———. "Les manufactures parisiennes de tapisseries au XVIIe siècle," *Mémoires de la Société de l'histoire de Paris* 19 (1892): 43-292.

Handlin, Oscar and John Burchard, eds. *The Historian and The City.* Cambridge, Mass.: The M.I.T. Press and Harvard University Press, 1963.

Hatin, Eugène. *Histoire de la presse en France.* 2 vols. Paris, 1859.

Hazard, Paul. *The European Mind.* Cleveland and New York: World Publishing Company, 1963.

Hénard, Robert. *La Rue Saint-Honoré.* 2 vols. Paris, 1908.

Herlaut, Commandant. "La disette de pain à Paris en 1709," *Mémoires de la Société de l'histoire de Paris et de l'Ile-de-France* 45 (1918): 5-100.

———. "L'éclairage des rues de Paris à la fin du XVIIe et au XVIIIe siècles," *Mémoires de la Société de l'histoire de Paris et de l'Ile-de-France* 43 (1916): 129-265.

Hillairet, Jacques. *Évocation du vieux Paris.* 3 vols. Paris, 1951-1953.

Hoffbauer, Fedor. *Paris à travers les âges.* 2 vols. Paris, 1885.

Hull, Charles Henry, ed. *The Economic Writings of Sir William Petty, Together with Observations upon the Bills of Mortality.* 2 vols. Cambridge, 1899.

Hurtaut, Pierre Thomas Nicolas. *Dictionnaire historique de la ville de Paris* . . . 4 vols. Paris, 1779.

Isambert, Jourdan, Decrusy, Armet, and Gaillandier. *Recueil général des anciennes lois françaises* . . . *jusqu'à la révolution de 1789.* 29 vols. Paris, 1821-1833.

Jacquart, Jean. "Une paroisse rurale de la région parisienne: Morangis aux XVIe et XVIIe siècles," *Mémoires de la Fédération des Sociétés historiques et archéologiques de Paris et de l'Ile-de-France* 8 (1956): 187-211.

Joly, Claude. *Traitté historique des écoles épiscopales et ecclésiastiques.* Paris, 1687.

Jourdain, Charles. *Histoire de l'Université de Paris au XVIIe et au XVIIIe siècle.* 2 vols. Paris, 1888.

Kauler, Jean, ed. "Un projet d'assainissement de Paris au temps de Mazarin," *Bulletin de la Société de l'histoire de Paris* 10 (1883).

King, James E. *Science and Rationalism in the Government of Louis XIV, 1661-1683.* The Johns Hopkins University Studies in Historical and Political Science, series 66, vol. 2. Baltimore, 1949.

Kleindienst, Thérèse. "La topographie et l'exploitation des 'Marais de Paris' du XIIe au XVIIe siècle," *Mémoires de la Fédération des Sociétés historiques et archéologiques de Paris et de l'Ile-de-France* 14 (1963): 7-167.

Lagrange, C. V. de. *Le Registre de Lagrange (1659-1685).* Ed. B. E. and G. P. Young. 2 vols. Paris, 1947.

Lalanne, L., ed. "Mémoire des désordres en général qui se trouvent dans les prisons de Paris et les remèdes qui s'y peuvent apporter (1644)," *Bulletin de la Société de l'histoire de Paris* 19 (1892): 82-86.

Lallemand, Léon. *Histoire de la charité.* 4 vols. Paris, 1902-1912.

———. *Histoire des enfants abandonnés et délaissés.* Paris, 1885.

Lambeau, Lucien. *La Place Royale* . . . Paris, 1906.

Lancaster, H. C. *A History of French Dramatic Literature in the Seventeenth Century.* 9 vols. Baltimore, 1929-1942.

———. *Sunset: A History of Parisian Drama in the Last Years of Louis XIV, 1701-1715.* Baltimore and London, 1945.

————. *The Comédie Française, 1680-1701: Plays, Actors, Spectators, Finances*. Baltimore, 1941.

————. *The Comédie Française, 1701-1774: Plays, Actors, Spectators, Finances*. Philadelphia, 1951.

Lavedan, Pierre. *Histoire de l'urbanisme*. 3 vols. Paris, 1926-1954.

Lavisse, Ernest, ed. *Histoire de la France illustrée depuis les origines jusqu'à la révolution*. 9 vols. in 17. Paris, 1911-1926. Vols. 5, 6, and 7.

Lawrenson, T. E. *The French Stage in the XVIIth Century*. Manchester University Press, n.d.

Léaud, Alexis, and Emile Glay. *L'Ecole primaire en France*. Paris, 1934.

Lebeuf, Jean. *Histoire de la ville et tout le diocèse de Paris*. 6 vols. Ed. A. Augier and F. Bournon. Paris, 1883-1893. Vol. 1.

Lecestre, L., ed. "Etat de la dépense faite durant l'hiver depuis le 1 décembre 1685 jusques au 30 avril 1686 pour le secours et subsistance des pauvres des faubourgs de cette ville de Paris," *Mémoires de la Société de l'histoire de Paris* 49 (1927) : 85-92.

Lehoux, Françoise. "La cour du monastère de Saint-Germain-des-Prés dans les premières années du XVIIIᵉ siècle," *Fédération des Sociétés historiques et archéologiques de Paris et de l'Ile-de-France* 9 (1957-1958) : 89-104.

Le Maistre, Pierre. *Coutume de Paris*. Paris, 1741.

Le Masson, J. B. *Le Calendrier des confréries de Paris*. Paris, 1875.

Lemesle, Gaston. *L'Eglise Saint-Sulpice*. Paris, n.d.

Lemonnier, Henry, ed. *Procès-verbaux de l'Académie royale d'architecture, 1671-1783*. 8 vols. Paris, 1911-1924.

Le Roux de Lincy, A. J. V. *Histoire de l'Hôtel de Ville de Paris*. Paris, 1846.

Lespinasse, René de. *Les métiers et corporations de la ville de Paris*. 3 vols. Paris, 1886-1897.

Levasseur, Emile. *Histoire des classes ouvrières et de l'industrie avant 1789*. 2 vols. Paris, 1901.

Levy, Bernard. *The Unpublished Plays of Carolet*, New York, 1931.

Lister, Dr Martin. *A Journey to Paris in the Year 1698*. London, 1698.

Longnon, Auguste. "La vieillesse de Scaramouche (1690-1694)," *Mémoires de la Société de l'histoire de Paris* 2 (1876) : 106-29.

Lough, John, ed. *Locke's Travels in France, 1675-1679*. Cambridge, 1953.

————. *Paris Theater Audiences in the Seventeenth and Eighteenth Centuries*. London: Oxford University Press, 1957.

Magne, Émile. *Images de Paris sous Louis XIV*. Paris, 1939.

————. *Paris sous l'échevinage au XVIIᵉ siècle*. Paris, 1960.

Manneville, Charles. *Saint-Médard*. Paris, 1906.

Marana, Jean-Paul. *Lettre d'un Sicilien à un de ses amis*. Collection des Anciennes Descriptions de Paris, ed. V. Dufour, IX. Paris, 1883.

Marion, Marcel. *Dictionnaire des institutions de la France aux XVIIᵉ et XVIIIᵉ siècles*. Paris, 1923.

——. *Histoire financière de la France depuis 1715*. 6 vols. Paris, 1914-1931. Vol. 1.

Martin, Germain. *L'Histoire du credit en France sous le règne de Louis XIV*. Paris, 1913.

Martin Saint-Léon, Étienne. *Histoire des corporations de métiers depuis leurs origines jusqu'à leur suppression en 1791*. Paris, 1920.

——. *Le Compagnonnage*. Paris, 1901.

Martineau, Jean. *Les Halles de Paris*. Paris, 1960.

Mathorez, Jules. *Les étrangers en France sous l'ancien régime*. 2 vols. Paris, 1919.

Mélèse, Pierre. *Le Théâtre et le public à Paris sous Louis XIV (1659-1715)*. Paris, 1934.

Mettler, Cecilia C. *History of Medicine*. Philadelphia, 1947.

Meurgey, J. *Histoire de la paroisse de Saint-Jacques-de-la-Boucherie*. Paris, 1926.

Meuvret, Jean. "Le commerce des grains et des farines à Paris et les marchands parisiens, à l'époque de Louis XIV," *Revue d'histoire moderne et contemporaine* 3 (1956): 169-203.

Montorgueil, Georges. *Les eaux et les fontaines de Paris*. Paris, 1928.

Mousnier, Roland. *Paris au XVIIᵉ siècle*. Paris, 1961.

Nemeitz, Joachim-Christophe. *Séjour de Paris....* From the 1727 edition, in Alfred Franklin, *La Vie privée d'autrefois*. Paris, 1897.

Ormesson, Olivier Lefèvre d'. *Journal*. 2 vols. Paris, 1860-1861.

Parsons, William Barclay. *Engineers and Engineering in the Renaissance*. Baltimore, 1939.

Pasturier, Louis. *L'Assistance à Paris sous l'ancien régime et pendant la Révolution*. Paris, 1897.

Paultre, Charles. *La Répression du vagabondage et de la mendicité en France sous l'ancien régime*. Paris, 1906.

Picot, Georges. "Recherches sur les quarteniers, cinquanteniers et dizainiers de la ville de Paris," *Mémoires de la Société de l'histoire de Paris et de l'Ile-de-France* 1 (1874): 132-66.

Piganiol de la Force, Jean A. *Description de Paris...* 8 vols. Paris. 1742.

Pillement, Georges. *Les hôtels de Paris*. Paris, 1945.

Pinkney, David H. *Napoleon III and the Rebuilding of Paris*. Princeton, N.J., 1958.

Poete, Marcel. *La Promenade à Paris au XVIIe siècle*. Paris, 1913.

———. *Une Vie de cité: Paris de sa naissance à nos jours*. 4 vols. Paris, 1924-1925.

Porchnev, Boris. *Les soulèvements populaires en France de 1623 à 1648*. French edition, ed. Robert Mandrou and Fernand Braudel. Paris, 1963.

Pottinger, David T. *The French Book Trade in the Ancien Régime*. Cambridge, Mass.: Harvard University Press, 1958.

Pradel, Abraham de (Nicolas de Blégny). *Le Livre commode des adresses de Paris pour 1692*. Ed. Edouard Fournier. 2 vols. Paris, 1878.

Ravaisson, François, ed. *Archives de la Bastille*. 19 vols. Paris, 1866-1904.

Raynaud, Maurice. *Les médecins au temps de Molière*. Paris, 1862.

Recueil contenant l'édit du roi donné en 1656 pour l'établissement de l'Hôpital général de Paris, les déclarations, règlements et arrêts intervenus depuis à ce sujet. Paris, 1676.

Rigault, Georges. *Histoire générale de l'Institut des Frères des Ecoles Chrétiennes*. Vol. 1, *Saint Jean-Baptiste de la Salle*. Paris, n.d.

Rondonneau de La Motte. *Essai historique sur l'Hôtel-Dieu de Paris*. Paris, 1787.

Roulland, Léon. "La foire Saint-Germain," *Mémoires de la Société de l'histoire de Paris* 3 (1876): 192-218.

Saint-Germain, Jacques. *La Reynie et la police au Grand Siècle*. Paris, 1962.

———. *Les financiers sous Louis XIV: Paul Poisson de Bourvalais*. Paris, 1950.

Saugrain, Claude Marin. *Les curiosités de Paris*. Reprinted from the edition of 1716. Paris, 1883.

Sauval, Henri. *Histoire et recherches des antiquités de la ville de Paris*. 3 vols. Paris, 1724.

———. *La Chronique scandaleuse de Paris*. Paris, 1910.

Sellier, Charles. *Anciens hôtels de Paris*. Paris, 1910.

Soulié, Dussieux, et al., eds. *Journal du Marquis de Dangeau*. 19 vols. Paris, 1854-1860.

Tanon, L. *Histoire des justices des anciennes églises et communautés monastiques de Paris*. Paris, 1883.

Targe, Maxime. *Professeurs et régents de collège dans l'ancienne Université de Paris (XVIIe et XVIIIe siècles)*. Paris, 1902.

Thompson, E. D. *The Life of Jean-Jacques Olier*. London and New York, 1886.

Tirat, Jean-Yves. "Les voituriers par eau parisiens au milieu du XVIIe siècle," *XVIIe siècle*, no. 57 (1962), 43-66.

Tisserand, L. M. "Une querelle scolaire à Paris au XVIIe siècle," *Bulletin de la Société de l'histoire de Paris et de l'Ile-de-France* 17 (1890): 76-84.

Urbain, C., and E. Levesque, eds. *Correspondance de Bossuet*. 15 vols. Paris, 1909-1925.

Usher, Abbott Payson. *The History of the Grain Trade in France, 1400-1710*. Cambridge, Mass., 1913.

Vénard, Marc. *Bourgeois et paysans au XVIIe siècle: Recherche sur le rôle des bourgeois parisiens dans la vie agricole*. Paris, 1957.

Vidal, Pierre, and Léon Duru. *Histoire de la corporation des marchands merciers grossiers et jouailliers*. Paris, n.d.

Villefose, René Héron de. *Histoire et géographie gourmandes de Paris*. Paris, 1956.

Villers, Philippe de Lacke, Sieur de, et François de Lacke, Sieur de Potshiak. *Journal du voyage de deux jeunes Hollandais à Paris en 1656-1658*. Paris, 1899.

Vimont, M. *Histoire de l'église et de la paroisse Saint-Leu-Saint-Gilles à Paris*. Paris, 1932.

Voltaire, F. M. A. de. *The Age of Louis XIV*. Everyman's Library. London and New York, 1926.

Weigert, Roger-Armand. "Les feux d'artifice ordonnés par le Bureau de la Ville de Paris au XVIIe siècle," *Mémoires de la Fédération des Sociétés historiques et archéologiques de Paris et de l'Ile-de-France* 3 (1951): 173-215.

Wiley, W. L. *The Early Public Theater in France*. Cambridge, Mass., 1960.

Wolf, A. *A History of Science, Technology and Philosophy in the 16th and 17th Centuries*. 2d ed. 2 vols. New York: Harper Torchbooks, 1959.

INDEX

LE PLAN DE LA VILLE, CITE, VNIVE

Ceste ville est vn autre monde
Dedans vn monde florissant;
En peuples et en biens puissans,
Qui de toutes choses abonde.

Matheüs Merian Basiliensis. Fecit

PAR
Fac-simil